pc

POLICY EXPLORATION THROUGH MICROANALYTIC SIMULATION

Guy Orcutt

Steven Caldwell

Richard Wertheimer II

Steven Franklin, Gary Hendricks,
Gerald Peabody, James Smith,
Sheila Zedlewski

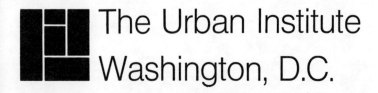 The Urban Institute
Washington, D.C.

THE URBAN INSTITUTE is a nonprofit research organization established in 1968 to study problems of the nation's urban communities. Independent and nonpartisan, the Institute responds to current needs for disinterested analyses and basic information and attempts to facilitate the application of this knowledge. As a part of this effort, it cooperates with federal agencies, states, cities, associations of public officials, and other organizations committed to the public interest.

The Institute's research findings and a broad range of interpretive viewpoints are published as an educational service. The interpretations or conclusions are those of the authors and should not be attributed to The Urban Institute, its trustees, or to other organizations that support its research.

The research and studies forming the basis for this report were supported by grants from the Department of Health, Education, and Welfare (grant number 31607/D/75-01) and the Ford Foundation.

Foreword

After a seven-year gestation period at The Urban Institute, the Dynamic Simulation of Income Model — DYNASIM — has come into being and is being put to use to help answer policy questions.

DYNASIM is a unique social science tool. It has been built in accord with some of the complexities of America's social and economic structure. Accordingly, its projections, which focus primarily on the U.S. household sector, have the characteristics of a census household sample and can be analyzed in the same fashion. Most other models are based on rather static and rigid assumptions, creating unrealistic distortions that become more serious as the forecasting time span is increased. In contrast, DYNASIM attempts to derive forecasts based on behavioral changes and relationships that maintain an inner consistency among the various demographic and economic factors traced by the model.

These features of DYNASIM are achieved by starting with a representative sample of individuals and families, incorporating their differences in age, education, race, sex, work experience, welfare benefits, and so forth. According to the best understanding available of behavioral relationships, the "individuals" in the model evolve from year to year — experiencing divorces and marriages, giving birth, becoming unemployed and finding new jobs, changing residence, and dying. Each year's simulation provides a new set of circumstances, such as different income distributions, the totality of which becomes the foundation for performing the next year's simulation. It is a *micro*simulation, adopted expressly to avoid many of the giant leaps of faith made by the widely accepted econometric models when they are used for *macro*simulation. This whole process of advancing or "aging" the population is well-geared to the analysis of proposed public policies because the year-by-year simulations of any single change or set of changes touches off a whole chain of reactions. Social science researchers typically use the caveat, "other things being equal," in their prognostications, paying tribute to the fact that other things do not remain equal. DYNASIM seeks to capture these real-world interactions and interrelationships.

Any new device, of course, needs to be used cautiously. This seems particularly appropriate for a model that appears somewhat awesome in its scope and that is still in an early stage in its evolution. One way of exercising caution with DYNASIM is to introduce its inner workings to critical examination. The authors of this book therefore lay bare the details of the development and operation of the separate parts of the model, stripping the instrument of mystery or fantasy. They pinpoint the facets of social science research that, when translated into the microsimulation equations, comprise the building blocks of the model.

DYNASIM might never have been created in this decade except for certain organizations that were willing to commit substantial funds to the enterprise. They did so at considerable risk, knowing it was a project which, even if ultimately successful, would bring benefits to them and their publics only in the long run. In the *social* sciences this kind of trust is rare. Those patient and generous organizations are the Office of Economic Opportunity, the Department of Health, Education and Welfare, the National Science Foundation, the Treasury Department, and the Ford Foundation.

The chief author of the microanalytic model, Guy Orcutt, was working on the idea for more than a decade when he brought the notion to The Urban Institute. He served full-time as first director of the project and then part-time on our staff until this book was completed; he continues to share his time and expertise with the Institute while serving as E. Whitney Griswold Professor of Urban Studies and Professor of Economics at Yale University.

This is not the place to catalog findings from uses of the model, but it is instructive to note some of the applications. One of the first uses of DYNASIM has been to forecast the future costs and caseloads of Aid to Families with Dependent Children (AFDC) through 1985. In another, DYNASIM was used to create a set of synthetic work and earning histories of Americans from 1960 through the year 2000 to get a better perspective on the functioning of the Social Security system. Projection to the year 2000 permits a view of the repercussions of recent and proposed changes in the system.

Income distribution projections have been made in connection with possible housing subsidies, the effect of teenage illegitimacy on future earnings, and the like. Chapter 14 presents findings from DYNASIM experiments designed to find policies that would help women achieve earnings parity with men. Chapter 15 includes forecasts in the growth of female-headed families and in the overall income distribution.

Anticipated work for DYNASIM included a simulation of changes in unemployment insurance rules. Several measures were pending to incorporate permanently some of the extended unemployment coverage enacted on an emergency basis during the 1974–75 recession. Simulations would reveal the budget dimensions and benefit distributions of these proposals. Another project called for simulating a negative income tax that would replace three welfare programs—AFDC, supplemental security income, and food stamps. One of the advantages of DYNASIM is that it can deal simultaneously with complex multiple programs of this type, and not merely for the next year or so but over extended periods of time.

DYNASIM can not provide definitive answers about the future. Unknowns continue to loom large. But this device does extend the ability of policy makers to make comparisons between policies, to perceive trends that otherwise would be hidden from view, and to get some idea of the magnitude of costs and effects that are far more reliable than estimates from other available means. However, in the end, the model is no better than the social research on which it relies. Thus, we hope that its presentation and use will spur other social scientists to enrich our understanding of the individual and social behavior upon which this model is based.

William Gorham
President
The Urban Institute

Washington, D.C.
July 1976

Table of Contents

PART III   ECONOMIC OPERATING CHARACTERISTICS

PART IV   EXPLORATIONS OF THE MODEL

TABLES

FIGURES

CHARTS

Acknowledgments

Given the joint nature and long duration of this venture, it is impossible to portray adequately the many and varied contributions made by each of the participants and by a host of other individuals and organizations. Guy H. Orcutt provided the original thrust and along with Harold W. Guthrie served as project codirector from 1969 through 1972. Since then Orcutt has functioned as project director, with Richard F. Wertheimer serving as project manager. John Bossons has worked on development of a successor to the present macro submodel and on development of wealth portfolio operating characteristics. Steven B. Caldwell has developed the demographic operating characteristics of the model, except for birth and education which were developed by Gerald E. Peabody. Gary Hendricks began the work on transfer income and has also carried out an error analysis of the model. Sheila R. Zedlewski developed the operating characteristics for disability and transfer payments. James D. Smith is responsible for developing a data base which can be used in specifying family wealth in the initial population samples and in developing operating characteristics relating to saving and intergenerational transfers of wealth. Wertheimer developed the labor income related parts of the model with assistance from Sheila Larkin, and, along with Sara Delano Kelly, he helped Orcutt develop the present macro submodel. Philip B. Nelson contributed a useful working paper on home-ownership and substantially improved the description of the model presentation in the second chapter.

George Sadowsky is the inventor and prime developer of MASH, the computer simulation system underlying our simulation studies. Kenneth R. Jacobs took over responsibility for the continuing development of MASH in 1973. (Sadowsky 1976). Roberta C. Carey, Zedlewski, and Jacobs programmed the model in the MASH system and ran most of the simulations. Erskine J. Underwood provided valuable assistance in preparing the 1960 and 1970 Census samples for use. Wendy Armstrong for the first three years of the project and then Brenda Brown have been invaluable in meeting the demanding secretarial needs of the project.

The project's advisory committee includes Martin Greenberger of Johns Hopkins University, Leslie Kish of the University of Michigan, James N. Morgan of the University of Michigan, Jeanne C. Ridley of Georgetown University, Alice M. Rivlin of the Congressional Budget Office, James H. Schulz of Brandeis University, and Harold W. Watts of the University of Wisconsin. They have been of enormous help with respect to data, data analysis, model specification, model application, and moral support.

Several government agencies and foundations have financed this and related projects. Six have played critical roles—the Office of Economic Opportunity, the National Science Foundation, the Social Security Administration, the Ford Foundation, the Department of Health, Education, and Welfare, and the Treasury Department. Many individuals within these organizations have been helpful. In particular, we must recognize the support and constructive suggestions made by James H. Blackman of NSF, Judith Dernburg of HEW, Edward Gramlich of Cornell University, Ronald Hoffman of the Congressional Budget Office, Nelson McClung of Treasury, Larry L. Orr of HEW, Florence Setzer of HEW, and Wayne Vroman of the University of Maryland.

PART I.
AN INTRODUCTION TO MICROANALYTIC MODELS

Chapter 1
MICROANALYTIC SIMULATION: AN OVERVIEW

This book describes an Urban Institute-based effort to develop microanalytic simulation as a significant new tool for policy exploration. A sample representation of the U.S. population is one of the key ingredients of the simulation capability which has been developed. A second is a microanalytic model which is used in simulating changes in the sample representation of this population over time. The simulated activities of individuals and families during the first year produce a population of a different size with changed income distribution, new places of residence, different educational status, and the like. The totality of these simulated changes produce a new sample population for the second year. This second year sample in turn becomes a suitable basis for simulating the succeeding year and so on.

This chapter indicates in greater detail what microanalytic models are and why microanalytic simulation is now both a feasible and attractive way of bringing basic research to bear on social and policy issues.

New Possibilities

To select prudent governmental policies affecting unemployment, social services, income distribution, national output, inflation, education, health, and the like requires the capability of predicting what the results will be, based on a realistic model of the economy. If policy makers are considering one tax law as compared to some other tax law, or one spending policy as compared to some other spending policy, they should know what the consequences of all the laws and policies under consideration are likely to be. One way to find out is to try out the policies and see what happens. This has often been done, but it can be a costly and painful way of smoking out errors, not very satisfactory from the standpoint of the affected citizens or the economy. Policies should be selected on the basis of their fruit; but it would be preferable to sample the fruit

1

before applying policies to the real world. If a sufficiently accurate model of the economy were available, it would make such sampling possible.

Clearly the policy relevance of any model depends critically on the understanding built into it. Predictive scope depends on what theories of the real world have been explicitly or implicitly used in specifying the relations or operating characteristics of the model. Predictive accuracy depends on the adequacy of the specification and linkages of these operating characteristics as descriptors of pertinent real world processes.

Of the many severe difficulties facing modelers of social systems, clearly the most intractable has been that of achieving a useful level of understanding of how social processes actually work and how they respond to human actions. This difficulty is not about to go away, at least not in this century. Nevertheless, three interlocking developments of the last twenty-five years do open up radically new and hopeful possibilities for development during the last quarter of this century of a basic understanding of social processes adequate to the building of social system models of great utility for policy analysis.

First and perhaps the most fundamental of these has been the remarkable growth during the last two decades of microdata—that is, data relating to individuals, families, firms, and other key behavioral units of the economy or government. These microdata are in contrast to macrodata which deal with aggregates and which sacrifice the richness of individual detail to focus on averages and generalities. Most microdata have been obtained by survey techniques and thus derive from natural events rather than planned experiments (Lansing and Morgan 1971). Two of the most important domestic organizations involved in collecting data about microunits have been the University of Michigan Survey Research Center and the U.S. Bureau of the Census with its ongoing Current Population Surveys and its public use samples drawn from the 1960 and 1970 population censuses.

A potentially very important new source of data relating to microbehavioral units has been opened up by the field experiments—some completed and others ongoing—bearing on family income maintenance programs. The impact of such experiments upon hypothesis testing and estimation is still small because the resulting flow of data has just begun to emerge. By the end of this century, however, field experimentation should have become a basic tool of social science research just as it already has in agriculture, medicine, and physical sciences. Both the Poverty Institute of the University of Wisconsin and Mathematica, Inc., have played major roles in sparking the development under way with their negative income tax experiments (Watts 1969).

A possible development which may spur the creation of valuable bodies of microdata is set forth in a proposal to build national accounts on a continually maintained, extended, and updated base of microlevel accounts of microbehavioral units. For an excellent description of this proposal, which would link the production of research useful microdata sets to the production of administratively useful macrodata, see Ruggles and Ruggles (1973).

The *second* major development of great importance for social science research is the advent during the 1950s of high-speed computers and associated devices for storage and retrieval of massive amounts of data. This revolutionary development is of obvious importance to our work but it has been so widely recognized that no further comment is needed here.

The microanalytic pattern or paradigm for modeling a social system is a *third* relatively new development which, in close interaction with the first two, opens up exciting new possibilities for modeling large-scale social systems and subjecting them to policy analysis. Such an approach appears to offer an excellent framework for consolidating and applying past, present, and future research work of many individuals in varied areas of the social sciences. This approach builds on developments in computer science and statistics and provides a fruitful way of mobilizing for policy analysis the large and varied bodies of microdata which already are or soon will be available. Microanalytic models are no substitute for microanalytic behavioral research. Rather they guide research and enhance the usefulness of research by providing a loom upon which the different strands of microbehavior can be woven together. Without microanalytic modeling, the results of behavioral research on microunits often are confined to a kind of Procrustean bed—that is, amputated or stretched beyond recognition to fit the commonly used macromodels.

This report gives an overview of microanalytic modeling and simulation with a focus on the specific Urban Institute model which is now operational. Clearly what is called for in this relatively new approach to social science research and policy analysis is an ongoing cumulative effort. We hope we have provided a good start.

Alternative Approaches to Modeling an Economy

The oldest and most widely utilized approach to the construction of quantitative models of the United States economy dates back to the path-breaking work of Tinbergen (1939). Models used in this approach may be referred to as aggregate-type national income models. These models use major sectors, such as the household and business sectors, as basic components. Macroeconomic relationships for these components are estimated and tested on the basis of annual or quarterly time series data of such variables as aggregate consumption and income of the household sector. The relationships developed have been finite difference equations of a stochastic or probabilistic nature. Both recursive and simultaneous equations systems have been developed. Examples of models of this general type include those by Tinbergen, Clark (1949), Klein (1947, 1950), Klein and Goldberger (1955), Duesenberry, Eckstein and Fromm (1960), Smithies (1957), and Suits (1962), to name only a few. The Social Science Research Council-Brookings econometric model building effort (1965) represents the most ambitious attempt in this general direction, containing as it does several hundred equations and an industrial sector with several subsectors.

The second oldest and the second most widely utilized approach to construction of models of the United States stems from Leontief's highly important work (1951, 1953). Industries are used as basic components in these models. Emphasis is placed on the cross-sectional structure of the economy rather than on its dynamic features. Physical outputs of industries are assumed to be strictly proportional to physical inputs classified by industry of origin. Models of this type have been stated in a nonprobabilistic form. Solution of such models with as many as one hundred industries has been achieved by the numerical inversion of a matrix of the same order. Richard Stone (1966) among others has contributed substantially to the extension of this modeling paradigm to social accounting.

The newest and least developed approach to the construction of models of socioeconomic systems is the microanalytic approach, developed by Orcutt (1957) and Orcutt, Greenberger, Korbel, and Rivlin (1961). While being of the same general statistical type as other models of national economies, microanalytic models are, nevertheless, the most general in terms of their statistical structure. Each major type of model of a national economy may include stochastic or random elements, each may use previous values of variables as part of what is treated as given, and each may be expressed as a system of equations. However, microanalytic models are more general in that they may contain a population of any kind of component instead of a single case of each kind, as is true with both Leontief-type and aggregate-type national income models.

The Need for Microanalytic Models

Microanalysis is a novel approach to modeling, but the concern for the behavior of individuals, as opposed to masses or aggregates, returns to a traditional economic perspective. Up until about four decades ago it was widely believed that economics, perhaps like mechanics, should consist of an elegant deductive structure resting upon a few simple premises about the behavior of microcomponents. It also was believed that individual introspection, self-observation, and observation of familiar components would be adequate for achieving the essential inductive substructure. However, three factors led to the virtual abandonment of the microanalytic approach to social system modeling when economists initiated the modeling of national economies.

In the first place, it came to be appreciated that households and firms are too complicated to yield the essential secrets of their behavior to unsophisticated, inductive attempts based on introspection and then available data. In the second place, it began to be apparent that as models of microcomponents became more complex, deductions about the results of their interaction would become extremely formidable if not impossible to achieve with tools that were then available. In the third place, governments responded to pressing socioeconomic problems by trying to accumulate data about their overall dimensions — and this reinforced a growing general belief in the value of this kind of aggregated information.

Economists, being unable to deliver what was needed by the microanalytic approach, turned to a more direct approach which we will refer to as the macro time series approach. This approach was facilitated by a rapidly expanded body of national income data. These data, being already at the level of aggregation that seemed attuned to such central interests as national economic stabilization and growth policies, appeared to permit the econometrician to sidestep the apparently intractible interpretation problems associated with the microanalytic approach. Also, by making use of these macro time series data that others were developing, the econometrician could happily retreat from the painstaking and substantial effort associated with data collection.

However, the micro-macro pendulum gradually started to swing back again during the last two decades. The inadequacy of highly aggregative national accounts for certain purposes became apparent. It has come to be realized that these accounts to not provide a satisfactory data base for predicting the effects of governmental actions. At the same time, major data gathering and computer related developments came along that are stirring revolutionary changes in social science research while making the more indirect microanalytic approach feasible.

The need to develop microanalytic models of economic systems, given the feasibility of doing so, arises because of the following considerations:

1. A substantial part of the theory and of the output of current research cannot be applied effectively in models restricted to macrocom-

ponents and macrorelations. Much of social science theory and research relate to the behavior of individuals, families, and firms. While it is generally a simple matter to aggregate behavior of microcomponents, we do not know how to aggregate microrelations appropriately. Sometimes macrorelations are specified to look like underlying microrelations, but clearly this may be very unsatisfactory. For example, if family consumption depends on family income and wealth as well as on various life cycle variables, then aggregate consumption will in general depend on the joint distribution of family incomes, family wealth, and family life cycle characteristics. Not only would such a relation be difficult to specify and essentially impossible to estimate directly, but it could not be used in a macromodel unless the joint distribution of all these micro variables were available for use as an input.

2. Satisfactory estimation and testing of highly aggregative models cannot be achieved because of the relatively few macro time series observations available for testing implications of such models against actual developments. Multicollinearity, autocorrelation, feedbacks, and errors of observations only serve to complicate and worsen what is already a very precarious situation insofar as satisfactory testing is concerned. The information available for estimation and testing can be enormously increased by appropriate use of the data relating to microcomponents.[1]

3. Models built only in terms of the interaction of major sectors cannot yield several important kinds of predictions. For example, not only is it important to predict how unemployment or income would be affected by alterative policies, but it also is important to predict how unemployment and income would be distributed among individuals and families by various characteristics. Such characteristics might well include previous unemployment, age, sex, race, and family size.

Some Previous Efforts

An example of an early useful development and application of a static microanalytic model without a significant behavioral content is provided by Joseph A. Pechman (1965) for estimating federal income tax revenues. A model used by Nelson McClung and Gail Wilensky (Wilensky 1970) in analyzing negative income tax and family maintenance programs represent an evolution of this type of microanalytic modeling with limited provisions for advancing the initial sample representation of the

1. The interested reader is referred to Orcutt (1968), Orcutt, Watts and Edwards (1968) and Edwards and Orcutt (1969) for a fuller treatment of the need for a microanalytic research strategy in order to improve hypothesis testing and estimation.

population forward in time. It was developed for President Johnson's Income Maintenance Commission and has been further developed at The Urban Institute where it has been used for estimating the cost and distributional impacts of a variety of welfare and health programs.

In addition to the dynamic demographic microsimulation model reported on in the book by Orcutt, Greenberger, Korbel and Rivlin (1961), several other microanalytic models have been developed. Ridley and Sheps (1966) developed REPSIM to study the relative importance of various demographic and biological factors on natality. Barrett (1967) reported on a human reproduction model similar to REPSIM. Hyrenius and Adolffson (1964) developed a fertility simulation model for use with age cohorts. A demographic microsimulation model has been reported by Hyrenius et al. (1964, 1967) and results obtained with this model have been reported by Holmberg (1968). Schultz (1968) reported on a microanalytic model which traces out twenty-year implications of the existing and alternative social security laws for individuals 45 or over in 1960. Horvitz et al. (1969) and Giesbrecht et al. (1968, 1969) described POPSIM, a dynamic model designed for computer microsimulation of the principal demographic processes, which produces either cohort or cross sectional data. Foster and Yost (1968) describe a microsimulation focussed on population and rural development. Sprehe and Michielutte (1969, 1971) report on the development of a microanalytic simulation model as a step in the development of a system of social accounts and Pryor (1973) reports on the development and use of a microanalytic model for investigating the impact of social and economic institutions on the distribution of income and wealth. Bryan and Carleton (1967, 1971) used microanalytic simulation as a tool for policy analysis in the monetary and fiscal area (1971). T. Mirer (1973) combined a nonbehavioral microanalytic approach with a macro time series approach in attempting to throw light on how various kinds of families would fare at different rates of inflation and unemployment. Finally, Barbara Bergman (1973) is using microanalytic simulation in researching and analyzing a variety of behavior but focussing on labor market phenomena, and Richard Nelson and Sidney Winter (1973) are using such an approach in their development of a new paradigm for research and theory development in the area of firm and market phenomena.

Outlines of a Microanalytic Model of an Economy Including Markets

Both for research purposes and for convenience of presentation, it is important and perhaps even essential to consider an overall model of an economy as an ensemble of interacting building blocks. Each type of block becomes a focus of research activity, and presentation of the overall model is facilitated by presentation of submodels of each type of block along with a description of the way in which interaction between blocks is to take place.

Alternative ways of breaking an overall model into blocks are possible but some ways seem definitely preferable. In general, the objective is to select blocks in such a way that each block or type may be studied with a minimum of concern about interrelationships with other blocks.

The major building blocks are called *components*. In microanalytic models of an economy the components represent recognizable entities met in everyday experience. The type of component occupying center stage is called a *decision unit*. Decision units include individuals, nuclear families, households, manufacturing firms, retailers, banks, insurance companies, labor unions, and local, state, and federal government units. Individuals are imbedded within more extensive family or household units. Firms are imbedded within industry units.

The decision units in microanalytic models interact with each other either directly or indirectly through a second major type of component called a *market*. The markets in a model represent markets in the economy, and it is through them that the third type of component flows from decision unit to decision unit. For brevity, components of this last type will be referred to as *goods*. But it must be noted that such components include not only goods which may be provided, held, sold, bought, or consumed by decision units, but also instruments used to represent wealth—such as money, bonds, shares of stock, deeds, and mortgages.

A description of any decision unit would include a listing of its own input, status, and output variables along with those relationships which are used in updating status variables and in generating output variables. The behavioral relationships used to generate values of the updated status variables and of the output variables are called *operating characteristics* of that component. Other relations of a definitional or tautological character may be used as convenience dictates. In principle there could be explicitly recognized operating characteristics for other than decision unit components. Thus, for some purposes physical depreciation equations might best be regarded as operating characteristics associated with physical entities such as houses or cars. However, this has not proved necessary in the work reported on in this book.

Finally, any variable used by an operating characteristic may be referred to as an *input* of that operating characteristic and any variable determined by an operating characteristic may be referred to as an *output* of that operating characteristic.

While the intent of interaction of many different types of decision units through markets remains as part of the original conception of microanalytic modeling of social systems, the implementation presented in this book still falls short of the dream in this as in some other respects. In fact, close examination will reveal that interaction through richly specified multiple markets is replaced by interaction through a simple macromodel.

Solution of Social System Models

Solution of a model consists of deriving implications from it. Solutions may be more or less complete, and a wide variety of ways of solving a model may be possible. The various approaches to solution of social system models may be classified into three broad classes, which for present purposes will be referred to as the analytic approach, the transitional matrix approach, and the simulation approach.

The Analytic Approach

In the analytic approach an attempt is made to deduce a relationship for each endogenous or output variable of a model that will express it explicitly as a function of initial conditions and exogenous or input variables of the model. The set of such relationships is the general solution of the model. Specific solutions of a model are obtained by evaluating these functions for specific sets of endogenous variables for specific time periods, and for given values of initial conditions and exogenous variables.

When feasible, the analytic approach has much to commend it and is greatly preferred by mathematicians. However, this approach has not been successfully applied to social system models of moderate complexity and realism. Either it has proved impossible to deduce general solutions or, if they can be deduced in a formal way, they are too complicated to understand or even to use as a basis for calculating specific numerical solutions.

In some cases in which a full analytic solution cannot be obtained, researchers lower their objectives and instead seek to analytically determine the dependence of expected or mean values of dependent variables on initial conditions and exogenous variables. Conditional probability functions are replaced by conditional expected value functions, and expected values of endogenous variables are sought instead of their probability distributions.

For some purposes approximation of probability distributions by their means is a sensible idea for arriving at a first approximation. And, if expected values of endogenous variables are all that are needed, then it may be ideal for single period prediction. The major practical difficulty with this approach is that for many purposes policy interest centers on distributional questions as well as on mean value questions. A potential user of a model will be upset to discover that, while he or she may have started with a model which was potentially capable of predicting the effect of policy on income distribution, the capability was lost in solving the model by replacement of distributions by mean values.

Transitional Matrix Approach

A numerical approach, which has been used effectively in obtaining specific solutions for some models, is the transitional matrix approach. It has been used by demographers, among others, and is the computational technique used by the United States Bureau of the Census in making population projections.

A transitional matrix is a rectangular array of transitional probabilities which, when multiplied by a vector (a one-dimensional array) of frequencies representing the state of population at a point in time, yields the vector of frequencies specifying the state of the population one period later. There would be one transitional probability for each combination of initial and final values of the variables by which components are classified.

With restricted models the transitional matrix approach may be an attractive approach to their solution and use. In the first place, it is easily specified in terms of repetitions of simple matrix operations. Secondly, if the number of components is very large relative to the number of cells into which components are classified, this technique groups components to minimize computation costs. The difficulty which prevents this method of solution from being satisfactory for solution of microanalytic models such as ours arises because the number of cells essential for a suitable specification of the state of a population of decision units would be many times larger than the number of decision units in the United States economy.

The transitional matrix technique seems attractive because it appears to avoid unnecessary repetition of calculations by grouping those components which are to be similarly treated. However, this grouping and regrouping becomes less and less attractive as the number of groups into which a population must be classified becomes large relative to the size of the population.

Even an extremely modest microanalytic model of the economy would involve substantially more than ten endogenous variables per family since even specifying ages and educational levels would take two variables for each family member. And, even if only ten values were permitted for each variable, the number of cells needed to classify families without loss of information would be 10^{10} or ten billion. The full matrix of transitional probabilities would then have ten billion squared elements! No doubt, if one were determined to use the transitional matrix technique, one would look for methods of avoiding the handling of empty cells and the calculation of transitional probabilities which would apply only to empty cells. Of course, any notion of direct estimation of each transitional probability from any conceivable body of data no matter how large would have to be abandoned. The computational problem would be increased by the fact that while most of the cells would be empty at any point of time, it would not be the same set which would be empty in successive time periods. Even if one were able, without great cost, to reduce the number of cells at time t to one-millionth of ten billion, one would still have ten thousand cell frequencies and the matrix of transitional probabilities would have one hundred million elements. Since current microanalytic attempts to model the economy involve several times as many variables per family as used in the above example, and since one-digit specification of variables would be highly unsatisfactory, it seems clear that the transitional matrix technique will not provide a satisfactory technique for solution of microanalytic models involving any serious attempt at realism. It seems equally clear that explicit estimation and testing of hypotheses relating to individual transition probabilities would not be a very attractive general approach to microanalytic modeling of social systems.

The Simulation Approach

Simulation, a general approach to the study and use of models, furnishes an alternative approach to that offered by conventional mathematical techniques. In using conventional mathematical techniques to solve a model the objective is to determine, deductively and with generality, the way in which the model relates endogenous variables to initial conditions and time paths of exogenous variables.[2] By contrast in any single simulation run the solution obtained is highly specific and consists of only a single set of time paths of endogenous variables. To determine how behavior of the endogenous variables is more generally dependent on initial conditions, parameters, and exogenous variables may require many simulation runs; and even then induction from specific results to general solutions will be required.

An individual simulation run may be thought of as an experiment performed upon a model. A given experiment involves operating a

2. There are many areas in which simulation is of importance to social scientists and to policy makers and the interested reader is referred to such useful starting points as provided by Adelman (1968), Clarkson and Simon (1960), Guetzkow (1962), Orcutt (1960), Shubik (1960a, 1960b).

model after first completely specifying a set of initial conditions appropriate to the model, a set of values of the parameters used in specifying relations contained in the model, and the time paths of those variables used in the model and treated as exogenous. Additional experiments would involve operating the model after respecifying the initial conditions, the parameters, and/or the exogenous variables. The problem of inferring general relationships from specific results obtained in individual experiments performed on a model is the same as that of inferring general relationships from specific experimental results in the inductive sciences. The scientist studying natural phenomena has no alternative. In principle the research worker, studying or using a model, could conceivably use a purely deductive approach, but with many models, including ours, this alternative has not proved feasible with known mathematical methods.

Solution of The Urban Institute's
Microanalytic Model

The simulation approach does permit, in principle at least, the solution of microanalytic models of economic systems and it is the basic approach we have used. However, two difficulties must be dealt with.

The first is that the operating characteristics of our model do not produce *events* such as death, but rather the *probabilities* of such events. For purposes of within-period tabulations, having the probability of each event for each microunit is ideal. However, it is not a substitute for updating the initial population so that it may be used as an initial population for the following year's simulation. This need is met by use, along with simulation, of what is widely known as the Monte Carlo technique. For example, the occurrence of death is determined, in effect, by a random draw from a container of black and white balls containing the same proportion of black balls as the predicted probability of death. If a black ball is drawn, as it were, the person is simulated to die. In actual practice this is done by assigning death if the predicted probability of death is more than a random number drawn from a uniform distribution running from zero through one. A similar procedure is used with other predicted probabilities. This method of dealing with probabilities is an unsophisticated yet powerful method which has come into wide use as a result of the development of the modern computer. This method capitalizes on two facts: first, it is possible to empirically approximate a multivariate probability distribution as closely as desired on the basis of an adequate number of random drawings from the distribution; secondly, it frequently is a great deal easier to obtain random drawings from a distribution than it is to analytically deduce the form of the distribution.

The second remaining difficulty to be dealt with is that we wish to simulate the behavior of very large populations composed of entities characterized by many attributes. But as a practical matter how can the state of a population be specified or updated if it involves, say, ten or more variables for each of, say, 200 million components?

The solution is as simple as it is obvious. Any current or updated population may be represented by a random sample drawn from it. Means, variance, covariance, and other functions of the sample will be estimates of the corresponding functions of the population sampled. The properties of samples and of sample statistics in relation to populations and population statistics have been extensively investigated and are readily available. Clearly, for many purposes the United States population may be satisfactorily represented by a sample of a few thousand persons and larger samples can be used when the use justifies the added expense.

The Urban Institute's Dynamic Simulation of Income Model (DYNASIM) thus operates with a sample representation of the United States population composed of individuals in families and is solved by the simulation approach. During each simulated year the model is used to determine sequentially the simulated activity of each member of the sample of individuals and families so as to produce an updated sample suitable for use as an initial sample in simulating the succeeding year.

The imputation of births and deaths modifies the size and age distribution of the population. Families are formed, dissolved, and moved to different geographic locations by the imputation of marriage, divorce, and migration. Schooling attainment is simulated for those of school age. In the labor sector of the model, wage income is generated for individuals by imputing labor force participation, hours worked, and wage rate. Family income is completed by imputing government transfer payments and returns to family wealth. Net family income is obtained by taxing the family's total income. Savings are determined from net income and lead to asset accumulation.

Operating in conjunction with this micro model is a submodel of the macroeconomy. This model provides an environment within which the micro model operates so that activities at the microlevel can be influenced by macroeconomic conditions. It also allows an examination of the impact of microbehavior on the macroeconomy. The macro submodel determines the total wage income and the aggregate level of unemployment in the economy. Wages and unemployment are then distributed among individuals by the micro operating characteristics in conformity with these totals.

Output Possibilities

In microanalytic simulation, as in the Ruggles approach to national accounting, samples of microunits are conceived of as representing corresponding populations. One convenience of this in national accounting is that any possible aggregation or tabulation of the microdata can be done on request at low or moderate cost. This is not generally feasible with a cell frequency approach to representation of a multivariate population since, as pointed out in discussing the transitional matrix approach to solution, even a ten-way, single-digit classification scheme would require ten billion cells if loss of flexibility and information is to be avoided.

Projections

In DYNASIM the population of families and component individuals is represented at every stage in a simulation by a probability sample which can be made available to users on request for any analysis and tabulation which could be made of a corresponding sample of a real population of families and component individuals. Since a microanalytic simulation uses a behavioral model which advances a sample representation of a population in time, future states of a population can be projected by carrying out a simulation. Thus, it is possible to analyze, tabulate, or otherwise aggregate the sample representation of a projected population in any way which was feasible with the initial sample of an actual population.

Microunit Histories

A second possibility, which is distinct but follows closely on the first, also emerges. A microanalytic model, such as ours, can be used to advance an initial sample based on, say, the 1960 Census public use sample, year by year until the present. Time series outputs can be compared with available national accounts time series, and cross sectional outputs can be compared with sample and census data over the years since 1960. The model can then be aligned so as to yield results in agreement with actual developments, the actual initial state of the real population in 1960, and what is known about accounting and behavioral relations. When this has been achieved, running the aligned model over the historical period since 1960 would yield a pieced together microunit data bank of a historical period in terms of time paths of a sample of microunits.

This way of merging and melding many disparate bodies of data and of available understanding could be regarded as yielding an augmented census-type public use sample of individuals and families for each year starting with 1960 up to the present. Such generated samples could be used in ways similar to the ways actual public use samples are used. The advantages would lie (1) in having such samples for years not otherwise possible, (2) in having samples for successive years actually linked between years at the individual and family level, such as might be desired for considering tax averaging schemes, for example, and (3) in having a richer description of microunits than is possible on the basis of any single survey. Inclusion of wealth and portfolio attributes along with income and demographic attributes would have obvious advantages for exploring the burden at the family and individual level of different approaches to taxation.

Policy Experiments

A third class of output capabilities which is inherent in our microanalytic simulation approach is that of carrying out policy experimentation by altering the time paths of input variables of the model or by altering the parameters or other specifications of the model. Tax laws, social security laws, or income maintenance arrangements might then be simulated — both with and without changes that are being considered — so that the likely consequences of proposed policy changes could be estimated.

Sensitivity Experiments

The capability of predicting implications of policy changes also means that sensitivity studies can be made of the dependencies of simulation outputs on parameter specification. Results from such studies can help guide subsequent behavioral research studies in fruitful directions by showing where improved precision in estimation would really matter.

Controlling Monte Carlo Variation

For a number of reasons, it is desirable in simulated policy experiments to control the Monte Carlo variability of the microanalytic model. The variability results from the use of pseudo-random numbers to decide which events are simulated to occur and which are not. We have designed a technique of dispensing random numbers which causes the same decisions to be made with the same random numbers from run to run. This procedure yields three related but distinct advantages.

The most important advantage is the separation of the Monte Carlo variability of the model from the effects of a treatment or experiment. This allows the social scientist to approximate the method used by a physical scientist, whose experiments consist of a control group and a treatment group. The only difference between the two groups is the fact of the treatment. The environments (in our case, the random numbers) are the same for both groups. Our technique means that an observed change between a control run and an experiment run can be attributed to the effect of the treatment with less uncertainty.

A second advantage is that alignment of the model with historical data is easier and more precise. With Monte Carlo variation controlled from run to run on identical populations, a changed probability for an event such as a marriage or death will reduce the number of occurrences of that event proportionally. Thus, if we find that the model simulates too many births in a particular year, we can reduce the birth probabilities by the proper percentages to align the model as closely as desired to historical marginal distributions or cross-tabulations.

The third advantage of the method is that it permits smaller sample sizes. Since the total Monte Carlo variation declines with increasing sample size, we might normally desire to run with as large a sample as possible. But when we are looking at differences between control and treatment runs, the Monte Carlo variability will be the same in the two runs, regardless of sample size.[3]

The random number technique used in the model was implemented by giving each population member (person, family, and interview unit) a random number stream of its own. Random numbers are taken from this stream at the same rate whether or not events are simulated to occur. The stream is defined by a kernel or seed that is used to generate subsequent random numbers. When an operating characteristic requires one or more random numbers, it uses the current value of the appropriate seed to generate them and then stores the seed associated with the last random number drawn as an attribute of the population entity for use by the next operating characteristic.

Other processes, aside from microsimulation within the MASH system (microanalytic simulation of households) and the current model,

---

3. In mathematical terms, we have taken two previously uncorrelated random variables (the control run determination being X and the experimental value being Y), and correlated them by using the same random numbers to make the stochastic decisions. For uncorrelated X and Y, the variance of the difference is the sum of the variances:

$$\text{Var}(X - Y) \text{ is given by } \text{Var}(X) + \text{Var}(Y)$$

For correlated random variables, however, the variance of the difference is the sum of the variance minus the covariance:

$$\text{Var}(X - Y) \text{ is given by } \text{Var}(X) + \text{Var}(Y) - \text{Cov}(X, Y)$$

The covariance of X and Y is almost equal to the sum of the variances because the random numbers used to determine X and Y are the same. (It is not quite equal because a treatment might result in different people dying or being born, but that effect is small for most treatments).

employ random numbers. For each such process, an independent stream of random numbers has been defined. Thus, it is possible to have a random variable in a macromodel, or as part of survey output, and achieve different but repeatable results by varying the starting point of the random number stream.

Modeling Paradigms and Data Bases

The close and highly interactive development of aggregate-type national income models and of national income accounts is, of course, well known and has been commented on many times. A similar association between inter-industry type models and the development of inter-industry accounts is also a fairly familiar phenomenon. Thus it should occasion no great surprise to be told that a close relation exists between the development of microanalytic models of social systems and the development and use of publicly available microdata sets.

Public use samples such as those of the Bureau of the Census from the 1960 and 1970 population censuses are of vital importance to the development and application of microanalytic models in many ways but one of the most direct is in furnishing initial populations for simulation runs. At present, solution and use of microanalytic models involves making simulation runs in which sample representations of populations of interest are moved forward in time in accordance with model-generated probabilities of microunit behavior. But, since predicted probabilities do depend on lagged attributes of members of the population as well as on model-specified behavioral relationships, initial samples are obviously needed. In the absence of appropriate real samples, synthetic initial populations would be created. However, the use of samples from real populations for this purpose has obvious advantages in generating predictions relating to real populations.

Joint frequency distributions associated with populations of individuals or other microunits can be represented in many ways. Complete listing is one way but, while it has the advantage of retaining all of the information assembled, it is unduly cumbersome for populations measured in the hundreds of millions. Approximation of joint frequency distributions by means of fitted multivariate normal or other analytically specified frequency distributions is possible but becomes economically less and less attractive as the number of measured characteristics per entity becomes large. In any case this approach runs the risk of imposing extensive and unrealistic regularities. Representation of multivariate distributions by moments such as means, variances, covariances, etc., is another possibility which loses its attractiveness as the number of variates per entity increases and as the need for higher moments is recognized. Tabular representation of multivariate frequency distribution is of course the traditional way of presenting census data. This method does not work too badly on bivariate distributions but the attempt to use such tabulations to calculate a multiple regression relating to individuals or families readily shows how unsatisfactory tabular representation is for this purpose.

In microanalytic modeling, populations both actual and synthetic are given sample representations. Public use samples drawn from real populations use the identical way of representing key entities which play roles in microanalytic modeling and simulation. The advantages of this idea in microanalytic modeling contributed to the creation of public use samples and in turn the creation of these public use samples has been and is contributing immeasurably to the development and policy application of microanalytic models.

Public Use Samples as Aids in Estimation and Testing of Behavioral Relations

Estimation and testing problems still abound even if observations on microunits are used, but at least it becomes possible to obtain and use data on an enormous body of unplanned experiments.[4] These unplanned experiments may be observed via surveys in great detail at frequent intervals and often with wide ranges of variations in the variables. In real life, there frequently are situations at the microlevel in which those variables, which an experimenter would have liked to have varied, do in fact vary and in which other variables, which an experimenter would have liked to hold constant, do remain constant. Furthermore, at the microlevel it is possible to relate differential responses to differential treatment as a means of eliminating the biasing effect of major feedbacks and as a means of identifying causal relationships.

Microanalytic models were devised to improve estimation and testing possibilities. And one central reason why they do this is that, although many microunits are introduced, all of these units are treated as members of one or another of a small number of populations of similar entities. Thus a single model of a household and its component units might be used for every household. The number of observational points that can be brought to bear in estimation or testing such a household

---

4. Much experience, if viewed retrospectively from a satisfactory perspective and with sufficient knowledge of the factors that were brought into play, may be considered "experiments" to the social scientist. Experiences that were not specifically charted out in advance are thus termed "unplanned."

model can thus be thousands of times as large as the number of parameters to be estimated.

Of course the ratio of observational points to parameters that must be estimated is not the only thing that matters. It is essential to work with the right variables measured for the same components for appropriate time intervals. Multicollinearity, autocorrelated errors, rapid feedbacks and errors of observation are problems associated with microdata sets as well as with macro time series. Nevertheless all of these problems are more manageable if the ratio of observational points to parameters is large. Such difficulties must be completely ignored if this ratio is low and even estimation becomes impossible as this ratio drops below one. No experimentalist would be very satisfied to estimate and test a particular relationship with a ratio of observational points to parameters of the order of ten or less. Yet this is what is attempted when primary reliance is placed on the use of national accounts data. However, given the development of large microdata sets such as provided by the Census public use samples, and given the growing body of sample survey data provided by the University of Michigan Survey Research Center and others, reasonable alternatives now exist.

Time Series Development Possibilities
Given Successive Public Use Samples

Responses of behavioral components are typically distributed over time and lag the situations which give rise to them. In addition some important determinants of behavior probably change to slowly to have observable consequences in the short run. Individual public use samples are useful for establishing appropriate initial conditions and do provide a variety of possibilities for testing hypotheses. Nevertheless, both short- and long-run time series data for microcomponents, or at least for numerous similar groups of microcomponents, are essential.

Public use samples drawn from decennial censuses cannot meet the need for frequently measured microcomponent time series. However, if public use samples could be developed from microdata sets obtained in the 1950, 1940, and 1930 and earlier population censuses it would be possible to construct a large number of extremely useful time series for distinguishable but similar cohorts of individuals.

The possibility of doing this stems from the fact that while no practical way seems to exist for linking data for identical individuals from different censuses it is possible to link data relating to distinguishable cohorts of individuals given public use samples from each of the censuses to be linked. To see this possibility, consider the group of white males aged 30 to 35 in 1930 who have completed 12 or more years of schooling. Except for deaths and emigrants and excluding immigrants, this group will show up in 1940 as white males aged 40 to 45 who have completed 12 or more years of schooling. In fact, the aged remnant of this group will show up in each succeeding census. Obviously a public use sample from each of the decennial census years starting with 1930 would permit the construction for this cohort of forty-year time series of every variable measured in each of the censuses. Of course, each time series would have only five points, but even so, such series would be of great research value, especially so since they could be obtained for innumerable cohorts of microunits.

Clearly, the development of public use samples from earlier censuses is extremely important on many grounds. However, foremost among these is the fact that the provision of such series would enable microanalytic researchers and model builders to avoid a myopic view of the world which might result from sole focus on data drawn from rather recent two-to-five-year panels.

Generation of Predictions for Individuals and Small Groups

The applications of the microanalytic models we have under development all involve deriving unconditional or conditional predictions about the U.S. population or about *major* subpopulations of the U.S. population. Expected output includes tabulations resulting from classification of the U.S. population according to selected variables. This type of output will be like the innumerable tables derived from U.S. census data. A wider range of variables will be available for use in classifying individuals and families into cells. Annual instead of decennial output will be possible. In addition, output for hypothetical development and use of policy will be feasible. Averages, variances and covariances of all microvariables will be available and development of aggregate time series will be possible.

While the richness of potential output about the U.S. population and about major subpopulations is great, compared with available macroanalytic models, our present approach does not permit generation of predictions relating to relatively small subpopulations such as the population of a city, county, state, or single-year age cohort. Neither does our present approach permit generation of useful predictions about specific families or specific individuals.

The fundamental reason for these limitations is that we represent any population and its associated distributions by a sample of individuals from the population. With a sample of ten to one hundred thousand individuals it is possible to achieve an excellent representation of the U.S. population in its full multivariate richness. Unfortunately the laws of sampling are such that, for a given adequacy of representation, nearly as large a sample is needed to represent a population of a few hundred thousand as is needed to represent a population of two hundred million. This sample might be large enough to permit calculation of some mean values for small groups, but even these would have large variances. Estimation of even single variate distributions would be out of the question.

When it comes to generating predictions relating to specific families or individuals, the problem is of a slightly different nature. Our operating characteristics are designed to predict aspects of individual and family behavior and experience. But it is stressed that these are probabilistic relationships. That is, they predict for individual units in any given year the probabilities of death, probabilities of marriage, probabilities of divorce, and so forth. The reliance on probabilistic operating characteristics reflects the limited nature of our knowledge about behavior of individual units. As our understanding grows, the probabilistic component of prediction at the micro level may be narrowed down. Nevertheless, it is bound to be a dominant feature of our understanding and hence of our models for the forseeable future.

The difficulty in using our models to generate predictions for individuals or for individual families is that such predictions should be in the form of probability distributions. Unfortunately while our models implicitly contain a basis for such predictions, our present provisions will not enable us to obtain explicit estimates of probability distributions for specific individuals or families. The problem is that only one concrete life is traced out for any one individual in any one simulation of the entire U.S. population. It is obtained by translating each probability distribution as it is computed for the individual into a concrete action by means of a random drawing from the distribution. This provides a fine Monte Carlo method of obtaining information about derived distributions relating to the U.S. population, since tens of thousands of life paths are traced out in any simulation run. It does not do for any one individual because only a single life path, out of the innumerable number of possible life paths for the individual, is traced out. In general this may result in but a single drawing from each derived distribution of interest.

The range of application of our microanalytic models could be extended to predictions about specific individuals and families as follows: The data set for a specific family, or for a specific individual and associated family, could be repeated one or more thousand times and used as a second sample along with the main sample representing the U.S. population. Members of this second sample would be tagged so as not to be included in tabulations for the U.S. population. Nevertheless, members of this second sample would be subjected to the repeated application of the same operating characteristics as are applied to members of the U.S. sample. Since concrete behavior for each member of this second sample would also be obtained by the use of random drawing from computed probability distributions, it is evident that each of the thousand or more replications of any individual would each go their own way. A given simulation run would thus generate a thousand or more life paths for the individual or family. Each such life path would represent a random drawing from the population of life histories implicitly determined by the operating characteristics of the model used. Since a thousand or more such life paths would be traced out, it would be feasible to summarize and tabulate results so as to estimate derived probability distributions of interest for the replicated individual and his family.

By making successive runs with everything held constant except the behavior or treatment of a replicated individual, it would be possible to determine the implied consequences for the individual of given behavioral or treatment changes. For example, such changes might consist of introduction of family limitation, extension of schooling, postponement of marriage, etc.

In presenting the basic idea for extending the range of application of our models, one important consideration has been glossed over. Why not run simulations with just the replicated individual or family of interest? Just as we must provide a family to serve as part of an environment for an individual to grow within and to interact with, we also need the U.S. population to complete the environment needed for an individual or family over time. The need could occur in a number of different ways, but the most pressing reason for needing the U.S. population is to permit replicated individuals to find suitable mates as determined by application of the marriage operating characteristics.

Interaction of the sample composed of a replicated family with the main sample could influence the behavior of the main sample in undesirable ways if steps were not taken to avoid this. Tabulations for this secondary sample can and would be kept quite separate from tabulation for the U.S. sample. Output generated with the main sample would be available for use in applying operating characteristics to members of the replicated sample; the reverse would not be permitted. Marriage between members of the replicated sample would not be permitted since this would be equivalent to marrying brothers and sisters. Members of the replicated sample would marry in the regular way with members of the main U.S. sample with one difference. Any member of the main sample marrying a member of the replicated sample would be replicated at the time of marrying. The replication would be transferred into the sample of replicated individuals and families. The individual replicated would be left in the main sample and his or her marriage would be completed in the usual way with someone from the main sample.

Extending the range of application of our models to yield results about subpopulations which, while numbering in the tens of thousands or more, are still small relative to the total U.S. population also seems possible. The appropriate approach seems to involve use of a second sample to represent the subpopulation along with a primary sample to represent the U.S. population. Operation and interaction of the two samples would be carried out much as in the above case of a second sample made up of replicated individuals. Again, output from the main sample would be available in applying operating characteristics to members of the second sample but the reverse would not be permitted. Tabulation for the two samples would be kept separate and of course different blow-up factors would be needed since individuals and families would have a higher probability of being in the sample for the subpopulation than in being in the sample for the U.S. population. Some additional complications might result in handling marriage and migration. These have not been fully worked through but are thought to be manageable.

Chapter 2

DYNASIM – SIMULATING THE POPULATION AND ITS INCOME

The foundation of The Urban Institute's dynamic microsimulation system is a sample representation of the U.S. population. This population is modified over time by a behavioral model known as *DYNASIM* (*Dyna*mic *S*imulation of *I*ncome *M*odel). Activities of individuals and families during the first year are simulated to produce a new sample population for the second year. This sample is in turn transformed into a suitable basis for simulating the succeeding year and so on for as many years as is desired.

The Microsimulation Process in Perspective

DYNASIM is composed of an interrelated set of processes or *operating characteristics*. These operating characteristics are behavioral relationships that specify for each entity – given its previous state and the new influences at work on it – what outputs are generated for the entity. In this way, the demographic sector of the model modifies the size and age distribution of the population and its family structure over time. The behavioral characteristics, expressed in terms of probabilities, are based in all cases on best available social science research.

The imputation of births and deaths changes the size and age distribution of the population. Families are formed, dissolved, and moved to different geographic locations by the imputation of marriage, divorce, and migration. Schooling attainment is simulated for those of school age. In the labor sector of the model, wage income is generated for individuals by imputing labor force participation, hours worked, and a wage rate. Family income is simulated by imputing government transfer payments and returns to family wealth. Net family income is obtained by applying tax regulations to the family's total income. Savings are determined from net income and lead to asset accumulation.

Operating in conjunction with this micromodel is an auxiliary model of the macroeconomy. This permits activities at the microlevel to be influenced by macroeconomic conditions. It also allows an examination of the impact of microbehavior on the macroeconomy. The auxiliary macromodel determines total wage income and total wealth income given the weighted hours of labor and population change as derived from the micromodel. The micromodel in turn determines the distribution of wage income, wealth income, and unemployment among individuals and families given the level of unemployment and total wage income and total wealth income from the macromodel. The unemployment rate, treated as a macropolicy input, influences developments at both the micro and macro levels.

There are two types of units in the sample population: persons and families. Families are taken to be nuclear families, i.e., families consisting of a married couple and their children who live with them; single persons, whether previously married or not, and their children, if any, are also included as families. Each individual unit and each family unit has its own identification number, and all persons carry a list which contains the identification numbers of their parents and children. Genealogical linkages can be maintained through use of these identification numbers.

Each individual or family unit is characterized by a set of attributes such as age, marital status, income level, educational attainment, and so forth. The micromodel functions deal sequentially with each family and its members. All appropriate operating characteristics are applied to each unit, thereby updating the status or conditions of the unit by simulating specific activities such as deaths, marriages, or labor force participation.

Operating characteristics are not applied automatically to each unit. Rather, they take account of distinctive features of the individual or family whose activities are being simulated. To take an obvious example, the operating characteristic of giving birth would not be applied to males, nor to females below and above child-bearing ages. Thus, the original attributes of each unit — or "current" attributes at the stage of a new simulation — play a role in determining what happens next.

Given that a unit is eligible to be subjected to possible modification by an operating characteristic, the attributes of the unit interact with the operating characteristic to determine the output of the operating characteristic. If any activity is imputed as a result of the interaction, the original attributes of the individual may be altered. For example, years of schooling may be increased by one year if a person is simulated to spend one more year in school. The output of an operating characteristic may also involve the creation of new units or the destruction of existing ones. For example, the fertility operating characteristic uses as inputs a number of attributes of the potential mother including her marital status, her age, her current number of children, and so on. If the woman does not have a birth, no change is made in her set of attributes. However, if she does give birth, her "number of children" is increased by one, and a new person unit, the newborn child, is created.

In determining whether or not an event such as a divorce will occur, a divorce operating characteristic is used in connection with appropriate attributes of a couple and their environment to estimate the probability of the event occurring. After the probability that an event will occur has been determined, a random number between 0 and 1 is generated by the computer. If this random number is less than the probability specified by the operating characteristic, the unit is treated as if the event had occurred. Otherwise the event is assumed not to have occurred. For example, if the operating characteristic were to generate a probability of .16 and the random number were .14 (or any other number less than .16), the event is simulated to have occurred. If the random number were .70 (or any other number greater than .16), the event is not simulated to have occurred.

An interactive computer system, MASH (*M*icro*a*nalytic *S*imulation of *H*ouseholds), has been designed to implement the model. MASH allows the user flexibility in operating the model and contains a sophisticated file-handling capability which is used to manipulate the microdata files that are required by simulation runs. Interaction between the user and the computer during the course of a simulation is permitted so that the progress of the simulation can be monitored or small changes, in the model or population, can be made. Capabilities for obtaining a wide range of output from the simulation are also provided by MASH. Included in MASH are a data bank, which contains time series such as birth rates, marriage rates, employment, and unemployment and the capability of drawing a sample survey from the simulated population for any year of the simulation. This sample survey can be fed into programs for computing cross-tabulations or regressions, or for conducting other analyses. A more complete description of MASH can be found in Sadowsky (1976).

Program Sectors

DYNASIM is specified by a sequenced set of program modules. Each module contains the description of an operating characteristic plus accounting identities, necessary summations, and provisions for random draws in accordance with specified probabilities.

For convenience the program modules are grouped together into program blocks. Program blocks present in DYNASIM are demographic, labor, transfer, and tax and wealth blocks. These program blocks are in turn grouped together in the MICROPASS program sector.

Other program sectors are the **MARRIAGE UNION** sector and the **MACROMODEL** sector. The **MICROPASS** and **MARRIAGE UNION** sectors are used to specify a microanalytic model of the United States population. The **MACROMODEL** sector consists of an auxiliary macro time series model developed to facilitate and extend use

FIGURE 2-1

RELATION OF MAJOR PROGRAM SECTORS TO
UPDATING OF MICRO AND MACRO DATA FILES

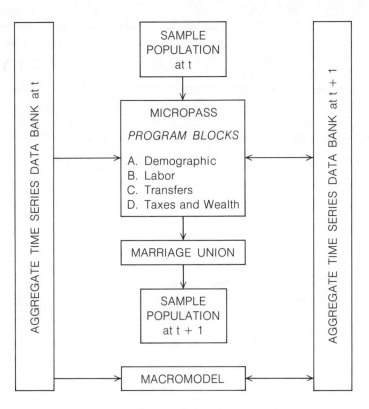

of the microanalytic population model. Figure 2-1 indicates the annual sequencing of the three sectors and how they relate to the micro and macro data files. We now describe each of the three sectors in turn.

The MICROPASS Program Sector

Except for the matching of persons previously selected for marriage, (which takes place in the **MARRIAGE UNION** sector), all microlevel operating characteristics are described by the program modules which comprise MICROPASS. These program modules are listed in Table 2-1 by name according to program block. Table 2-1 also provides sequencing and eligibility information which indicate to which units and in which order program modules are to be applied for each year simulated. The remainder of this section describes the modules which constitute the MICROPASS sector. The presentation is organized according to block membership.

Demographic Program Block

1. *INCREMENTATION:* This module updates values of age and years at current school levels. Inputs include the prior year's age and years at current school level.
2. *LEAVING HOME:* For each never-married member (aged 14 to 34) of a multiperson family, this module computes the probability that a person leaves home. If a person leaves home, he forms a new one-person family for which he is the head. The family that loses a member has its family members reduced by one. Inputs are age, sex, and race.
3. *DIVORCE:* For each married couple this program module computes the probability that a couple gets divorced. If a divorce occurs, a new one-person family is established with the former husband as its head. Children stay with the former wife, and assets are divided. Year of most recent marital status change is reset. Inputs include year of most recent marital status change; year; head's race and age; the family's region and SMSA size last year; and head's disability status, unemployment status, and wife's earnings last year.[1]
4. *BIRTH:* For each female aged 14 to 49 years of age this program module calculates the probability that a female gives birth. If a woman does give birth the number of children she has (one, two, or three) is probabilistically determined along with the sex of each child. The mother's race is assigned to all of her children. Her year of last birth is reset. Inputs include the female's race, age, previous number of offspring, marital status, and last year's grade completed.
5. *DEATH:* For each person this program module computes the probability that a person dies. If a person dies, the marital status and year of most recent marital status change of a spouse, if one exists, is reset. A flag is set so that if an inheritance module is included it will be triggered at the appropriate time and so that the deceased will be passed over during the remainder of the simulation run. Inputs include the year and the person's race, sex, and age; and

---

1. The term "last year" refers to the previous year in relation to the year being simulated (not to the year before the current calendar year).

TABLE 2-1

PROGRAM MODULE SEQUENCING FOR EACH FAMILY
IN MICROPASS PROGRAM SECTOR

Order	Program Module	Eligibility
A. Demographic Program Block		
1	Incrementation	Each family and each person
2	Home Leaving	Each never married person aged 15 to 35
3	Divorce	Married couple if any in each family
4	Birth	Each female person aged 14 to 50
5	Death	Each person
6	First Marriage Selection	Each never married person over 14
7	Remarriage Selection	Each previously married person
8	Disabled	Each person over 13
9	Education	Each person aged 5 to 30
10	Location	Each family
B. Labor Program Block		
11	Wage Rate	Each person over 13
12	Labor Force Participation	Each person over 13
13	Hours in Labor Force	Each person in labor force
14	Fraction of Hours Unemployed	Each person in labor force
15	Earnings	Each family and each employed person
C. Transfers Program Block		
16	Social Security	Each family
17	Other Pensions	Each family
18	Unemployment Compensation	Each person in labor force
19	AFDC	Each family
20	SSI	Each family
21	Food Stamps	Each family
22	Transfer Income	Each family
D. Taxes and Wealth Program Block		
23	Wealth Income[a]	Each family
24	Federal Income Taxation and Disposable Income[a]	Each family
25	Saving and Wealth[a]	Each family

a. This module was not included in the 1975 version of DYNASIM, although it has been specified.

the person's last year marital status, number of offspring, and grade completed.

6. *FIRST MARRIAGE SELECTION:* For each never-married person over 14 and under 35, this program module calculates the probability of first marriage. If the person is selected to be married, the person enters the MARRIAGE UNION sector after MICROPASS. Inputs include the year; the person's race, sex, and age; the person's grade completed, hours worked, and wage rate last year; and the family's transfer income last year.

7. *REMARRIAGE SELECTION:* For each previously married single person this program module calculates the probability of remarriage. If a person is selected to be married, the person enters the MARRIAGE UNION sector after MICROPASS. Inputs include the person's sex, age, marital status, year, and year of most recent marital status change.

8. *EDUCATION:* For each person aged 5 to 30 this program module calculates the grade completed, years at current school level, and whether the person is currently in school. Inputs include the person's race, age, sex, and school status and his last year's grade completed, years at current school level, and the family head's grade completed.

9. *LOCATION:* For each family this program module calculates the probability that a family moves; if it moves, the probability that it migrates; if it migrates, the family's new region, SMSA city size and whether its members live in a central city or a suburb of an SMSA are obtained. The family's new location is recorded. Inputs include the sex, age, race, marital status, and year of most recent marital status change for the family head; and last year's region and SMSA size.

10. *DISABLED:* For each person over 13 this program module calculates the probability that a person is disabled and updates the disability status of the individual. Inputs include the person's race, sex, age, marital status, grade completed, and previous year disability status.

Labor Program Block

11. *WAGE RATE:* For each person over 13 this program module calculates the person's wage rate. Inputs include the person's age, race, and sex; current and last year's age, grade completed, marital status, disability status, and region, last year's labor force participation and wage rate, and a normal random component.

12. *LABOR FORCE PARTICIPATION:* For each person over 13 this program module calculates the probability of labor force participation and updates labor force status. Inputs include the person's race, sex, age, marital status, disability status, and previous year labor

force participation, the family's last year's transfer income, and whether or not there is a child under six in the family, and last year's national unemployment rate. If the individual is a married woman, family income other than her own earnings in the last year is also an input.

13. *HOURS IN LABOR FORCE:* For each person in the labor force this program module calculates labor force hours. Inputs include a normal random component; the person's age, race, and sex; the person's last year's hours in the labor force and labor force participation status; current and last year's marital status, grade completed, and disability status; and last year's values of family transfer income, total family income less the person's earnings, and whether the family contains a child under six.

14. *FRACTION OF HOURS UNEMPLOYED:* For each person in the labor force this program module calculates the probability of unemployment. The unemployment status is updated. If the person is unemployed, the fraction of total labor force hours during which the person is unemployed is calculated and recorded. Inputs include the person's race, sex, age, marital status, and grade completed; and a random draw. If the person suffers some unemployment, the fraction of labor force hours spent unemployed is calculated as a function of a normal random component; the fraction of labor force hours spent unemployed last year; sex; current and lagged values of age, marital status, grade completed, disability status, whether the family contains a child under six, and region.

15. *EARNINGS:* For each family and each employed member of the family this program module calculates the earnings of each employed member of the family and the family's earnings. Inputs include the wage rate, hours in labor force, unemployment status, and fraction of hours unemployed.

Transfer Program Block

16. *SOCIAL SECURITY:* This program module assigns social security income to families with a retired, deceased or disabled worker with sufficient contributions to the social security system. Contributions to the social security fund are simulated for persons in the labor force in covered employment and are a function of hours worked and earnings. Primary benefit eligibility is a function of contributions, age, disability status, and earnings. Dependent's benefit eligibility is a function of marital status, age, school status, disability status, and earnings. The benefit amount is dependent upon contributions, current earnings, and the number of eligible family members.

17. *PENSIONS:* For families whose head is over 59 years old, this program module determines whether or not some income from pensions other than social security is received and, if so, the amount of the pension. The probability of receiving a pension is a function of the sex, age, and education of the head of the family. If it is determined that a pension is received by the family, the pension amount is specified to be a function of the education, sex, marital status, and race of the head of the family, and the social security and asset income of the family.

18. *UNEMPLOYMENT COMPENSATION:* This program module assigns unemployment benefits to insured workers with at least 40 hours of unemployment. A worker's insured status depends upon: a stochastic design which determines if he works in covered employment, earnings in the previous year, hours worked in the previous year, and the number of weeks for which unemployment compensation was received in the previous year. If a worker is insured, a stochastic decision determines if benefits are denied because the unemployment was voluntary. For all insured eligible workers, a weekly benefit is calculated as a function of the worker's average weekly wage in the previous year, the average wage replacement rate, and maximum weekly benefit for the census region in which he lives. Annual unemployment compensation is a function of this weekly benefit, the number of hours of unemployment, and the number of weeks during which unemployment compensation was received last year.

19. *AFDC:* This module assigns income from aid to families with dependent children to families who meet the program's categorical and economic eligibility criteria. The categorical criterion is a function of the age and school status of the children in the family and the sex, disability, and employment status of the head of the family. The economic criterion is a function of the family's assets, other transfer income, and earnings less imputed work-related expenses. If a family meets these criteria, the benefit is computed as a function of the family size, earnings less disregards,[2] other family income, the standard of need, benefit rate reduction, and maximum allowable benefit for the census region in which the family lives.

20. *SSI:* This program module assigns income from supplemental security income to families who meet the categorical and economic eligibility criteria. The categorical criterion is a function of the age, disability status, and labor force participation of each family member. The economic criterion is a function of the assets, earnings less disregards, and other income of the family. If the family is eligible, the

---

2. Disregards are earnings which are not counted in determining the benefit level.

benefit is computed as a function of the national income guarantee, state supplementation payment, family size, and family income less disregards.

21. *FOOD STAMPS:* This program module assigns the bonus value of food stamps received by eligible families. Family eligibility is a function of family size, receipt of AFDC income, receipt of SSI income, earnings less disregards, asset income, and other transfer payment income. If a family is eligible, the bonus value is computed as the difference between the allotment value for that family size less the required purchase amount. The purchase amount is a function of the family size and family income less disregards.

22. *TRANSFER INCOME:* This program module sums the dollar transfer outputs of the SOCIAL SECURITY, PENSION, UNEMPLOYMENT COMPENSATION, AFDC, SSI, and FOOD STAMP modules to generate the total transfer income received.

Taxes and Wealth Program Block

23. *WEALTH INCOME:* This module, although fully specified, was not included in the 1975 version of DYNASIM.

24. *FEDERAL INCOME TAXATION AND DISPOSABLE INCOME:* This module, although fully specified, was not included in the 1975 version of DYNASIM.

25. *SAVING OPERATING CHARACTERISTIC:* This module, although fully specified, was not included in the 1975 version of DYNASIM.

The MARRIAGE UNION Program Sector

The first marriage and remarriage operating characteristics merely select those who "intend" to marry in a given year. To complete the marital process the eligible males must then be matched with the eligible females. Since the selection of eligible males is done independently from the selection of eligible females, there is no guarantee that a reasonable mate can be found for each person in the marriage pool. Matches can be made more precise by overselecting potential partners and returning those who happen to "fit" least well to the population of single persons; this in effect makes the criterion of "goodness of fit" a determinant of marriage probability. The matching process is often handled this way.

    An arbitrary ranking algorithm was conceived based on race, age, education, and region of the country. This algorithm ranks the pool of males and the pool of females. A minimum distance function computes the minimum number of rank orders which must be crossed for the predicted number of marriages to occur. After the two rank orderings are merged, the excess males or females who happened to fit least well are returned to the single population.

The MACROMODEL Program Sector

The microanalytic model described above is designed to provide a microanalytic and dynamic representation of the United States population for use in exploring consequences of alternative government policies. However, this model which is focused on the behavior and well-being of individuals and families, cannot generate variables which depend on developments and interactions involving the whole economy. The macro time series model is intended to fill some of the gaps left by the microanalytic model.

The value of providing closure is twofold. In the first place, the microanalytic model needs an environment in which to operate. In the second place, economists think they know something about the control of some macrovariables such as the unemployment rate. It clearly would be useful to trace out the impact of fiscal, monetary, and other macro-level policies on the behavior and well-being of individuals and families. The macroanalytic model presented here represents a first step in providing such a facility.

The simplest expedient for providing a needed environment for the microanalytic model would be to treat unemployment, real GNP, price level changes, and earned fractions of GNP as exogenous inputs. The disadvantage of doing this is that no explicit account would be taken of the close interrelatedness of these variables or of the impact of these variables on what is going on in the microanalytic model. Instead the results would give a very unrealistic view of the extent to which outcomes could be independently manipulated by use of macrolevel policy tools. While the auxiliary model presented here does take a useful step towards capturing the close interconnectedness of household inputs from the macrolevel, it still leaves points at which policy assumptions could be entered either by alteration of specified unemployment, government expenditure net of transfers, or by alteration of parameter values. Also, by having a macromodel designed to receive inputs from the microanalytic model, it is possible to extend the micromodel's range of application.

In developing a macro time series model extensive simplification has been achieved by assuming that the federal government controls the fraction of the labor force which is unemployed through use of macro policy tools. The advantage of this assumption is that if the unemployment rate is controlled by the federal government it becomes less critical and possibly unnecessary for present purposes to account accurately for the role of the private sector in generating aggregate demand. Private sector behavior in this area is simply regarded as being supplemented or offset as necessary to achieve a desired unemployment rate given balance of payment problems and past price movements. Of course this would not do for a model intended to be useful in guiding short-run stabilization efforts. It is hoped, however, that the model developed will be useful in tracing out first order consequences of unemployment policy for household behavior and welfare.

The auxiliary macro model presented here should be regarded as but a first step in establishing useful links between macro economic policy and the microanalytic model of the United States population. It also is of interest in that it provides for and makes important uses of outputs of the microanalytic model as inputs into a macro time series model. Obviously this macromodel has several deficiencies which could be reduced with additional effort. Perhaps the most serious of these is the gap between the action which policy makers might take (such as increasing the rate of growth of the money supply) and the resulting impact upon unemployment and other exogenous variables. Also, while relationships used in the macromodel do fit historical data fairly well, important causal relations may not have been successfully captured. In addition, while it may be possible to use fiscal policy and monetary policy to control the level of aggregate demand and the unemployment rate while also influencing the earned income share of GNP, such a possibility has not yet been provided for in the model.

A Schematic View

Figure 2-2 presents a view of the macromodel. The arrows in the diagram indicate which variables are used directly to determine the generated values of each variable when that variable is being treated as endogenous to this model. The programmed version of the model provides a means by which all parameters in the model may be altered and also a way by which variables may be specified rather than generated. These provisions have many potential uses, but in any case they do make it possible to introduce a wide variety of hypothetical policy inputs into the model. They also make it easy to use outputs from the microanalytic model as inputs in this model.

The primary function of the causal chain represented by the left-hand side of this schematic diagram is to determine real Gross National Product, GNP1. Values of this variable are the output of a production function using employment and lagged values of capital stock, K1, as inputs. K1 results from the cumulation of noninventory gross private domestic investment, I1, less capital consumption, CC1. I1 in the present version of this model is determined by current and lagged values of GNP1 and of population change.

    The primary function of the uni-directional set of relations represented by the upper right-hand side of this schematic diagram is to generate major components of gross national product in current billions of dollars. The primary relation used in converting to a current price basis is currently a form of Phillip's curve used to generate P, the implicit

FIGURE 2-2

SCHEMATIC DESCRIPTION OF DYNASIM MACROMODEL

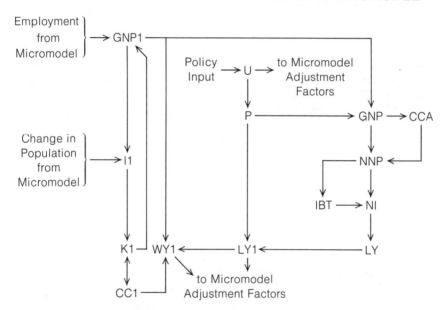

GNP1 = Gross national product in 1958 dollars
I1   = Gross private domestic investment in 1958 dollars
K1   = Capital stock in 1958 dollars
CC1 = Capital consumption in 1958 dollars
U   = Unemployment rate
WY1 = Wealth Income in 1958 dollars
LY1 = Labor Income in 1958 dollars
P   = GNP price deflator
GNP = Gross national product in current dollars
CCA = Capital consumption allowance in current dollars
NNP = Net national product in current dollars
IBT   = Indirect business tax in current dollars
NI   = National income in current dollars
LY   = Labor income in current dollars

price deflator for GNP. Alternatively the price deflator might be explicitly specified. Given GNP, the capital consumption allowance, CCA, is computed by a function involving parameters which may be set by the user to adapt the model to actual or hypothetical laws governing computation of capital consumption allowances by business for tax purposes. Net national product, NNP, is taken as equal to GNP less CCA. Indirect business tax and non-tax liability, IBT, is obtained as a distributed lag function of NNP. The included parameters may be used to adapt the model to actual or hypothetical laws governing such taxes. National Labor income, LY, is obtained as a distributed lag function of NI; and LY1 in billions of constant dollars is obtained as LY_t/P_t. An identity is used to determine real wealth income, WY1, prior to taxes other than indirect business taxes, IBT.

Provision for Distributed Lags

A somewhat limited provision is made in almost every nonidentity equation of the model for the introduction of a distributed lag of those variables, other than the lagged dependent variable, which appear on the right-hand side of each equation. This is done by inclusion of the lagged dependent variable among the predictor variables used in each such case. What has been done is to make use of the well-known fact that if k_1 is between minus and positive one, then if

$$Z_t = k_1 Z_{t-1} + X_t$$

it also is true that

$$Z_t = X_t + k_1 X_{t-1} + k_1^2 X_{t-2} + k_1^3 X_{t-3} + \ldots$$

For purposes of this exposition Z_t is taken to be the dependent variable of any given equation and X_t is everything that appears on the right-hand side of the equation in question except k_1 times the lagged value of the dependent variable. The average length of the distributed lag obviously depends on the size of k_1. If k_1 is positive then all the lagged weights will be positive and decline exponentially towards zero with increasing lags so long as k_1 is less than 1. The sum of the series of declining weights starting with $k_1^0 = 1$ as the first weight will be $1/(1 - k_1)$.

Provision for Autocorrelated Disturbances

A provision is made in almost every nonidentity equation for introduction of a disturbance term denoted by u_t. The term is generated by a linear first order autoregressive process driven by a random variable, denoted by e. It is assumed that e is normally and independently distributed with a mean of zero and either a fixed variance or a variance which increases as the square of the value of some suitable predetermined variable.

The value of including autocorrelated disturbances is twofold. First, omitted variables are likely to be autocorrelated and taking account of this fact makes it possible to take advantage of the recent past in predicting the value of subsequent disturbances. This could be of substantial help in improving short-run forecasting even if all parameter values were known perfectly. Secondly, taking proper account of the presence of autocorrelated disturbances should be of value in improving the precision with which parameter values can be estimated from historical data.

Linearity

In this initial specification of the model all variables are used in a linear form. The objective is to keep the number of parameters to be estimated as few as possible while still paying attention to distributed lags and autocorrelated disturbances. This is done in the belief that it is more important to get the right variables in with the right lag structure than it is to worry about possible nonlinearities. Given that we estimate the equations of this model with highly aggregated time series data, it is obvious that we must be very parsimonious with parameters to be estimated. If in running this model it becomes apparent that introduction of nonlinearities would be valuable, then an effort will be made to incorporate them in a sensible way.

Recursive Structure

The model, as specified, is completely recursive. This has obvious advantages for both estimation and simulation since simultaneous equation problems are avoided. The justification of working with an annual recursive model rests upon the notion that the federal government can and will cause aggregate demand to vary so as to approximately control the fraction of the labor force which is unemployed in each year. The otherwise normal feedback from aggregate income to unemployment through aggregate demand is thus largely offset by governmental action. Of course, this assumed ability and behavior of the federal government was not much in evidence before 1950, and we may be over-rating the government as far as the future is concerned. In any case, we have selected what strikes us as a sensible recursive structure starting with the unemployment rate. Implications of partial breakdown of our assumptions about government behavior can be explored after we have a well-functioning model and simulation system.

The Programmed Version

In the present implementation the error terms are suppressed, and the entire model or parts of it can be run in a tracking or non-tracking mode over specified time intervals as desired. When operating in a tracking mode the output of an equation is computed as specified by the equation. This output is available for printout but is then modified to track exactly a historically or otherwise specified time series. Among other things this facilitates checking how individual equations are functioning without propagating errors throughout the system.

Appendix A gives a more detailed specification of DYNASIM and appears at the end of this volume.

PART II.
DEMOGRAPHIC OPERATING CHARACTERISTICS

Chapter 3
DEATH, BIRTH, AND IMMIGRATION*

Death

Role in the Model

Mortality is a major determinant of the size of the population as well as its distribution by age, race and sex. The central importance of mortality to socioeconomic issues is not its inevitability but rather the fact that the probability of death is distributed very unevenly across the population. Death rates are higher for the aged than for the young, for nonwhites than for whites, and for males than for females. Alongside these familiar differentials exist less familiar ones: death rates are lower for adults with greater educational attainment as compared to adults with less schooling, death rates are lower for married persons than for single, widowed or divorced persons, and they are lower for women with three children than for women with either more or fewer children. Mortality is thus a process of *selective* attrition which generates continuous changes in population composition.[1] Since mortality is heavily concentrated at older ages, and since the consequences of differential mortality are cumulative, the size and composition of the aged population are especially affected.

---

* Steven B. Caldwell and Gerald Peabody had the main responsibility for this chapter and the work it represents. Caldwell was mainly responsible for the sections on death and on immigration; Peabody for the research on birth.

1. An interesting example of a political consequence of differential mortality has to do with a substantial differential which has existed between the death rates of northern vs. southern Democrats in the U.S. House of Representatives. Given the impact of the mortality differential on the distribution of seniority in the House, McCann (1972) has demonstrated that the low death rates of southerners vis-á-vis northerners were an important factor in the numerical advantage that southerners long held among senior House Democrats.

An Overview of the Mortality Submodel

From the end of the 18th century to 1960, reduction in mortality rates — primarily through the control of disease — added about 40 years to the expectation of life for a newborn child. As the mortality rate declined, so did its year-to-year variation. The pronounced variation characteristic of mortality series in the 19th century has been replaced by a smoother pattern in the 20th century (Sutton, 1971). Consequently, projections of mortality rates for various age groups have become considerably more reliable. Historically the decline in death rates has been the most important factor in the rapid acceleration of population growth, yet the relatively low and stable mortality rates within developed countries in recent decades have led to a diminished interest in the role played by mortality in population increase. For example, in the United States, recent changes in population growth rates were due mainly to changes in fertility rates. As the rate of mortality has become more stable and its variance has declined, attention has turned to the existence of substantial socioeconomic differentials in mortality. In fact, it has been suggested that further reductions in mortality are more likely to be based on socioeconomic epidemology than on biomedical epidemology (Kitagawa and Hauser, 1973).

Our goal in constructing a mortality submodel has been to combine evidence about past levels and past distributions of mortality in the United States. We have drawn from three sources to construct the submodel:

1. Vital statistics data covering the period from 1933 to 1968 give central death rates by age, race, and sex. These data were used to estimate the parameters of a functional form which specifies that mortality declines as an exponential function of time toward some positive asymptotic level within separate age, race, and sex subpopulations.
2. Data from the censuses of 1940, 1950, and 1960, combined with vital statistics for the three-year periods surrounding each of these censuses. The data were used to estimate parameters capturing marital status differentials in mortality.
3. The 1960 Matched Records Study (Kitagawa and Hauser, 1973), which includes evidence on differentials in mortality by education, income, and the number of live births (for females only).

Parameters estimated from all three sources have been combined in a comprehensive mortality submodel. This submodel generates a probability of death in a particular year for each individual as a function of the individual's age, race, sex, marital status, education, and parity (if applicable). A random number between 0 and 1 is drawn in the computer. If the random number is less than the death probability generated by the submodel, the person "dies." If not, the person survives and, of course, one year is added to that person's age.

Estimating the Age, Race, Sex and Calendar Year Parameters

In the United States, annual collection of mortality statistics was begun in 1900. Not until 1933, however, were all states included in the Federal Death Registration Area. It is believed that in recent years underregistration of deaths has been less than 1 percent (Shryock, et al., 1971). From death registration data and from midyear estimates of the U.S. population by age, race, and sex, based on surveys and census data, the national death rates have been calculated by age, race, and sex for each year since 1933.

Figure 3-1 gives for selected groups the pattern of mortality decline over the period 1933 through 1968. The examples given are death rates for persons who were less than 1 year old by race and sex. The patterns for other race-sex-age classes are generally similar. The full set of 76 age, race, sex specific time series constitutes striking testimony to the enormous success in the nation's mortality reduction efforts over this period.

For any group, the overall death rate is the sum of a set of cause-specific death rates. Since age patterns of death are different for different causes, and since environmental conditions probably affect the intensity of various causes in different ways, a complete parameterization of the age curve of mortality would contain as many parameters as there are statistically unique causes of death (Preston, 1972). For our current purposes, however, it is sufficient to achieve a reasonable approximation of the trend in the *sum* of cause-specific rates, rather than the trends in each cause-specific rate separately. Time, of course, is simply a proxy for changes in public health, medical and other conditions with some casual influence on mortality.

Two major assumptions underlie the specification of the mortality submodel. First, the level of mortality is assumed to be changing as a declining exponential function of time with each subpopulation. Second, it is assumed that the level of mortality within each subpopulation is approaching an asymptote, and the asymptote itself is a parameter to be estimated from the data. The specification incorporating these two assumptions is given by:

$$P_{it} = a_{i1} + a_{i2} \cdot e^{a_{i3} \cdot (t - 1950)} \tag{1}$$

FIGURE 3-1

DEATHS PER THOUSAND PERSONS BY RACE AND SEX
FOR PERSONS LESS THAN ONE YEAR OLD

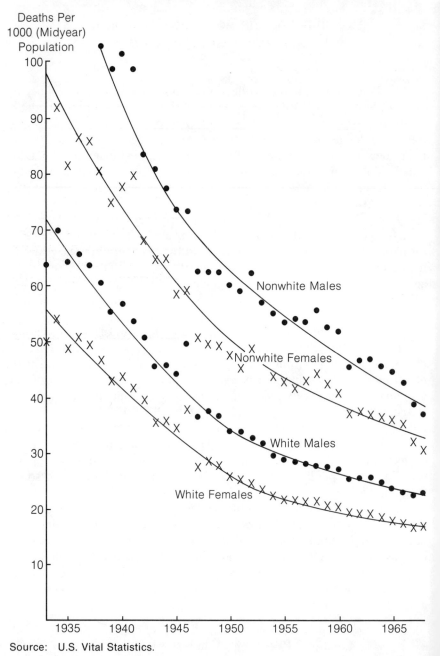

Source: U.S. Vital Statistics.

where P_{it} = central death rate for the ith age, race, sex group ($i = 1, 2,$ . . . ,76) in calender year t;

a_{i1} = the asymptote, or lower bound, for the level of mortality in the ith age, race, sex group;

$a_{i1} + a_{i2}$ = predicted mortality level for 1950 for group i (arbitrarily set by letting $t = 1950$ be the origin)

$$\frac{dP_{it}}{dt} = a_{i3}a_{i2}e^{a_{i3} \cdot (t-1950)} = \text{the predicted rate of mortality over time; as}$$

$$t \to \infty, \frac{dP_{it}}{dt} \to 0, \text{ assuming that } a_{i3} < 0.$$

t = calendar year (1933, 1934, . . .)

The notion of an asymptote, or lower bound, can be conceived of as partitioning all causes of death into (1) endogenous and (2) exogenous causes. Endogenous causes of death are resistant to scientific progress, whereas exogenous causes are relatively preventable and treatable. Bourgeois-Pichat (1952) has suggested that extrapolating the trend in endogenous mortality would be one approach to measuring the limit to the decline in mortality. By this very definition, exogenous mortality ought to be declining toward a *lower* bound of zero. On the other hand, endogenous mortality rates could be *increasing* toward an upper bound, since in effect the existence of a larger pool of survivors of exogenous mortality creates a larger population at risk of succumbing to endogenous causes. The asymptote which we are estimating using death rates from all causes, and which we hypothesize is a lower limit to mortality from all causes, might approximate this theoretical upper limit toward which endogenous causes are tending.

By taking logarithms, equation (1) can be converted to a form which, although nonlinear, is nonetheless estimable.[2]

$$\ln (P_{it} - a_{i1}) = \ln(a_{i2}) + a_{i3} (t - 1950) \qquad (2)$$

The parameters estimated using the nonlinear estimation technique from the central death rate data[3] for all 76 age, race, sex groupings are given

2. An iterative, nonlinear estimation algorithm was used which employed both Gaussian and steepest descent methods to achieve convergence. Convergence was achieved for all but two subpopulations: nonwhite males 65–69 and 70–74.

3. Central death rates are computed by dividing the number of persons whose age at last birthday was, e.g., 40–44 years, who die in a given year by the midyear estimated total of persons 40–44 years of age. Rivlin (Orcutt, 1961) used an adjustment technique to convert central death rates to approximate life-table mortality rates. A life table mortality rate is an estimate of the probability that a person of exact age x in a given year will die before his next $(x + 1)$ birthday. The ideal number for our purposes would be the probability that a person in a given age group at a point in time, e.g., 40–44, will die within a year, even if by the time he dies he is no longer in that age group. Different from both the central death

TABLE 3-1

MORTALITY: ESTIMATED PARAMETERS AND R^2:
UNITED STATES, 1933–68[a]

$$Pr(\text{death}) = a_1 + a_2 e^{a_3(t-1950)}$$

AGE IN YEARS	WHITE MALES				BLACK AND OTHER MALES			
	a_1	a_2	a_3	R^2	a_1	a_2	a_3	R^2
0–1	10.84	25.57	−0.050	.97	20.79*	43.87	−0.047	.96
1–4	0.64	0.86	−0.098	.98	1.12	1.72	−0.087	.97
5–9	0.32	0.43	−0.075	.97	0.47	0.56	−0.070	.99
10–14	0.34	0.40	−0.069	.98	0.48	0.58	−0.075	.98
15–19	1.21	0.24	−0.091	.85	1.15	1.24	−0.071	.95
20–24	1.26**	0.84**	−0.046**	.60	2.00	2.14	−0.069	.94
25–29	1.28	0.61	−0.078	.90	3.00	1.80	−0.087	.93
30–34	1.39	0.81	−0.074	.95	3.75	2.25	−0.084	.93
35–39	2.00	1.14	−0.064	.94	5.51	2.06	−0.094	.91
40–44	3.53	1.31	−0.067	.96	7.72	3.23	−0.079	.90
45–49	6.17	1.56	−0.065	.96	9.76	5.71	−0.052	.89
50–54	9.50	2.99	−0.035	.92	4.29**	18.75**	−0.019**	.88
55–59	15.15	3.97**	−0.030**	.82	18.66*	11.02**	−0.026**	.78
60–64	26.37	1.73	−0.068	.85	38.40	0[d]	0[d]	.35
65–69	40.11	0.94**	−0.111	.68	57.70[c]	0[d]	0[d]	b
70–74	57.81	2.38**	−0.091	.73	69.50[c]	0[d]	0[d]	b
75–79	79.47	11.53	−0.060	.89	72.11	8.36**	−0.065*	.66
80–84	115.26	23.12	−0.046*	.83	90.64	6.70**	−0.118	.71
85+	208.82	11.81	−0.073**	.51	−286.73**	449.82**	−0.004*	.79

Notes:
   a. All variables are significant at the .01 level unless indicated by a single asterisk (*) which indicates significance at the .05 level, or by a double asterisk (**) which indicates significance at the .10 level or less.
   b. No solution obtained.
   c. Because of coefficient unreliability the mean for the 1960–68 period was used.
   d. Because of coefficient unreliability the slope was set equal to zero.

in Table 3-1. Seventy-four percent of all the coefficients were significant at least at the 0.01 level and another eight percent are significant at the 0.05 level.[4] The estimated asymptote parameters (a_1), when plotted against age, are consistent with an intuitive conception of a reasonable age pattern of lower limits to death reduction (Figures 3-2A, 3-2B, and

---

rate and the life table mortality rate, this number may be either larger or smaller than the central death rate depending on the age distribution of the population and on the change in mortality probabilities with age. Since the correction is both complicated and of little consequence we have used the uncorrected central death rates.
   4. As can be seen from Figure 3-1, the residuals are highly auto-correlated, which lends a downward bias to the estimates of standard error though the parameter estimates themselves are unbiased. Consequently significance tests based on the standard errors must be treated conservatively.

TABLE 3-1 (continued)[a]

	WHITE FEMALES				BLACK AND OTHER FEMALES			
AGE IN YEARS	a_1	a_2	a_3	R^2	a_1	a_2	a_3	R^2
0–1	7.51*	20.30	−0.050	.97	16.93*	34.50	−0.046	.96
1–4	0.55	0.69	−0.104	.98	0.92	1.53	−0.086	.97
5–9	0.26	0.26	−0.092	.98	0.34	0.49	−0.075	.98
10–14	0.20	0.25	−0.082	.97	0.16*	0.61	−0.077	.98
15–19	0.41	0.28	−0.095	.97	0.80[c]	0[d]	0[d]	.96
20–24	0.41	0.47	−0.094	.98	1.30[c]	0[d]	0[d]	.97
25–29	0.48	0.58	−0.093	.98	0.52**	3.05	−0.063	.97
30–34	0.69	0.73	−0.083	.98	1.33	3.45	−0.063	.98
35–39	1.05	0.98	−0.073	.97	2.41	3.90	−0.057	.95
40–44	1.88	1.08	−0.076	.98	1.07**	8.34	−0.037	.96
45–49	2.98	1.52	−0.069	.97	−2.92**	15.63	−0.022	.97
50–54	4.10	2.79	−0.053	.97	−11.80**	30.57*	−0.016*	.98
55–59	5.22	5.23	−0.043	.97	8.81*	15.15	−0.034	.96
60–64	8.22	7.93	−0.043	.99	26.29	5.04	−0.074	.87
65–69	14.05	11.58	−0.041	.97	37.22	1.51[^^]	−0.113**	.37
70–74	11.30**	31.35	−0.024	.98	45.22	3.30*	−0.103	.81
75–79	24.44**	46.22	−0.026	.97	26.15**	38.36	−0.018**	.84
80–84	59.05*	55.44*	−0.027*	.93	71.80	3.16**	−0.137	.70
85+	189.81	13.87**	−0.068*	.65	114.98	12.15**	−0.082*	.69

Notes:
a. All variables are significant at the .01 level unless indicated by a single asterisk (*) which indicates significance at the .05 level, or by a double asterisk (**) which indicates significance at the .10 level or less.
b. No solution obtained.
c. Because of coefficient unreliability the mean for the 1960–68 period was used.
d. Because of coefficient unreliability the slope was set equal to zero.

3-3). To the extent these estimated lower limit parameters have substantive significance, they might be useful in evaluating efforts to further reduce mortality. Of course, mortality data have long been used as an indication of health and medical progress (National Center for Health Statistics, 1964). The traditional indicator of progress in mortality reduction has been the rate of decline in the level of mortality *toward zero*. But if mortality is declining toward non-zero lower bounds, the more appropriate yardstick would be the difference between the lower bound and the current level and the rate at which that difference was diminishing rather than the difference between zero and the current level. Where the difference between the estimated lower bound and the current level is already low, it suggests that efforts to further reduce mortality have a low potential pay-off. For example, in Figure 3-3 the plots indicate that the mortality level of white females aged 50 through 54 is close to an irreducible minimum, whereas the levels for white females aged 80

FIGURE 3-2A

COMPARISON OF THE ESTIMATED ASYMPTOTE PARAMETERS IN THE MORTALITY MODEL FOR WHITE MALES AND BLACK MALES AT ALL AGES

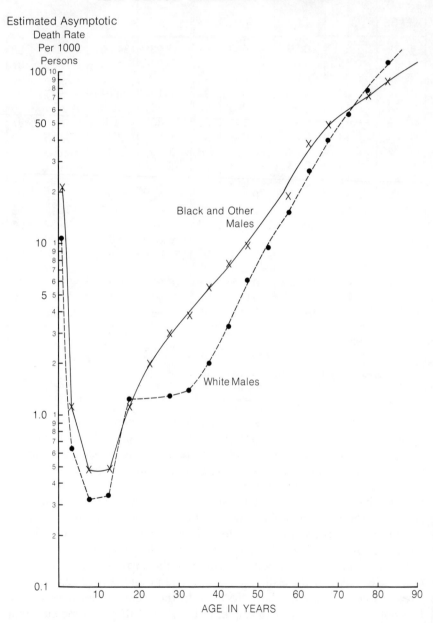

Note: See text for method of estimating asymptotes.

FIGURE 3-2B

COMPARISON OF THE ESTIMATED ASYMPTOTE PARAMETERS IN THE MORTALITY MODEL FOR WHITE FEMALES AND BLACK FEMALES AT ALL AGES

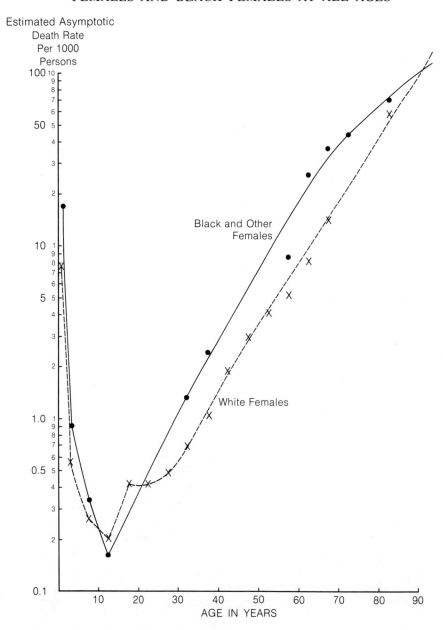

Note: See text for method of estimating asymptotes.

FIGURE 3-3

CENTRAL DEATH RATE LESS ESTIMATED ASYMPTOTE FROM 1933–1968 FOR WHITE FEMALES, AGES 0–1, 50–54, 60–64, AND 80–84

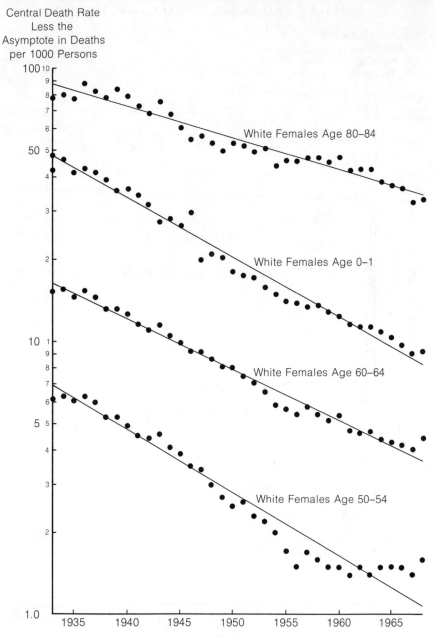

Central Death Rate
Less the
Asymptote in Deaths
per 1000 Persons

White Females Age 80–84

White Females Age 0–1

White Females Age 60–64

White Females Age 50–54

Note: See text for method of estimating asymptotes.

through 84 have the most room for improvement and the levels for the 0-1 and 60-64 groups are intermediate in potential for reduction. Clearly not all deaths are equally preventable. To identify in this manner those age groups with the largest remaining number of "preventable" deaths might add precision to intuitive notions on how to measure progress in mortality reduction, and might target mortality reduction efforts more efficiently.

However, obvious problems exist in applying this interpretation to the parameters as estimated. The most important problem is that the asymptotes are different for males compared with females, and for whites compared with blacks. The long controversy concerning the true causes of male and female differentials has not yet reached a consensus as to whether the differences are biological or socioeconomic in origin. But strong consensus does exist that racial differences in mortality are not due to genetically-based biological differences between blacks and whites.[5] Thus it would be quite wrong to argue that the lower bounds estimated for blacks, which are higher than the lower bounds estimated for whites (see Figures 3-2A and 3-2B), represent a suitable goal for mortality reduction for blacks. The discrepancy in the white/black lower bound estimates suggests that socioeconomic differentials in mortality are affecting the estimation of the asymptotes.[6] Thus, it is clearly incorrect to claim that the lower bounds as currently estimated are uncontaminated indicators of purely biological limitations to death reduction.

Tables 3-2A and 3-2B report trends in sex and race mortality differentials for the United States from 1900 to 1964. The sex differential

5. It has been suggested that black-white differences in mortality based on uncorrected census and death registration data are partly overstated due to measurement error (Kitagawa, 1972). Black deaths (the numerator) are probably counted more completely than the black population in censuses and surveys (denominator). We have made no attempt to correct central death rates for such possible undercounting. The sample used to represent the United States population for simulations is drawn from the same data files used to provide the denominators in calculating mortality rates. Consequently the mortality submodel will generate, initially at least, the correct *number* of deaths. However, since the *rates* may be too high (if the above argument is correct) the black population could be depleted too rapidly during simulations.

6. Another possible indicator that socioeconomic variables are affecting the asymptote estimates can be observed in the plots of the asymptote parameters for whites (Figures 3-2 and 3-3). For white females and even more so for white males, the asymptotes for the late teens and early twenties seem out of line with the rest of the curve. Specifically, the lower limits on mortality at these ages seem higher than might be expected from the rest of the pattern. This observation may be an indication that whites at these ages face unusually severe nonbiological risks of mortality, which have resisted the usual methods of treatment. Possible examples of such risks are suicide and motor vehicle accidents, which are in fact two of the principal causes of death at these ages. Death rates from these sources have been increasing over the past 15 years, and the causes appear to lie in complex social and psychological factors not amenable to the usual biomedical treatments.

TABLE 3-2A

TRENDS IN SEX AND RACE DIFFERENTIALS IN MORTALITY, BY AGE GROUPS, UNITED STATES: 1900 TO 1964

Year and Age	SEX DIFFERENTIAL (Ratio male rate to female rate)			RACE DIFFERENTIAL (Ratio nonwhite rate to white rate)		
	Total population	White	Nonwhite	Both sexes	Male	Female
1964 All Ages	1.35	1.35	1.35	1.03	1.04	1.04
Under 1 year	1.29	1.32	1.25	1.90	1.86	1.96
1–4 years	1.11	1.12	1.13	2.00	1.89	1.88
5–14 years	1.67	1.67	1.40	1.50	1.40	1.67
15–24 years	2.67	2.50	2.10	1.60	1.40	1.67
25–34 years	1.82	1.89	1.72	2.54	2.53	2.78
35–44 years	1.65	1.79	1.51	2.54	2.35	2.79
45–54 years	1.85	1.96	1.45	1.94	1.74	2.35
55–64 years	2.01	2.15	1.36	1.70	1.42	2.24
65–74 years	1.79	1.83	1.49	1.38	1.26	1.55
75–84 years	1.39	1.39	1.30	0.84	0.80	0.86
1954 All Ages	1.37	1.39	1.29	1.11	1.08	1.16
Under 1 year	1.31	1.32	1.26	1.89	1.85	1.96
1–4 years	1.18	1.10	1.16	1.82	2.00	1.90
5–14 years	1.50	1.50	1.33	1.40	1.33	1.50
15–24 years	2.29	2.50	1.79	1.90	1.67	2.33
25–34 years	1.82	1.89	1.48	2.69	2.53	3.22
35–44 years	1.58	1.70	1.20	2.44	2.12	3.00
45–54 years	1.74	1.88	1.21	2.16	1.80	2.80
55–64 years	1.18	1.90	1.33	1.72	1.49	2.13
65–74 years	1.57	1.59	1.35	1.16	1.08	1.27
75–84 years	1.28	1.29	1.28	0.82	0.80	0.81
1900 All Ages	1.08	1.08	1.05	1.47	1.45	1.50
Under 1 year	1.23	1.23	1.23	2.09	2.10	2.10
1–4 years	1.07	1.08	1.00	2.24	2.15	2.33
5–14 years	0.97	1.00	0.77	2.37	2.05	2.66
15–24 years	1.02	1.04	1.05	2.02	2.03	2.00
25–34 years	1.00	1.00	1.07	1.49	1.54	1.44
35–44 years	1.09	1.10	0.91	1.47	1.34	1.62
45–54 years	1.10	1.11	1.03	1.64	1.59	1.71
55–64 years	1.11	1.12	1.00	1.56	1.48	1.65
65–74 years	1.11	1.11	1.08	1.23	1.21	1.24
75–84 years	1.08	1.08	1.16	0.98	1.02	0.85

Source: U.S. Public Health Service, *Vital Statistics of the United States,* reports 1964, 1960, 1950 and earlier decennial census years. *1940, 1920, 1900–1950 Vital Statistics,* 1950, Vol. I, Table 8.40.

has continued to widen, while the racial differential has been fairly stable since 1945. It is possible that the standard mode of mortality data collection and tabulations which highlights the traditional demographic categories of age, race, and sex but without simultaneously controlling for socioeconomic differences have contributed to an overstatement

TABLE 3-2B

TRENDS IN SEX AND RACE DIFFERENTIALS IN MORTALITY, UNITED STATES: 1900 TO 1964 (BASED ON AGE-STANDARDIZED DEATH RATES)

Year	SEX DIFFERENTIAL (ratio male to female rate)			RACE DIFFERENTIAL (ratio nonwhite to white rate)		
	Total population	White	Nonwhite	Both sexes	Male	Female
1964	1.65	1.70	1.42	1.45	1.36	1.62
1960	1.61	1.64	1.36	1.42	1.32	1.59
1955	1.52	1.60	1.31	1.41	1.31	1.60
1950	1.45	1.48	1.25	1.54	1.42	1.68
1945	1.39	1.43	1.22	1.44	1.36	1.59
1940	1.29	1.32	1.17	1.60	1.52	1.70
1930	1.19	1.21	1.09	1.72	1.64	1.81
1920	1.06	1.08	0.97	1.50	1.44	1.60
1910	1.16	1.16	1.07	1.54	1.48	1.61
1900	1.09	1.10	1.06	1.58	1.56	1.61
Percent chance 1900 to 1964	+51	+54	+34	−8	−13	+1

Note: The above ratios were based upon age standardized death rates age composition of 1940 used as standard.
Source: Computed from Public Health Service, *Vital Statistics of the United States: 1964*, Table 1.2. Data for 1900 to 1930 are for death registration states.

of racial differentials. Indeed, analysis including a measure of family income with the 1960 Matched Records Study suggested that racial differences were, in part, socioeconomic (Kitagawa and Hauser, 1973, p. 102).

The ratio of black to white mortality rates, which is fairly high in the very early years of life, declines over the childhood period, reaching a low in the late teenage years. The ratio worsens for blacks very rapidly thereafter and becomes most disadvantageous for them during ages 30 through 39. Apparently the gap in relative situations with respect to factors which cause or prevent death is at its worst at this age (although the bias due to undercount may also be a factor here). The ratio declines steadily after age 39, reaches unity at around age 75, and then goes below one. The fact that nonwhite mortality rates are lower than white rates at older ages may be due to the fact that those who survived the higher death rates at earlier ages tend to be extremely hardy.

Females have lower mortality rates than males at all ages in virtually all parts of the world (Madigan, 1957). The differential in mortality rates in the United States is particularly noticeable during the economically most productive decades of life. Both biological and environmental hypotheses have been advanced to account for the excess male mortality. Women, according to the biological thesis, are better suited to withstand disease. Environmentalists, on the other hand, have stressed the role differentiation which has emerged as a result of the increased complexity of modern industrial society. They have hypothesized that the poor relative mortality status of males in the United States is due at least partly to the socioeconomic roles they assume. One implication of this is that as females move into more typical male roles — that is, toward equal participation in the labor force and with a comparable occupational distribution — their superior mortality status relative to males will tend to be reduced.

The mortality module of DYNASIM specifies that in the future mortality rates will decline at a decreasing rate in all age, race, and sex subpopulations, except for a very few in which rates will remain constant. After a very rapid decline in mortality from prior to World War II to the mid-fifties, rates have since remained quite stable. The rapid decline was probably due to reductions in mortality from infectious and parasitic diseases accomplished through antimicrobial therapy. By the mid-fifties, changes in the death rate from infective and parasitic diseases were no longer significantly influencing the general mortality trend. The result was a general stabilization of the overall trend (Moriyama, 1968). Indeed, if trends were estimated using death rates for the period 1955–1968 only, the resulting projections would look quite different, and in some cases mortality increases would be projected.

However, we will not argue that, because the last fifteen years do not appear to fit the overall thirty-three year pattern very well, the evidence from the earlier period ought to be disregarded. Ideally, past patterns in the overall rate should be explained on the basis of the behavior of the several cause-specific rates, and these cause-specific rates should be projected into the future. However, projecting cause-specific rates is also difficult. For example, we simply do not know whether breakthroughs in the prevention or treatment of particular chronic diseases will be forthcoming, or whether various social causes of death — violence, alcohol, accidents, drugs, and the like — will fall in severity. Who, for instance, could have predicted that the fuel crisis of the early 1970s would trigger reduced highway speed limits, leading to a significant drop in traffic deaths? Identifying factors that will account for substantial changes in cause-specific death rates seems no easier than finding such factors to account for changes at the aggregate level.

We do know that other nations have lower mortality rates than the United States, and that certain subpopulations in the United States have rates considerably below the average. If we hypothesize that differences in mortality between different populations are mainly a result of their different environmental experience, it follows that the lowest observed mortality risk is a goal obtainable in any other population. Moriyama (1968) among others concludes that the death rates in the United States should decline toward the favorable levels now enjoyed by other countries.

Marital Status

Within age-race-sex groupings, marital status is strongly related to mortality rates. For males or females, whites or nonwhites, mortality rates have been consistently lower for married persons than for persons of other marital status. Published statistics using evidence from the censuses of 1940, 1950, and 1960, combined with death registration statistics, document this differential (National Center for Health Statistics, 1968, Table 58).

Marital status-specific mortality rates by age, race, and sex from the 1940, 1950, and 1960 census periods were used to estimate marital status differentials. The mortality rate for each of the four marital status groups (single, married, divorced, widowed) within a particular subpopulation was first divided by the mortality rate for the whole subpopulation, yielding a set of marital status-specific mortality ratios for each of the three periods. Inspection of the ratios within subpopulations over the three points in time revealed no apparent trends. Therefore, for each ratio the mean of the values for each of the three periods was calculated. Table 3-3 gives these mean mortality ratios for marital status groups.

The requirements of the simulation model make inescapable the question of the exact nature of the marital status differentials.[7] For example, does being married add to longevity, or are people with greater chances of longevity the ones who become and stay married?

If marital status is causal, that is, if a change in marital status brings about a change in environment sufficient to account for the change in mortality associated with being in the new status, then mortality ratios

---

7. Of course, the causal hypothesis is implicit for all differentials in DYNASIM, and not just this one.

TABLE 3-3

MARITAL STATUS MORTALITY DIFFERENTIALS, UNITED STATES, 1940–1960
Mortality Ratios[1]

Color, Sex, and Marital Status	AGE GROUPS								
	20–24	25–34	35–44	45–54	55–59	60–64	65–69	70–74	75 and over
White Males									
Single	1.2	1.6	1.8	1.5	1.4	1.3	1.3	1.2	1.1
Married	0.7	0.8	0.8	0.9	0.9	0.9	0.9	0.9	0.8
Widowed	3.1	3.0	2.3	1.8	1.5	1.4	1.3	1.2	1.2
Divorced	2.1	3.0	3.0	2.4	2.0	1.8	1.7	1.6	1.5
White Females									
Single	1.1	1.5	1.4	1.1	1.0	1.0	1.0	1.0	1.0
Married	0.9	0.9	0.9	0.9	0.9	0.9	0.9	0.9	0.7
Widowed	3.2	2.1	1.5	1.3	1.2	1.1	1.1	1.1	1.1
Divorced	2.1	1.9	1.6	1.4	1.3	1.3	1.3	1.4	1.3
Nonwhite Males									
Single	1.1	1.6	1.8	1.5	1.3	1.3	1.3	1.3	1.1
Married	0.7	0.8	0.8	0.8	0.8	0.8	0.8	0.8	0.8
Widowed	2.6	2.6	2.2	2.0	1.8	1.6	1.4	1.3	1.2
Divorced	1.4	1.8	1.9	1.8	1.5	1.5	1.5	1.4	1.4
Nonwhite Females									
Single	1.2	1.5	1.4	1.2	1.0	1.1	1.0	1.1	1.0
Married	0.9	0.9	0.9	0.8	0.8	0.7	0.8	0.8	0.8
Widowed	1.8	2.0	1.6	1.5	1.3	1.3	1.1	1.1	1.0
Divorced	1.2	1.2	1.2	1.1	1.1	1.1	1.3	1.4	1.2

1. The ratios are derived by dividing the mortality rate for the marital status group (e.g., for *single* white males, age 25–34) by the overall mortality rate for the same race-sex-age group (all white males, age 25–34). The ratios given are the mean of ratios for 1940 and 1960.
Source: United States National Center for Health Statistics, *Vital Statistics Rates in the United States, 1940–1960*. Department of Health, Education and Welfare, Washington, D.C., 1968, Table 57.

based on marital status can be applied directly to rates based on age, race, and sex for any calendar year, whatever the distribution of the population with respect to marital status.

At the other extreme, the observed marital status differentials may be entirely due to selection. That is, one or more unknown attributes may be affecting both marital status and death probability. Carter and Glick (1970, pp. 340–43) have suggested that the proportionately greater decline in mortality among married persons, especially women. over the period 1940–1960, was in part due to the increase in the proportion of women in the upper educational levels with high probabilities of survival who married, thus "skimming the cream" from the ranks of the unmarried.

If selection accounts for some or all of the effect, the best way to introduce more realism and consistency in the model at the individual level would be to incorporate appropriate independent variables. Failing that, the mortality ratios could be scaled up or down as composition changed to prevent changes in the marital composition of a subpopulation from affecting its mortality level.[8] Intermediate positions along the continuum between causation and selection could be accomodated by scaling the mortality ratios so as to reduce, but not eliminate, the effects on mortality of changes in marital composition.

In the uses of the model prior to this publication, the mortality ratios had not been scaled to account for changes in marital composition; i.e., marital status is treated as a causal variable. However, a scaling option is possible if one prefers to simulate using selection as the explanation.

Education and Income

By far the most important study of mortality in the United States in recent years has been the 1960 matched records study by Kitagawa and Hauser (1974). The study matched a sample of 340,000 deaths which

---

8. Although the mortality ratios in Table 3-2B are age, race, and sex specific, they are not specific to marital status. Since marital status is related to education, we might be incorporating the same effect twice. However, Kitagawa and Hauser (1973) presented separate tabulations (for whites only) for family members and unrelated individuals. These exhibit little or no differences in educational differentials by family status. Although the family status distinction is not the same as a marital status distinction, there is a rough correspondence, especially for males. However, no differences in the educational ratios for males show up across family status categories. Thus it seems likely that the error introduced by applying an education parameter which is not marital status specific, at least for whites, is small. Lacking any similar data for nonwhites, the same assumptions are made for them.

occurred between one and five months after the 1960 Census against the 1960 Census records to obtain the decedents' social and economic characteristics that are not available on death certificates. A strong in-

TABLE 3-4

MORTALITY DIFFERENTIALS BY EDUCATION, UNITED STATES, 1960

Race and Years of School Completed	25–64 Years of Age	65 and Over	25–64 Years of Age	65 and Over
White	*Males*		*Females*	
0–4 years	1.15	a	1.60	1.17
5–7	1.14		1.18	1.04
8	1.07		1.08	1.03
9–11	1.03		0.91	0.94[b]
12	0.91		0.87	0.94[b]
13–15	0.85		0.82	0.70[b]
16 or more	0.70		0.78	0.70[b]
total	1.00		1.00	1.00
Black and Other Races				
0–4	1.14	a	1.26	a
5–8	0.97		1.06	
9 or more	0.87		0.74	
total	1.00		1.00	

a. Ratios either not significant or else, as in the case of white males 65 or over, the ratios are sufficiently close to 1.00 as to make it unlikely that they could make any significant difference in mortality rates in the simulation model.

b. The ratios for white females 65 and over, where they are equal for two contiguous education groups, have in fact been derived by collapsing the two groups and deriving a single value.

Source: Evelyn M. Kitagawa and Philip M. Hauser, *Differential Mortality in the United States: A Study in Socioeconomic Epidemiology,* Vital and Health Statistics Monograph Series, American Public Health Association, Cambridge, Mass.: Harvard University Press, 1973, Tables 2.1 and 2.2.

verse relationship between mortality and the level of educational attainment was found for white and nonwhite males and females. Table 3-4 shows the age-adjusted mortality ratios calculated by Kitagawa and Hauser which are suitable for use in our model.

An inverse relationship between mortality and income was also uncovered by Kitagawa and Hauser but they point out that serious problems of interpretation exist. First, much of the relationship may be an artifact due to the effects of approaching death on income, rather than the reverse. Second, since education and income are clearly related, each must be controlled in estimating the effect of the other.

The causation versus selection question is no less unavoidable in dealing with income than with education. Further, there is the question of whether relative or absolute education/income is the appropriate variable. The absolute level of education has been treated as causal by this submodel. Thus, in DYNASIM rising levels of education would tend to reduce the levels of mortality. Income is not used because of the reservations noted above.

Parity

For white women who have ever been married Kitagawa and Hauser (1973) have presented mortality ratios standardized for age and education which indicate significant differentials by the number of children ever born (Table 3-5).

The differences are not particularly large. For the 45 through 64-year-old group the highest mortality ratio (for a parity of 7 or more) is 28 percent greater than the lowest (3). The differences for the over 65

TABLE 3-5

MORTALITY DIFFERENTIALS BY PARITY FOR WHITE
WOMEN: UNITED STATES, 1960

Mortality Ratios[a]

Total Number of Children Ever Born (Parity)	45–64 years	65 years and over[c]
For All White Women Who Have Never Been Married[b]	1.00	1.00
no children	1.07	
1 child	1.04	
2 children	0.94	
3 children	0.89	
4 children	0.96	
5 or 6 children	1.05	
7 or more children	1.14	

a. The ratios are standardized for age and education because of the known negative associations between fertility and education and between mortality and education.

b. Ratios are given only for white women in source (below). However, given this strong evidence for the existence of parity differentials for white women, and given the choice of either using the same differentials by assumption for nonwhite women or using no differentials at all, we opt to assume that the same differentials hold also for nonwhite females.

c. No clear pattern was observable in the differential ratios for white women over 64 nor was the deviation from the average for the whole group ever more than 6 percent. Thus we opt not to use differentials for females over 64 (i.e., the differentials are assumed to be zero).

Source: Kitagawa and Hauser, *Differential Mortality in the United States,* Table 6.11.

group are so small and so inconsistent that we do not retain them in the model.

A J-pattern appears, with mortality lowest in the 2–4 parity women and higher at both extremes. This may be the combined result of (1) very high fertility *per se* causing higher mortality rates, and (2) the presence in the very low parity groups of sub-fecund, sterile, or otherwise impaired women who for those reasons may have higher-than-normal mortality rates. It is also possible that women with fewer children tend to have higher rates of divorce, separation, or widowhood, and that such changes in marital status have an adverse effect on mortality. Parity composition in DYNASIM affects the aggregate race-sex-age specific mortality rates; i.e., parity is treated as a causal factor.

Kitagawa and Hauser do not present parity data for nonwhite women. However, it seems more defensible to use the ratios and parameters estimated for whites than to assert, in effect, that no differentials exist among nonwhites.

Birth

Changing patterns of fertility are the single most important factor in determining the size and age distribution of the population in the long run (assuming that mortality rates do not change drastically). Since the size and age distribution of the population are central to many other phenomena, it would be highly desirable to have an understanding of the determinants of fertility incorporated into DYNASIM.

Unfortunately, knowledge of the behavioral relationships underlying childbearing has not proceeded to the stage where it is possible to

TABLE 3-6

PROBABILITY OF A MARRIED WOMAN, AGED 14–49, DESIRING A CHILD

Number of Children Already Born	Probability of Desiring Another Child
0	0.96
1	0.96
2	0.70
3	0.30
4	0.20
5 or more	0.20

Source: Adapted from Peabody (1971).

predict future fertility rates with any high degree of confidence. Furthermore, it has proven to be difficult to transfer the behavioral knowledge we do possess into a successful microanalytic operating characteristic.

Consequently we have chosen to include in DYNASIM an interim birth operating characteristic which does not fully incorporate all existing knowledge about underlying behavioral relationships. This operating characteristic has the virtues, nevertheless, of capturing some of the most important relationships, as well as being a manageable program module in DYNASIM.

A more complete birth operating characteristic, not currently being used, is presented in Peabody (1971). In the interim operating characteristic, Peabody's results have been heavily drawn upon, but extensive modifications have been introduced in the interest of manageability and simplicity.

The first step in the interim birth operating characteristic is the determination of whether a woman of child-bearing age (14–49 years old) desires to have a child. If she is not married, it is assumed she does not. If she is married, her probability of desiring a child is a function of the number of children she has already had. This function is given in Table 3-6.

If a woman desires to have a child, the probability that she will have a child, P(BIRTH), depends upon her age as follows:

$$P(BIRTH) = .36 \ e^{[- .105 \ \{max(0,AGE-24)\}]}$$

where the parameters have been selected to reproduce the distribution of live births by age of mother given in Table 1-69 in Section II of Volume I, 1969, *Vital Statistics* (U.S. Public Health Service, 1969). This function captures the decline in natural fecundity which accompanies advancing age as well as the tendency women have to space their children a few years apart rather than to have them at one year intervals.[9] It is assumed that no contraceptive technique is used.

If a woman does not desire to have a child, the probability that she will have a child depends upon her age, race, and education as follows:

$$P(BIRTH) = [.36 \ e^{[-.200 \ \{max(0,AGE-24)\}]}] \ x$$
$$[1 - F_2(RACE, EDUCATION)]$$

where F_2 is given in Table 3-7. This function includes declining natural fecundity with age, but fertility is reduced according to the efficiency of contraception used by the woman. Contraceptive efficiency depends upon the education and race of the woman.

---

9. In Peabody's original specification (Peabody, 1974), fecundity and interval between births are treated as separate functions. From a conceptual standpoint, separation of these two functions is desirable, but they have been combined in the interim version for simplicity.

TABLE 3-7

CONTRACEPTIVE EFFICIENCY FUNCTION (F_2)

EDUCATION	RACE	
	Nonwhite	White
Less than 12 years	0.75	0.975
12 years	0.80	0.985
More than 12 years	0.85	0.99

Source: Adapted from Peabody (1971).

Once a probability of giving birth has been calculated, the woman is simulated to give birth if a random number drawn from a uniform distribution bounded by zero and one is less than the probability of birth.

If a birth is simulated to occur, the probability of a multiple birth is determined as a function of race. This is shown in Table 3-8. A random number drawing decides whether the mother has a single child, twins, or triplets.

TABLE 3-8

MULTIPLE BIRTH PROBABILITY FUNCTION

RACE	NUMBER BORN		
	1	2	3
Nonwhite	0.9760	0.0237	0.0003
White	0.9812	0.0185	0.0003

Source: Adapted from Peabody (1971).

Finally the sex of the child is determined as a function of race. This function is shown in Table 3-9. A random number less than the probability in the table results in a boy being born. Otherwise a girl is born.

TABLE 3-9

SEX OF NEWBORN FUNCTION

RACE	SEX
	Male
Nonwhite	0.5059
White	0.5134

Source: Adapted from Peabody (1971).

Immigration

Net civilian immigration data for the United States for the 1960–70 period are given in Table 3-10. Using these data we calculated a multiplicative scaling factor to adjust populations over this period for observed net immigration. For years beyond 1970 we use the standard estimate of 400,000 net immigrants per year.

TABLE 3-10

NET IMMIGRATION: CALCULATING A SCALING FACTOR
FOR THE PURPOSE OF INCORPORATING NET CIVILIAN
IMMIGRATION OVER THE NINETEEN-SIXTIES INTO
THE POPULATION OF THE MODEL

Year	(1) Net Immigration, from July 1 to June 30[a] (in '000's)	(2) Cumulative Net Immigration (in '000's)	(3) Official U.S. Midyear Population Estimates[b] (in '000's)	(4) Scaling Factor $\left[\dfrac{(3)}{(3) - (2)}\right]$
1960–61	461[c]	461	182,992	1.00253
1961–62	365	826	185,771	1.00447
1962–63	356	1182	188,483	1.00631
1963–64	341	1523	191,141	1.00803
1964–65	323	1846	193,526	1.00963
1965–66	425	2271	195,576	1.01175
1966–67	429	2700	197,457	1.01386
1967–68	420	3120	199,399	1.01590
1968–69	383	3503	201,385	1.01770
1969–70	351[d]	3854	203,235[e]	1.01933

Notes:

a. From Irwin, Richard, and Robert Warren, "American Immigration in the Sixties," *Proceedings of the Social Statistics Section, 1970,* American Statistical Association, 1971, 278–283. The figures cited are net values composed of five major components: net alien immigration, net arrivals from Puerto Rico, net arrivals of citizens, conditional entrants, and emigration. The 400,000 net additional Armed Forces personnel overseas in 1970 as compared to 1960 are not included.

b. Estimates as of July 1; e.g., as of July 1, 1961 for 1960–61.

c. Includes net civilian immigration from April 1, 1960 to June 30, 1961.

d. Includes net civilian immigration from July 1, 1969 to March 31, 1970.

e. Census count as of April 1, 1970.

Chapter 4
FAMILY FORMATION*

The formation of new families in DYNASIM occurs primarily through marriage.[1] This chapter describes how individuals in the sample population are selected for first marriage or remarriage, and how the mate-matching processes operate. The bulk of this description is devoted to the research on entry into first marriage.

The first marriage submodel incorporates age, period, cohort and social structural influences.[2] Age, period, and cohort parameters are estimated from evidence derived from 1960 and 1970 Census data on age at first marriage. Using both 1960 and 1970 Census data makes possible a test on the reliability of part of the data. The social structural parameters are estimated from the 1971 Current Population Survey. Combining the two sets of parameter estimates yields a submodel of first marriage selection which generates a probability of first marriage for each person over 14 years old in the sample who has never been married. A random number is drawn and compared to the generated probability to decide whether or not the person is selected for first marriage.

For all persons widowed or divorced, a remarriage operating characteristic generates a similar probability of marriage selection. Again, a random number is drawn to decide selection.

All persons selected for either first marriage or remarriage constitute a pool of eligibles who then enter the mate-matching process. Males and females are given scores according to their race, age, education, and region. Matches are then made by linking partners whose scores are as close as possible. If there is an excess of one sex in the pool of eligibles, those for whom no potential mate exists are considered to have been victims of a marriage squeeze and are returned to the population to await next year's lottery. If the size of the simulation population is small or if the actual number of eligibles selected is allowed to

---

* Steven B. Caldwell had the main responsibility for this chapter and the work it represents.

1. New (single person) families are also formed when unmarried persons leave the parental unit to set up their own households (see Chapter 2, program module 2—"Home Leaving"). Birth (Chapter 3) adds new members to existing families.

2. "Period" means the marriage year. "Cohort" means the individual's birth year. For example, if a 22-year old person is married in 1973, age would equal 22, the period would be 1973, and the cohort would be 1951. Each of these factors is presumed to affect the probability of a person getting married in any particular year. "Social structural influences" include such things as income, education, and race.

fluctuate randomly around the expected value (based on the sum of the selection probabilities), the number of squeezed out persons may be unrealistically high. Consequently an option has been made available to multiply all selection probabilities by some constant term greater than one so as to create an outsized pool. In this manner, the number of matches in the model can be made to approximate the number of matches expected from marriage statistics analysis.

Post-marriage residential rules are deterministic. If both partners are living with parents, a new family unit is created with the same locational characteristics (region and city size) as the male's prior family. If either partner is a single person family, the other partner is moved into that family unit. If both are single person families, the female moves into the male's family unit. Financial assets of each partner and any prior children are merged in the new marriage unit.

Theoretical Perspective

It is a truism that the analysis of social change has been hindered by a failure to appreciate its complexity. One aspect of that complexity is the existence of three separate conceptually distinct sources of change: aging, cohort succession, and time (period) effects (Mason et al., 1973; Riley et al., 1972; Schaie and Strother, 1968; Buss, 1974; Laufer and Bengtson, 1974; Johnson et al., 1974). A cross-sectional design samples different ages at one point in time and therefore confounds age changes and cohort differences. Since groups may differ conceptually in age on the one hand and cohort on the other hand, no unambiguous interpretation which assigns an effect to age and cohort is possible with this design. Similarly, a longitudinal design which samples only one cohort at various ages through time is unable to assess cohort-related effects (Buss, 1974; Baltes, 1968).

These three effects — age, period, and cohort — need not all be operative in a given process. But if they are, to ignore one is to misinterpret the relative impact of the remaining two. Although the three effects, as usually measured, are logically confounded[3], we argue here that they are conceptually distinct. Aging is associated with life-cycle and maturational effects; period is associated with short-term environmental effects; and cohort is associated with the longer-term social climate.

In the particular case of first marriage, the hypotheses would be: (1) that physiological and psychological aging would have major effects on the likelihood of a person's entering the marriage market and finding a

3. To know any two uniquely determines the third. For example, a cohort "born" in 1930 observed in the period 1960 will, as usually measured, necessarily have an age of 30.

partner; (2) that economic, political, and military conditions in a particular period could affect first marriage likelihood for all ages and cohorts; and (3) finally, that different social and cultural circumstances affecting successive cohorts at similar points in the careers of successive cohorts could generate intercohort differences in propensity to enter first marriage.

However, even if we accept that the three effects are conceptually distinct, logical confounding of the three effects generates serious estimation problems. As opposed to a cross-section or (single cohort) longitudinal design, a multi-cohort longitudinal design in which age, period, and cohort can all vary is required to separate the three effects empirically. Moreover, the greater the variation in age, cohort, and period the more advantageous the design. However, maximizing variation in all three variables in the same design requires enormously large data bases, a requirement made even more stringent since first marriage is a relatively rare event.

Moreover, influences other than age, period and cohort are likely to be at work. Consequently, the enormous set of observations required should also contain information on a number of other relevant attributes. Not all members of a given cohort are likely to behave identically in the same period. Class, race, sex, subcultural and attitudinal differences are likely sources of heterogeneity in the population. Moreover, these sources of heterogeneity may interact with the age, period, and cohort variables, rather than being simply additive. Following Land (1975), we label these further sources of heterogeneity "social structural" effects. Thus, for example, if the social structural variable "proportion of the year spent working" positively affects the probability of entering first marriage independently of age, period, and cohort, then it follows that changes in age-specific labor force participation patterns will affect aggregate first marriage rates independently of aggregate age, period, and cohort composition. Moreover, such social structural changes might have different effects for different cohorts, i.e., they might interact. For example, imagine the relatively sharper effect that a booming economy might have on the first marriage probability of a young woman belonging to a recent cohort who has been socialized in a climate of women's liberation as compared to one 15 years older.

Ideally, these questions about the exact relationship of age, period, and cohort effects, on the one hand, to social structural effects, on the other, in the determination of first marriage rates would be tested in the context of the appropriate data file. However, such over-time files are seldom available. If a relatively small range of cohorts and of periods were sufficient, then, for example, the Michigan Panel Study of Income Dynamics might be useful. However, since we desired to observe first marriage over a much longer time period than five or seven years, we used the two-stage approach to estimating and testing outlined below, in each stage testing and estimating parameters from those data deemed most suitable and combining parameter estimates into a single model afterwards.

Model Specification

We first used an additive model for first marriage in which historical changes in the rate of entry into first marriage are separated into five components:

    (1) age effects (AGE)
    (2) cohort effects (COH)
    (3) period effects (PER)
    (4) social structural effects (SOCSTR)
    (5) residual change (U)

Then the probability of first marriage for person i in year t (PROBFSTMAR$_{it}$) is given by:

$$PROBFSTMAR_{it} = a_o + \Sigma b_h \ SOCSTR_{ih} + \Sigma c_j \ AGE_{ij} + \Sigma d_k \ COH_{ik}$$
$$+ \Sigma e_m \ PER_{im} + U_{it} \quad (1)$$

where:

a_o = intercept.

$SOCSTR_{ih}$ = value of hth social structural variable for ith person in year t.

b_h = effect of hth social structural variable.

AGE_{ij} = 1 if ith person is in jth category in year t; = 0 otherwise.

c_j = effect of being in jth age category.

COH_{ik} = 1 if ith person is in kth birth cohort category in year t; = 0 otherwise.

d_k = effect of being in kth cohort category.

PER_{im} = 1 if ith person is in mth period category in year t; = 0 otherwise.

e_m = effect of being in mth period category.

U_{it} = residual effects for person i in year t.

Over-Time Data from the 1960 and 1970 Censuses

The basic data were drawn from Table 2 of the report, *Age at First Marriage,* of the U.S. Censuses of Population of 1960 and 1970. The data were compiled from a question asked of a 5 percent sample of the population. If a person had ever married, a question was asked as to when he or she was married. In the case of those married more than once, the question was asked when he or she first married.

These sample data, weighted by the Census to represent the entire population, provided estimates of the total number of persons in various cohorts who were first married at single years of age beginning at age 15 up to 34.

The first step toward deriving estimates of first marriage probabilities was to create four separate files (white males, white females, black males, black females) for both 1960 and 1970. Each file contained the total number first married by single years of age at the census date. Also included in these four files was the number never married and ever married combined for each year, i.e., the number of persons in each cohort on the census date.

These eight data files were then used to calculate the probability that any single person of a particular age at the census interview would have married for the first time at some earlier age. This was done by comparing the total number of persons of a given age at census interview who married for the first time at some particular earlier age with the total population of the cohort less the persons who had already been married for the first time by that earlier age. The output from this operation is eight sets of first marriage probabilities.[4]

The last step in preparing the data for analysis, after merging the 1960 and 1970 files,[5] was to convert the data to rectangular file form and to assign appropriate values for age, period, and cohort to each probability based on its row and column position in the original files. After merging the 1960 and 1970 files, the result was four rectangular data files — one each for white males, white females, black males, and black females.

Each rectangular file contained four variates (probability, age, period, cohort) on each of 1290 observations.[6] Single years of *age* at marriage from 15 through 34 (i.e., 20 years) were included. Ages at 1970 Census interview, 16–89, were included. Accordingly, the data span nearly three-quarters of a century, the period 1896 through 1969 (i.e,, 74 years or periods).

4. These tables can be obtained by writing to the author at The Urban Institute.

5. The files were merged by using the 1970 Census to provide first marriage probabilities for the years 1959–1968.

6. Although unequal numbers of persons were represented by each data set, e.g., there were far more white than black males, still the number of observations is the same, since each probability applies to a *category*.

Age, Period, and Cohort Effects

All analyses use the merged 1960–1970 data files, each of which contains 1290 observations for 20 ages at first marriage (15–34), 74 birth cohorts (1880–1953) and 74 periods (1896–1969). The results of 64 regressions performed on these files using alternate equations are displayed in Table 4-1.

A first set of questions concerns the most appropriate categories to omit in order to make the equation estimable (Mason, et al., 1973) or in order to specify a more parsimonious equation. Where it was necessary for estimating purposes to omit more than one category in a dimension we omitted adjoining categories. To omit more than a single category from a given dimension is to offer the hypothesis that the effects of the omitted categories are identical. In addition, we decided to omit those categories for which the number of observations was smallest, i.e., the earliest periods and the latest birth cohorts.

Reasoning that cohort-based change ought to be relatively gradual, we decided to use a smaller number of cohort categories than period categories. Since we believed that the data were likely to be less reliable for older cohorts and periods, for older cohorts and periods we used a smaller number of categories than for more recent cohorts and periods. For example, for the final estimations we created a separate variable for each year after 1945, in order to generate a reasonably long time series of period coefficients for further analysis.

Another consideration concerns the form of the dependent variable. It can be argued that using the probabilities as dependent variables is less desirable than using the natural log of the odds ratio ($\ln \frac{P}{1 - P}$).

The logit form does not generate predicted probabilities of less than zero or greater than one. It helps correct for the inevitable heteroscedastic error term arising from the bounded dependent variable.

Our major hypothesis was that significant, independent contributions of age, period, and cohort existed. The appropriate test for this question is the F-test for the significance of additional R^2 generated by an entire set of variables. An approximately equivalent but slightly less conservative test is to simply compare the corrected coefficients of determination (R^2) when the set of variables is included versus when they are not included. Using the former test, we conclude that age, cohort, and period have significant independent effects on first marriage probability. Age has by far the strongest effect and in general period has a slightly stronger effect than cohort. For example, compare equations 17, 18, and 19 for white males 18–21 in Table 4-1. For equation 17, with all three effects included, $R^2 = 0.9897$ (only $\bar{R}^2$ shown in table). For equation 18, without period effects, $R^2 = 0.9874$. Yet, despite the virtually identical

TABLE 4-1

SUMMARY OF REGRESSIONS WITH MERGED 1960–70 FIRST MARRIAGE PROBABILITY DATA

No.	Age[a]	Number of Categories Included — Age	Cohort	Period	Dependent Variable[b]	$\bar{R}^2$	N
			WHITE MALES				
1	15–34	19	33	34	P	.9029	1290
2		19	25	25	P	.9074	
3		19	25		P	.8816	
4		19	33		P	.8808	
5		19		25	P	.8999	
6		19		34	P	.8957	
7		19		51	P	.9067	
8			25	25	P	.4205	
9		19			P	.7682	
10	15–26	11	35	35	P	.9611	822
11		11	35		P	.9142	
12		11		35	P	.9208	
13	18–2b	7	23	35	L	.9869	540
14		7		35	L	.9805	
15		7	c	35	L	.9849	
16	18–21	3	23	36	P	.9701	278
17		3	23	36	L	.9867	
18		3	23		L	.9776	
19		3		36	L	.9852	
20		3			P	.5073	
21		3			L	.5903	
22	22–25	3	12	32	P	.9263	262
23		3	21	35	L	.9653	
24		3	c	35	L	.9611	
25		3	12		P	.8948	
26		3			P	.9210	
27		3			L	.9492	
28		3			P	.0137	
29	26–34	8	23	35	P	.9410	531
30		8	23	35	L	.9411	
31		8	23		P	.7265	
32		8	23		L	.7492	
33		8		35	P	.8436	
34		8		35	L	.8665	
35		8			P	.4799	
36		8			L	.5222	

(see notes on next page)

TABLE 4-1 (continued)

No.	Age[a]	Number of Categories Included Age	Cohort	Period	Dependent Variable[b]	$\bar{R}^2$	N
		WHITE FEMALES					
37	15–19	4	24	36	L	.9832	360
38		4		36	L	.9480	
39	20–23	3	22	36	P	.9723	270
40		3	22	36	L	.9743	
41		3		36	L	.9679	
42	24–34	10	23	35	P	.9539	660
43		10	23	35	L	.9618	
44		10		35	P	.9032	
45		10		35	L	.9369	
46		10			P	.6998	
47		10			L	.7525	
		BLACK MALES					
48	18–21	3	23	36	L	.9051	274
49	22–25	3	12	32	P	.8441	258
50		3	21	35	L	.8636	
51		3		35	L	.8453	
52		3		32	P	.8365	
53		3	12		P	.7897	
54			12		P	.3028	
55	26–34	8	23	35	P	.7688	522
56		8	23	35	L	.7376	
57		8		35	L	.7084	
58		8			L	.1741	
		BLACK FEMALES					
59	15–19	4	24	36	L	.9191	360
60	20–23	3	22	36	L	.7597	270
61	24–34	10	23	35	P	.6942	660
62		10	23	35	L	.6833	
63		10			P	.3553	
64		10			L	.3540	

a. Ages at first marriage included in the regressions. For males 15–17, probabilities are set to .001, .004, and .015 for whites respectively and .002, .005, and .015 for nonwhites respectively.

b. P: probability of first marriage. L: $\ln \frac{P}{1-P}$.

c. In this regression each cohort's birth year (C) and the square of the birth year (C²) were substituted for the dummy variable representation of the cohort effect.

fit to the data generated by these three equations, the .0023 additional R^2 explained by adding the 36 period terms to equation 18 is significant at the .01 level (F = 2.1) and the .0099 additional R^2 gained by adding the 23 cohort terms to equation 19 is significant at the .01 level (F = 5.5). For the age at marriage of the 22–25 white male group, the cohort terms add .0164 (F = 5.0) to the variance when added to the period and age effects, and for the 26–34 white male group the cohort terms add .0711 (F = 29) to the variance. Period terms add a substantial .1843 additional to R^2 for this latter group. It appears that for white males at least, period and cohort have increasing importance with age.

To allow for such interactions, separate equations were estimated for separate age at marriage categories. These separate regressions are an attempt to weaken the additivity assumption. Additivity implies that each effect operates independently of the other two effects. We performed separate regressions by age at marriage as an obvious way to specify a class of interactions. This approach, which seems theoretically more defensible than the purely additive model, also yielded statistically superior fits. Corrected standard errors of estimate were lower for each of three white male equations (i.e., nos. 16, 22, and 29) covering ages 18–21, 22–25, and 26–34, and for each of two white male equations (nos. 19, 29) covering ages 15–26 and 26–34 than for either comparable white male equation (nos. 1 or 2) covering the entire age group 15–34. Multiple correlation coefficients cannot be compared directly, but an overall indicator of fit for a set of several separate regressions was computed by first adding together the residual sums of squares for each regression, subtracting the residual sum of squares from the total sum of squares for a simple regression on all the data, and dividing by the total sum of squares over all data. For example, equation 13 (for ages 18–26) has a higher $\bar{R}^2$ than either of equations 17 (for ages 18–21) or 23 (for ages 22–25). However, summing the residual sums of squares for equations 17 and 23 (2.0141), subtracting that from the total sum of squares for equation 13 (116.3226), and dividing by the latter, yields an R^2 of .9921, which is better than equation 13's $\bar{R}^2$ (.9885). We conclude equations 17 and 23 together provide a statistically superior fit to that of equation 13 alone, thus supporting the interaction hypothesis.

With these initial explanations complete, we proceeded to estimate twelve final equations for the twelve age-race-sex groupings, the results of which are given in Tables 4-2 and 4-3. It is these equations which are used in DYNASIM. (For males, both white and black, age group 15–17 was not included in the estimations since the nuptiality probabilities are quite small. For these groups the mean value over the 1946–69 period is used.) The $\bar{R}^2$ for each of the twelve final equations is given in Table 4-4.

In all cases $\bar{R}^2$ declines with age. For whites the decline is only

TABLE 4-2

FINAL REGRESSIONS ON FIRST MARRIAGE
PROBABILITIES BY RACE, SEX, AND AGE
Regression Coefficients ($\times 10^2$)

	MALES				FEMALES			
	18–21		22–25		15–19		20–23	
	White	Black	White	Black	White	Black	White	Black
Equation No.:	(17)	(48)	(23)	(50)	(37)	(59)	(40)	(60)
Age								
15					a	a		
16					64	38		
17					112	65		
18	a	a			154	85		
19	57	43			171	94		
20	99	69					− 7	9
21	133	82					3	4
22			−21	0			5	2
23			−10	1			a	a
24			− 3	2				
25			a	a				
Cohort								
1880–84	a	a	a	a	a	a	a	a
1885–89	− 4	−21	3	12	4	0	− 2	15
1890–94	− 1	−15	2	18	6	4	− 2	13
1895–99	2	− 3	− 7	19	15	8	2	31
1900–02	4	− 8	−17	− 3	22	14	−14	9
1903–05	9	− 9	− 9	4	25	21	−12	27
1906–08	13	− 4	−12	8	31	20	−10	31
1909–11	15	− 5	− 8	14	35	23	−15	31
1912–14	14	− 9	−12	9	42	25	−14	32
1915–17	12	−11	−11	10	44	39	−19	32
1918–20	7	−13	−12	− 4	46	39	−23	25
1921–23	5	−16	− 7	−17	46	45	−20	28
1924–26	13	− 1	− 3	−20	35	44	−20	20
1927–29	2	− 7	7	−28	23	42	−16	20
1930–32	3	−12	12	−34	2	30	−12	16
1933–34	25	−14	22	−46	−10	21	− 2	9
1935–36	36	−19	38	−40	−27	5	4	1
1937–38	42	−33	56	−36	−46	−13	9	− 1
1939–40	43	−52	72	−35	−68	−40	14	− 6

a. Category omitted from regression equation.

| | MALES | | | | FEMALES | | | |
| | 18–21 | | 22–25 | | 15–19 | | 20–23 | |
	White	Black	White	Black	White	Black	White	Black
Equation No.:	(17)	(48)	(23)	(50)	(37)	(59)	(40)	(60)
1941–42	41	−75	90	−27	−103	−81	22	− 1
1943–44	39	−101	99	−24	−134	−119	21	− 1
1945–46	33	−121	113	−27	−177	−158	19	− 3
1947–48	36	−143			−228	−218	12	−12
1949–50	33	−165			−280	−283		
1951–53					−344	−365		
Period								
1896–1904	a	a	a	a	a	a	a	a
1905–14	10	17	a	a	0	− 4	11	− 5
1915–19	18	13	2	8	− 5	− 4	13	− 2
1920–24	25	22	24	9	− 1	− 6	29	− 6
1925–29	22	26	26	15	−10	−10	30	−12
1930–31	10	14	20	?	−25	−20	23	−25
1932–33	0	11	7	−12	−38	−37	14	−34
1934–35	11	24	28	6	−28	−29	37	−20
1936–37	17	26	37	22	−28	−35	46	− 18
1938–39	22	27	38	21	−32	−39	47	−17
1940–41	48	40	64	36	−10	−32	76	1
1942–43	67	44	58	40	0	−28	78	3
1944–45	45	22	39	28	− 5	−40	61	− 8
1946	73	36	85	78	37	−13	104	29
1947	80	46	89	89	50	− 6	109	32
1948	85	50	81	86	53	− 3	104	27
1949	81	50	73	76	55	− 5	95	23
1950	92	56	71	80	73	4	98	24
1951	102	52	70	83	81	4	97	24
1952	93	53	54	76	84	0	89	25
1953	91	55	57	85	93	7	92	33
1954	82	58	61	93	99	15	90	36
1955	80	69	67	109	117	32	99	49
1956	82	74	70	118	127	43	99	54
1957	81	78	69	125	139	51	97	63
1958	78	90	58	116	142	57	90	60
1959	76	93	55	127	159	75	90	66
1960	64	90	38	103	162	87	76	47

a. Category omitted from regression equation.

TABLE 4-3

FINAL REGRESSION ON FIRST MARRIAGE PROBABILITIES BY RACE, SEX, AND AGE
Regression Coefficients ($\times 10^2$)

Eq. No.	White Males 26–34 (30)	Black Males 26–34 (56)	White Females 24–34 (43)	Black Females 24–34 (62)
Age				
24			93	40
25			86	34
26	45	33	78	32
27	42	30	68	30
28	39	26	62	29
29	35	25	53	25
30	29	21	42	17
31	21	13	30	5
32	14	8	20	3
33	7	2	9	− 7
34	a	a	a	a
Cohort				
1880–84	a	a	a	a
1885–89	− 5	6	3	14
1890–94	− 9	− 4	− 2	7
1895–99	−10	−11	− 3	− 3
1900–02	−14	−19	− 4	− 1
1903–05	− 5	− 1	1	15
1906–08	− 1	− 2	3	27
1909–10	2	− 2	9	38
1911–12	4	8	16	33
1913–14	10	5	19	32
1915–16	14	2	15	29
1917–18	19	6	18	40
1919–20	28	3	24	38
1921–22	31	16	38	46
1923–24	36	5	30	46
1925–26	49	20	38	54
1927–28	63	17	49	61
1929–30	79	24	54	73
1931–32	91	36	62	87
1933–34	104	39	70	85
1935–36	119	53	76	95
1937–38	131	62	89	105
1939–40	143	62	100	110
1941–44	160	67	118	120

a. Category omitted from regression equation.

TABLE 4-3 (continued) 79

Eq. No.	White Males 26–34 (30)	Black Males 26–34 (56)	White Females 24–34 (43)	Black Females 24–34 (62)
Period				
1905–14	a	a	a	a
1915–19	0	13	5	14
1920–24	18	20	20	24
1925–29	13	11	9	4
1930–31	2	− 9	− 6	− 7
1932–33	−12	−23	−18	−42
1934–35	9	3	3	−24
1936–37	17	6	11	−11
1938–39	12	4	7	−20
1940–41	28	23	21	− 5
1942–43	16	29	18	8
1944–45	3	18	0	− 4
1946	45	51	41	7
1947	43	50	38	2
1948	29	41	28	1
1949	16	30	20	− 3
1950	12	38	14	− 6
1951	5	32	10	−13
1952	− 6	20	1	− 8
1953	− 9	28	0	−15
1954	−18	27	− 5	−13
1955	−20	33	− 6	− 5
1956	−26	28	− 8	−13
1957	−31	38	−11	−17
1958	−38	28	−18	−23
1959	−43	30	−22	−24
1960	−56	12	−35	−52
1961	−68	−11	−48	−68
1962	−75	−10	−55	−71
1963	−79	− 6	−56	−71
1964	−85	−10	−59	−72
1965	−83	0	−57	−68
1966	−95	−11	−64	−80
1967	−98	−10	−72	-83
1968	−99	2	−67	−76
1969	−103	5	−69	−87
Intercept	−246	−275	−289	−268

a. Category omitted from regression equation.

TABLE 4-4

CORRECTED MULTIPLE CORRELATION COEFFICIENTS FOR FINAL FIRST MARRIAGE REGRESSION EQUATIONS BY RACE, SEX, AND AGE

Age	WHITE MALES		WHITE FEMALES		BLACK MALES		BLACK FEMALES	
	$\bar{R}^2$	Eq. No.	$\bar{R}^2$	Eq. No.	$\bar{R}^2$	Eq. No.	$\bar{R}^2$	Eq. No.
18–21 (M)	.9867	17			.9051	48		
15–19 (F)			.9832	37			.9191	59
22–25 (M)	.9653	23			.8636	50		
20–23 (F)			.9743	40			.7497	60
26–34 (M)	.9411	30			.7376	56		
24–34 (F)			.9618	43			.6833	62

slight, but for blacks the decline is quite strong. The fit is much better for whites than blacks. Other research on the reliability of the data suggests that one possible reason for the poorer fit for blacks is the lower reliability of the data for blacks; however, it is also possible that factors not taken into account in these equations simply play a larger role in the first marriage decisions of blacks.

The slope of first marriage change with age is much sharper for whites than blacks, both male and female. Cohort patterns are quite different by age. For all females, the youngest age group exhibits a sharp decline in cohort coefficients. The middle age group exhibits no particular cohort trend. Finally, the oldest age group exhibits a substantial increase in cohort coefficients. The overall picture is consistent: for more recent cohorts there has been a decline in first marriage likelihood at young ages and an increase in first marriage rates at older ages. For males, the picture is the same, with the sharpest increase in first marriage rates in the older age groups.

One caution seems in order. Although the evidence seems reasonably strong for the existence of independent age, period, and cohort effects, the estimation of magnitudes of effects is clearly hampered by the difficulty of separating cohort and period effects, apparently because of their collinearity. The pattern of the estimated cohort effects appears to be compensating for the pattern of trends in period effects (and vice versa). Although annual fluctuations in period coefficients track major wars and economic events, as we would expect, such intuitively reasonable movements are sometimes overridden by sharp trends that seem to be essentially responses to trends in the estimated cohort parameters. This confounding of effects does not always occur, but its frequency suggests that difficult problems exist in empirically separating the two dimensions.

Social Structural Effects: Data and Estimation Technique

A disadvantage of the first marriage probability data is the lack of information on other variables besides race, sex, age, period, and cohort. It is reasonable to expect that other variables, for example labor force status, do have strong effects. If so, such other variables should be taken into account when estimating the age, period, and cohort effects. Not including the variables in the equations, if indeed they are influencing first marriage, means that we have misspecified the equations and our parameter estimates are biased. Unfortunately, appropriate data do not exist for simultaneous testing and estimation of all relevant parameters in a complete model of first marriage. We cannot regard age, period, and cohort parameter estimates presented as unbiased structural coefficients. Rather, they are more or less biased estimates of the "true" structural parameters, but their usefulness derives from the relatively long time series evidence which has been used in their estimation. If the net effect of the social structural variables within race, sex, age-specific groups has remained relatively constant over the periods and cohorts with which we are concerned, we have relatively unbiased estimates of the "true" age, period, and cohort effects by race and sex. To the extent that the net effects have not remained constant, the changing effects of the social structural variables on the distribution of first marriage have been confounded with changes in the period and/or cohort effects. In short, any collinearity between the period and cohort variable on the one hand and the social structural variable on the other hand leads to biased period or cohort parameter estimates. The second stage of our analysis attempts to gauge the effects of some of those variables left out of the first stage estimates. For this purpose, the March 1971 Current Population Survey provides an excellent empirical source. The monthly Current Population Survey interviews roughly 50,000 families in the United States, largely for the purpose of eliciting labor market information; however, the survey is supplemented for the March interview by questions on other social and demographic characteristics, including for our purposes current marital status, the year of first marriage, and current age.

The first step of the analysis used an extract taken from the March 1971 Current Population Survey. This extract consisted of persons between the ages of 15 and 30 inclusive and included information on roughly twenty variables describing each person ($N = 36,783$). A small subsample ($N = 500$) from this extract was used for initial exploratory analyses. These analyses, as well as the age, period, and cohort results reported above, suggested performing separate regressions for groups defined simultaneously by race, sex, and age. Consequently, twelve new extracts broken by race, sex, and age (three groups) were drawn from the initial extract.

In drawing these twelve second-stage extracts, the eligible population was restricted to those who reported their marital status as either: (1) single (never married) or (2) married, widowed, or divorced (ever-married), if and only if the person reported the year first married as either 1970 or 1971. In other words, those eligible for inclusion were (1) those who had either first married in the one and one-quarter years prior to the interview, or (2) who had never married.

As the twelve extracts were drawn, the initial dependent variable (DEP1) was created as follows:

(1) if a person reported his (her) marital status as single (never married) set DEP1 = 0;

(2) for all other persons, i.e., those persons who first married in the one and one-quarter year prior to the interview, set DEP1 = 1.

The mean of DEP1 therefore is an estimate of the proportion of the race-, sex-, and age-specific group who first married in the period January 1, 1970 through March 1, 1971. For example, Table 4-5, which contains the relevant summary statistics from all twelve files, provides the means of DEP1, which shows that, e.g., 14.7 percent of the cohort of white females who reported an age of 18–20 years in March 1971 (and who thus are in the age group 17–19, approximately, at the beginning of 1970) married for the first time in the fourteen months between January 1, 1970 and March 1, 1971. The first row of Table 4-5 gives the mean first marriage proportions (probabilities) for the twelve groups. However, more important than these aggregate group probabilities is the underlying micro data; i.e., for each person we know whether he or she first married in the prior one year and two months. Thus, DEP1, a dichotomous (0 or 1) dependent variable can be regressed on suitable micro-level characteristics in order to locate those variables related to propensity to first marriage in that year and one-sixth.

However, the question of choosing the most appropriate dependent variable is linked with the problem of integrating the two steps of analysis: (1) the first-stage analysis using age, period, and cohort to explain the over-time aggregate nuptiality histories, and (2) the second-stage analysis using dichotomous, micro nuptiality decision data. Our strategy is to create a linking dependent variable by residualizing DEP1. We accomplish this by subtracting from DEP1 the *predicted* first marriage probability generated by the model from the first stage based on period and cohort, as well as race, sex, and age. The variable which results from this residualizing procedure, which we call DEP2, is thus used as the appropriate dependent variable and regressed on relevant social structural variables. The reasoning behind this procedure will now be described.

We have assumed an additive model for first marriage probability (specific to a given age-race-sex grouping) in which changes in the rate of entry into first marriage are decomposed into five components as previously described in equation (1).

Simultaneous estimation of the four kinds of effects requires data which range over reasonable numbers of age, periods, and cohorts as well as having information on social structural variables. If we tried to estimate model (1) directly from the C.P.S. data, the single (1970) "period" effect would be absorbed into the intercept. Moreover, the cohort effects, since they would be confounded with the age affects, could not be separately

TABLE 4-5

SUMMARY STATISTICS FOR FIRST MARRIAGE DATA FROM 1971 CURRENT POPULATION SURVEY

	WHITE FEMALE			WHITE MALE			BLACK FEMALE			BLACK MALE		
	17–19	20–22	23–27	18–20	21–23	24–28	17–19	20–22	23–27	18–20	21–23	24–28
Proportion First Married	.147	.245	.213	.117	.220	.197	.117	.184	.123	.051	.157	.148
Residual Proportion First Married	.036	.016	.019	.034	.022	.000	.019	.031	−.009	−.024	.006	−.008
Earned Income	1265	2718	4790	2203	3553	6271	825	1908	3301	1648	2775	4033
Proportion Worked												
0 weeks	23	13	11	12	13	8	44	27	24	25	20	12
1–13	23	14	3	23	14	5	21	14	8	21	11	7
14–26	17	15	6	16	13	8	11	12	9	14	14	8
27–39	10	11	8	11	11	6	6	9	8	9	6	14
40–47	5	7	6	6	6	7	3	7	1	4	8	8
≥48	22	42	65	33	43	65	15	31	50	27	42	52
Proportion in												
Northeast	26	29	31	27	29	31	16	20	21	13	17	28
North Central	31	29	26	28	30	26	16	20	20	21	19	14
South	24	22	24	25	23	22	55	43	48	51	53	51
West	19	20	19	19	18	22	14	17	11	14	10	8
Proportion Education												
0–11 grades	23	8	11	17	12	15	41	26	37	36	30	42
12	53	35	37	39	35	35	40	40	43	36	38	31
13–15	24	40	17	44	32	20	20	28	10	27	24	10
≥16	0	17	36	0	22	30	0	7	10	0	8	17
Proportion Hourly Wage												
≤0.50	37	19	14	21	19	11	56	34	28	35	25	21
0.51–1.50	31	22	9	26	15	6	23	23	18	23	22	10
1.50–2.50	22	28	21	23	19	16	14	28	22	22	19	26
2.51–4.00	9	25	39	21	27	32	6	11	21	14	23	26
≥4.01	2	6	17	9	20	36	2	3	11	6	11	18
N	2792	1402	775	2439	1559	948	443	269	197	339	211	139

estimated. Instead, the regression coefficient for age would be the sum of the respective structural coefficients for cohort and age. We can see this formally if we observe that for cross-section data equation (1) collapses into:

$$PROBFSTMAR_{it} = (a_0 + e_{1970}) + \Sigma b_h \; SOCSTR_{ih}$$
$$+ \; \Sigma(c_j + d_k) \; AGE_{ij} + U_i \quad (2)$$

The possibility of estimating distinct period and cohort effects is important, since we are attempting to imbed in DYNASIM a dynamic model which is responsive to major period- and cohort-based sources of social change. Aggregate features of the national demographic and economic structures can shift year by year in important ways in response to policies. It is desirable that the micromodel of first marriage behavior should be sensitive to these period-specific changes. Moreover, in order to use the model for projecting into the future, we want to capture intercohort changes. Thus, even if the patterns of period and cohort effects are difficult to project into the future, at the very least knowledge of past variation ought to be helpful in suggesting probable limits to future period-and-cohort-specific shifts in first marriage rates.

As we have seen, if equation (2) were estimated from the cross-section data only, a period effect would not be estimable, since all observations are for one period, and only the sum of the age and cohort effects would be estimable. Nevertheless, to estimate the entire model from cross-section data does have the very attractive feature that, assuming model (1) is correct, unbiased estimates of both the social structural factors and the sum of the age and cohort effects are obtained. This is true because no relevant variables are omitted from the estimation process. However, the problem of how to use parameter estimates from the over-time data would be unsolved. Lacking such parameters it would be impossible to project first marriage probabilities into the future, i.e., to project either the constant term (i.e., the true constant plus a period effect) or the summed age-plus-cohort coefficient. Of course, one could insert age, period, and cohort parameters as estimated from the over-time data into the cross-section model, but if, as is likely, these parameters were biased one would thereby lose most of the advantages of estimating using cross-section data. The predictions could be considerably off target using an equation which mixed biased and unbiased parameter estimates.

Instead, the procedure we used assumes the age, period, and cohort parameters are most appropriately estimated from the over-time data. We then substitute these parameter estimates directly into equation (1) prior to estimating the remaining parameters from the C.P.S. data. That is, the parameters c_j, d_k and e_m were substituted into equation (1). The parameters as estimated were subtracted from original dependent variable (DEP1) before estimating a_o and the social structural set b_h. Stated formally, set

$$\text{PROBFSTMAR}_{i,1970} = \text{DEP1}_i \text{ then} \qquad (3)$$

$$\text{DEP1}_i - (c_j \text{AGE}_{ij} + d_k \text{ COH}_{ik} + e_{1970}) = \text{DEP2}_i \qquad (4)$$

which yields the specification used for estimating the remaining parameters:

$$\text{DEP2}_i = a_o + \Sigma b_h \text{ SOCSTR}_{ih} + u_i \qquad (5)$$

The new dependent variable, DEP2, is regressed on the appropriate social structural variables in the cross-section data. The disadvantage of this procedure, as we have discussed, is that the age, period, and cohort parameters are likely to be biased upward, and the social structural variables will consequently be biased downward. However, the advantage of this method is that the bias in one set of estimates at least takes account of the bias in the other set of estimates. For projection purposes at least, such offsetting biases are preferable to a mixture of unbiased and biased estimates. The final argument in favor of this approach is that the bias in the estimates of the social structural coefficients is probably small, since the correlation between DEP1 and the residualized DEP2 is very high.

Social Structural Effects: Results

Several hypothesis guided the choice of the appropriate social structural variables. Region of residence was included as a possible index of underlying cultural differences affecting nuptiality behavior. Education was included because we hypothesized that persons still completing their education would delay marriage. In addition, more education might make males more attractive, but on the other hand, for females higher levels of education might make it more difficult for them to find a suitable partner. For males we expected that better economic status would lead to both greater readiness to enter marriage and greater attractiveness to potential partners. We decided to use two independent measures of economic status: (1) amount of time worked, and (2) wage rate earned per unit of time worked. For females, it was difficult to predict in advance the effect of economic status on marriage probabilities. However, if part of the reason women enter marriage is for economic protection, then we would hypothesize that the more economically self-sufficient a woman becomes the lower her probability of entering marriage.

Whether or not a person received any asset income was used as another indicator of economic status. Again, we expected positive effects for males and negative effects for females. Finally, a variable which was set equal to one if a woman received welfare or other public assistance was included. It was expected that for such women, marriage, at least "reported" marriage, might be less desirable, given the loss of benefits ordinarily entailed. Finally, we hypothesized that the above patterns would be different for different sexes, races, and ages. Hence, separate regressions, to allow for interactions, were performed for white and black males by age (18–20, 21–23, 24–28) and white and black females by age (17–19, 20–22, 23–27). However, the results for blacks are not reported since the number of observations was small.

Regressions incorporating these hypotheses were performed separately on the twelve appropriate extracts drawn from the 1971 C.P.S. using DEP2 as the dependent variable and all using the sample weights. The results for whites are displayed in Table 4-6. For white males statistically significant regional differences in first marriage probabilities were located. The South and West consistently had the highest nuptiality, and the Northeast the lowest. Educational differences behave roughly as hypothesized. For the youngest age group, years of education is inversely related to nuptiality; many persons were delaying marriage because they were in school. For the 21–23 age group, the group with 13–15 years of education completed was significantly lower in nuptiality than the 0–11 group. Finally, in a pattern which was repeated for other race-sex groups, the oldest group displays no significant differences in nuptiality by educational attainment. Apparently, differences in education disappear as a force affecting nuptiality by the time a cohort normally completes its education.

Probably the clearest and most important result is the strong effect of *both* labor market variables — time worked and earnings rate — on the nuptiality of white males. Hourly wages, which are estimated from the data by taking the midpoint of the weeks worked variable, multiplying it by forty hours and dividing the result into total earned income, have a clear, monotonically increasing relationship to nuptiality for white males at all ages. For the oldest age category, the relationship is nearly a step function, with nuptiality increasing sharply as wages reach about $1.50 per hour. In addition to the wage relationship, the number of weeks worked has a strong, monotonically increasing, relationship to first marriage probabilities. Only for the oldest age group is the relationship somewhat weak. Still, full-time workers (48 weeks or more), who constitute nearly two-thirds of the oldest group, have higher nuptiality than part-time workers, though the difference is not quite significant. Whether an improved economic position leads a male to be more prepared to take on marital responsibilities, or whether it makes him more attractive as a

TABLE 4-6

SOCIAL STRUCTURAL REGRESSION COEFFICIENTS FROM 1971 CURRENT POPULATION SURVEY DATA BY SEX AND AGE FOR WHITES[a]

	WHITE MALES			WHITE FEMALES		
	18–20	21–23	24–27	18–20	21–23	24–27
Intercept	−60*	−13	−224*	129*	113*	−46**
Region						
Northeast	b	−95*	b	−105*	−90*	
North Central	38*	−31**	68*	−60*	−31**	
South	83*	b	99*	b	b	
Education						
0–11	b	b	b	b	b	
12	−37*	−41**	−42**	−19**	52**	
13–15	−81*	−94*	1**	−131*	−66**	
16 or more	c	−42**	−2**	c	−76**	
Weeks Worked						
0	b	b	b	25**		71**
1–13	−78*	−150*	b	2**	−147*	b
14–26	−25**	−24**	b	12**	−115**	b
27–39	54**	7**	b	12**	−63**	190*
40–47	68**	30**	b	b	−149*	178*
48	76*	77**	44**	b	−172*	−73**
Hourly Wage						
a. $ per hour (continuous)	19.6*d	16.2*d	3.3**d	17.5*d	9.5**d	11.6**d
b. 0.50/hr	b	b	b	−34**	b	b
0.51–1.50	48*	44**	b	8**	100*	59**
1.51–2.50	104**	98*	155*	48**	130*	99**
2.50–4.00	147*	147*	138*	b	159*	134**
4.01	150*	193*	171*	b	68**	88**
Asset Income						
0	b	b	b	b	b	b
1	14**	52*	71*	−63*	−66*	−37
Welfare or Other Public Assistance						
0						b
1						−155**

TABLE 4-6 (continued)

	WHITE MALES			WHITE FEMALES		
	18–20	21–23	24–27	18–20	21–23	24–27
Unempl., Workman's Comp., gov't. pensions, veterans						
0			b			
1			86*			
Mean of dep. var.						
F	17.6	8.1	4.1	9.9	3.9	4.7
d.f	142,424	161,542	12,935	132,778	161,385	10,764
$\bar{R}^2$	.0864	.0676	.0371	.0395	.0309	.0439

a. All variables are significant at the .01 level unless indicated by a single asterisk (*), which indicates significance at the .05 level, or by a double asterisk (**), which indicates significance at the .10 level or less.
b. Omitted category.
c. No observations in category (therefore omitted).
d. Estimated in continuous form, but dummy categories proved preferable using $\bar{R}^2$ criterion—consequently dummies to be used in simulation.

partner in the marriage market, or both, remains unanswered. The important finding is the evidence that *both* components of labor force status, wages and hours, have simultaneous independent effects. Often total earned income is automatically used as the simple indicator of economic status in social research; insufficient attention is given to the fact that earned income is the *product* of two quite separate components, hours and wages. Both appear to have effects on nuptiality.

A third economic variable, being the recipient of asset income, also has a direct positive effect, at least for the two older groups. However, it appears the *amount* of asset income is not related to nuptiality. When the amount was entered in the equation rather than, or in addition to, simple recipient status, amount was not significant. Perhaps being a recipient of asset income is a proxy for other variables, e.g., class of origin, which affect marital attractiveness. Finally, for the oldest group, recipients of certain government transfer payments (unemployment, workmen's compensation, government pensions and veteran's pensions) have higher nuptiality. Again, the amount proved less important than simple recipient status, and again we are drawn to the proxy interpretation.

For white females, the region variable behaves as it does for white males, although the effect disappears altogether for the oldest group. The education variable also behaves quite similarly; once again, the effect disappears for the oldest group. The major difference between men and women lies in the sharply different effects of the economic variables. For women, the effect of both weeks worked and wage rate is bell-shaped, i.e., lower at the two ends than in the middle range. Also for women the effect of receiving asset income on nuptiality is *negative*. White females who worked full time or earned the highest wages had significantly lower nuptiality than those who worked part time or earned middle-range wages. It is possible the effect is in the other direction, since we are measuring the labor force variables as of the year of marriage. Consequently, it could be that for some a first marriage led to less time spent working. But first marriage seems less likely to have led to lower wage rates. Finally, it seems quite unlikely that first marriage could have led to a lower probability of being a recipient of asset income. Consequently, we suggest an alternative explanation, that to some extent improved economic status for a female has an independence effect, enabling her to delay marriage or not to enter marriage at all. At the very least this sex difference in the affected economic status confirms the importance of viewing the social structural determinants separately by sex. Finally, for the oldest group of women, to be a welfare recipient is to have lower (legal) first marriage rates, although the relation is not quite significant.

The final product of these regressions is a set of estimated parameters on the social structural variables. These parameter estimates can be combined with the age, period, cohort parameters estimated previously. The result is a dynamic model of first marriage behavior at the individual level in which the probability of first marriage for a particular individual is a function of the individual's race, sex, age, and cohort, a set of social structural attributes, and the particular period of time in which the person is located. Change in first marriage behavior at the aggregate level can be decomposed into the five sources cited above:

(1) period
(2) cohort
(3) age
(4) social structural
(5) residual

Given a method of projecting cohort and period parameters, the model can be used to project first marriage rates into the future for a population with a given set of attributes.

Remarriage

Remarriage probabilities, which are quite different from first marriage probabilities, are drawn directly from published tabulations of the 1967 Survey of Economic Opportunity (U.S. Bureau of the Census, 1971). Variations in remarriage by duration of current marital status, current marital status, sex, and age are incorporated (Table 4-7). Since DYNA-SIM treats both separated persons and persons whose spouse is absent for other reasons as if they were divorced, the population at risk of remarriage is too large. Consequently, simulation totals for remarriages

TABLE 4-7

REMARRIAGE PROBABILITIES BY DURATION OF
CURRENT MARITAL STATUS, CURRENT MARITAL
STATUS, SEX, AND AGE

Duration of Current Marital Status (yrs.)	Age (Divorce or Widowhood)	MALE		FEMALE	
		Divorced	Widowed	Divorced	Widowed
0–4	<25	.304	.199	.300	.145
	25–34	.262	.199	.184	.145
	35–44	.222	.181	.117	.033
	45+	.152	.102	.048	.019
5–9	<25	.253	.142	.214	.075
	25 34	.130	.142	.117	.075
	35–44	.084	.049	.039	.040
	45+	.049	.060	.025	.009
10–14	<25	.195	.061	.170	.033
	25–34	.085	.061	.077	.033
	35–44	.087	.029	.043	.012
	45+	.021	.020	.019	.005
15 or more	<25	.100	.061	.115	.033
	25–34	.104	.061	.052	.033
	35–44	.043	.029	.035	.012
	45+	.028	.020	.049	.005

Source: U.S. Bureau of the Census, "Social and Economic Variations in Marriage, Divorce and Remarriage: 1967," Tables 8 and 9.

over the 1970–72 period were adjusted using historical data and adjustment factors specific to both race and sex. These adjustment factors are used for simulation in other time periods in order to effectively reduce the number of remarriages so that they will correspond to realistic proportions of all marriages.

Chapter 5
FAMILY DISSOLUTION*

To construct a submodel of family dissolution in the United States, evidence is drawn from two sources of data: (1) vital statistics on marriages and divorces for the period 1949–1971, and (2) the five-year Michigan Panel Study of Income Dynamics (PSID). For a particular married couple, the submodel generates a probability of dissolution for reasons of marital discord (includes separations, divorces, annulments)[1] in a given calendar year. The actual decision to dissolve a marriage in the model is made by comparing the generated probability with a random number.

Morgan (1974) has found that changes in family composition, along with labor force participation, so dominate changes in family economic well-being that "nothing else seems to matter very much." Certainly the level and distribution of family dissolution significantly affect family income and wealth distribution in direct and indirect ways, such that the overall effects can best be explored within the DYNASIM framework. Incorporated in DYNASIM, the family dissolution submodel should make possible more realistic simulations of family income and wealth distribution during experiments on the impact of public policies.

Model Specification

Following Land (1975), observed historical changes in marriage dissolution probabilities are separated into the following five components:
   (1) duration effects; change associated with increasing duration of marriage of the marriage cohorts that make up the population.
   (2) cohort effects; change associated with the replacement of older marriage cohorts in the population by younger marriage cohorts.
   (3) period effects; change associated with unique historical characteristics of a given observation period.

* Steven B. Caldwell had the main responsibility for this chapter and the work it represents.
   1. Family dissolution may also occur for reasons of mortality (Chapter 3). Unmarried members of a family may leave the family in order to marry (Chapter 4), or simply to set up a one-person family of their own (Chapter 2, demographic program module 2, "home leaving").

(4) social structural effects; change associated with the varying efficacy of socioeconomic institutions involved in particular distributional processes.

(5) residual change; unaccounted for by duration, cohort, period, or social structural effects.

A marriage *cohort* is here defined as all those marriages which take place in a particular year rather than, as previously used, all those persons born in a particular year. The *duration* of a marriage is its duration in number of years, and the particular calendar year during which the marriage is at risk of dissolving is the *period*.

Cohort effects represent conditions which affect marriage cohorts at approximately the same stage in the "careers" of successive cohorts. For example, changes in the laws affecting the ease of divorce, or long-term changes in attitudes toward the desirability of divorce might lead successive cohorts to have different patterns of divorce. Duration effects reflect the high dissolution rates early in marriage as the higher risk marriages dissolve; longer duration marriages display a declining tendency to dissolve. Period-specific shifts are caused by conditions in particular years which affect all marriage cohorts simultaneously, each at a different stage in its "career". Examples of such conditions might be wars, sharp macroeconomic fluctuations, and faddish attitude changes. Numerous social structural aspects bearing on dissolution have been suggested by previous research, among them education, income, location, presence of children, age difference of partners, and race.

Combining the components in an additive specification yields the following model for the probability of dissolution of marital unit i in year t ($PROBDIS_{it}$):

$$PROBDIS_{it} = a_o + b_h SOCSTR_{ih} + c_j DUR_{ij} + d_k COH_{ik} + e_m PER_{im} + U_{it} \quad (1)$$

where:

$PROBDIS_{it}$ = probability that marital unit i will dissolve (by marital discord) in year t.

a_o = intercept.

$SOCSTR_{ih}$ = value on hth social structural variable for ith marital unit in year t.

b_h = effect of hth social structural variable on divorce probability.

DUR_{ij} = 1 if ith marital unit in jth duration-of-marriage category in year t; otherwise = 0.

c_j = effect of being in jth duration category on divorce probability.

COH_{ik} = 1 if ith marital unit in kth cohort category in year t; = 0 otherwise.

d_k = effect of being in kth cohort category on divorce probability.

PER_{im} = 1 if ith marital unit in mth period category in year t; = 0 otherwise.

e_m = effect of being in mth period category on divorce probability.

U_{it} = residual (effect) for marital unit i.

A major drawback of this specification is the additivity assumption. Yet, attempts to specify models in which age, period, and cohort interact do not prove conclusively superior to the additive approach.

Estimation Strategy

A large and rich longitudinal data file would be required for simultaneous estimation of the parameters for all four types of effect. Estimating independent duration, period, cohort, and social structural effects require data ranging over large numbers of durations, cohorts, and periods, as well as containing information and variation in appropriate social structural variables. Such data do not exist to our knowledge. Consequently, two data files have been used: the Michigan Panel Study of Income Dynamics (PSID) for social structural parameter estimates, and vital statistics data for the duration, period, and cohort parameter estimates. If the PSID were used to estimate the entire model, given that the 1968–72 interval is treated as a single period, it would be impossible either to estimate the effects of being in other periods or to separate duration and cohort effects. Formally, equation (1) collapses as follows:

$$PROBDIS_{it} = (a_o + e_{1968\text{-}72}) + \Sigma b_h \, SOCSTR_{ih}$$
$$+ \Sigma \, (c_j + d_k) \, DUR_{ij} + U_{it} \quad (2)$$

The period effect, since it is a constant, is collapsed into the intercept and the coefficients of duration and cohort are summed, since the two variables become completely confounded in a single period. Although subject to these disadvantages, estimating parameters from the PSID does have the advantage that it would generate less biased estimates than would estimating alternative partial models.

However, since we are interested in constructing a dynamic model that is useful in projecting over considerable historical periods, we are particularly interested in the period effects. Since the PSID cannot be used to estimate period effects, we have instead used the two-stage strategy of estimating partial models from two different data files.

For the first stage, in which duration, period, and cohort effects were tested and estimated, vital statistics data were used. Data on divorces by duration of marriage, together with marriage data giving initial cohort size, were manipulated to yield estimates of divorce probabilities for cohorts 1949–71 over periods 1949–71 for durations less than one through nine years. A variety of models were fit to these data. Significant independent duration, period, and cohort effects were estimated. A logit transformation performed best.

In the second stage of the analysis, the PSID was used to estimate the parameters of the social structural variables, having first subtracted out the effects of duration, period, and cohort drawn from the first stage. The drawback of this strategy is that the duration, period, and cohort parameter estimates are likely to be biased upward and the parameter estimates for the social structural variables biased downward. Fortunately, in practice the bias was small, since the correlation between the original dissolution probability variable and the residualized variable was quite high. The advantage of the strategy is that each of the parameter sets were estimated from the data file most suitable.

Stage One: Age, Period, and Cohort Effects

Marriage and official divorce statistics are based on information from two sources: (1) complete counts of events obtained from all states and (2) samples of marriage and divorce certificates from states meeting certain reporting criteria. The states meeting the reporting criteria for divorce, called the Divorce Registration Area (DRA) were formally established in 1958 with 16 states included. The DRA numbered 28 states in 1969. Divorces in the DRA in 1969 accounted for 59 percent of all divorces in the United States. Prior to 1958 detailed statistics were based on pretabulated data provided by certain state offices of vital statistics. Consequently, as estimates for the entire United States, the data are not completely reliable; some error may be attributed to the unrepresentativeness of the states in the DRA. Moreover, the marriage number (first, second, etc.) is a poorly reported item; it was entered on less than 50 percent of the records from five states in 1969 (National Center for Health Statistics, 1972, pp. 3–8). Fortunately a sample study of all state divorce records was made in 1960 enabling a test of the estimate of divorces by duration of marriage (National Center for Health Statistics, 1964; Carter, Ortmeyer and Plateris, 1962). The DRA estimate was within one standard error of the estimate based upon the sample from all state divorce records in 6 of the 10 years of marriage duration categories. In two others the DRA estimate was within two standard errors of the sample estimate and in one it was slightly more than two standard errors away from the sample estimate (which meant that the DRA estimate was about 10 percent lower than the sample estimate). We interpret this as meaning that the reliability of the data is tolerably high. However, the reliability probably deteriorates seriously for the older periods in which few states met the reporting criteria.

Data on total number of marriages by calendar year provides initial marriage cohort sizes:

N_C = initial size of cohort C (i.e., number of marriages in year C)
  (C = 1949, 1950, . . . 1971)

Data on the percentage distribution of divorces by duration of marriage in the DRA alone multiplied by the number of divorces in the entire United States (from vital statistics) provide estimates of the number of divorces by duration of marriage in the nation in a given year:

$D_{P,A}$ = number of divorces of duration A
  (A = 0,1, . . . 9) dissolved in period P
  (P = 1949, 1950, . . . 1971)

The cumulative proportion of divorces by duration of marriage by cohorts (Table 5-1) can then be calculated:

$$T_{C+A,A} = \frac{\sum_0^A D_{C+A,A}}{N_C} = \text{cumulative proportion of cohort C divorced by duration A (implied period} = C + A) \quad (3)$$

From (3) we can derive the *probability* of divorce for still intact couples in cohort C married A years:

$Pr_{C,A}$ = probability of divorce to a marital unit in cohort C of duration A
  (implied period = C + A)

$$= \frac{D_{C+A,A}}{N_C - \sum_0^{A-1} D_{C+A,A}} \quad (4)$$

$$= \frac{T_{C+A,A} - T_{C+A-1,A-1}}{100 - T_{C+A-1,A-1}} \quad (5)$$

However, we need to correct (4) and (5) for the marriages which are dissolved by mortality. The number dissolved by mortality should be subtracted from the denominator. We calculated $M_{C+A,A}$, the number of marriages of cohort C which are dissolved by death during duration year A, using marital status-specific mortality rates. Utilizing these numbers we correct the denominators in (4) and (5):

$$Pr_{C,A} = \frac{D_{C+A,A}}{N_C - \sum_0^{A-1} D_{C+A,A} - \sum_0^A M_{C+A,A}} \quad (6)$$

TABLE 5-1

CUMULATIVE PERCENT OF DIVORCES BY DURATION OF MARRIAGE FOR MARRIAGE COHORTS

Year Married	Less than 1	1	2	3	4	5	6	7	8	9
1949	1.54	3.94	6.21	8.32	10.10	11.55	12.80	13.95	14.99	15.82
1950	1.36	3.46	5.73	7.71	9.43	10.86	12.12	13.20	14.15	15.07
1951	1.44	3.85	6.37	8.47	10.25	11.81	13.09	14.20	15.27	16.29
1952	1.82	4.37	6.87	9.01	10.82	12.38	13.66	14.88	15.95	17.03
1953	1.68	4.17	6.71	8.80	10.58	12.03	13.40	14.61	15.68	16.71
1954	1.50	4.00	6.50	8.58	10.26	11.84	13.32	14.69	15.90	16.95
1955	1.53	3.98	6.38	8.37	10.20	11.79	13.30	14.62	15.74	16.86
1956	1.52	3.91	6.32	8.39	10.03	11.62	12.96	14.30	15.61	16.80
1957	1.51	3.81	6.18	8.28	10.28	12.20	13.76	15.24	16.57	17.81
1958	1.42	3.65	6.00	8.19	10.07	11.76	13.37	14.85	16.23	17.46
1959	1.55	3.81	6.02	8.13	10.06	11.93	13.57	15.12	16.49	17.94
1960	1.53	4.08	6.32	8.44	10.43	12.29	14.06	15.67	17.32	18.91
1961	1.50	3.79	6.11	8.25	10.39	12.34	14.14	15.95	17.68	19.34
1962	1.34	3.67	6.06	8.49	10.67	12.67	14.71	16.61	18.47	20.27

Year										
1963	1.35	3.73	6.25	8.59	10.79	12.91	15.00	17.16	19.06	20.94E
1964	1.38	3.96	6.55	9.01	11.45	13.82	16.14	18.28	20.27E	22.23E
1965	1.42	3.88	6.33	9.09	11.75	14.49	17.01	19.25E	21.33E	23.32E
1966	1.49	4.04	6.96	8.89	12.85	15.50	18.03E	20.39E	22.52E	
1967	1.58	4.21	7.26	10.41	13.40	16.27E	18.92E	21.43E		
1968	1.44	4.10	7.35	10.62	13.70E	16.61E	19.22E			
1969	1.55	4.38	7.78	11.14E	14.37E	17.34E				
1970	1.58	4.68	8.33E	11.97E	15.37E					
1971	1.61	4.90E	8.82E	12.61E						
1972	1.81E	5.27E	9.27E							
1973	1.96E	5.61E								
1974	2.14E									

Note: E = estimated.

Source: (1) For 1949–1967 divorces: Ferriss, Abbott L., "An Indicator of Marriage Dissolution by Marriage Cohort," *Social Forces*, 1970, 48 (March), 356–364.

(2) For 1968–1969 divorces: *Vital Statistics of the U.S., 1967 and 1968, Vol. III, Marriage and Divorce*, National Center for Health Statistics.

(3) For 1970–71 divorces: Unpublished final statistics, phone communication with National Center for Health Statistics (Ms. Mary Flaer).

(4) For 1972–74 divorces: The mean of the percentage distributions of divorces by duration for the three years 1969–71 was applied to preliminary divorce statistics for 1972–74 (839,000; 913,000; 96,000) for a rough estimate of the 1972–74 cohort cumulative figures, which should, of course, be taken only as an estimate.

$$= \frac{T_{C+A,A} - T_{C+A-1,A-1}}{100 - T_{C+A-1,A-1} - \left(\sum_{0}^{A} M_{C+A,A}/N_C \right)} \qquad (7)$$

The corrected divorce probabilities by duration, period, and cohort are displayed in Table 5-2. These corrected probabilities are taken to be our best estimates of the phenomenon whose variation we want to explain.

Using published (1949–1969) and unpublished (1970–71)[2] final statistics on divorce in the DRA by duration yields 185 observations. An additional 30 observations (N = 215) were derived by using the mean percent of divorces in each duration category for 1969–71 (Table 5-3). These means were applied to preliminary national divorce totals for 1972–74, in order to generate expected divorce probabilities for 1972–74. The purpose of this exercise was to incorporate additional evidence from the recent period, one characterized by sharp rises in divorce rates, in order to observe any effect on parameter estimates. Since these 30 observations are only expected values, however, they are omitted from most analyses, including the final versions.

Given these data, three major classes of specification were attempted: (1) additive analysis of variance (all dummy variables); (2) additive analysis of covariance (some dummy variables and some polynomials) and (3) interactive models using polynomials.[3]

Additive (all dummies)

The least restrictive additive specification treats duration, cohort and period as sets of dummy variables. One category is omitted from each dimension to avoid singularity; one additional category omitted from any dimension is necessary to make the model estimable because of the logical confounding of the three dimensions (Mason, et al., 1973). In practice, a minimum of one duration, two period, and two cohort categories were omitted. (The least recent two periods and the most recent two cohorts were omitted, since they included the fewest observations.) Omitting several categories from a dimension implies the hypothesis that the effect on dissolution for all the omitted categories in a single dimension is identical.

Table 5-4 shows the results of ten regressions using the dummy variable specification, five with the augmented (N = 215) data set in-

2. We thank Ms. Mary Flaer of the National Center for Health Statistics; received by phone communication, August 19, 1974.
3. The covariance and polynomial models did not perform as well as the additive model and are not reported here. These models are given in Caldwell (1975).

TABLE 5-2

PROBABILITY OF DIVORCE BY DURATION OF MARRIAGE FOR MARRIAGE COHORTS

Year Married	Less than 1	1	2	3	4	5	6	7	8	9
					DURATION IN YEARS					
1949	1.54	2.44	2.37	2.27	1.96	1.63	1.44	1.34	1.24	1.00
1950	1.36	2.13	2.36	2.12	1.88	1.60	1.44	1.25	1.12	1.10
1951	1.44	2.45	2.63	2.26	1.96	1.76	1.47	1.30	1.27	1.23
1952	1.82	2.60	2.63	2.31	2.01	1.77	1.48	1.44	1.28	1.32
1953	1.68	2.54	2.66	2.26	1.97	1.64	1.58	1.42	1.23	1.25
1954	1.50	2.54	2.62	2.24	1.85	1.78	1.70	1.61	1.45	1.28
1955	1.53	2.49	2.51	2.14	2.02	1.79	1.74	1.55	1.34	1.36
1956	1.52	2.43	2.52	2.22	1.81	1.79	1.54	1.57	1.56	1.44
1957	1.51	2.34	2.47	2.25	2.20	2.16	1.80	1.74	1.60	1.52
1958	1.42	2.27	2.45	2.34	2.07	1.90	1.95	1.74	1.65	1.50
1959	1.55	2.30	2.31	2.28	2.12	2.10	1.89	1.82	1.64	1.77
1960	1.53	2.59	2.34	2.28	2.19	2.10	2.05	1.90	1.99	1.96
1961	1.50	2.33	2.42	2.29	2.35	2.20	2.08	2.14	2.10	2.06
1962	1.34	2.37	2.49	2.60	2.40	2.26	2.37	2.26	2.27	2.25
1963	1.35	2.44	2.61	2.51	2.43	2.40	2.43	2.58	2.34	2.37
1964	1.38	2.62	2.71	2.65	2.70	2.70	2.73	2.59	2.48	2.51
1965	1.42	2.50	2.56	2.96	2.95	3.14	2.98	2.74	2.62	2.58
1966	1.49	2.59	3.05	3.17	3.31	3.07	3.03	2.92	2.72	
1967	1.58	2.68	3.20	3.42	3.36	3.35	3.20	3.14		
1968	1.44	2.70	3.40	3.55	3.74	3.40	3.17			
1969	1.55	2.88	3.57	3.66	3.66	3.50				
1970	1.58	3.15	3.84	3.99	3.89					
1971	1.61	3.35	4.14	4.17						
1972	1.81	3.53	4.24							
1973	1.96	3.73								
1974	2.14									

Source: Calculated from cumulative percents in Table 5-1, making correction for mortality according to method described in text.

TABLE 5-3

PERCENTAGE DISTRIBUTION OF DIVORCE BY DURATION OF MARRIAGE IN THE DIVORCE REGISTRATION AREA OF THE U.S., 1967–1971

Duration in years	1967[1]	1968[2]	1969[3]	1970[4]	1971[4]
<1	5.8	5.1	5.2	4.8	4.6
1	9.1	8.7	8.6	8.5	8.8
2	8.4	9.3	9.2	9.4	9.5
3	8.1	8.5	8.5	8.5	8.8
4	6.9	7.2	7.5	7.7	7.5
5	6.0	6.0	6.4	6.9	6.4
6	5.3	5.5	5.4	5.6	5.9
7	4.7	4.8	4.7	5.0	4.8
8	3.9	4.3	4.2	4.1	4.1
9	3.4	3.7	3.8	3.6	3.7
10–14	14.4	14.2	13.8	13.8	13.5
15–19	10.0	9.6	9.5	9.0	9.0
20–24	7.1	7.3	7.1	7.0	7.0
25–29	3.9	3.6	3.5	3.3	3.6
≥30	2.8	2.4	2.5	2.6	2.6
Total	99.8	100.2	99.9	99.8	99.8

1. Source: *Vital Statistics of the U.S., 1967, Vol. III, Marriage and Divorce.* National Center for Health Statistics.
2. Source: *Ibid.,* 1968.
3. Source: *Ibid.,* 1969.
4. Source: Unpublished final statistics, via phone communication with National Center for Health Statistics.

cluding the expected values and five with the primary (N = 185) data set. Figures 5-1 through 5-3 display the duration, period, and cohort coefficient profiles for selected regressions and yield some insight into the behavior of the parameter estimates under alternative theoretical assumptions.

It is useful to visualize the dependent variable (i.e., the divorce probabilities) as a surface in three dimensional space which we are trying to approximate, though in fact it is a discrete set of points, not a continuous surface. If the X axis represents changing age, and the Y axis changing cohort, then a plane parallel to the X-axis gives the age profile within a particular cohort. A plane parallel to the Y-axis gives the profile for successive cohorts, holding age constant. A line sloping down to the right, and making a 45 degree angle with both the age and cohort axes, represents the points for a particular year. If a particular year has high divorce rates for "period" reasons, one would see a ripple above

FIGURE 5-1

COHORT EFFECTS FROM REGRESSIONS
ON DIVORCE PROBABILITY DATA

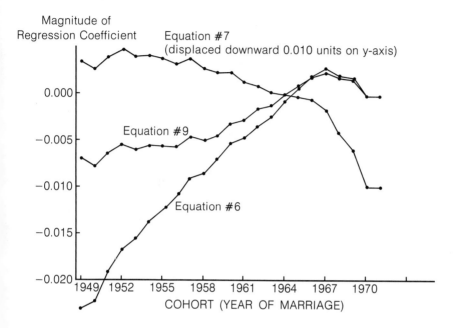

the line for that year. A plane perpendicular to that line would give the profile of ripples, or period effects.

In short, there exists a high degree of interdependence among the three effects. Sharp changes occur in, e.g., duration and cohort parameter estimates, as we make different assumptions about period effects. A dramatic example can be seen in the difference between equations 6 and 7. The substantive difference between the two equations is that in equation 6 we assume that the two years 1949 and 1950 had identical period effects while in equation 7 we assume that the seven years 1949–1955 had identical period effects. As a consequence, in equation 7 the duration and cohort parameters have the burden of explaining the variance previously explained by the 1951–1955 period parameters. The first effect is a change in the cohort parameter estimates prior to 1956 (see Figure 5-1) and the duration parameter estimates (see Figure 5-2); moreover, since duration parameters change, *all* cohort parameters may be affected. The statistical confounding means that a different substantive hypothesis affecting one dimension may affect the parameter estimates for all three dimensions.

TABLE 5-4

REGRESSIONS ON DIVORCE PROBABILITY USING ADDITIVE ANALYSIS OF VARIANCE MODELS

Dependent Variable: Probability of divorce in one year ($\times 10^4$)

	ESTIMATED COEFFICIENTS (b's)									
	N = 215					N = 185				
	Equation Number									
Independent Variable	1	2	3	4	5	6	7	8	9	10
Duration of Marriage										
<1	-55	-18	3	-47	-12	-105	49	10	-23	0
1	58	91	110	64	96	6	144	111	80	101
2	82	116	129	87	116	31	151	125	95	116
3	72	98	113	76	102	26	130	108	82	100
4	57	77	91	59	80	17	104	86	63	79
5	43	59	70	44	61	11	80	66	47	60
6	29	41	50	29	42	6	57	47	32	41
7	18	27	33	19	27	3	37	30	21	26
8	6	10	13	6	10	-1	17	13	8	11
9	a	a	a	a	a	a	a	a	a	a

Period (Year Marriage at Risk)										
1949	a	a	a	a	a	a	a	a	a	a
1950	a	a	a	a	a	a	a	a	a	a
1951	−35	a	a	a	a	−38	a	−18	a	a
1952	−31	a	a	a	a	−38	a	0	a	a
1953	−43	a	a	a	a	−56	a	−3	a	a
1954	−62	a	a	a	a	−80	a	−11	a	a
1955	−73	−21	−8	a	a	−97	a	−13	a	a
1956	−82	−26	−10	a	a	−113	0	−14	a	a
1957	−95	−35	−14	a	a	−132	−2	−19	a	a
1958	−110	−46	−21	a	a	−154	−7	−26	a	a
1959	−111	−42	−12	a	a	−161	3	−17	a	a
1960	−121	−48	−11	a	a	−177	4	−16	a	a
1961	−121	−43	−2	a	a	−183	16	−7	a	a
1962	−132	−50	−6	a	a	−200	16	−11	a	a
1963	−138	−52	−5	a	a	−212	22	−10	a	a
1964	−134	−44	5	a	a	−215	35	0	a	a
1965	−131	−37	15	a	a	−219	49	10	a	a
1966	−133	−35	20	a	a	−227	58	14	a	a
1967	−135	−33	23	a	a	−236	66	18	a	a
1968	−117	−11	46	a	a	−223	96	41	a	a
1969	−107	4	61	a	a	−217	120	56	a	a

a. Omitted category.

(continued on next page)

TABLE 5-4 (continued)

ESTIMATED COEFFICIENTS (b's)

Independent Variable	N = 215					N = 185				
	Equation Number									
	1	2	3	4	5	6	7	8	9	10
Period (cont.)										
1970	−88	28	85	a	a	−199	156	80	a	a
1971	−82	39	96	a	a	−192	178	91	a	a
1972	−68	56	112	a	a	b	b	b	b	b
1973	−50	75	130	a	a	b	b	b	b	b
1974	−36	89	144	a	a	b	b	b	b	b
Cohort (Year of Marriage)										
1949	−124	−54	a	−138	a	−230	137	a	−68	a
1950	−122	−59	a	−147	a	−223	128	a	−77	a
1951	−96	−40	a	−133	a	−191	141	a	−63	a
1952	−78	−27	a	−124	a	−167	149	a	−54	a
1953	−72	−26	a	−128	a	−155	143	a	−58	a
1954	−60	−17	a	−125	a	−137	144	a	−55	a
1955	−53	−14	a	−126	a	−124	140	a	−56	a
1956	−48	−13	a	−127	a	−113	134	a	−57	a
1957	−31	0	a	−115	a	−89	140	a	−45	a
1958	−31	−5	a	−119	a	−83	129	a	−49	a
1959	−25	−2	a	−113	a	−70	125	a	−43	a

	1	2	3	4	5	6	7	8	9	10
1960	−13	5	a	−101	a	−53	125	a	−31	a
1961	−11	3	a	−96	a	−46	115	a	−26	a
1962	−4	6	a	−85	a	−33	110	a	−14	a
1963	−2	4	a	−76	a	−23	103	a	−11	a
1964	6	7	a	−60	a	−6	102	a	1	a
1965	10	8	a	−46	a	8	99	a	11	a
1966	19	13	a	−33	a	22	96	a	21	a
1967	28	18	a	−19	a	29	86	a	25	a
1968	21	6	a	−20	a	22	61	a	19	a
1969	24	a	a	a	a	18	41	a	16	a
1970	32	a	a	a	a	a	a	a	a	a
1971	33	a	a	a	a	a	a	a	a	a
1972	23	a	a	a	a	b	b	b	b	b
1973	a	a	a	a	a	b	b	b	b	b
1974	a	a	a	a	a	b	b	b	b	b
Intercept	319	190	128	277	168	474	−41	134	200	150
$\bar{R}^2$	.9434	.9358	.9228	.8033	.3772	.9552	.9542	.9053	.7829	.5453
R^2	.9587	.9507	.9335	.8308	.4061	.9678	.9658	.9212	.8193	.5699
Corrected standard error of estimate	1.65	1.75	1.92	3.07	5.46	1.19	1.20	1.73	2.62	3.79
F	63.9	64.9	89.6	31.3	15.6	78.3	84.8	60.0	23.3	25.8

a. Omitted category.
b. Inapplicable category (no data).

FIGURE 5-2

DURATION EFFECTS FROM REGRESSIONS
ON DIVORCE PROBABILITY DATA

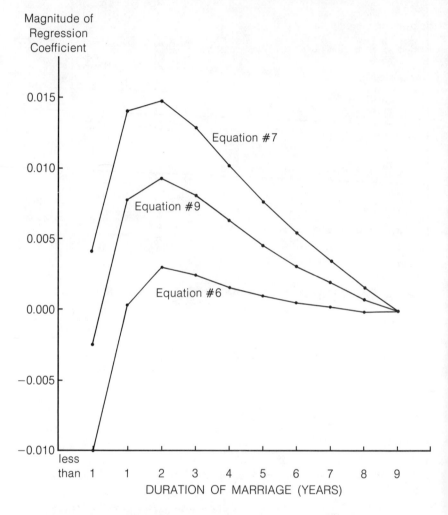

Perhaps the most important question is whether significant[4] independent period, duration, and cohort effects exist, or whether two, or even one, of the variable sets is sufficient. Equations 5 and 10 fit to the probability observations in Table 5-2 incorporate duration effects only. Equations 4 and 9 add cohort effects; the change in R^2 is significant. Equations 1 and 6 add period effects to the duration and cohort effects; again,

4. In what follows, significance is assumed to refer to the .01 level.

FIGURE 5-3

PERIOD EFFECTS FROM REGRESSIONS
ON DIVORCE PROBABILITY DATA

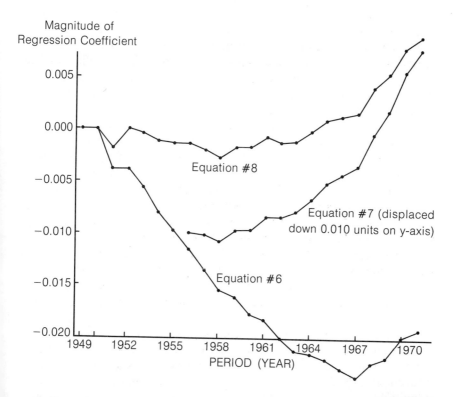

the change in R^2 is significant. Adding cohort last yields a smaller (but still highly significant) gain in R^2 than adding period last, indicating that cohort is a weaker influence on divorce probabilities than period. Nevertheless, each set adds significantly to the variance explained. This contrasts with the results in Mason, et al. (1973) in which three sets of hypothetical data, with only duration, cohort, or period effects respectively built in, were fit to models of this additive form. In no case[5] did the addition of a second or third dimension significantly improve R^2 if the appropriate dimension had already entered. Assuming the additive specification is appropriate, we conclude that there exist independent duration, cohort, and period effects on divorce probabilities.

A second set of testable hypotheses involves collapsing (or omitting) categories, i.e., hypothesizing that two or more categories in a single

5. There is one exception, but it occurs when two out of seven period categories are omitted (Mason, p. 250).

dimension have identical effects. For example, equation 7 compared to equation 6 omits five additional period variables without significantly reducing R^2, although, as pointed out above, dramatic shifts in the parameter estimates result. Nevertheless, although parsimony would suggest using the minimal number of categories necessary, we are reluctant to search for collapsible categories. Statistical tests alone, we would argue, should not be the only criterion. Since we have no solid theoretical reasons for expecting that duration, period, or cohort effects should remain constant over particular intervals, we prefer to use only the minimum collapsing necessary to make the model estimable (in fact, we have used one more than necessary, for symmetry's sake). This logic suggests equation 6 as the most appropriate additive specification.

One reasonable hypothesis is that the cumulative proportion of a cohort still married by a certain duration would be related to the proportion likely to divorce at that time span. For example, if an unusually high proportion have already divorced, one might expect a somewhat lower rate than usual, as the cohort approaches its "normal" state. However, the cumulative proportion still married is very highly correlated (.99) with duration of marriage. Such multicollinearity makes the separate parameter estimates for both duration and cumulative proportion still married highly unstable when estimated simultaneously; usually only one proved to be significant. On this basis it was decided to continue using duration and to drop cumulative proportion from further estimations.

The logit transformation of the dependent variable prevents predicted values of p greater than one or less than zero. It reduces the estimation inefficiency due to heteroscedasticity, and is a more reasonable theoretical form for the relationship, since it does not assume the same magnitude for effects whatever the probability level. Consequently, equation 6 was re-estimated in logit form as equation 18, and the results appear in Table 5-5. The resulting patterns of the period and cohort coefficients (Figure 5-4) are generally similar to those of the non-logit equation 6 although the period effects begin increasing earlier (1964 vs. 1968) and more sharply, and the cohort profile shows a downturn in the late sixties. The coefficient of determination is higher, though to make a direct comparison, predicted logits should be converted back to predicted probabilities whose correlation with the observed probabilities would yield a directly comparable R^2.

Drawing substantive implications from the duration, period, and cohort effect profiles in equation 18 is difficult because of the sensitivity of the profiles to alternative specifications. However, illustrative conclusions can be drawn from equation 18 (see Figure 5-4), the logit analysis-of-variance specification with five omitted categories (duration 9, periods 1949–50 and cohorts 1970–71). The period effect profile falls steadily

TABLE 5-5

REGRESSION ON LOGIT USING ADDITIVE ANALYSIS OF VARIANCE EQUATIONS

Dependent Variable: $\ln \dfrac{P}{1-P}$, where P = probability of divorce in 1 year

Independent Variables	Equation #18 ($\times 10^4$)	Independent Variables	Equation #18 ($\times 10^4$)
Duration[1]		1968	−380
1	−129	1969	−309
1	407	1970	−202
2	474	1971	−143
3	420		
4	343	**Cohort**	
5	272	1949	−316
6	195	1950	−317
7	131	1951	−184
8	55	1952	−93
9	a	1953	−68
		1954	−2
Period		1955	24
1949	a	1956	46
1950	a	1957	130
1951	−125	1958	118
1952	−78	1959	143
1953	−140	1960	187
1954	−235	1961	183
1955	−286	1962	195
1956	−330	1963	191
1957	−397	1964	213
1958	−485	1965	218
1959	−467	1966	227
1960	−509	1967	211
1961	−496	1968	128
1962	−545	1969	90
1963	−563	1970	a
1964	−528	1971	a
1965	−501	$\bar{R}^2$	.9762
1966	−491		
1967	−482	R^2	.9829

a. Omitted category.
1. For duration of marriage greater than nine years, the following values are used for duration categories (and no period or cohort effects are added):

Duration	Probability of Dissolutions
10–14	.0184
15–19	.0131
20–24	.0085
25–29	.0055
30+	.0016

FIGURE 5-4

PERIOD AND COHORT EFFECTS FROM FINAL
LOGIT EQUATION FIT TO DIVORCE
PROBABILITY DATA

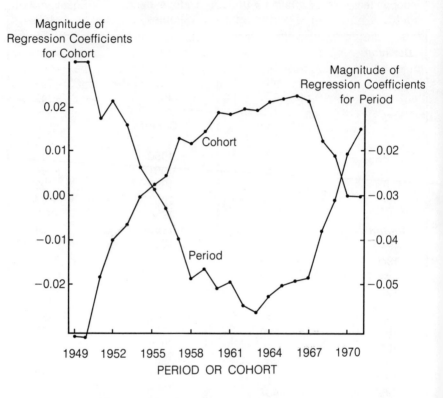

from 1949 to 1963, then rises thereafter, and especially sharply after 1967. This relatively smooth profile with no major turning point is somewhat at variance with our expectations for sharp yearly fluctuations and no particular trend. It is not clear what events are generating this profile. The cohort profile is more intuitively appealing. It is quite smooth, as we might expect of a more long-run, aggregate social change. The profile rises at a decreasing rate. It reaches a maximum in the first half of the sixties, then begins declining in 1967. The implication is that a long-term shift toward increased marital dissolution has ceased, and an era of more stable marriages may be beginning, though masked for the present by still sharply increasing period effects. The duration profile indicates that length of marriage does have a strong independent effect on dissolution probability.

Stage Two: Social Structural Effects

The data used to estimate the social structural influences on divorce were drawn from Waves I–V of the Panel Study of Income Dynamics.

For the present study an extract was created with the relevant variables for all families intact in 1968 and for which it could be ascertained if the family was still intact or not in 1972. The initial dependent variable (DEP1) equals one if the husband-wife family intact in 1968 was no longer intact for reasons of marital discord at the time of the 1972 interview, and equals zero otherwise. The residualized dependent variable (DEP2) was created by subtracting from DEP1 the expected probability of divorce based on the cohort of the marital unit in 1968 and taking account of changing duration and period as the unit passes through the years 1968–72. Consequently, the unit of time is here defined as four years. To convert to an annual period in DYNASIM the predicted dissolution probability from this stage is manipulated appropriately.[6]

While DEP1 measures dissolution, whether by divorce or separation, the age, period, and cohort parameters were estimated from over-time data which counted divorces only. In effect this measurement discrepancy forces the social structural variables to account for the differences between the divorce probability predicted using stage one and the separations and/or divorces measured by DEP1.

In practice the correlation between DEP1 and DEP2 is very high (.992 for units with white heads and .994 for units with black heads). Consequently, we expected the bias on the social structural parameter estimates introduced by residualizing with (probably) biased estimates of the age, period, and cohort effects to be quite small. A number of models were estimated using both DEP1 and DEP2 and no significant differences were detected.

The conceptual specification of the particular variables to be entered in the regressions using DEP2 was based on previous work in the area (Carter and Glick, 1970; Bumpass and Sweet, 1972; Farley and Hermalin, 1971; Sweet, 1972; Ross and Sawhill, 1975). This work

---

6. If P_4 is the predicted dissolution probability from the second stage for the four-year period, to convert it to P_1, the annual equivalent, we assume that no other attrition of marriages exists and that P_1 is constant over the four-year period; then

$$P_4 = 4P_1 - 6P_1^2 + 4P_1^3 - P_1^4$$

Since P_1 is considerably less than one, we ignore the third and fourth powers. Then

$$6P_1^2 - 4 P_1 + P_4 = 0,$$

Solving,

$$P_1 = \frac{1}{3} - \frac{\sqrt{16 - 24P_4}}{12}$$

suggested that separate regressions by race of head be performed to allow for interactions of all the variables with race. We excluded units whose head was 55 years old or older and units whose head was not in his first marriage, since the duration of marriage variable measured duration since head's *first* marriage and not since head's most recent marriage. We hypothesized that age of head at first marriage would be positively related to stability. Homeownership, as an index of degree of commitment and possibly also as a rough indicator of economic status, was hypothesized to be positively related to stability. Past findings on the presence of children suggested including the variable but we had no clear hypothesis on expected direction of effect. Regular church attendance was used as an indicator of religious beliefs and traditional attitudes which would be positively related to stability. Living in the central city of a large metropolitan area, as an indicator of a less traditional sytle of life and perhaps also more contact with potential alternative partners, was expected to be negatively related to stability. Possible economic strains hypothesized to be negatively related to stability were indexed by three variables: (1) head experienced serious recent unemployment; (2) head experienced serious recent disability, and (3) family income recently dropped. A recent increase in an income variable was included to see if it had positive effects. Finally, both husband's and wife's annual earnings were included. We expected husband's earnings to be positively related to stability. However, it was not clear whether wife's earnings should generate an "independence effect" and thus be negatively related to stability or whether wife's earnings should reduce the economic strains of marriage.[7]

Results

Separate regressions using weighted observations from the PSID were run using the basic equation specified above for (1) the entire population (N = 1657); (2) the population split into those of duration less than ten years (N = 589) and greater than nine years (N − 1068); and (3) each duration category split by race of head. Significance tests indicated, however, that splitting the duration-specific categories by race or by duration produced no statistically significant improvement in fit. Consequently, the entire sample of marriage units whose head was less than 55 and in his first marriage was used. However, very strong regional differences by race were observed in separate regressions by race. Therefore, for the final model both race and race-region interactions were

7. In cases such as this, where the duration of effect could not be clearly hypothesized, two-tailed tests of significance were used.

included. The limitation to first marriages was unfortunate, though it seemed desirable in view of the importance of adequately measuring the duration of marriage variable. For males who had just entered their second marriage after a long first marriage, the measured duration of marriage would be large (since measured from date of first marriage). This would seriously distort the residualization, which was based on duration of marriage. Consequently, we are limiting the analysis to first marriages, or equivalently, assuming that second and later marriages dissolve identically to first marriages.

Many variables, e.g., regular church attendance, which are significantly related to dissolution in the PSID, are not available in DYNASIM. One strategy would be to leave these variables out of the final equations, thus generating biased parameter estimates for the included variables insofar as they shared variance with the excluded variables and DEP2. The premise of this strategy is that the covariation of the excluded with the included variables will remain constant. Our strategy, however, is the more conservative one: estimating with all relevant variables. Variables not in DYNASIM then have their coefficients collapsed into the intercept.[8] This approach is more defensible given the causal implications of DYNASIM experiments. If, for example, the husband's income is positively related to marital stability, then an experiment using the model that affects male incomes will also necessarily affect marital stability. By avoiding upwardly biased regression coefficients on independent variables, the implications of such experiments are kept more realistic.

Table 5-6 displays the results of estimating the basic model with race and race-region interactions for the eligible sample. The second column shows the re-estimated results after dropping the insignificant terms from the model. The version to be programmed into DYNASIM is shown in the last column after the variables unavailable in DYNASIM are collapsed into the intercept.

For whites, the Northeast is the region which seems to induce the lowest split probabilities, but for blacks the Northeast region is the most hostile to family stability. Whites living in the West have by a large margin the lowest marital stability. Blacks have higher levels of marital stability than whites in the West, about the same levels in the South and North Central regions, and lower stability in the Northeast. As expected, both age of head at marriage and being a homeowner have positive effects on stability. For the head to experience recent serious unemployment seems to have a strong destabilizing effect on the family. Both head's disability and living in a central city of a large metropolitan area have negative effects on stability, but the effects both fall just short of 0.05

---

8. This is done by multiplying the sample mean of the variable by the estimated coefficient, and adding the product to the intercept.

116

TABLE 5-6

REGRESSIONS OF RESIDUALIZED PROBABILITY OF
MARITAL DISSOLUTION (DEP2) ON SOCIAL STRUCTURAL
VARIABLES USING THE MICHIGAN PANEL FOR FAMILY
HEADS LESS THAN 55 YEARS OF AGE AND IN
THE FIRST MARRIAGE[a]

Variable	REGRESSION COEFFICIENTS (×10³)		Final Model Used in DYNASIM (Significance Tests not Applicable)
	Initial Model	Reestimated Model	
Intercept	102*	100*	.088
Region:			
South (all)	22**	21**	.021
South (black only)	−113*	−111*	−.111
West (all)	91	93*	.093
West (black only)	−172	−171	−.171
North Central (all)	11**	11**	.011
North Central (black only)	−95**	−95**	−.095
Northeast (all)	b	b	
Race:			
Black	92*	92*	.092
White	b	b	
Lives inside central city of large metropolitan area	31**	31**	.031
Age of head at marriage	−5.6	−5.7	−.0057
Nonhomeowner	46	45	.045

significance. Nevertheless, because we believe there was sufficient theoretical and other empirical evidence for these effects, we retained both variables in the final equation. Neither a sharp increase nor a sharp decrease in income has a significant effect.[9] The presence of children has no detectable effect. Families who attend church regularly seem to be the sort who have significantly more stable marriages.

Husband's earnings have no effect. However, wife's earnings have a destabilizing effect, though one which is not very strong statistically. Nevertheless, again we decide to retain the latter variable. Another factor influencing our decision on all three borderline variables is the fact that all three were clearly significant when weighted regressions were performed, as opposed to unweighted regressions. Although in a

9. Perhaps this is because this variable is not proximate enough in time to most of the period at risk.

TABLE 5-6 (continued)

| | REGRESSION COEFFICIENTS ($\times 10^3$) | | Final Model Used in DYNASIM |
| | Initial | Reestimated | (Significance Tests |
Variable	Model	Model	not Applicable)
Head experienced serious unemployment recently	92	96	.096
Head experienced serious disabilities recently	28**	29**	.029
Have no children under 18 present	−18**		
Attends church regularly	−32	−32	
Income increased compared to prior year	−8**		
Income decreased compared to prior year	10**		
Wife's earned income (000's)	6.8**	5.7**	.0057
Husband's earned income (000's)	−0.2**		
R^2	.0544	.0534	
$\bar{R}^2$	.0440	.0453	
F	5.23	6.61	
N	1657	1657	

a. All variables are significant at the .01 level unless indicated by a single asterisk (*) which indicates significance at the .05 level or by a double asterisk (**) which indicates significance at the .10 level or less.
b. Omitted category.
Two-tailed tests used for the intercept, race, region, children and wife's earned income since expected direction of effect was not clear beforehand. One-tailed tests used for all other coefficients.

well-specified model with homogeneous coefficients the sampling plan does not have to be incorporated into a regression analysis (Porter, 1973), in the real world of less than perfectly specified models with complex sampling designs, the outcome of the analyses often, as in this case, depend on whether weighted or unweighted regressions are performed.

It is possible, of course, that the onset of marital difficulties sent some women into the labor force, but given that income was measured for 1967 and marital dissolution over the 1968–72 period, the direction of causality seems fairly assured.

Dropping those variables judged to be not significant (children, increase or decrease in family income, husband's earnings), we reestimated the equation; the results are in the second column of Table 5-6. Regular church attendance is not an attribute carried in DYNASIM. Therefore, as the last step, the coefficient for the variable was multiplied by its mean sample value and added to the intercept.[10] This yields a final version for programming which is given in the last column. These social structural variables do yield considerable heterogeneity in predictions. Consider a high-risk couple that is white and living in the West, that resides inside the central city of a large metropolitan area, that was married when the male was young (e.g., 20), that does not own its home, whose head is experiencing disability and serious unemployment, and whose wife is earning a high salary (e.g., $10,000 in 1967 dollars). Such a couple, *apart* from duration, period, and cohort effects, has a predicted (four-year) dissolution probability of 0.325. Consider on the other hand a low-risk couple that is black and living in the West, not in a central city in a large metropolitan area, whose head is older when married (e.g., 30), a homeowner, and without disabilities or serious unemployment, and whose wife is without her own income. The couple has a predicted dissolution probability, *apart* from duration, period, and cohort effects, of −0.162.[11] The range is about 0.49. Thus the basic duration, cohort, and period prediction is spread quite considerably according to the socioeconomic characteristics of the marital unit.

Conclusions

As implemented in DYNASIM the family dissolution component generates a probability of marital splits due to discord in two stages. The first stage generates a probability as a function of duration, period, and cohort, while the second stage generates a probability as a function of region, race, age of head at marriage, homeownership, unemployment and disability of head, living in central city, and wife's annual earnings. After transforming the logit from the first stage to a probability, and the four-year period of the second stage to one year, the final probability is the sum of the two. A stochastic decision is made in simulations. In case of a split, all children stay with the mother, though this custody rule is easily altered. Wealth is split equally; that too is easily altered. The male leaves and begins a new single-person family. Both male and female become immediately eligible for remarriage.

---

10. For church attendance: −0.032 × 0.38 = 0.012. Added to the intercept: −0.012 + 0.100 = 0.088.

11. If an overall predicted probability happens to be less than zero, it is set equal to zero.

Chapter 6
EDUCATION*

Schools play a major role in effecting the transition from the home to the world of work. Further, the number of years of school completed appears to have a significant impact upon income and other measures of well-being in adult life. Consequently it is crucial to incorporate into a model of the dynamics of income and wealth the role that schooling plays. The schooling operating characteristic predicts the number of years of school each individual has completed on the basis of the person's age, race, sex, and the education of a parent. Although we do not know how directly these variables are related to the true causes of attainment, we rely on relationships implied by statistical analysis.

Historically the social class of a child's parents has affected how he or she will fare in the school system. Children of the upper classes have consistently obtained more education than have the children of the lower classes (Bowles, 1972). The variable most consistently used in a variety of studies and for different levels of the school system to assess the influence of class is parents' education. This variable is used in this study.

Parents' occupation, income, or wealth may also have important effects, although the evidence that they do is less complete than it is for parents' education; in future versions of the model they may also be included. In particular, human capital theory (Becker, 1964) suggests that income is an important variable. In this theory education is viewed as an investment and additional years of school are attended if the present value of the gain from the extra years of school is more than the cost of acquiring them. However, Eckland's (1964b) empirical study shows that a parent's education and occupation have much more influence on college graduation than does a parent's income.

A number of additional factors known to influence schooling attainment have not been incorporated into the current version of the education sector because they are not simulated in DYNASIM. An individual's intelligence or ability is also a factor that affects one's chances for success in school. Most studies (for example, Berls, 1969, Folger et al., 1970, and Sewell and Shah, 1967) find that ability and social class have independent effects on college attainment that are roughly of the same order of magnitude, although their relative effects differ for men and

* Gerald Peabody had the main responsibility for this chapter and the work it represents.

119

women. Sewell and Shah (1968) and Trent and Medsker (1968) found that parental encouragement to attend college had a strong influence on their children's aspirations and attainments. An individual's psychological attitude is also important for understanding motivation to attend and complete college. Adams (1970) found that students with high grades or who think they are smarter than their peers are more likely to enroll in college and to have a lower dropout rate. Other variables such as high school curriculum, size of community in which one is reared, or distance to the nearest college also affect the probability of attending college.

Finally, it should be noted that this model generates a demand for education on the part of individuals, but there is no guarantee that society will, in fact, provide facilities for the enrollment projected by this model.

In the next section the general structure of the model for simulating schooling attainment is reviewed. In successive sections the sources of data and the estimation of the transition probabilities used in the model to simulate attainment are described.

Overview of Model Structure

The major function of the education model is to simulate each person's passage through the *grades* — year by year — and through the four major *levels* of schooling — grade school, high school, college, and graduate school. The model distinguishes between the highest grade completed (GRADECOM) and the number of years spent at each level (INT) in order to account for the fact that many persons are retained in the same grade for more than one year.

Within the simulation it is assumed that people who have left school do not return to school and so never re-enter the school routine. In fact, a large number of people do return to school either to complete a degree or to acquire additional training. We attempt to account for these people by having the graduation rates and dropout rates reflect the completed experience of the cohort. This approach introduces some distortions into the time pattern of schooling attainment for the cohort. This approximation also means that enrollment rates for the different grade levels will not correspond exactly to the historical rates.

To run the model the initial population must be assigned appropriate schooling status so this education operating characteristic can proceed. The samples from which the initial population is drawn give for each individual the highest grade completed, whether he or she is currently attending school and, if so, which grade. For a person attending school we retain the information on the grade being attended and from that person's age determine a value for INT. Persons not enrolled in school who are younger than age 14, and some of those who are older than 14, are reinserted into school at the level of the highest grade they will attend. Remaining people who are not enrolled have their highest grade completed made a permanent part of their attribute list and do not enter the schooling routine.

Children in the initial population who have not yet entered school and children born during the course of the simulation are entered into the first grade during the course of the simulation when they reach age five, six, or seven. They are entered on a random basis since we do not keep track of the month of birth, a major determinant of entrance age.

A very small fraction of each cohort never enters school. In March, 1967 (U.S. Bureau of the Census, 1968), the last year in which the Current Population Reports had a separate category for no years of school completed, 0.3 percent of the population aged 14-17 had not completed at least one year of school. (Interestingly, whites outnumbered blacks in this category; 0.1 percent of the blacks had not entered school while 0.3 percent of the whites had not.) It seems reasonable to speculate that severe mental or physical handicaps, extreme isolation, or very unstable home location (migrant farm workers, for example) might be some of the reasons for never enrolling. Since nonenrollees constitute a very small portion of each cohort they are ignored in this work.

In the following sections the structure of the model for each grade level and the data used to estimate the probability functions are discussed.

Grade School

There have been few studies of the determinants of dropping out of grade school, perhaps because grade school graduation has become almost a universal norm in this country. However, there are still children who drop out of school before or upon eighth grade graduation, and their opportunities in adult life are generally severely limited by leaving school so early. Further, children who fall behind in school do so in the early years of grade school. This retardation affects their chances of later completing high school so the lifetime schooling pattern for many individuals is set early during grade school.

We can obtain data on age of enrollment in the first grade from the reports of the 1966, 1969, and 1970 Current Population Surveys. These reports include a table on enrollment in specific grades by age, race, and sex. Typically in these years 9 percent of the cohort entered first grade when they were five years old, 86 percent entered when they were six, and the remaining 5 percent entered when they were seven. These values are used in the model for age at entry into grade school. There are slight variations in these figures by race and sex which have been ignored. The data are not available as a function of the education of the parent.

Grade school attendance is the next function to be estimated. To simplify the model it has been assumed that all grade school students attend for at least eight years. But some attend longer. Two Census data sources provide information on grade school enrollment. The school enrollment tables from the 1960 Census give how many 14- and 15-year-olds were enrolled below their modal grade[1] as a function of their parent's education. The 1970 Current Population Survey gives more detail on how many years a student is enrolled below the modal grade but has no information on parental education. The 1960 Census shows the difference in the probabilities of being retained one extra year depending upon parental education. We have assumed the same relative differential by parental education also holds for being retained more than one extra year. The relative probability of being retained one extra year as opposed to two or more extra years was obtained from the 1970 CPS. (In all cases in these discussions, the parent whose level of education is measured is the father *if* he is present in the family; otherwise, the reference is to the mother.)

The enrollment probabilities obtained from these assumptions and used in the model are given in Table 6-1. The values for being retained for two or more extra years for whites and blacks with parents having graduated from at least the eighth grade are rough estimates, since the number of people in these cells in the original data was too small for meaningful calculations.

For the first seven years of attendance in grade school, it is assumed that each year of attendance results in an additional year of school completed. Persons entering the eighth year of school face three possibilities. The most likely is that they will successfully complete eighth grade and leave grade school. In this case, GRADECOM is recorded as eight. A second possibility is that they attend eighth grade for an additional year. In this case INT is increased to eight, but GRADECOM remains at seven. The third possibility is that they drop out of school permanently, regardless of whether they have been retained one or more extra years. Enrollment data are not very accurate for obtaining dropout rates since non-enrollees sometimes re-enroll at a later date and complete the grade. To get final completion rates it is therefore necessary to consider the cohort several years after the modal age of graduation.

The best available national study for determining the influence of parental education on the probability of dropping out of grade school is

---

1. The modal grade is the grade in which the largest number of students of a given age are enrolled.

TABLE 6-1

PROBABILITY OF ENROLLMENT IN GRADE SCHOOL BY RACE, SEX, AND PARENT'S EDUCATION, AND YEARS IN ATTENDANCE AT GRADE SCHOOL

INT[b]	Race	Sex:[c]	EDUCATION OF PARENT[a] (Grades Completed)					
			0 through 7th		8th through 11th		12th and over	
			M	F	M	F	M	F
7 and under	White		1.0	1.0	1.0	1.0	1.0	1.0
	Black		1.0	1.0	1.0	1.0	1.0	1.0
8	White		.25	.14	.08	.02	.01	.0
	Black		.33	.22	.17	.09	.06	.03
9 and over	White		.26	.30	.20[d]	.20[d]	.20[d]	.20[d]
	Black		.37	.40	.20[d]	.20[d]	.20[d]	.20[d]

a. Parent is the father, if present in the family; otherwise it is the mother.
b. INT is the number of years the child has been in attendance at grade school.
c. Sex refers to the child who is being considered.
d. These numbers are rough estimates.
Source: Calculated from 1960 Census and 1970 CPS data.

the 1962 Current Population Survey. In this survey, data were obtained relating the school attainment of the men in the sample who were at least twenty-five years of age in 1962 to the educational level of their fathers. These data were used to obtain the relative dropout probabilities for different parental education groups for white males. It was assumed that the same ratios apply for white females. In the absence of better data, the 1960 Census non-enrollment data for blacks were used to get their ratio of dropout probabilities. The sum of these probabilities for different parental education groups weighted by the population of each group, which was obtained from the 1960 Census, gives the total dropout rate. Values for the total dropout rate for each race and sex group were taken from the 1970 CPS schooling attainment data for the 18 and 19-year-old group. With numerical values for the total dropout rate and the relative probabilities for different parental education categories, the dropout probability for each parental education group can be calculated. The results of these calculations are contained in Table 6-2. Each cell in this table gives the probability that a person currently enrolled in the eighth grade (regardless of the total number of years enrolled in grade school) will drop out of school permanently. Persons who drop out receive a completed education of seven years. Persons who are not retained an

TABLE 6-2

PROBABILITIES FOR FAILURE TO COMPLETE AT LEAST THE EIGHTH GRADE BY RACE, SEX, AND PARENT'S EDUCATION

Race and Sex	PARENT'S EDUCATION			
	0 through 7th	8th through 11th	12th	13th and over
Black				
Female	.044	.028	.011	.006
Male	.086	.054	.022	.011
White				
Female	.043	.014	.007	.004
Male	.060	.020	.010	.005

Source: Calculated from 1960 Census data and the March 1962 Current Population Survey.

extra year and who do not drop out are given an education level of eight years and are considered for enrollment in high school. Persons who are retained an extra year have their grade level left at seven years but are cycled through the same process the following year and, thus, have a chance to complete eighth grade after one or more extra years of attendance in grade school.

High School

High school *enrollment* is rapidly becoming universal since most states have compulsory attendance laws. However, an examination of enrollment data shows that enrollment falls off rapidly for the 16 and 17-year-old group for whom enrollment is no longer mandatory. Consequently, high school *graduation* is not yet close to being universal.

The probability of entering high school for eighth grade graduates has been obtained from the 1970 CPS educational attainment data based on the 18 and 19-year-old group. These data give the total fraction of each race and sex group in the cohort that leaves high school after the eighth grade. The difference in the dropout probabilities by parental education were estimated using the same procedure as outlined above for grade school. (The same difference was used.) The results of these calculations, contained in Table 6-3, are expressed in terms of the probabilities of *not* entering high school.

For each person enrolled in high school 3 years or less (INT $\leq$ 3),

TABLE 6-3

PROBABILITY THAT AN EIGHTH GRADE GRADUATE
WILL NOT ENTER HIGH SCHOOL AS A FUNCTION OF
RACE, SEX, AND PARENT'S EDUCATION

Race and Sex	EDUCATION OF PARENT[a]			
	0 through 7th	8th through 11th	12th	13th and over
Black				
Female	.065	.040	.016	.008
Male	.076	.047	.019	.010
White				
Female	.053	.018	.009	.004
Male	.049	.016	.008	.004

a. Parent is the father, if present in the family; otherwise it is the mother.
Source: Calculated from 1960 Census data and the March 1962 Current Population Survey.

two possibilities exist. The person may enroll for an additional year
(whereupon his grade completed is increased by one year) or drop out.
For persons enrolled for four years or more (INT $\geq$ 4), three possibilities
exist. The person may graduate from high school (whereupon his grade
completed is set to 12 years), may be retained for an extra year, or may
drop out without graduating.

The total dropout rate for each race and sex group was obtained from
the 1970 CPS educational attainment data for the 20- and 21-year-old
group. Spady (1967) calculated from the 1962 Current Population
Survey the conditional probability that a male who graduated from
the eighth grade would become a high school graduate as a function
of his father's education. These results were used to get the relative
dropout probabilities for white males and females in different parental
education groups. The ratios obtained from Spady's data are consistent
with results obtained from the Project Talent survey (Berls, 1969). For
blacks non-enrollment rates from the 1960 Census were used to get the
ratio of dropout probabilities. These data enable us to calculate the total
number of dropouts within each race, sex, and parental education category.

We next need to allocate the dropouts to a specific year in school.
To do so we work backward from the senior year. In recent years one-
third of the total number of high school dropouts reach their senior year
(U.S. Bureau of the Census, 1969). Further, one-half of the senior year
dropouts come from the seniors 18 years of age or older (Jaffe and
Adams, 1969). The dropout probability for seniors who are 17 or

TABLE 6-4

PROBABILITY OF DROPPING OUT OF HIGH SCHOOL FOR STUDENTS WHO HAVE ATTENDED FOUR YEARS OR MORE AS A FUNCTION OF AGE, RACE, SEX, AND PARENT'S EDUCATION

Age	Race	Sex:	Total		PARENT'S EDUCATION							
					0 through 7th		8th through 11th		12th		13th and over	
			F	M	F	M	F	M	F	M	F	M
17 and younger	Black		.100	.140	.13	.17	.077	.100	.046	.061	.031	.041
	White		.069	.066	.13	.13	.064	.060	.032	.033	.016	.016
18 and over	Black		.12	.14	.15	.17	.097	.10	.056	.061	.036	.041
	White		.17	.11	.33	.21	.16	.10	.085	.050	.042	.027

In terms of the model, INT $\geq$ 4.

younger is therefore taken to be one-sixth the total dropout rate of each age, race, parental education group. The dropout probabilities for seniors 18 years or older was determined by calculating how many people would remain in school to that age and then finding the dropout probability that made the total number of dropouts of that age equal to one-sixth of the total. These results are contained in Table 6-4.

Finally, the probability of attending one additional year of school for those not yet seniors was determined as follows. The number of dropouts who are not yet seniors are equal to two-thirds of the total. The age dependence was calculated by assuming that the age dependence of dropping out is the same as the age dependence of non-enrollment. The age-dependent enrollment rates used were an average of the 1960 Census data and the 1970 CPS data. The probability of enrollment in high school for an additional year by number of years already attended (INT), age, race, and parental education is given in Table 6-5.

College

The time pattern of attendance at the college level is not as well defined as it is at the primary and secondary levels. Many who attend college delay their entrance one or more years after high school graduation, and many students leave school for awhile after entering and then return. Eckland (1964a) found from a study of the male enrollees of one university that only 47 percent of those who would ultimately graduate (within a ten-year period) attended school continuously and graduated within four years. Another 24 percent attended school continuously but took more than four years to complete their degree, while 24 percent of the graduates had left school for awhile and graduated in the sixth year or later. In this version of the model no attempt is made to capture this time pattern of college attendance.

A number of educational opportunities are open to high school graduates. The major ones are vocational schooling, two-year college, and four-year college. One's relative chances for entering and successfully completing one of these options is very dependent upon the characteristics of the individual, including the parents' socioeconomic class. (A review of these data is contained in Peabody, 1972). In the current version of the model no attempt is made to simulate attendance at vocational schools. We only consider college attendance and no distinction is made between two-year and four-year schools.

College entrance probabilities for white males and females are calculated from the Jaffe-Adams study (1969) and are given in Table 6-6. In this table the total enrollment rates for males and females combined

TABLE 6-5

PROBABILITY OF ENROLLMENT IN HIGH SCHOOL AS A FUNCTION OF AGE, RACE, SEX,
PARENT'S EDUCATION, AND NUMBER OF YEARS IN ATTENDANCE AT HIGH SCHOOL

Age	INT[a]	Race	Sex:[c]	Total		PARENT'S EDUCATION[b]							
						0 through 7th		8th through 11th		12th		13th and over	
				M	F	M	F	M	F	M	F	M	F
14	<4	All		1.0	1.0	1.0	1.0	1.0	1.0	1.0	1.0	1.0	1.0
15	<4	White		.99	.99	.98	.98	.99	.99	1.0	1.0	1.0	1.0
		Black		.97	.98	.95	.97	.97	.98	.98	.99	.99	1.0
16	<4	White		.97	.97	.94	.95	.97	.97	.98	.99	1.0	1.0
		Black		.91	.94	.89	.92	.93	.95	.96	.97	.97	.98
17	<4	White		.93	.94	.86	.88	.93	.94	.97	.97	.98	.98
		Black		.86	.90	.83	.87	.90	.92	.94	.95	.96	.97
18+	<4	White		.89	.89	.79	.80	.90	.90	.95	.95	.97	.97
		Black		.86	.90	.83	.87	.90	.92	.94	.95	.96	.97
All	4	White		.05	.03	.09	.06	.05	.03	.02	.01	.01	.01
		Black		.05	.03	.08	.04	.05	.02	.03	.01	.02	.01
All	5	White		.35	.40	.66	.75	.33	.38	.17	.19	.08	.09
		Black		.50	.60	.62	.74	.39	.46	.23	.28	.15	.19

a. Number of years in attendance at high school.
b. Father, if present in family; otherwise, the mother.
c. Sex of student.

for high school graduates aged 17 or less are taken directly from the Jaffe-Adams study after removing those who did not report their parent's education.

The Project Talent study (Berls, 1969 and Folger, et al., 1970) and the Sewell and Shah study (1967) indicated there is a difference in the enrollment rates for men and women as a function of parental education. The enrollment rate for females with parents having some college education was 90 percent of the enrollment rate for comparable males. When the parent was a high school graduate, a woman's enrollment rate was 80 percent that of a male's; when the parent had an incomplete high school education the woman's rate was 70 percent of the male's; and when the parent attended only grade school the woman's rate was 60 percent of the male's. These ratios have been used to calculate the separate probabilities for men and women within each parental group from the total for both sexes found by Jaffe-Adams (see Table 6-6).

Jaffe and Adams found that 18-year-old high school graduates were half as likely to enroll in college as younger graduates; this is reflected in the enrollment probabilities for this older age group in Table 6-6. This table also gives the total enrollment rate for males and for females. These totals were obtained by weighting the parental education dependent probabilities by the relative population size, from the 1960 Census, of each group. These calculated totals agree favorably with the long-term trend in enrollment rates found by Jaffe and Adams (1964). They found that for an extended period about 50 percent of white male high school graduates have entered college, and 40 percent of white female graduates have entered.

TABLE 6-6

PROBABILITY OF COLLEGE ENTRANCE BY AGE OF HIGH SCHOOL GRADUATION, SEX, AND PARENT'S EDUCATION

			PARENT'S EDUCATION			
Age	Sex	Total	0 through 7th	8th through 11th	12th	13th and over
17 and younger	Female	.44	.14	.27	.47	.78
	Male	.55	.24	.39	.59	.86
	Both	.50	.19	.33	.53	.82
18 and over	Female	.22	.07	.14	.24	.39
	Male	.27	.12	.19	.29	.43

Source: Calculations based on data from Jaffe and Adams (1969) and other sources.

Not available are data on dependence of college enrollment upon parental education for blacks and other racial minorities. Furthermore, there are no enrollment figures available, as there are for grade school and high school, that might provide some insight on this dependence. In the initial experiments with the model, the figures in Table 6-6, which are total values for all races, are being used for blacks and whites. These rates are probably slight underestimates for whites and overestimates for blacks.

Recently about one-third of all college entrants delay their entrance by at least one year after high school graduation. Thus, rather than insert all college entrants immediately into college, we delay the entrance for one-third of them by one year. These people are tagged in the model as college attenders but are not actually put into college until one year after they have completed high school.

The enrollment probabilities used in the model are designed to reproduce the final attainment rates of years of college completed and do not necessarily bear any relation to the actual attendance pattern in college. Jaffe and Adams (1969) found that among ultimate college dropouts, one-half failed to enroll as sophomores, and 50 percent of the remainder failed to enroll as juniors. A study by Marshall and Oliver (1970) of the University of California system also found that enrollment figures for that system could be described by a constant rate of dropout in each year. We therefore assume for this model that within each race, sex, and parental education group there is a fixed probability of dropping out during each year of college. Those who do not drop out are retained.

In the senior year we will hold some students in college an extra year to make again a mild increase in the realism of the timing of college attendance. About one-half of the ultimate number of graduates do so within four years. Therefore, in the fourth year we assume that one-half of the students attend for an extra year. Of those not retained, one-half of the senior-year dropouts leave school and the remainder graduate. In the fifth year everyone either graduates or drops out. No one remains in college past the fifth year.

To allocate the dropouts to the appropriate year of school we need the total dropout rates for each group. Spady (1967) gives the conditional probability that a white male aged 25-34 in 1962 would complete college, given that he had completed at least one year, as a function of his father's education. Using his data we assume that 45 percent of the white males whose father had less than an eighth grade education graduate, 55 percent graduate if the father attended or graduated from high school, and 70 percent graduated if their father had attended college. The probability of enrollment in college for an additional year by number of years already attended (INT), age, race, sex, and parental education is given in Table 6-7. (It is assumed that there is a constant dropout prob-

TABLE 6-7

PROBABILITY THAT A COLLEGE STUDENT WILL BE
ENROLLED IN SCHOOL AN ADDITIONAL YEAR AS A
FUNCTION OF SEX, RACE, NUMBER OF COLLEGE
YEARS ATTENDED, AND PARENT'S EDUCATION

| Race and Sex | INT[a] | PARENT'S EDUCATION[b] | | | |
		0 through 7th	8th through 11th	12th	13th and over
Black					
Male	1–3	.82	.86	.86	.91
	4	.5	.5	.5	.5
	5	.0	.0	.0	.0
Female	1–3	.82	.86	.86	.91
	4	.5	.5	.5	.5
	5	.0	.0	.0	.0
White					
Male	1–3	.82	.86	.86	.91
	4	.5	.5	.5	.5
	5	.0	.0	.0	.0
Female	1–3	.76	.80	.80	.85
	4	.5	.5	.5	.5
	5	.0	.0	.0	.0

a. Number of years of college attended.
b. Father, if present in family; otherwise the mother.
Source: Calculations based on data from Spady (1967) and other sources.

ability for each school year.) The dropout probabilities for seniors are given in Table 6-8. (It is assumed that the senior-year dropouts are split evenly between four-year and five-year students.)

No data is available to calculate the education dependence for white females. Data discussed above indicate that females have slightly more dependence upon parental education than do males. However, there are no good data to provide a guide for adjusting the parental education dependence. Consequently, the probability for women in each group has been reduced by the ratio of the total graduation rates for females to that of males. From the Jaffe-Adams data for recent cohorts about 55 percent of the males that enter college graduate, while about 40 percent of the females do. Thus, the dropout rate in each parental education category for males was multiplied by the ratio .40/.55 to get the educational dependence for females.

For blacks there again is no information available on the effect of parental education. Initially the same probabilities for black females and males as those for white males are used. The values for white males are

TABLE 6-8

PROBABILITY THAT A STUDENT WHO HAS SPENT AT
LEAST FOUR YEARS IN COLLEGE WILL DROP OUT
WITHOUT GRADUATING AS A FUNCTION OF RACE,
SEX, AND PARENT'S EDUCATION

Race and Sex	PARENT'S EDUCATION			
	0 through 7th	8th through 11th	12th	13th and over
Black				
Male	.18	.14	.14	.09
Female	.18	.14	.14	.09
White				
Male	.18	.14	.14	.09
Female	.24	.20	.20	.15

In terms of the model, INT ≥ 4.
Source: Calculations based on data from Spady (1967) and other sources.

being used because both black males and females have had a graduation rate higher than white females, 45 percent as compared with 40 percent for white females.

Graduate School

College graduates face a variety of further educational opportunities. The most important include professional schools, such as dentistry, law and medicine, or graduate training in an academic area. The latter can lead to a further degree, an M.A. or Ph.D., or a related title. In the current version of the model no distinction is made between these alternative forms of schooling in simulating attendance beyond the college level.

The length of time a person spends in graduate school varies considerably from individual to individual. As with college we do not attempt in this version to adequately account for the time spent in graduate school. Indeed, for simplification we make the assumption that everyone who attends graduate school does so for two years and then leaves.

The total enrollment rates for white males and females are taken from Census Bureau data. The enrollment rate is chosen so that the model generates the correct number of people who have completed at least one year of school beyond four years of college. In recent years (U.S. Bureau of the Census, 1970) about 45 percent of white males, 30

TABLE 6-9

PROBABILITY OF ENTRANCE TO GRADUATE SCHOOL BY RACE, SEX, AND PARENT'S EDUCATION

Race and Sex	PARENT'S EDUCATION			
	0 through 7th	8th through 11th	12th	13th and over
Black				
Female	.09	.17	.31	.55
Male	.12	.22	.40	.73
White				
Female	.10	.18	.32	.57
Male	.15	.27	.48	.86

percent of white females, 38 percent of black males, and 29 percent of black females who have at least an A.B. degree have completed at least one additional year of school.

The parental education dependence of the entrance rates has been taken from Project Talent data (Beils, 1969). These data suggest that the probability of graduate school enrollment increases by a factor of roughly 1.8 for each successive level as one moves up the parental education scale. Folger et al. (1970) give enrollment rates for men and women by only the high ability group, so their data can not be used to obtain overall male and female rates. It is assumed that the same ratios hold for men and women. The entrance probabilities were calculated using population weights for each category from Spady (1967). The resulting probabilities for whites are contained in Table 6-9. Again there is no information available for blacks so the white data is initially used for blacks.

Chapter 7
GEOGRAPHIC MOBILITY*

Role in the Model

Americans are a mobile people. About one in five moves to a different address each year. Between March 1970 and March 1971 about 38 million persons moved to a different address, including about 13 million persons who moved across a county line and about 7 million persons who moved across a state line. Moreover, annual surveys conducted since 1948 reveal remarkable stability over that period in rates of local and nonlocal mobility (Figure 7-1).

Such massive circulation of people has major personal and public consequences. For individuals, moving often ends in substantial economic improvement; in fact geographic mobility is so closely associated with gains in income and occupation status and with reductions in unemployment that it appears to offer a major escape route for disadvantaged members of the population (Morrison, 1972; Wertheimer, 1970). Moreover, the move to a new social environment can alter individual behavior patterns. Everett Lee (1971) has suggested that rural-to-urban migration has done more to lower fertility than the birth control pill.

Taken in the aggregate, individual mobility decisions have enormous collective effects. Lansing and Mueller (1967), among others, assert that the geographic mobility of labor is one of the basic processes of adjustment in the economy of the United States. The unfettered responses of workers to changes in the location of productive activity, resulting from new developments in technology, demand and transportation have generally been viewed as economically desirable. Other collective consequences seem less favorable. The concentration of persons in urban regions—the population implosion—has disadvantageous environmental consequences as well as advantageous efficiency advantages. Outmigration from central cities and depressed areas leads to racial separation, the concentration of poverty, and other types of stratification that appear detrimental to a democratic society.

The submodel which generates geographic mobility in DYNASIM differs from other submodels described in this volume in that it does not attempt to capture the behavioral dynamics of geographic mobility. One

---

* Steven B. Caldwell had the main responsibility for this chapter and the work it represents.

FIGURE 7-1

MOVERS BY TYPE OF MOBILITY AS PERCENT OF
THE POPULATION 1 YEAR OLD AND OVER, FOR
THE UNITED STATES: APRIL 1949–MARCH 1971

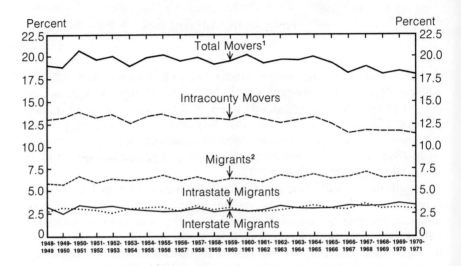

1. 'Movers' are those persons who move to different residences.
2. 'Migrants' are those persons who move their residence to a different county.
Source: U.S. Bureau of the Census, *Current Population Reports,* Series P-20, No.
          235, "Mobility of the Population of the United States: March 1970 to March
          1971," U.S. Government Printing Office, Washington, D.C., 1972.

reason is that location does not figure at all prominently as an independent variable in other operating characteristics in the current version of
DYNASIM. For example, location has little effect on the birth, death,
marriage, or divorce processes. However, location has some effect
on the labor market. A regional variable influences labor force participation and wage rates for certain demographic groups. Consequently, it is
possible to use the model to explore the consequences of particular assumed mobility patterns on earned income and labor force participation.
However, the causes of mobility patterns are not specified, other than
certain primitive demographic differentials. Partly this is because many
of the variables which might condition mobility flows are not generated
by DYNASIM. For example, no genuine region-specific labor demands
are generated. Also, although specific regional location is imputed in
DYNASIM, other locational characteristics (such as the size of the area)
are generic identifications. That is, a particular person is located in
a specific region (South, Northeast, North Central, West) but only in
generic size-type categories. Consequently, the characteristics of partic-

ular states, SMSAs, central cities, etc., have no application in the current DYNASIM and are unavailable as conditioning characteristics. The mobility submodel, while providing a base for further development and application work, does not have any genuine behavioral content. Its spirit is actuarial; it attempts to generate a reasonable number of certain demographic categories of movers and migrants, and to maintain approximately realistic locational distributions of families and persons.

Macro and Micro Approaches to Mobility

An important distinction can be made between macro and micro models of geographic mobility. Macroanalytic models focus on the ecological determinants of population flows among locations. Ginsberg (1972a) points out that most macro models use one of two forms of regression analysis. In the first approach the flows into and out of a few selected regions are studied over a long period of time and related to changes in the properties of the regions (Hagerstrand, 1957). The second approach, which includes the vast majority of macro models, selects a cross section of areas and analyzes the flows between them for one or perhaps two time periods. The dependent variables are the absolute sizes of the flows in number of persons and the independent variables are properties of the locations. Mechanical attraction models, whose formal structure was derived from physical concepts such as inertia, potential, and gravity, are of this kind. Important explanatory variables in these early demographic models include population size, distance from origin to destination, the size of a flow, and intervening opportunities (Stouffer, 1940).

Another group of macro models of this kind relates flows to the differential economic attractiveness of locations. Directional attractiveness models analyze gross place-to-place flows; nondirectional models analyze net migration at a single location. Directional economic attraction models have used as measures of attractiveness per capita income, per unit unemployed, degree of urbanization, recreational resources, and quality of dwellings (ter Heide, 1963).

Other examples of directional models are those of Fabricant (1970) which treats migration between any two regions as a function of the excess demand-for-labor gap between the two regions, and Blanco (1963) and Olvey (1970) who take the more traditional view and regard relative wages as the pivotal factor. Examples of nondirectional models are those reported by Kelley and Weiss (1969) and Greenwood (1970). A very influential directional model is the one reported by Lowry (1966), who employed manufacturing wage rates as measures of attractiveness and unemployment rates and intervening distances as deterrents. For metropolitan areas Lowry found no evidence that labor market conditions at the origin had any influence on the rate of out-migration. Rather, the propensity to migrate seemed to depend on personal and family characteristics, especially age, education, and family status. Persons leave prosperous areas as readily as they leave depressed areas. The volume of outmigration from an area thus depends on the size and characteristics of the population residing in the area. On the other hand, the choice among alternative destinations is influenced by both distance between origin and destination and labor market conditions at the destinations. A depressed community is unable to attract enough immigrants to replace its losses, while a prosperous area, although it may have the same or higher rates of outmigration (due to the presence of young, mobile elements) more than replaces its losses.

Microanalytic models of geographic mobility have in the past been the poor stepchild of migration studies. However, in recent years an increasing number of efforts have been reported which use survey and residence history data on individuals and families (Wolpert, 1967; Land, 1969; Morrison, 1967, 1971, 1972; Lansing and Mueller, 1967; Long, 1973; Taeuber, et al., 1968). Other semi-microanalytic approaches use the migration probabilities of various subpopulations as dependent variables (Shryock and Nam, 1965; Bowles, 1970; Apgar, 1970). All such models attempt in some degree to suggest the actual behavioral processes which underlie mobility decisions, and from which the aggregate relationships represented by the macro approaches presumably derive. Some of these studies have investigated the relationship between personal and family characteristics and the choice of destination. Most, however, have addressed the relationship of these characteristics to the decision to move.

Morrison (1973) has proposed that the decision to move be analyzed in relation to a variable decision threshold. For a decision to move to take place, a situational inertia must be overcome. Families and individuals are arrayed along a continuum on this variable and their position can change over time. Sources of threshold variability include life cycle position (age, family, and marital status), socioeconomic characteristics (education and labor market experience), occupationally induced constraints, and prior migration experience (duration of residence, number of previous moves).

Morrison further suggests that a complete operating characteristic which both generates movers and allocates movers among competing destinations requires a conjunctive framework that integrates both micro and macro aspects of the mobility process. In the first stage, a microanalytical model, incorporating the family and personal characteristics which are related to differential responsiveness to mobility, would generate a pool of movers. This pool can be more finely differentiated, e.g., into local vs. nonlocal movers. In the second stage the pool of movers is allocated by a directional macroanalytic model using aggregate locational measures of attraction. In such a dynamic two-stage submodel both the characteristics of the population and of the various locations would be updated annually, an updating pattern determined by the consequences of the previous year's mobility. The DYNASIM submodel is structured in this fashion, though without any rich behavioral content.

Specification of the Model

In DYNASIM, the family can be appropriately treated as the unit of geographic mobility. However, the national surveys (largely censuses) from which initial population representations for DYNASIM are drawn typically suppress considerable locational detail in the released data files for fear of violating confidentiality assurances. Consequently, the limited locational information currently available in typical initial populations is used to specify only two locational attributes:

(1) Census region: (Northeast, North Central, South, West)
(2) A size-type variable with the following seven categories:
   (a) SMSA population of 2,000,000 or more
   (b) SMSA population of 750,000 to 2,000,000
   (c) SMSA population of 500,000 to 750,000
   (d) SMSA population of 250,000 to 500,000
   (e) SMSA population under 250,000
   (f) urban, non-SMSA
   (g) rural, non-SMSA

For example, a particular family might be identified by DYNASIM as located in an SMSA whose population is over 2 million persons and which is located in the Northeast. Clearly, only the regional attribute identifies a particular geographic location; the other attribute is a categorical identifier.

The operating characteristic specified for geographic mobility proceeds in two stages. First, a pool of movers is generated. For each family (and unrelated individuals) a probability of moving (changing residence) is calculated as a function of demographic, economic, life cycle and life history (e.g., duration of residence) characteristics of the family and its members. The usual random number drawing selects those families and individuals who are to move in a given year. This first stage also further sifts the movers. From those families who move, a subset is selected by a second function as movers across county lines. The result of the first stage is three sets of families and persons: (1) nonmovers,

(2) intramovers, and (3) intermovers. The purpose of this stage is to account for the retention of certain persons in their current location, current county, or current state. Since the relevant question is who moves and who is retained, this first stage has been called a *retention model* by Morrison (1973).

The second stage of the operating characteristic is an *allocation model*. Transition probabilities distribute the pool of movers among the set of competing destinations. While the first stage is necessarily microanalytic, the second stage could be macroanalytic. In the second stage, destinations compete for their share of the pool of movers using

TABLE 7-1

THE PROBABILITY OF MOVING TO A NEW RESIDENCE
FOR FAMILIES AND UNRELATED INDIVIDUALS BY SEX,
MARITAL STATUS, AND AGE OF FAMILY HEAD,
EXCLUDING MALE HEADS WITH WIFE PRESENT

SEX OF HEAD	AGE				
Male	14–24	25–34	35–44	45–64	65 and over
Family heads, excluding males with spouse present[1]	.646	.334	.191	.092	.052
Unrelated individuals	.707	.556	.368	.241	.147
Female	14–24	25–34	35–44	45–64	65 and over
Family heads	.593	.379	.218	.095	.050
Unrelated individuals	.771	.483	.288	.152	.110

1. This exclusion is dealt with in Table 7-2.

Source: These probabilities are derived from Table 6 of *Current Population Reports,* Series P-20, No. 235, "Mobility of the Population of the United States: March 1970 to March 1971," U.S. Government Printing Office, Washington, D.C., 1972. That table gives the mobility status of the population 1 year old and over in March 1971 by relationship to head of household, age and sex. Mobility status is determined on the basis of a comparison between the place of residence of each individual at the survey date and the place of residence one year earlier, *movers* consisting of all persons who were living in a different house in the United States at the end of the period than at the beginning of the period.

        Since the mover rates apply to persons rather than families and since the information on the persons is as of the *end* of the period rather than the beginning, the following adjustments were made to convert, insofar as possible, the rates into ones applying to families given information about the families and persons included as of the beginning of the period:

        a. Those residing abroad on March 1, 1970, but counted in the United States on the survey date in 1971 are counted as movers.

        b. Only heads of families are considered, i.e., heads of primary families, primary individuals, and "others." Rates applying to primary individuals and "others" are used in proportion to the number in each category to determine rates for all unrelated individuals.

their attractiveness variables. Since movers have been classified by the distance of their move, each allocation model operates on the appropriate class of mover. For example, only those who have been selected to move across a state line are subject to competition from the four potential regional destinations.

Estimation of Parameters

Parameters for the first stage of the above specification were derived from published tabulations of the March 1971 Current Population Survey. The limitations of such tabulations as a basis for analysis need no repetition. Not only is the range of variables presented in the tabula-

TABLE 7-2

THE PROBABILITY OF MOVING TO A NEW RESIDENCE FOR FAMILIES WITH A MALE HEAD, SPOUSE PRESENT, BY DURATION OF MARRIAGE

For families which have a male head with spouse present, the probability of moving will depend on the years since first marriage as follows:

Less than one year: i.e., this is the situation in which a male will have been selected to marry for the first time during the same year in which the location decision is applied (assume the marriage decision is applied first). The rule will be that if the male is living alone then the female will come live with him, but he will live in the same location, i.e., the probability of a move will be zero. If the male is not a head, i.e., in his parents family, then it will be assumed that he moves to a new house with probability of 1. His initial location characteristics will be the same as those of his previous family, and whether or not they change in the first year will depend on whether or not it happens that he crosses county lines, moves to a new region, etc. If his marriage is a remarriage, then of course whether or not he is to "move" that year depends on the number of years since his first marriage. For females, if they marry they are always assumed to move in with the male, either at his old address, or with him to a new address. Thus the probability of a move is always 1.

Duration of Marriage	Probability of Move
1 year:	.583
2–4 years:	.436
5–9 years:	.281
10 or more:	.100

Source: See Table 7-1, *op. cit.,* Table 6.

tions highly limited, it is also not possible to interpret multiple relationships effectively.

Two sequential decisions constitute the first stage (retention). First, a decision simply to move is made as a function of the size of the family, the sex and age of the head of the family, and for husbands with wives present, the number of years since first marriage (Tables 7-1 and 7-2). The product of this decision is a pool of families and persons who move. Second, for all movers, an additional function selects the families and persons who move across a county line (i.e., nonlocal movers). This decision depends on the sex, age, and educational attainment of the family's head (Table 7-3).

TABLE 7-3

INTERCOUNTY MIGRANTS: THE PROBABILITY OF MOVING ACROSS A COUNTY LINE GIVEN THAT THE FAMILY HAS DECIDED TO MOVE TO A DIFFERENT HOUSE: BY SEX, AGE, AND EDUCATION OF HEAD

(Families at risk are those which have been selected to move to a different house by the functions in Tables 7-1 and 7-2.)

MALE HEAD

Age	GRADES COMPLETED				
	0–8	9–11	12	13–15	16 or more
25–34	.306	.329	.370	.367	.461
35–44	.192	.368	.381	.401	.464
45–64	.282	.307	.370	.391	.348
65 or over	.271	.435	.348	.452	.533

FEMALE HEAD

Age	GRADES COMPLETED				
	0–8	9–11	12	13–15	16 or more
25–34	.286	.319	.374	.447	.450
35–44	.251	.251	.396	.401	.559
45–64	.216	.326	.371	.360	.408
65 or over	.228	.360	.439	.204	.528

Source: *Current Population Reports*, Table 4, Series P-20, No. 235.
For male and female heads less than 25 years old, the following probabilities apply:

    male head, wife present: .363   female head: .213
    male head, wife not present: .205
    male unrelated individual: .355   female unrelated individual: .425
Source: Table 6, *Ibid.*

The second stage (allocation) exposes the two classes of movers to (nonbehavioral) transition probabilities which select destinations. The pool of intercounty movers is exposed to interregional transition proba-

TABLE 7-4

INTERREGIONAL MIGRATION PROBABILITIES AS A FUNCTION OF RACE, REGION OF ORIGIN AND REGION OF DESTINATION

This matrix is meant to operate on the set of all migrant families and persons. A migrant family or person is defined as one which has moved across a county line. Thus a family becomes eligible to enter the interregional matrix only if it has been selected in a given year to (1) move and (2) move across a county line.

		WHITES Year t + 1			
		Northeast	North Central	South	West
Year t	Northeast	.652	.067	.166	.115
	North Central	.047	.652	.188	.112
	South	.065	.084	.764	.087
	West	.043	.100	.140	.717
		BLACK AND OTHER RACES Year t + 1			
		Northeast	North Central	South	West
Year t	Northeast	.587	.158	.230	.026
	North Central	.023	.523	.354	.100
	South	.103	.125	.681	.090
	West	.054	.128	.121	.698

Source: U.S. Bureau of the Census, *Current Population Reports,* Series P-20, No. 235, "Mobility of the Population of the United States: March 1970 to March 1971," U.S. Government Printing Office, 1972. Table 13.

bilities separately by race (Table 7-4). Intercounty movers are also exposed to transition probabilities which determines the size-type destination for the next period (Table 7-5).

The current mobility submodel is clearly no more than a skeleton version awaiting further behavioral content as the need and opportunity arise. A major block is the lack of locational detail in major surveys. Such detail could be imputed, however, for purposes of exploring aspects of mobility patterns. The major advantage of the DYNASIM framework is the future possibility it offers for integrating micro and macro insights on the mobility process.

TABLE 7-5

PROBABILITIES OF MOVING AMONG SMSA SIZE CATEGORIES BY SIZE OF ORIGIN AND SIZE OF DESTINATION[1]

		12 largest SMSAs (over 2 million)	750,000 or more	500,000 to 750,000	250,000 to 500,000	Under 250,000	Urban, not SMSA	Rural, not SMSA
		Year t + 1						
Year t	12 largest	.50	.14	.12	.07	.07	.04	.04
	750,000 or more	.18	.50	.11	.06	.06	.04	.05
	500,000 to 750,000	.17	.12	.50	.06	.06	.04	.05
	250,000 to 500,000	.16	.11	.10	.50	.06	.03	.04
	Under 250,000	.16	.11	.10	.06	.50	.03	.04
	Urban, not SMSA	.15	.11	.10	.05	.05	.50	.04
	Rural, not SMSA	.15	.11	.10	.05	.06	.03	.50

1. Computed from the 1960 and 1970 census distributions of the population in the above categories using the following assumptions: that one-half of all the families or persons which migrate, i.e., cross a county line and who lived in each size category, moved out of that category; that the number who move out of each category, based on the 1970 distribution, is in proportion to the number who move in, as the national population growth rate for 1960–70 is to the growth rate for that size category 1960–70; that to achieve that gross immigration, from all other categories a given category draws from the other six in roughly similar proportions of their migrants.

PART III.
ECONOMIC OPERATING CHARACTERISTICS

Chapter 8
LABOR: PARTICIPATION, WAGE RATES, AND UNEMPLOYMENT*

This chapter describes the research performed to estimate the employment and earnings sector of the model.[1] The chapter is divided into four parts describing (1) the labor force participation decision, (2) hours in the labor force, (3) wage rate, and (4) unemployment.

Labor Force Participation

Role in the Model

Participating in the labor force is the most common means of receiving income. Since a central focus of DYNASIM is the distribution of income, simulating the decision to participate in the labor force is an essential element.

In the model the decision to participate is largely dependent upon the demographic characteristics of each individual. Thus, this decision rests upon much of what has happened in the demographic sector. For example, a woman's decision to participate in the labor force depends in part upon whether she is married and has young children.

The decision to participate in the labor force also depends upon the alternatives to earned income available to the potential worker. Presumably, eligibility for a transfer payment discourages labor force participation.

In addition, this decision depends upon the level of national unemployment since high rates of unemployment discourage participation. Finally, the decision depends upon the previous year's decision since

---

* Richard F. Wertheimer II had the main responsibility for this chapter and the work it represents. A more technical description of the operating characteristics discussed in this chapter is given in Wertheimer (1975).

1. Chapter 2 describes how this research fits into DYNASIM.

there is a certain degree of consistency in a person's behavior from one year to the next.

The decision to participate in the labor force, in turn, has an important impact upon the rest of the model. If a person participates, we must simulate hours worked, and a wage rate. (If not, these parts of the model can be skipped.) Participation influences a person's eligibility for payments from government transfer programs. Finally, whether or not an individual participates in the current year influences whether he participates the next year.

Ultimately, through its effect on earnings and receipt of transfer payments, the decision to participate in the labor force has an important effect upon each person's income and the income of the family to which he may belong.

Economic Theory and Labor Supply

In recent years there have been many efforts made by economists to estimate micro labor supply functions.[2] These studies have in common similar underlying theories and the same underlying motivation. The theory is that of the work-leisure tradeoff with the wage rate as the price of leisure. The underlying motivation of this research has been to estimate the income and substitution effects[3] associated with changes in wage rates or nonwage income so that the impact upon labor supply of programs providing transfer payments could be predicted. Of particular interest have been the various negative income tax schemes proposed to replace the Aid for Families with Dependent Children program.

No attempt will be given here to provide a complete theory of labor supply; see especially Kosters (1966). Briefly, the theory is that persons are faced with a decision about how to allocate their time between work and leisure. (Sometimes a three-part division is made among market work, home work, and leisure.) Leisure is considered to be an economic good like food, clothing, and automobiles. The price of leisure is the wage rate which one could earn if one were to work for an hour rather than to consume an hour of leisure.

When leisure is viewed this way, the economic theory of consumer demand for goods can be applied. The amount of leisure which a person

2. See, for example, Boskin (1970), Cain and Watts (1973), Fleisher and Porter (1971), Greenberg and Kosters (1970), Hall (1970), Kalachek and Raines (1970), and Kosters (1966).

3. The income effect is the impact upon work behavior of an increase in income (holding the wage rate constant). The substitution effect is the impact upon work behavior of an increase in the wage rate (holding income constant).

will consume depends upon the person's income and the price of leisure relative to other goods. If leisure is assumed to be a noninferior good, then, *ceteris paribus,* he will consume more of it as his income increases. As the price of leisure increases (i.e., the wage rate increases), there will be both an income effect tending to increase consumption of leisure and a substitution effect tending to decrease it. The net effect of the price increase could be either positive or negative.

There have been many problems with this approach both from a theoretical and an econometric point of view. These have resulted in a rather inconclusive current state of affairs.

From a theoretical point of view there have been two major problems—(1) the interdependence of the decision making by members of the same family and (2) the treatment of economic production done in the home and not involving market transactions. These two problems then lie in the background when econometric estimation takes place since they impose upon the researcher the unpleasant choice between an improperly specified model and a model which has a very large number of parameters which may be difficult or impossible to estimate.

The interdependence problem arises from the fact that individuals are not necessarily independent economic units. A wife's decision to participate in the labor force is not dependent merely upon her own wage rate and income but also upon the labor decisions of other members of the family. For example, there may be more pressure for a wife to work if her husband's earnings are low. Likewise, the husband's decision is dependent upon what the wife may do. Under some circumstances, one member's labor force involvement may be a substitute for another's. Under other circumstances it may be a complement. This still ignores the issue of other members of the family who may have a major role in the family's economic decision making or no role at all.

The "home" problem arises from the fact that in some families one spouse does a major amount of work in the home (e.g., cleaning, child-rearing, etc.) which is never recorded as an economic transaction, while in other families some or all of this work is done by someone outside the family (e.g., domestic worker, day care center) and is explicitly paid for by the family. Thus, each member of the family faces a tripartite choice—working in the labor market for an explicit wage rate, working at home for an implicit wage rate, and leisure. Needless to say, facing this three-way decision is analytically more complicated than a two-way decision would be.

Even after the analyst has made the necessary theoretical compromises to work around these complexities, he faces serious econometric problems—quite apart from the problems of misspecification and multiple parameters. How does one measure a wage rate for someone who does not work? What is the wage rate for work in the home? Do various kinds of nonemployment income have the same effect upon work behavior (e.g., can the effect upon work behavior of a change in income from stocks and bonds be used to infer the effect upon work behavior of a change in income from transfer payments)? Does one measure hours of work or hours in the "labor force" (i.e., time employed plus time unemployed)? Is the work response continuous or discontinuous? How does one account for differences in individual tastes and differences in market conditions?

Economic theory to date offers little help in making all of these choices. Thus, economists who have actually made estimates have arrived at different choices, according to their own justification. For a summary and evaluation of these choices and the results that followed, see Cain and Watts.

However different their analyses were, nearly all of the analysts have been most interested in estimating the income and substitution effects of changes in wage rates. If one wishes to predict the effect upon work behavior of changes in welfare programs, these changes can often be translated into changes in nonemployment income and changes in the net wage rate received. For example, most negative income tax schemes supply an income floor plus a tax rate applied to earnings up to a "break-even" point. Different minimum support levels and different tax rates imply different nonemployment income levels and different net wage rates. These, in turn, can be translated into changes in work behavior via the income and substitution effects.

The focus of DYNASIM is somewhat different. Since it is necessary to simulate each persons's labor force behavior rather than to predict the response to a change in just two parameters, the focus has been more on accurate micro predictions rather than on the accuracy of a limited number of parameters. Furthermore, the purpose of the model has been primarily as a synthesizer of research rather than as a producer of new research.

Given the unsettled state of affairs in the economic theory plus the synthesizing role of this study, it was decided that the best solution was to incorporate a relatively simple and flexible submodel of these labor force responses.

Specification of the Labor Force
Participation Function

The goal in specifying the function to be estimated was to construct a function which did a good job of predicting the labor force behavior of individuals over time (utilizing economic theory and other analysts' insights and experiences where possible), while at the same time preserving the ability to manipulate parameters as a means of simulating changes in either government policy or human behavior.

The first decision to be made was whether to represent labor force participation as a continuous function of a set of explanatory variables or to treat it instead as a discontinuous function with a threshold effect (i.e., the pressure to participate must build up to a certain point before one participates at all; once the threshold is reached, participation may be much greater than nominal). Following Kalachek and Raines, and Hall, we decided to pursue the latter course. First, it permits a straightforward means of altering the labor force participation rate in the simulation model. Second, it recognizes that there are significant fixed costs of employment (search costs, commuting, child care, etc.) as well as institutional barriers which discourage persons from working fewer than some minimum number of hours per time period.

We define a variable PINLABORF to be the probability of an individual participating in the labor force. We wish to estimate a function to predict PINLABORF for members of the sample population. Given this function, we can then have another function determine the level of participation (measured in hours) *given* that the person participates. (This function is described later.)

The general form of the desired function is

$$PINLABORF_{it} = f(PART_{i,t-1}, X_{it})$$

where $PART_{i,t-1}$ is a dichotomous variable taking on the value one if person i participated in the previous year and zero otherwise and X_{it} is a vector of other variables related to the probability of participating in the current year. Lagged participation is included in the function to represent a set of variables also related to current year participation but unobservable. These variables change only slowly over time and their effect upon participation remains constant. (For example, an intense dislike of housework and child-rearing is likely to be correlated with a person's probability of participating in the labor force and also is likely to persist from year to year.)

In order to provide for maximum interaction among the variables affecting participation, while avoiding the various statistical problems associated with regressions with dichotomous dependent variables, we constructed a simple table of probabilities of participation. This table consists of a cross-tabulation of the labor force participation rates of a large number of distinct groups of persons defined by their age, race, sex, family transfer income in previous year, disability status, and marital status, as well as by whether they participated in the labor force the previous year and (for women) whether they had a child under six years old.

Age was included as one of the explanatory variables in order to capture the impact of the life cycle. During youth formal investments in human capital are a strong competitor for a person's time, while in old age physical problems plus the ability to draw on nonwage income cause declines in participation. Since physical problems which interfere with work are likely to become more frequent with age and since some of these are irreversible, we expected a gradual decline in the probability of participation beginning in middle age with a sharp dropoff coinciding with the institutionally important retirement age of 65.

Race has been included to reflect the fact that black women have tended to have higher participation rates than white women, while white men have tended to have higher rates of participation than black men.

Sex has been included to reflect the traditional differences in labor force behavior of men and women. Sex not only has an independent effect but also influences the effect of other variables upon participation. For example, having a child under six would likely reduce the probability of a woman working but have no effect on the probability of a man working.

Family transfer income the previous year was used as a proxy for the availability of transfer income in the current year. As a possible substitute for transfer income, total family income in the previous year less the person's total earnings that year was also tried for wives only.

TABLE 8-1

LABOR FORCE OPERATING CHARACTERISTIC VARIABLE DEFINITIONS

Name	Description
$AFDCY_{k,t-1}$	AFDC Income
AGE_{it}	Age
$CHILDSIX_{kt}$	Child under six in Interview Unit
$DISABLED_{it}$	Disability status
$EARNS_{i,t-1}$	Earnings the previous year
$FOODY_{k,t-1}$	Food stamp income
$GRADCOM_{it}$	Highest grade of school completed
$PART_{i,t-1}$	In labor force
$PENSIONY_{k,t-1}$	Pension income
$RACE_i$	Race
SEX_i	Sex
$SOCURY_{k,t-1}$	Social Security Income
$SSIY_{k,t-1}$	Supplemental Security Income
$TFINCOME_{k,t-1}$	Total family income the previous year
$WAGEE_{it}$	Expected wage rate
$WEDSTATE_{it}$	Marital status

Disability status was used for obvious reasons. It should be noted that this variable is somewhat suspect since persons out of work may attempt to rationalize their behavior by magnifying a physical problem.

Marital status and whether a person had a child under six years of age were both used to reflect the division of labor which often takes place between spouses—especially when there is a small child present.

Definitions of variables used in the labor force participation function are given in Table 8-1.

Estimation of the Labor Force Participation Function

The function was estimated using the University of Michigan Institute for Social Research Panel Study of Income Dynamics (PSID). Survey years 1968–73 were available at the time the estimates were made. Since the PSID contains information on the same group of individuals over the six years, it was possible to use lagged participation as one of the explanatory variables. (This causes the loss of one year of data.) Since the questions on labor force participation refer to the preceding calendar year, a full set of observations on participation and all of the explanatory variables are defined for the period 1968–72. (The data for 1967 was used only for determining lagged participation.)

In order to maximize the sample size we have pooled the data for all of the years before estimating the function. This means that the observations are not fully independent.

Since two consecutive years of information are required for each observation, observations had to be dropped whenever either year's information was missing. If, for example, a person joined the sample in 1970 by marrying someone already in the sample, participation in the previous year and participation in the current year would be defined for the three observations, 1970–72, but not for the two observations, 1968–69.

Results

The results of cross-tabulating the labor force participation rates are shown in Table 8-2. The results, in general, are in line with expectations. For all groups, participation in the previous year and disability status cause splits into high participation rate categories and low participation rate categories, respectively. In addition, marginal groups such as teenagers and the elderly have low rates.

TABLE 8-2
LABOR FORCE PARTICIPATION FUNCTION (F_{LF1})

MALES AGED 21–64

	WHITE							NONWHITE					
	Did not participate previous year		Participated previous year					Did not participate previous year		Participated previous year			
	Disabled	Able-bodied	Disabled		Able-bodied			Disabled	Able-bodied	Disabled		Able-bodied	
			Transfer Income		Transfer Income					Transfer Income		Transfer Income	
Age			<1,000	>1,000	<1,000	1,000–2,000	>2,000			<1,000	>1,000	<1,000	>1,000
21–25	.33	.47	.99	.88	.97	.93	.86	.19	.33	.86		.90	
26–45	.12	.47	.98	.83	.99	.95	.92	.24	.32	.93	.69	.97	.86
46–55	.07	.25	.97	.79	.99	.92	.96	.10	.29	.88		.97	
56–60	.24	.15	.91	.78	.98	.88	.77	.12	.19	.83		.98	
61–64	.09	.13	.89	.56	.93	.80	.78	.07	.07	.94		.94	

(see notes at end of table)

TABLE 8-2 (continued)

UNMARRIED FEMALES AGED 21–64

	WHITE							NONWHITE									
	Did not participate		Participated					Did not participate			Participated						
			No child under 6			Child <6					No child <6			Child <6			
	Disabled	Able-bodied	Disabled		Able-bodied	Trans. Inc. t−1		Disabled	Able-bodied		Disabled	Able-bodied		Disabled		Able-bodied	
Age			Trans. Inc. (t−1)			<1,000	>1,000		Trans. Inc. (t−1)			Trans. Inc. (t−1)		Trans. Inc. (t−1)		Trans. Inc. (t−1)	
			<1,000	>1,000					<1,000	>1,000		<1,000	>1,000	<1,000	>1,000	<1,000	>1,000
21–25		.41	.88	.88	.89	.96	.73		.28	.23	.83	.83	.78	.81	.60	.90	.78
26–45		.29			.95	.98			.27	.14	.83	.95	.85			.93	
46–55		.39			.97	.78			.20	.12	.83	.95	.90			.97	
56–60	.09	.21	.84	.73	.95	0	0	.11	.18	.06	.75	.88	.75			.87	
61–64		.06			.92				.11	0	.50	.73	.73				

(see notes at end of table)

TABLE 8-2 (continued)

MARRIED FEMALES AGED 21-64

WHITE

AGE	Did not participate			Participated							
	Disabled	Able-bodied Non-Wife Income		Disabled	No Child <6 Able-bodied	Child <6 Able-bodied Non-Wife Income					
		<15,000	>15,000			0–3,000	3,000–6,000	6,000–9,000	9,000–12,000	12,000–15,000	>15,000
21–25	.35	.25	0	.56	.91	.85	.77	.74	.71	.71	.63
26–45		.18	.12		.90	0	0	0	0	0	0
46–55	.11	.10	.09		.90						
56–60	.07	.07	.05		.88						
61–64	.04	.04	0		.77						

NONWHITE

AGE	Did not participate			Participated	
	Disabled	Able-bodied Transfer Income		Disabled	Able-bodied
		<1,000	>1,000		
21–25	.10	.34	.23	.61	.84
26–45		.22	.15		
46–55		.15	.11		
56–60					
61–64		.09			

TABLE 8-2 (continued)

PERSONS UNDER 21

RACE	WHITE				NONWHITE			
Sex	Male		Female		Male		Female	
Participated?	No	Yes	No	Yes	No	Yes	No	Yes
A 14–15	.29	.65	.19	.49	.11	.49	.09	.50
G 16–17	.47	.69	.36	.68	.21	.52	.18	.48
E 18–19	.42	.79	.45	.75	.29	.63	.28	.67
20	.28	.87	.37	.79	.28	.76	.27	.71

LABOR FORCE PARTICIPATION FUNCTION, PERSONS AGED 65 AND OVER

RACE	WHITE				NONWHITE			
Sex	Male		Female		Male		Female	
Participated?	No	Yes	No	Yes	No	Yes	No	Yes
A 65–69	.11	.81	.05	.75	.13	.86	.03	.69
G								
E 70+	.05	.77	.02	.66	.04	.61	.02	.63

Notes:

1. Transfer income $= AFDC_{k,t-1} = FSTAMP_{k,t-1} + PENSION_{k,t-1} + SOCURY_{k,t-1} + SSI_{k,t-1}$
2. Non-Wife Income $= TFINCOME_{k,t-1} - EARNS_{k,t-1}$
3. Variable definitions appear in Table 8-1.
4. Blank spaces indicate a single number applies to the entire space.

Among able-bodied persons who participated in the preceding year, white men generally have higher rates of participation than black men in all age and transfer categories. (Virtually all able-bodied white men participated if they worked the previous year, received little or no transfer income last year, and are aged 26–60.)

Although women generally had lower rates of participation than comparable men, the rates of participation for unmarried women who worked the previous year and had no young children were quite high, and there was little difference between whites and blacks. The rates for married women were somewhat lower, but those married women under age 60 who participated in the previous year and had no young children had rates of 85 to 90 percent.

Two alternative measures of income were tried for married women – total family income the prior year less their own earnings plus total family transfer income that year. Total family transfer income was tried for the remaining groups where sample size permitted. (The non-participant male groups and the disabled groups were usually too small for reliable estimates of income effects.) Family income produced a more statistically significant effect for white wives, while transfer income produced a more statistically significant effect for black wives. Both measures of income had the predicted negative effect upon participation. The effect was particularly dramatic for white wives, where participation rates (for able-bodied women who worked the previous year and had children under six) declined from 85 percent for the lowest income group to 63 percent for the highest with a steady decline in between. Transfer income had a strong negative effect upon unmarried women with children and upon nonwhite married women. (Even though transfer income is lagged by one year, it is still possible that causality is also running in the opposite direction, i.e., women who do not work are more likely to receive transfer payments.)

The age variable worked as expected. Participation rates tend to peak in the 26–45 age category and decline for both younger and older groups.

Hours in the Labor Force

Role in the Model

If an individual does not participate in the labor force, the hours sector of the model is skipped. Thus, the first important influence upon this sector is the determination of whether or not a person participates at all.

Given that he does participate, the number of hours he participates is largely dependent on his demographic characteristics.

The number of hours an individual is in the labor force obviously affects that person's earnings and—when all individuals are considered—the distribution of income among all persons and families. In addition, it influences a person's eligibility for receipt of transfer payments since some programs have requirements that an individual have worked certain amounts of time to be eligible for certain levels of payments. Thus, there is a second connection to the distribution of income.

Theory and Specification of the Hours Equation

The theory of labor supply was discussed in the previous section on labor force participation and need not be repeated.

The goal in specifying the hours-in-the-labor-force equations was to do a good job of predicting the number of hours per year that individuals spend in the labor force, while at the same time preserving the ability to manipulate parameters as a means of simulating changes in either government policy or human behavior.

Since we represent the decision to participate or not as a separate and prior decision, the hours equations are specified for those persons who did in fact participate. For them, we define a continuous variable, HOURS, equal to the number of hours per year that an individual spends employed plus the number of hours per year he spends unemployed.

We specify the general form of the regression equations to be estimated for hours in the labor force as

$$\text{HOURS}_t = X_t\beta + u_t \qquad \text{and} \qquad (1)$$

$$u_t = \gamma u_{t-1} + \epsilon_t, \qquad (2)$$

where HOURS_t is a vector of cross-section observations taken at time t of the dependent variable, X_t is a matrix of comparable observations of a set of explanatory variables, β is a vector of parameters, u_t is an autoregressive error term, and ϵ_t is a random error term.

The purpose of specifying the pair of equations is to capture the autocorrelation of the dependent variable without allowing the lagged value of the dependent variable to dominate the relationship. The error term is presumed to be autocorrelated because of autocorrelated variables omitted from the equation. The reasoning is the same which led us to include lagged participation in the participation function.

Separate equations were estimated for eight demographic groups—males aged 21–64 by race, females aged 21–64 by race and marital status, persons aged 14–20, and persons older than 64. For men this permits a complete set of interactions between race and sex, on the one hand, and the explanatory variables in the regression equation, on the other. For women this permits a complete set of interactions between race, sex, and marital status, on the one hand, and the explanatory variables, on the other.

The explanatory variables used in each equation were as follows: Several age dummies were included. These were expected to capture a tendency for both young and old people to work less than persons of prime working age. For teenagers and persons over 65 a continuous age variable was used to account for rapid rise in hours worked as a person ages from 14 to 21 and the correspondingly rapid decline in hours worked after one reaches 65.

Disability status was used for obvious reasons. Marital status was included for men and teenagers. (Being married confers work responsibilities upon men and teenagers.)

A predicted wage rate was used to represent the price of leisure. This predicted wage was calculated using a set of regression equations

TABLE 8-3

VARIABLE DEFINITIONS FOR HOURS WORKED

Variable	Variable Definitions
AGE01	Equals 1 if AGE is 21 through 25, 0 otherwise
AGE02	Equals 1 if AGE is 26 through 44, 0 otherwise
AGE03	Equals 1 if AGE is 45 through 54, 0 otherwise
AGE04	Equals 1 if AGE is 55 through 60, 0 otherwise
AGE05	Equals 1 if AGE is 61 through 64, 0 otherwise
DISABLED	Equals 1 if person is disabled, 0 otherwise
MARRIED	Equals 1 if person is married, 0 otherwise
WAGEE	Expected wage rate
TRANSINC	Transfer income previous year
CHILDSIX	Equals 1 if there is a child under six years old in family, 0 otherwise
DNONWIFINC	Family income less own earnings previous year
NONWHITE	Equals 1 if nonwhite, 0 otherwise
FEMALE	Equals 1 if females, 0 otherwise
YRSGT14	Age minus 14
YRSGT65	Age minus 65
ED01	Equals 1 if education is 8 years or less, 0 otherwise
ED02	Equals 1 if education is between 9 and 11 years, 0 otherwise
ED03	Equals 1 if education is between 12 and 15 years, 0 otherwise
ED04	Equals 1 if education is 16 years or more, 0 otherwise

described in the next section. This instrumental variable technique eliminates transitory influences and errors in reporting on an individual's wage rate. The sign of this variable depends upon the relative strengths of the income and substitution effects.

Transfer income the prior year was used as a proxy for the likelihood of receiving transfer income in the current year. We expect a negative influence. Family income less a person's own earnings last year was used for white wives only.

Having a child of preschool age increases the need for a person to have income but it also increases the opportunity cost of a person's working (particularly for the mother). For this reason an appropriate dummy variable was included for both men and women.

A complete list of variables and definitions is given in Table 8-3.

Estimation of the Hours Equation

The same sample (the PSID) was used to estimate the hours equations as was used to estimate the labor force participation function. The data were pooled as before.

Equation (1) was estimated using ordinary least squares for the survey years 1968–72. Residuals, $\hat{u}_t$, were calculated by

$$\hat{u}_t = \text{HOURS}_t - X_t b_t \tag{3}$$

where b_t is the OLS estimate of β. Then, using the survey taken in 1969, residuals, $\hat{u}_{t-1}$, were calculated by

$$\hat{u}_{t-1} = \text{HOURS}_{t-1} - X_{t-1} b_t \tag{4}$$

Then γ was estimated by regressing $\hat{u}_t$ upon $\hat{u}_{t-1}$, using ordinary least squares. (For this latter equation, observations were dropped whenever either of the two consecutive years of data were missing.)

With this procedure our estimate of β is unbiased, but our estimate of the standard errors of β is biased because u is autocorrelated. Consequently significance tests must be viewed with caution.

Results

The regression results are given in Table 8-4. An entry of zero indicates that the variable was omitted from the equation. Standard errors of estimate (corrected for degrees of freedom) are shown for each equation in

TABLE 8-4

HOURS EQUATIONS $(F_h)^{b,c}$

Variable[a]	White Male	Nonwhite Male	White Female Unmarried	Nonwhite Female Unmarried	White Female Married	Nonwhite Female Married	<21	≥65
CONSTANT	2003	2005	1909	1883	1454	1263	572	896
AGE02	98	51**	158*	60**	-21**	3**	0	0
AGE03	56*	8**	153*	-48**	52**	-81**	0	0
AGE04	-74*	-132	9**	-61**	44**	-170**	0	0
AGE05	-251	-259	-150*	-546	-268	-415*	0	0
DISABLED	-218	-329	-216	-332	-559	-384	-15**	-348
MARRIED	176	99	0	0	0	0	270	0
WAGEE	23	46	-35**	-53**	34**	133	0	178
TRANSINC	-.15	-.20	-.19	-.19	0	-.09	0	-.14
CHILDSIX	111	22**	-131*	-41**	-286	-92*	0	0
DNONWIFINC	0	0	0	0	-.02	0	0	0
NONWHITE	0	0	0	0	0	0	-55	0
FEMALE	0	0	0	0	0	0	-277	-218
YRSGT14	0	0	0	0	0	0	212	0
ED02	0	0	0	0	0	0	-94	0
ED03	0	0	0	0	0	0	-72**	0
ED04	0	0	0	0	0	0	-57	0
ρ	.57	.43	.57	.43	.66	.59	.39	.70
SEE	501	494	505	517	529	575	652	445

Combined $R^2 = 0.82$

a. See Table 8-3 for definitions.

b. The predicted number of hours for each individual is obtained by multiplying each coefficient from the appropriate column by the value which the corresponding variable takes on for that individual and then taking the sum of the products. For example, the predicted hours for a white male, aged 26–44, able-bodied, married, expected wage of $4.00, no transfer income, and no children would be

$$2003 + (98 \cdot 1) + (56 \cdot 0) - (74 \cdot 0) - (251 \cdot 0) - (218 \cdot 0) + (176 \cdot 1) + (23 \cdot 4.00) - (0.15 \cdot 0) + (111 \cdot 0) = 2369 \text{ hours}$$

c. All coefficients are significant at the 0.01 level unless indicated by one asterisk (*) which indicates a significance only at the 0.05 level or two asterisks (**) which indicates significance at the 0.10 level or lower.

the "SEE" row. The autocorrelation coefficient is shown in the "ρ" row. The combined $\bar{R}^2$ — the fraction of the total variance explained in the combined sample — is shown at the bottom.

Both prime age males and prime age unmarried females tended to work fulltime. Married women, teenagers, and the elderly worked much less. Adults under 25 tended to work fewer hours than those 26–45 (except for married white females). Hours generally peaked for the 26–45 age group and then declined with increasing age.

The effect of disability was not uniform across the groups. The two married female groups had the two highest hour losses. For the men and the unmarried women disability had a much stronger impact upon nonwhites than whites. There is no obvious explanation for these findings.

Being married and having a child under six increased hours for men, while they decreased hours for women.

The substitution effect was strong enough for men and married women to give the expected wage coefficient a positive sign. The negative coefficients for the unmarried women were not significant. The effect was strongest for married nonwhite females, where an increase in the expected wage rate of $1.00 per hour led to a 133 hour increase in expected work. This is nearly four times as strong an effect as for white married females. The effect was also stronger for nonwhite men than for white men.

With the exception of white married females (for whom the variable was not used) transfer income in the previous year has a negative effect. Transfer income of $1,000 was associated with 100–200 hours reduction in expected work. For white married females, family income less their own earnings the previous year had a negative effect on hours. Each $5,000 in income was associated with a 100-hour reduction in work.

The level of autocorrelation was generally quite high — although it tended to be somewhat lower for nonwhites than whites. The combined $\bar{R}^2$ was .82 — a high figure for cross-section work. Part of this is attributable to the autocorrelation.

Wage Rates and Earnings

Role in the Model

The distribution of income is greatly influenced by the distribution of earnings. The distribution of earnings, in turn, depends upon both the amount of work done by each person and the rate at which the person earns income. Since most primary earners (the breadwinners of economic units) work fulltime and constitute a large fraction of the labor force, it is the wage rate which becomes a central focus. (Of course, accumulated wealth plays a large role in determining the distribution of income as well.)

In DYNASIM, persons' wage rates depend upon their age, race, sex, education, and location. These factors are all determined in the demographic sector of the model.

A person's wage rate affects the hours worked and is an input to the sector which calculates the distribution of income and wealth.

The Economic Theory of Wage Determination

Hypotheses about wage rate determination follow in straightforward fashion from the theory of investment in human capital (Becker, 1964). According to this theory individuals (in many cases subsidized by society) invest in themselves by getting a formal education, enrolling in formal training programs, and receiving on-the-job training (either formal or informal). These activities are viewed as investments because they involve an outlay of funds (e.g., tuition, foregone earnings) in return for higher earnings in the future.

If this theory is correct, we should expect persons with larger stocks of human capital to have higher wage rates. The stock of human capital can be measured (imperfectly) by a person's education, age (a proxy for experience and training), and occupation (also a proxy for training).

In addition to differences in the stock of human capital from person to person, there may also be differences in the price paid for human capital. A college or a high school education may be less valuable in geographic areas where there is little demand for skilled labor than it is in places where there is a high demand. The supply of labor of various skill levels also plays a role. If there is a glut of college graduates in a particular area, it may depress the rate for college graduates in that area. Migration from areas where the price of human capital is low to areas where it is high would tend to eliminate these differences, and achieve significant wage gains for the migrants (Wertheimer, 1970). However, in spite of the high mobility levels of Americans, substantial differences still exist, and, because of this, we have included location as an explanatory variable in our model.

The price of human capital may also depend upon the race and sex of its owner. This difference, quite thoroughly documented (Becker, 1964, and Weiss, 1970), can be largely attributed to discrimination.

The estimation of the returns to human capital by regressing earnings upon human capital stock and price has some serious problems, however. First, the variables which are used to measure the stock of human capital are imperfect measures which are often correlated with other factors related to earnings. For example, education level does not measure knowledge acquired or ability to perform a task but merely the grade level reached. Furthermore, education is correlated with the individual's intelligence and the economic and social status of his parents—both of which are related to his earnings. If these other variables are included in the regression analysis, multi-collinearity makes it difficult to disentangle the independent effects of the explanatory variables. If some of these variables are omitted from the equation, then earnings attributable in fact to the omitted variables may be partially attributed statistically to the variable that remains in the equation.

In addition, there are many factors which influence earnings which are simply not understood. This is reflected in the relatively low fraction of explained variance in human capital equations. This means that persons with exactly the same measured personal characteristics may have vastly different earnings rates. This point has been pursued in depth by Jencks (1972).

It does not necessarily follow, however, either that estimating these functions is a useless exercise or that government policy actions taken to affect explanatory variables in the equation (e.g., education) and thereby influence income are meaningless. It simply means that we should not expect equality of human capital stock and the price of human capital to lead to equality of earnings. Earnings can be influenced by altering human capital but can only be partially controlled in this fashion.

A major goal in estimating our model was to obtain accurate predictions of earnings over time rather than to focus exclusively on measuring the rate of return on various investments in human capital. (We are, of course, interested in measuring these returns accurately too.) Consequently, the studies which have been done were not ideal for our model although they certainly have influenced its specification. We have tried (as in sectors discussed earlier) to use judiciously lagged values of the wage rate to improve our predictions, while at the same time preserving the relationship betweeen the wage rate and the human capital variables.

Specification of the Model

The goal in specifying the wage rates equations was to do a good job of predicting a person's position in the wage distribution over time, while at the same time preserving the ability to simulate changes in either government policy or human behavior.

The variable which we wish to predict is an individual's average hourly relative wage, WAGE, defined as annual earnings divided by hours worked per year for each person divided by the aggregate wage rate for the economy. We specify the general form of the regression equations to be estimated as

$$\text{WAGE}_t = X_t\beta + u_t \quad \text{and} \tag{5}$$

$$u_t = \gamma u_{t-1} + \epsilon_t \tag{6}$$

where WAGE_t is a vector of cross-section observations taken at time t of the dependent variable, X_t is a matrix of comparable observations of a set of explanatory variables, β is a vector of parameters, u_t is an autoregressive error term, and ϵ_t is a random error term.

The purpose of specifying the pair of equations, (5) and (6), is to capture the autocorrelation of the dependent variable without allowing the lagged value of the dependent variable to dominate the relationship. Presumably the autocorrelation is caused by explanatory variables whose values do not change much from year to year and whose influence upon the dependent variable does not change much from year to year. If some of these variables are not included in the estimated equations, than the error term, u_t, will be autocorrelated. (For example, having a father who is president of U.S. Steel Corporation is likely to be associated with a high wage rate but is not included in the equation. In the following year the chances are high that the father will still be president of U.S. Steel, and the wage rate will still be high.)

In order to permit a rather full set of interactions among the explanatory variables, separate equations were estimated for demographic groups. The groups were adults aged 21–64 by race and sex, teenagers, and the elderly.

Years of education were included in the equation in dummy variable form. This form permits jumps in the return to education as important milestones (such as high school and college graduation) are passed.

Age was used as a proxy for on-the-job training and experience. In theory a better measure of experience would be years of work experience (or, better yet, "depreciated" years of work experience[4]). This variable was not available on the PSID, although it could have been approximated by subtracting six plus the years of education from a persons age. This latter procedure assumes a continuous history of work—an unreasonable assumption for married women, the group for whom accurate measurement of years of experience would be the most important. Since

4. This assumes that experience depreciates in value during periods in which a person does not work.

it seemed unlikely that this transformation would add much, and since using years of experience would have increased the size and cost of the model, age was used instead.[5]

An additional problem with using age in a cross-section regression is that the age-earnings profile observed at a point in time is not necessarily an accurate picture of the changes in any age cohort's earnings over its members' lifetimes. Ruggles and Ruggles (1974) have demonstrated this using longitudinal data from Social Security. The particular problem that causes cross-section studies to be misleading is that earnings actually go up all the way through age 65 (albeit at a slower rate during the last years of work), while the cross-section studies show a decline during the last few years and a less steep upward slope through a person's entire lifetime. The reason for this discrepancy is that the growth in the economy over time is increasing virtually everyone's earnings year by year. Old people's earnings decline *relative* to younger people as they approach retirement, but their absolute level of earnings continues to rise.

In DYNASIM the wage rate function determines the relative wage distribution only. The total amount of labor income, determined by the macroeconomic model, is then distributed according to the relative distribution. Thus, the assumption made in DYNASIM is that snapshots of the relative wage distributions remain the same over time.

A regional dummy variable was used to capture the difference in the price of human capital between the South and the rest of the country.

A marital status dummy variable was used for men (and tried unsuccessfully for women) to test the hypothesis that married men would select higher-paying (but possibly less satisfying) jobs because of their need for extra income.

Disability was included to test the hypothesis that being disabled would lower one's own human capital.

A complete list of variables is given in Table 8-5.

Estimation of the Wage Rate Equations

The relative wage rate equations were estimated using a procedure analogous to that used in the hours function. The relative wage rate was calculated by dividing the absolute wage rates by the mean wage rate for the appropriate year.

---

5. Sawhill (1974) has shown that women who have never married have a flat age-earnings profile, almost the same as for females who have ever been married. This suggests a rather low pay-off for years of experience for women.

TABLE 8-5

VARIABLE DEFINITIONS FOR WAGE RATES

Variable	Variable Definitions
ED1	Equals 1 if Education is 8 years or less, 0 otherwise
ED2	Equals 1 if Education is 9 through 11 years, 0 otherwise
ED3	Equals 1 if Education is 12 through 15 years, 0 otherwise
ED4	Equals 1 if Education is 16 years or more, 0 otherwise
AGE1	Equals 1 if Age is 21 through 25, 0 otherwise
AGE2	Equals 1 if Age is 26 through 30, 0 otherwise
AGE3	Equals 1 if Age is 31 through 40, 0 otherwise
AGE4	Equals 1 if Age is 41 through 50, 0 otherwise
AGE5	Equals 1 if Age is 51 through 60, 0 otherwise
AGE6	Equals 1 if Age is 61 through 64, 0 otherwise
AGE2ED4	AGE2 · ED4
AGE3ED4	AGE3 · ED4
AGE4ED4	AGE4 · ED4
AGE5ED4	AGE5 · ED4
AGE6ED4	AGE6 · ED4
SOUTH	Equals 1 for South; 0 otherwise
MARRIED	Equals 1 if Married; 0 otherwise
DISABL	Equals 1 if Disabled; 0 otherwise
NONWHITE	Equals 1 if Race = nonwhite; 0 otherwise
FEMALE	Equals 1 if Sex = 1; 0 otherwise
YRSGT14	Age minus 14
YRSGT65	Age minus 65

Results

The results of the wage rate regressions are shown in Table 8-6. In general, the results are in line with human capital theory. Education pays off for all groups, and college education pays off for men even more when combined with age.

The age-wage profile for white men without college educations is steeper than for the other groups. The profile for black men and all women is rather flat, except for college-educated black men whose profile is similar to that of college-educated white men. (The profile declines sharply relative to white men in the last two age categories, however.) Separate regressions (not shown) run for each year of the survey revealed some year-to-year change but no clear trends in (1) the age-earnings profiles for blacks relative to whites, (2) the age-earning profiles for women relative to men, or (3) the rewards from education for blacks or women. While others (Welch, 1973; Freeman, 1973) have

TABLE 8-6

RELATIVE WAGE RATE EQUATIONS (F_w)[b]

Variable[a]	AGE: 21–64				Age <21	Age ≥65
	White Male	Nonwhite Male	White Female	Nonwhite Female		
Constant	.604	.753	.642	.675	.518	1.062
ED2	.250	.139	.070**	.053*	.058*	.268**
ED3	.428	.248	.249	.160	.125	.330*
ED4	.584	.193*	.709	.722	0	.792
AGE2	.178	.046**	.034**	.025**	0	0
AGE3	.370	.129	.042**	.017**	0	0
AGE4	.479	.127	.076*	−.024**	0	0
AGE5	.404	.062**	.092*	.023**	0	0
AGE6	.468	.022**	.059**	.074**	0	0
AGE2ED4	.243	.271*	.312	.353	0	0
AGE3ED4	.559	.669	.348	.089**	0	0
AGE4ED4	.714	1.947	.109**	.294*	0	0
AGE5ED4	.894	.411	−.037**	.068**	0	0
AGE6ED4	.700	.516*	.506	−.170**	0	0
SOUTH	−.256	−.294	−.145	−.203	−.087	−.140**
MARRIED	.216	.224	0	0	0	0
DISABL	−.083*	0	0	0	0	0
NONWHITE	0	0	0	0	−.042*	−.038**
FEMALE	0	0	0	0	−.079	−.424
YRSGT14	0	0	0	0	.040	0
YRSGT65	0	0	0	0	0	−.022*
ρ	.56	.72	.29	.17	.17	.36
SEE	.72	.51	.76	.56	.45	.92

Combined R^2 = .63

a. See Table 8-5 for definitions.

b. All variables are significant at the .01 level unless indicated by a single asterisk (*) which indicates significance at .05 level or by a double asterisk (**) which indicates significance at the .10 level or less.

found some changes in the rewards from education over the sixties, no trends in relative wage rates were incorporated into DYNASIM on the grounds that there were no strong indications that these trends would necessarily persist in the seventies — particularly during a period of high unemployment.

The South dummy variable takes on a similar value for the four major adult groups.

The disability variable was significant only for the white males and was dropped for the other groups.

The marital status was significant only for the men. It was dropped from the women's equations.

The continuous age variables worked as expected for the teenagers and adults.

The combined $\bar{R}^2$ was .63 — a relatively high figure for cross-section regressions, but the presence of much of the same sample over the years and the inclusion of the autoregressive error must be borne in mind in interpreting this statistic.

Unemployment

Role in the Model

Unemployment has been a critical issue for the federal government for decades. The unemployment rate is considered to be one of the most important indicators of the health of the national economy. The issue of the distribution of unemployment has received increasing attention in recent years. In particular it has been noted that teenagers and nonwhites experience much more unemployment than other groups.

In the model the determination of the national unemployment rate is taken as given. However, the distribution of unemployment is handled by the micromodel.

The distribution of unemployment (given some level of national unemployment) is dependent upon the demographic characteristics of the population in the model. Thus, how much unemployment a person is simulated to experience depends upon much of what has happened in the demographic sector described in the preceding chapters and what happens in the macro time series model.

Unemployment and its distribution can be considered an output of the model in its own right. However, it also influences other parts of the model. Unemployment influences receipt of transfer payments since, for example, the unemployed person may be eligible to receive unemployment compensation. In addition, hours of work are computed by subtracting hours of unemployment from hours in the labor force.

Theory of Unemployment

It is well known that certain groups within the labor force have much higher rates of unemployment than the average. Of particular concern has been the persistent 2:1 black-white unemployment ratio. However, other groups, notably teenagers, experience higher than average unemployment rates as well.

Various theories have been advanced to explain these differentials. Most have concentrated on the racial difference. Explanations include market segmentation, discrimination, human capital acquisition, and hiring queues. Smith and Holt (1971) have shown that the higher rates of unemployment for blacks stem from higher rates of separation from jobs rather than from inability to find jobs. Hall (1972) and Perry (1972) have done similar studies. Gramlich (1974) has shown that the distributional effects of unemployment are not borne equally by the various sectors of the labor force.

There was no practical way in which these studies could be directly incorporated into the model. Instead we have tried to reproduce the observed differentials by relating unemployment to demographic characteristics of the population.

Specification of the Unemployment Equations

The concept of unemployment in an annual model is somewhat different from the concept that receives the most public attention—the monthly unemployment rate. In the model unemployment is measured in two

TABLE 8-7

VARIABLE DEFINITIONS FOR UNEMPLOYMENT

Variable	Variable Definitions
ED1	Equals 1 if Education is 8 years or less, 0 otherwise
ED2	Equals 1 if Education is 9 through 11, 0 otherwise
ED3	Equals 1 if Education is 12 through 15, 0 otherwise
ED4	Equals 1 if Education is 16 years or more, 0 otherwise
AGE1	Equals 1 if Age is 21 through 25, 0 otherwise
AGE2	Equals 1 if Age is 26 through 30, 0 otherwise
AGE3	Equals 1 if Age is 31 through 40, 0 otherwise
AGE4	Equals 1 if Age is 41 through 50, 0 otherwise
AGE5	Equals 1 if Age is 51 through 60, 0 otherwise
AGE6	Equals 1 if Age is 61 through 64, 0 otherwise
SOUTH	Equals 1 if Region = South; 0 otherwise
MARRIED	Equals 1 if Married; 0 otherwise
DISABL	Equals 1 if Disabled; 0 otherwise
NONWHITE	Equals 1 if Race = nonwhite; 0 otherwise
FEMALE	Equals 1 if Sex = female; 0 otherwise

ways—(1) being unemployed or not at sometime during the year and (2) number of hours of unemployment during the year.

Since there is a sizable flow of persons through the state which we call unemployment, there are more than three times as many persons who experience unemployment at *some time* during a year than there are persons who are unemployed during the Current Population Survey survey week for each month. For example, the average monthly unemployment rate of the total labor force in 1970 was 4.8 percent, while the fraction of the labor force that was unemployed at *some time* during the year was 15.2 percent.

We specified a two-stage model. The first stage relates whether or not a person experiences any unemployment at all to his demographic characteristics—

$$\text{UNPROB}_{it} = f(X_{it})$$

where UNPROB_{it} is the probability of experiencing unemployment sometime during the year and X_{it} is a vector of other variables related to the probability of experiencing unemployment during the current year.

The explanatory variables used included race and sex, since there is a history of different rates for these four groups.

Education categories were used to account for the higher vulnerability to unemployment that the less skilled have. Less skilled persons usually have less bargaining power, less knowledge of the opportunities in the labor market, and a wage rate which is low enough to make unemployment compensation a possible temporary alternative to working. Finally, age categories were included to capture the higher vulnerability of young adults, who have much higher job turnover rates than older workers.

In the second stage, we specify a pair of equations which explain the person's own unemployment rate, UNRTHRS (i.e., the number of hours per year he is unemployed divided by the number of hours he is in the labor force), given that he experienced some unemployment. These are specified as follows:

$$\text{UNRTHRS}_t = X\,\beta_t + u_t \qquad (7)$$

$$u_t = \gamma u_{t-1} + \epsilon_t \qquad (8)$$

where the usual definitions apply.

The same set of explanatory variables was used at this stage as in the previous stage for much the same reasons. A complete list of the variables used in these regressions is given in Table 8-7.

TABLE 8-8

CALCULATIONS OF UNEMPLOYMENT PROBABILITIES (F_{u1})

MALES AGED 21-64

Age	WHITE						NONWHITE				
	Ed: 0–11 yrs.		Ed: 12–15 yrs.		Ed: 16+ yrs.		Ed: 0–11 yrs.		Ed: 12–15 yrs.		Ed: 16+ yrs.
	Unmarried	Married	Unmarried	Married	Unmarried	Married	Unmarried	Married	Unmarried	Married	
21–25	.46	.33	.26	.18	.16	.12	.38	.31	.40	.24	.03
26–64	.22	.19	.17	.10	.09	.04	.24	.20	.26	.17	

FEMALES AGED 21-64

Age	WHITE			NONWHITE		
	Ed: 0–11	Ed: 12–15	Ed: 16+	Ed: 0–11	Ed: 12–15	Ed: 16+
21–25	.43	.23	.12	.30	.28	.04
26–45	.20	.15	.11	.23	.21	
46–64	.18	.08	.03	.14	.12	

(continued on next page)

TABLE 8-8 (continued)

PERSONS AGED 14–20

Marital Status	WHITE				NONWHITE			
	Male		Female		Male		Female	
	Ed: 0–11	Ed: 12+	Ed: 0–11	Ed: 12+	Ed: 0–11	Ed: 12+	Ed: 0–11	Ed: 12+
Unmarried	.54	.24	.55	.16	.58	.43	.45	.34
Married	.28	.19			.53	.30		

PERSONS AGED 65+
.03

Estimation of the Unemployment Equations

A cross-tabulation of pooled data from the PSID was used to estimate the probability function.[6] The results are shown in Table 8-8.

The findings are strikingly regular for adult men. White men have a lower probability of experiencing unemployment than nonwhites within every age-education-marital status category. Married men have a lower probability than unmarried men in every race-education-age category. Men aged 26–64 have lower probability than men aged 16–25. Finally vulnerability to unemployment decreases with education for each race-age-marital status group.

The findings for adult women are almost as regular. Education and age have the same effects as for men. However, the least educated white women have higher vulnerability to unemployment than the least educated nonwhite women. The fact that data were restricted to family heads casts some doubt on the reliability of these findings.

The most striking thing about the results for teenagers is the high rates. Unmarried young men with less than a high school education had a better than 50 percent chance of experiencing unemployment. Otherwise, the results mirror those for the adults.

The results of the unemployment rate regressions are given in Table 8-9. In an initial version of these regressions (not shown) separate dummy variables were used for having completed 9–11 years, 12–15 years, and 16 or more years of education, respectively. The coefficients of these dummies were similar so a single dummy for having completed 8 or fewer years was used instead. Similar combining was done for age. For women, age was eliminated entirely. In the table a zero entry means that the particular dummy was dropped from the equation—thus collapsing its category into the omitted group.

Having less than nine years of education was associated with a higher rate of unemployment for three of the four adult groups. Middle age was associated with a higher rate for the men. This is likely to be caused by the difficulty older men have in finding new work once they have been laid off. Many people in the older group (but still under 65) have the option of withdrawing from the labor force altogether if jobs are too hard to find.

Being married has a negative effect on the unemployment rate. This is probably due to married men's greater need for jobs. They may accept an undesirable job more readily than single men.

Having a child under six had a strong positive effect on the expected unemployment rate of women. Having a child under six may act as a deterrent for accepting anything less than an ideal job and thus

---

6. Unemployment data were available only for family heads. This may have introduced a bias of unknown direction in some of the coefficients.

TABLE 8-9

UNEMPLOYMENT RATE FUNCTION $(F_{u2})^b$

Variable[a]	AGE: 21–64				Age <21	Age ≥65
	White Male	Nonwhite Male	White Female	Nonwhite Female		
Constant	.19	.26	.22	.26	.14	.04
ED1	.04	.03**	0	.06	0	0
AGE1	0	0	0	0	0	0
AGE2	0	0	0	0	0	0
AGE3	.03*	0	0	0	0	0
AGE4	.08	.06*	0	0	0	0
AGE5	0	0	0	0	0	0
SOUTH	−.04	−.03**	.10*	0	0	0
MARRIED	−.04*	−.07	0	0	0	0
DISABL	.05	.08	.06**	.12	0	0
NONWHITE	0	0	0	0	.08*	0
FEMALE	0	0	0	0	.18	0
CHILDSIX	0	0	.19	.12	0	0
ρ	.47	.40	.44	.53	—	—
SEE	.15	.15	.20	.21	.23	.30

Combined R^2 = .71

a. See Table 8-7 for definitions.
b. All variables are significant at the .01 level unless indicated by a single asterisk (*) which indicates significance at .05 level or by a double asterisk (**) which indicates significance at the .10 level or less.

prolong unemployment. It may also reflect the difficulty mothers may have in obtaining part-time employment.

The autocorrelation coefficients were high, indicating that persons with abnormally high rates of unemployment in one year are likely to have a high rate in the following year.

Chapter 9
DISABILITY AND TRANSFER INCOME*

This chapter describes the disability and transfer income operating characteristics of the model. These characteristics are designed to provide an appropriate framework in which to analyze the impacts of changes in relevant government policy or demographic trends on the existing transfer payment structure in this country. The impacts can be observed in the form of changes in program costs or in the "well-offness" of families in the sample population.

The disability operating characteristic is an auxiliary one. It is used to provide the right distribution and number of disabilities in the population each year. The labor market submodel takes a person's disability status into account. Subsequently, labor force behavior and disability status are used together to determine eligibility for many of the transfer programs.

In the transfer income operating characteristic the following cash payment programs are simulated: social security, pensions, unemployment compensation, aid to families with dependent children, (AFDC), supplemental security income (SSI), and food stamps. With the exception of pensions, the administrative rules of the specific programs governing eligibility, dollar amounts, duration of payments, and so forth are incorporated in the model.

Compromises are required to limit the size and processing burden of dealing with these transfer programs in the context of the entire microsimulation model. For example, program rules which are peculiar to particular states are collapsed into more general rules which apply either on a regional or national basis in the simulation. Survey data were used to build a module to approximate the distribution of income from pensions other than social security. In some respects the transfer payment operating characteristic serves as a base upon which one could selectively build a more elaborate set of rules for a particular program.

This chapter is primarily descriptive rather than a defense of the approximations used to simplify program rules or an explanation of the alternative approaches considered and discarded. Space does not permit such an extensive treatment here although some program modules have

---

* Sheila Zedlewski had the main responsibility for this chapter and the work it represents.

been described in more detail elsewhere and are referenced accordingly. It is hoped that this discussion focuses attention on the more important problems of simulating these characteristics.

The transfer programs are described in the order in which they are simulated. It is important to bear this in mind because some programs take into account transfer income provided by other payment systems. It should also be noted that the rate of participation in each program is controlled by the users; for example, it is generally known that not nearly as many families participate in the food stamp program as are eligible. To account for this, each module can eliminate eligible families from participation via a stochastic or random process. The historical caseload for a program can be matched in a simulation year by using a two-step process. First, one simulation produces the number of program eligibles given the module rules. Secondly, this number is compared to the number of actual participants that year. The percentage by which eligibles exceed participants is used to eliminate eligible persons or families on a random basis in subsequent simulations.

Disability

Disability is an important determinant of labor force participation and of the receipt of various transfer payments. In 1970 11 percent of persons aged 16–64 who were not in school or inmates of institutions were disabled to some extent. More than half of these disabled persons were out of the labor force, and many were eligible for public transfer programs such as social security, AFDC, and SSI. This operating characteristic predicts the disability status of each adult in the model's sample population. An adult is defined as one who is at least age 14, and thus may enter the labor market. Each year, entry into and exit from the status of being disabled is simulated.

The University of Michigan Institute for Social Research Panel Study of Income Dynamics (PSID) was used to estimate the disability entry and exit functions. Beginning in interview year 1969, disability status was recorded for each person in the PSID sample. The actual survey question was: "Is this individual disabled or does he require extra care?" The possible responses were: yes – disabled; yes – requires extra care; or no. This same question was asked again in interview years 1970 through 1972.[1] Thus the dependent variable in this analysis is a

---

1. More detailed information on disability, such as length and type of limitation, was recorded for heads of families. However, for simplicity it was decided to use only the disability information available for each person in the PSID sample.

dichotomous one. Specifically, the value of the dependent variable, disability status, was recorded as "1" for only those who answered: yes – is disabled. The value was set to "0" for all others. Furthermore, the analysis for purposes of the model was limited to only those persons who were in the panel study all five years and who were at least 14 by 1972.

The PSID disability data were organized with 1969 as a base year at which time each person's initial disability state is known. In subsequent years, those of the nondisabled population who report a disability are termed *entries*. Meanwhile, some of those who were disabled in any one or more of the years 1969 through 1971 report leaving that status, and these are termed *exits*. The probability functions to predict disability entries and exits were estimated using an average rate of disability over the three-year period so that any anomalies in the data in a single year would be obscured. The disability rates were computed by dividing the pooled entries and exits observations into various subgroups based on such characteristics as age and education level. The observed probability of being disabled, $\hat{P}_j$, of the jth subgroup of size N_j was defined as

$$\hat{P}_j = \sum_{i=1}^{N_j} \frac{X_i}{N_j}$$

where $X_i = 1$ if disabled
$ = 0$ is not disabled

Functional Form

In order to constrain the estimated probabilities to a 0-to-1 range for all values of the independent variables, a logit model was chosen which fits the disability probability to the independent variables with an S-shaped curve instead of with a straight line. This model can easily be put into a linear form for estimation purposes. For each observation (j) this model states:

$$Ln \left(\frac{P_j}{1 - P_j} \right) = \sum_{k=0}^{n} \beta_k X_{kj} + U_j$$

where $X_{oj} = 1$; where $\hat{P}_j$ was substituted for P_j to permit estimation of the β's; where X_k represents the independent variables; and where U_j is a random variable for the jth group. The ratio $P_j/(1 - P_j)$ constitutes the odds that a person is disabled, which gives rise to the popular expression of "log-odds" model for the logit transformation.

Because $\hat{P}_j$ is binomally distributed, the variance of U_j is not a constant as is normally assumed for least squares estimation. Thus weights[2]

2. This weighting procedure was developed in A. A. Cook and A. J. Gross, *Estimation Techniques for Dependent Logit Models*, The Rand Corporation, Rand Memorandum RM-5734 PR, November 1968.

were constructed to meet the condition of homoscedasticity which are of the following form:

$$W_j = [N_j \hat{P}_j (1 - \hat{P}_j)]^{1/2}$$

And the model,

$$W_j \, Ln \left(\frac{P_j}{1 - P_j} \right) = W_j \sum_{k=0}^{n} B_k \, X_{kj} + W_j \, U_j$$

was estimated using ordinary least squares regression analysis.

Disability Status Equations

The results of the logit regression forms used to predict disability, entries, and exits are presented in Table 9-1. An entry of zero indicates that the variable was omitted from the equation. Although numerous equations were tested only results of two are presented—those actually implemented in the model. Cell size imposed limitations on the

TABLE 9-1

LOGIT FUNCTIONS TO PREDICT DISABILITY STATUS[a,b]

Dependent Variable: $Ln \left(\frac{P_j}{1 - P_j} \right)$ where P_j = probability of being disabled for different subgroups

Explanatory Variable	Disability Entry Equation	Disability Exit Equation
Constant	−2.979	−.510
Age: <35	0	.639
Age: 35–44	.344**	0
Age: 45–54	.833	−.417
Age: 55–64	1.153	−.647
Age: 65+	1.521	−.516
Nonwhites	.301*	0
Married Female	−.306*	0
Female	0	.271
Nonwhite Female	0	−.364
Education < 12 years	0	−.201*
Corrected R²	.64	.81

a. A zero table entry indicates that the explanatory variable was omitted from the equation.
b. All variables are significant at the .01 level, except those indicated by a single asterisk (*), which are significant at the .05 level, or by a double asterisk (**), which are not significant.

number of ways in which the data could be categorized. The final explanatory variables included in the equation to predict disability entries are age, race, sex, and marital status. It was originally hypothesized that education level would also be an important explanatory variable. It was assumed that persons with a low education level would have a higher probability of being in jobs with a high health risk and would thus be more apt to become disabled. However, none of the variables tested to represent this differential proved significant.

In the entry equation results shown, the disability probability increases gradually with each ten-year age interval dummy. This phenomenon is supported by all of the available disability data. In addition, nonwhites have a larger chance of entering the disabled population than whites. But married females have a smaller risk of becoming disabled than single females or males. The equation does a fair job of explaining the variance among subgroups—the corrected R^2 was .64.

The disability exit function shown in Table 9-1 suggests that older persons, those with a low level of education, and nonwhite females have significantly lower probabilities of recovery than other population groups. But younger persons (under 35 years) and females have significantly greater odds of recovery than their counterparts. In contrast to the entry equation, education level did prove to be a significant explanatory variable. Specifically, those with a low level of education (less than high school completion) have a lower chance of recovery than those who at least completed high school. As discussed above this variable serves as a proxy for occupation. That is, those with a low education level are more likely to be in blue collar jobs and thus are more likely to be exposed to the risk of severe injury and long term disability. A substantial percentage of the variation, 81 percent, is explained by the exit equation.

Social Security[3]

The social security program, the largest transfer program in the United States, provides cash benefits to about one out of every eight persons in the country. The program, formally known as Old-Age, Survivors and Disability Insurance (OASDI), is designed to partially replace income from work that is lost to workers and their dependents because of the worker's retirement, disability severe enough to prevent substantial gainful employment, or death. Because of the program's importance, this module attempts to simulate its cash benefit provisions by modelling the

---

3. For a more detailed description of this program module, see "Simulation of Social Security," Sheila Zedlewski, Urban Institute Working Paper 980-4, December 1974.

administrative rules as closely as practicable. The following description of the module uses the 1970 social security. rules as its initial reference point. All of the changes in the law which occurred through 1974 are incorporated.

Eligibility or Coverage

The major principle underlying this transfer program is that security benefits grow out of one's own specific work experience. Entitlement to benefits is based on the duration of employment and the level of earnings under work covered by the social security system. Thus, there are two crucial pieces of information needed to properly simulate the rules of the program—the amount of time, measured in quarters of a year, a worker has been covered under social security and the worker's earnings during that period. A worker's experience under the system can be simulated fairly easily once his or her past work history is determined. The difficulty then, since the initial OASDI credits are unknown, is to assign representative work histories to the population in the model. Cumulative quarters of coverage and social security earnings must be estimated for each adult in the initial sample.

   The first step in the initial assignment process is to determine which persons in the initial sample population are in employment covered by the social security system. The insurance status of these persons is termed *currently covered*. In 1970, 90 percent of all paid employment was covered.[4] The major types of employment excluded were federal civil service, some of the self-employed, and some state and local government employees. Thus, some of the persons in the initial sample population who are employed in these categories are excluded from current coverage on a probabilistic basis.[5] The coverage status of each person, used in the assignment of initial credits and in determination of benefit eligibility, is maintained in the simulation. All persons in the model who have a currently covered status initially maintain it unless they drop out of the labor force. In addition, each new entry into the labor force is assigned a coverage status probabilistically. This procedure is an oversimplification because some persons do move in and out of covered employment during a continuous work career. The extent of the error introduced by this procedure is unknown, but is somewhat dependent upon the length of the simulation. That is, in longer simulations more employment movement would take place and not be represented.

4. Table 25, *Social Security Bulletin, Annual Statistical Supplement,* 1972.
5. See Zedlewski, op. cit., page 3, for details of this procedure.

TABLE 9-2

MALES NOT COVERED IN 1969 BY SOCIAL SECURITY

Probability of Obtaining Specified Quarters of Coverage

Age	40[b]	36	31	26	21	16	11	6	0
<19	.000	.000	.000	.000	.000	.000	.000	.006	1.0
19–23	.000	.000	.000	.001	.004	.018	.070	.260	1.0
24–28	.005	.016	.045	.103	.193	.313	.459	.625	1.0
29–33	.090	.141	.214	.298	.394	.491	.601	.697	1.0
34–38	.179	.225	.281	.366	.429	.512	.598	.701	1.0
39–43	.256	.292	.345	.398	.453	.530	.587	.623	1.0
44–48	.285	.320	.360	.406	.455	.512	.584	.690	1.0
49–53	.345	.374	.418	.463	.514	.580	.651	.737	1.0
54–58	.362	.453	.493	.538	.592	.648	.710	.783	1.0
59–63	.484	.517	.558	.602	.651	.704	.761	.826	1.0

Header spanning 40[b] through 0: QUARTERS[a]

a. The probabilities are given for having obtained the specified number of quarters *or more* of coverage.
b. Forty quarters assures benefits for life

TABLE 9-3

FEMALES NOT COVERED IN 1969 BY SOCIAL SECURITY

Probability of Obtaining Specified Quarters of Coverage

Age	40[b]	36	31	26	21	16	11	6	0
<19	.000	.000	.000	.000	.000	.000	.000	.003	1.0
19–23	.000	.000	.000	.000	.002	.012	.054	.216	1.0
24–28	.001	.004	.017	.051	.121	.241	.412	.634	1.0
29–33	.032	.060	.108	.180	.285	.414	.567	.733	1.0
34–38	.093	.129	.188	.263	.361	.475	.606	.752	1.0
39–43	.102	.177	.235	.307	.393	.490	.604	.737	1.0
44–48	.155	.190	.240	.304	.380	.472	.581	.709	1.0
49–53	.179	.213	.262	.320	.390	.473	.572	.694	1.0
54–58	.187	.224	.271	.325	.389	.465	.558	.682	1.0
59–63	.224	.255	.298	.348	.409	.484	.570	.688	1.0

QUARTERS[a]

a. The probabilities are given for having obtained the specified number of quarters *or more* of coverage.
b. Forty quarters assures benefits for life.

Data from the Social Security Administration's 1 percent Continuous Work History Sample[6] were used to estimate probabilities for the imputation of quarters of coverage in the base year. The original data show the number of persons – by insurance status, sex, and age – who fall into specific intervals of quarters of coverage. Tables 9-2 through 9-5 show the probability of having x or more quarters of coverage given that person's sex, insurance status, and age. The number of quarters assigned, x, ranges from 0 to 40, the maximum shown in the raw data which is enough to insure a person for life. Because of data limitations,

TABLE 9-4

MALES COVERED IN 1969 BY SOCIAL SECURITY

Probability of Obtaining Specified Quarters of Coverage

Age	QUARTERS[a]							
	40[b]	36	31	26	21	16	11	6
<19	.000	.000	.000	.001	.003	.021	.160	1.0
19–23	.000	.002	.009	.052	.176	.407	.732	1.0
24–28	.173	.305	.504	.707	.852	.939	.983	1.0
29–33	.787	.852	.906	.944	.966	.981	.991	1.0
34–38	.905	.929	.950	.969	.979	.987	.994	1.0
39–43	.942	.954	.967	.977	.985	.992	.996	1.0
44–48	.951	.961	.971	.980	.987	.993	.997	1.0
49–53	.956	.964	.973	.981	.987	.994	.997	1.0
54–58	.955	.963	.972	.979	.986	.993	.997	1.0
59–63	.949	.958	.967	.975	.983	.992	.997	1.0
64–68	.923	.940	.955	.966	.977	.991	.997	1.0
69+	.792	.799	.835	.869	.902	.946	.975	1.0

a. The probabilities are given for having obtained the specified number of quarters *or more* of coverage.
b. Forty quarters assures benefits for life.

coverage is not imputed to persons who are over age 64 and *not* currently covered. Most of the persons in this coverage-age category are already receiving a benefit if their coverage was sufficient for entitlement.

The quarters of coverage attribute is updated each year for each worker with current coverage. A quarter of coverage corresponds to a calendar quarter in which a worker was paid at least $50. The number of quarters credited to each worker is derived from the number of hours the worker was in the labor force, his unemployment rate, and earnings.

6. Unpublished data for 1969. Furnished by Michael Resnic of the Office of Research and Statistics, Social Security Administration.

TABLE 9-5

FEMALES COVERED IN 1969 BY SOCIAL SECURITY

Probability of Obtaining Specified Quarters of Coverage

Age	QUARTERS[a]							
	40[b]	36	31	26	21	16	11	6
<19	.000	.000	.001	.001	.003	.009	.092	1.0
19–23	.000	.000	.002	.012	.084	.255	.586	1.0
24–28	.049	.110	.233	.416	.620	.792	.927	1.0
29–33	.394	.485	.599	.705	.799	.883	.955	1.0
34–38	.538	.603	.686	.767	.841	.911	.965	1.0
39–43	.662	.703	.769	.835	.891	.938	.976	1.0
44–48	.705	.756	.814	.865	.911	.949	.980	1.0
49–53	.757	.796	.842	.885	.922	.953	.981	1.0
54–58	.776	.801	.846	.886	.921	.951	.979	1.0
59–63	.799	.834	.870	.902	.931	.962	.984	1.0
64–68	.785	.823	.862	.898	.928	.964	.989	1.0
69+	.615	.657	.711	.763	.819	.884	.942	1.0

a. The probabilities are given for having obtained the specified number of quarters *or more* of coverage.
b. Forty quarters assures benefits for life.

This module assumes a continuous spell of employment during the year and a continuous spell of unemployment. A quarter is earned with each 200 hours of work (employment two eight-hour days per week for 3 months) and any fraction of this, assuming earnings are sufficient. Of course, each worker is limited to a maximum of four quarters per year. But if unemployment was experienced, the maximum number of quarters that can be earned is reduced by the number of full quarters (480 hours) of unemployment. In addition, anyone whose earnings exceed the maximum taxable wages for the year automatically receives four quarters, as is provided by the law.[7]

The second crucial piece of information which is necessary to simulate cash benefits under OASDI is cumulative earnings while covered under the system. Again, this attribute must first be imputed to each adult in the initial sample and then updated during each year of simulation. In reality, earnings up to the taxable maximum are recorded each year a person works under employment covered by OASDI. At the time of benefit eligibility, this information is used to compute a worker's average monthly earnings. Essentially, total earnings are divided by the number of months in his "computation years"—five less than the

7. See "Annual Maximum Taxable Earnings," *Social Security Bulletin, Annual Statistical Supplement,* 1972, page 27.

number of calendar years since 1950 or age 21. The omission of five years permits the five lowest earning years to be excluded from the computation. Cumulative earnings under social security since 1955 or age 26, if later, are carried in the simulation model. This makes the simplifying assumption that the lowest earnings years for all persons are the earliest ones. Actually, for persons with continuous work careers under social security—those entitled to relatively high benefits—this assumption should be fairly realistic. But this procedure may understate the entitlement of persons with noncontinuous work careers. Their lowest earnings years, some of which may occur during the simulation, are those in which they are out of the labor force or not covered by OASDI.

In order to determine the initial cumulative earnings attribute at entry into the model, an earnings profile is imputed based upon a worker's current wages. Using the 1 percent Sample Longitudinal Employee-Employer Data File, Nancy and Richard Ruggles have provided some new insights into birth cohort patterns of earnings.[8] Although cross-sectional profiles of earnings versus age show earnings leveling, then declining with advancing age, they found a continual rise in earnings exhibited by every birth cohort up to the point of retirement at age 65 using longitudinal data. Thus, the imputation of cumulative earnings in this model makes the assumption that earnings continually rise over a work career. In conjunction with their work, the Ruggles produced tabulations showing the percent change in average earnings by age, sex, and race over the period 1957–1969. From this data, average annual rates of increase were derived using a standard compounded interest formula.[9] These average rates are shown in Table 9-6.

Given the current earnings of a worker and the annual rate of earnings increase for the particular age-race-sex category, the same formula can be used to approximate a worker's earnings in any year since 1955. Initial cumulative earnings are derived by summing a worker's estimated "social security earnings" over the years in which he or she worked in covered employment. By "social security earnings" is meant the estimated earned income up to the legal taxable maximum for that year.

To approximate the years during which a person worked in covered employment, two procedures are used, depending on whether the person is currently covered or not. All of the coverage is assumed to be in the most recent past for workers currently covered. Therefore, a worker's starting year of coverage is found by subtracting the number of years

---

8. Nancy and Richard Ruggles, "The Anatomy of Earnings Behavior," National Bureau of Economic Research, May 1974.

9. That is, $A = P(1 + r)^n$, where A = current earnings, P = initial earnings, r = average rate of increase and n = number of years.

of coverage (quarters ÷ 4) from the current year. Earnings are accumulated to the present beginning either in 1955, in the year in which the worker reached age 26, or in the starting year of coverage, whichever occurs *last*.

If a worker is not currently covered and is a recent dropout from the labor force, the starting year of coverage is calculated as the year in

TABLE 9-6

AVERAGE ANNUAL RATE OF EARNINGS INCREASE BY AGE, SEX, AND RACE

	WHITE		NONWHITE	
Age	Male	Female	Male	Female
25–29	6.42%	5.79%	7.39%	9.37%
30–34	4.72	3.94	5.58	6.38
35–39	4.82	3.94	5.58	6.33
40–44	5.02	4.37	5.49	6.25
45–49	5.21	4.60	5.58	6.29
50–54	4.82	4.20	5.90	5.85
55–59	4.57	4.60	4.97	6.16
60–64	4.47	5.31	5.16	7.19
65–69	4.60	4.92	4.26	4.77

Source: Computed from Percent Change in Average Earnings by Age, Sex, and Race, 1957–1969, in "The Anatomy of Earnings Behavior," Nancy, D. Ruggles and Richard Ruggles, National Bureau of Economic Research, May 1974, page 22.

which the person dropped out minus the number of years of coverage.[10] For all other persons who are not currently covered, the starting year of coverage is assumed to be 1937 or the year in which that person reached age 21, if later. Earnings are accumulated for these groups over whatever years of coverage extend into the period beginning in 1955 or the year in which the person reached age 26, if later, and ending in the year in which coverage is exhausted. There are some persons who are not currently covered and have no earnings recorded because they are out of the labor force. Their current expected earnings is estimated by imputing a wage rate using the proper labor market equation multiplied by average hours worked, arbitrarily set to 1600.

Each year of the simulation, the cumulative earnings attribute is updated for each worker covered under social security. Current earnings,

10. Recent dropouts—less than 10 years—can be distinguished on the Census Public Use Sample using the variable "Year Last Worked."

up to the legal taxable maximum for the year, are simply added to the cumulative amount.

Benefits

All social security benefits are based upon a person's primary insurance amount (PIA). At the time of the retirement, disability, or death of a worker with sufficient social security coverage, a PIA is computed based upon the worker's average monthly wages (AMW). A person's AMW is simply calculated as his cumulative earnings divided by the number of months which have elapsed since 1955 or the year in which the worker reached age 26, if later. From this, the primary insurance amount is computed according to the statutory formula for the current year.[11] This PIA determines the maximum amount of benefits a worker and his dependents can receive. It is computed and saved for a person at the time of initial benefit receipt.[12] But a person's PIA can change during the simulation. For example, a benefit can be "lost" or a legislated benefit increase may occur.

A person with sufficient quarters of coverage is eligible for retirement benefits at age 62, although the benefit is actuarily reduced prior to age 65. A worker has sufficient quarters for retirement if at least one quarter was ·earned for each calendar year elapsing after 1950 or the year in which he became 21. A primary insurance amount is computed in the model as soon as a person is eligible for any benefit. That person's earnings behavior determines whether the retirement benefit is actually accepted. That is, as long as current earnings do not drive the benefit to zero under the prevailing tax law, that person receives a payment. For example, in 1974 gross earnings of $2,400 or more prevent a person from receiving any benefit. (This assumes perfect knowledge of the system on the part of workers, which of course is not necessarily the case in real life.) Once a benefit is accepted, the basic PIA is frozen for the remainder of the simulation, except for legislated percentage increases. If the benefit is not accepted, new earnings will be included in the cumulative amount.

Dependents of the retired worker are also entitled to benefits. A wife or a husband age 62 or over may be a dependent, but the case of a husband receiving a benefit is relatively infrequent because he must have

---

11. For these formulas see the *Social Security Bulletin, Annual Statistical Supplement,* 1972, page 16.

12. The PIA of each person who is already receiving benefits in the initial sample is computed from the recorded benefit amount in an initialization process.

been receiving at least one-half of his support from his wife at the time of her entitlement. Therefore, the model omits this type of benefit. Furthermore, if a wife is entitled to a retirement benefit based on her own employment record as well as on her dependent status, she will receive the higher of the two benefits. A wife under age 62 who has in her care the retired worker's dependent child (under age 18) may also receive a benefit. In addition, any children under age 18 or age 18–22 and attending school full-time may receive benefits. The basic dependent's benefit is one-half the PIA of the retired worker. However, the total family benefit based on one worker's PIA is subject to a maximum.[13]

Disability benefits are available only if a worker is disabled to the extent he or she cannot engage in substantial work activity. The OASDI system generally regards average monthly earnings of $140 or more as a demonstration of substantial work activity. Thus, in this module, annual earnings above $1,680 are sufficient to disqualify a disabled worker from these benefits.

A special insured status is also required for the payment of social security disability benefits. In addition to being fully insured (at least one quarter earned for each calendar year since 1950 or age 21, if later), a disabled worker must have been engaged in covered employment for at least one-half of the quarters in the last ten years. In the simulation current social security coverage at the time of disability is used as a proxy for this test. The dependent's benefits and family maximum tests, described above, are also applicable for disability benefits.

When an insured worker dies, the surviving spouse and dependent children may be eligible for benefits based upon the deceased worker's PIA.[14] A widow may receive benefits if she is at least age 60, has a dependent child under 18 years of age, or is at least age 50 and disabled to the extent that she is totally unable to work.[15] Benefits are assigned to unmarried dependent children under age 18 or between age 18 and 21 and in school.

The benefit rate for a widow without dependent children is 100 percent of her husband's PIA. It is 75 percent for a widow caring for the deceased worker's child. The dependent child's rate is also 75 percent. The entire family benefit is subject to a maximum constraint as discussed previously.

13. The maximum is based upon the worker's AMW. See the *Social Security Bulletin, Annual Statistical Supplement,* 1972, page 21.

14. In reality, a worker's dependent parents may also be eligible. However, this provision applies very infrequently and is not simulated.

15. A widower is also entitled to benefits if he meets one of these conditions and has been dependent on the deceased wife for at least one-half of his support. This benefit is so infrequent — a fraction of one percent of the social security benefits awarded — that it is not simulated.

After the primary insurance amount and potential family benefit is calculated, each family member's current earnings are considered before the final family benefit is assigned. Under the annual earnings test, deductions may be made from the benefits of persons under age 72 if earnings are in excess of the yearly exempt amount.[16] Excess earnings of the primary beneficiary are charged against the total family benefit. But the excess earnings of an auxiliary or survivor (wife, widow, child, etc.) are only charged against that person's benefit.

It should be noted that during the simulation a change in a family member's status may cause the loss of a benefit or the conversion to a different type of benefit. A beneficiary must meet the proper categorical requirements described in this section in each simulation year.

Pensions

To predict which families receive pensions and for what amounts, use was made of the University of Michigan Panel Study of Income Dynamics (PSID). The pensions reported on this survey as one amount include government employee pensions (military and federal, state, and local government), private pensions, and veterans pensions. Because there are differences between these programs, it would be more desirable to treat them as separate payments. However, separate program modules which would attempt to model the administrative rules of these programs would be quite complex and impose heavy processing burdens on the model. This arises primarily because eligibility for pensions is a function of the employment experience of an individual over his entire work career. This type of information is not available from a survey and is burdensome to retain during a simulation. Thus, this pensions module is suitable to approximate only the distribution of this type of transfer payment among families in the model.

Four years of data from the panel study were used, representing years 1969–1972. The first year of data was used to estimate the probability that a particular family in an initial sample population receives a pension. The later three years of data were pooled and used to estimate the probability that a family receives a new pension in any simulation year. It is assumed that the head of the family receives and retains the pension from one year to the next. When that person dies the pension is removed from the pool of family income resources, although any survivor may later qualify separately. The observations were limited to only

16. The earnings tests for recent years can be found in the *Social Security Handbook,* 5th Edition, 1974, page 289.

those families whose head was over 59 years old, so that most families receiving a pension due to disability and not retirement were excluded.

Pension Receipt

The probabilities to predict the receipt of a pension were computed via simple cross tabulations. The explanatory variables chosen were those which reflect the commonality among the retirement programs noted earlier. These variables are sex, age, education, race, marital status, and hours worked.

Sex was included as one of the explanatory variables in order to capture the differences in work patterns between males and females. Pension programs provide retirement income to those who have left employment after a substantial length of continuous employment. Since this type of work pattern is more typical of males than females, they are more likely to receive a pension. In addition, females who are widows and report a pension may actually be entitled to it because of their deceased husband's employment rather than their own.

Age was included as an explanatory variable because it is an important factor in the receipt of a pension for all of the programs included. A full pension usually can only be received at age 65 in private pension systems. Federal employees may retire with full pension benefits at age 60 after completing 20 years of service.

Education and race were also used as explanatory variables. These variables are used as proxies to reflect the differences in pension entitlement between occupation groups. Professional and technical workers are more likely to receive a pension than other occupation groups.[17] Since occupation is not available in the PSID survey for retired workers, these proxies were used to indicate the likelihood of being in this occupation group. That is, persons who are white and persons who have a college education are more likely to receive a pension.

Hours worked was also used as an explanatory variable to predict pension receipt for persons over age 59. For all of the pensions included, persons who are currently employed are less likely to have pension entitlement than those who have retired. This reflects, in part, the greater likelihood of continued employment for persons in jobs without pension benefits since they are less likely to face mandatory retirement. It also reflects the hypothesis that the lack of retirement income is a factor in the need or willingness to continue working.

17. Walter Kolodrubetz reports this finding in "Private Retirement Benefits and Relationship to Earnings: Survey of New Beneficiaries," *Social Security Bulletin,* May 1973.

Tables 9-7 and 9-8 show the probabilities of a particular family head over age 59 receiving a pension in the base year and each simulation year, respectively. The results for the base year prediction follow the expectations described above. For example, males with at least twelve years of education, who are at least age 65 and who worked less than 1,000 hours for the year have a higher probability of receiving a pension than any other group. In addition, females who are widows are more likely to receive a pension than other single females. The hours worked explanatory variable was not used for females because so few were still in the labor force. In addition, race was a better discriminator than education for females to reflect probable differences in past socioeconomic status.

The results shown in Table 9-8 which are used to simulate whether a family receives a *new* pension were not as satisfactory. Male heads of families overall are no more likely to receive a new pension than females. Education does not prove to be a good discriminator: it makes little difference for males, and females with a high education level are only slightly more likely to receive a new pension than other females. Particularly among males, the probability of receiving a new pension is greatest for the age bracket 64–66, reflecting the typical retirement age of workers.

Pension Income

Observations on those who received a pension were extracted from the pooled PSID data to estimate a regression equation to predict the amount of pension income received. In general, the amount of pension income under all of these programs is positively related to years of service and past earnings. In the case of veterans pensions the amount is also negatively related to current earnings. One would expect highest private pensions to be reported by professional and technical workers and the lowest pensions to be reported by unskilled and semi-skilled workers. Again, in the absence of earnings histories, other variables were used to show these differences in pension incomes. Dummy variables for education were included. The level of family wealth assets was also used as an indicator of high past earnings. Because white males who are married typically reach the highest levels of earnings, these interaction terms were also included as explanatory variables.

Many private pension plans reduce the amount of a pension by some fraction of social security benefits. Thus, an explanatory dummy variable was included to indicate this. This variable may also show that those who are not eligible for social security are receiving higher pen-

TABLE 9-7

PROBABILITY OF RECEIVING A PENSION IN BASE YEAR (1969): FAMILY HEADS, 59 YEARS OF AGE OR OLDER

Male	Annual Hours Worked: 1000 Hours or Less		Annual Hours Worked: More Than 1000 Hours	
	Education less than 12 years	Education 12 years or more	Education less than 12 years	Education 12 years or more
AGE: 59–64	.40	.40	.03	.14
AGE: 65–69	.44	.75	.28	.19
AGE: 70+	.34	.55	.50	.50

Female	Widow		Not Widow	
	White	Nonwhite	White	Nonwhite
AGE: 59–64	.24	22	.15	.03
AGE: 65+	.40	.31	.45	.25

Source: Cross tabulations from the PSID, year 1969.

TABLE 9-8

PROBABILITY OF RECEIVING A NEW PENSION IN BASE YEAR (1969): FAMILY HEADS, 59 YEARS OF AGE OR OLDER

Male	Education: 0–11 Years	Education: 12–15 Years	Education: 16+ Years
AGE: 59–63	.05	.05	.03
AGE: 64–66	.12	.18	.07
AGE: 67+	.07	.09	.10

Female	Education: 0–11 Years	Education: 12–15 Years	Education: 16+ Years
AGE: 59–63	.04	.04	.12
AGE: 64–66	.07	.24	.01
AGE: 67+	.06	.09	.12

Source: Cross tabulations from the PSID, years 1970–1972.

sions under plans which are not just designed to supplement social security. The major example of this type of plan is the Federal Employees Retirement Program.

The regression results are shown in Table 9-9. The fraction of the population variance explained is .24. All of the variables discussed were

TABLE 9-9

AMOUNT OF PENSION INCOME
(in 1958 dollars)

Variables	Coefficient	T-Ratio
Constant term	1970.09	12.32
Education less than 12 yrs.	−974.70	6.97
Education 12–15 years	−373.51	2.42
Married Male	485.00	3.88
White Male	333.16	2.62
Some Social Security	−481.73	4.52
Assets in 1958 Dollars	0.19	9.15
Corrected R^2: .24 Standard Error: 1328.88		

significant at least at the .05 level. The higher pensions are received by those with a high education level, white males, married males, and those with substantial assets. The presence of concurrent social security benefits has a depressing effect on the pension amount.

Unemployment Compensation

Unemployment insurance is a federal-state system designed to provide temporary wage loss compensation to workers who are involuntarily unemployed. Federal law establishes the framework of this transfer program across all states. But outside of the minimum federal requirements, there is considerable variation in the program rules among states. In this program module the federal rules are simulated, and the state variability has been collapsed by region. Insurance coverage requirements are simulated for all members of the work force. Once a worker experiences a spell of unemployment, an annual benefit is computed if he is eligible. These procedures are described in the following two sections.

Coverage

Unemployment insurance coverage is similar among all states. The largest groups in the labor force with little or no protection are workers in local governments, domestic service in private households, and agriculture. These groups account for over 85 percent of the wage and salary workers not covered. The remaining types of employment not covered include some workers in state governments and in nonprofit organizations. In the simulation model neither industry group nor occupation is

TABLE 9-10

PROBABILITY OF UNEMPLOYMENT INSURANCE PROTECTION

| Year | EMPLOYMENT (in thousands) | | |
	Total	Covered by Unemployment Insurance	Probability of Coverage
1970	78,627	59,526	.757
1971	79,120	59,375	.750
1972	81,702	66,900	.819
1973	84,409	70,379	.834

Source: From Tables C-25 and C-28, *Economic Report of the President,* Washington, Government Printing Office, 1975.

simulated. Thus, exclusion from insurance protection is made to occur on a purely stochastic basis. Table 9-10 shows the probability that a worker is covered. Because there has been a trend toward greater coverage of workers during the 1970s, this has been incorporated into the model.[18]

A worker must also meet some qualifying requirements which are meant to demonstrate that he has a substantial and recent attachment to the labor force. There are no federal standards as to these qualifying requirements. States generally use employment experience in the five quarters preceding the quarter in which a worker becomes unemployed as the base period to determine this type of eligibility. In this module, the prior year's labor force experience is used as a proxy for the base period. The first qualifying requirement specifies the minimum earnings a worker must have had in the base period to become eligible for

18. The user may adjust the probability in years outside of the historical period shown.

TABLE 9-11

MINIMUM ANNUAL
EARNINGS REQUIREMENT

Region	Minimum
North Central	$537
Northeast	676
South	467
West	737

Source: Derived from Table 301, *Comparison of State Unemployment Insurance Laws,* Washington, Government Printing Office, 1974.

benefits. This type of requirement is used in all states. Table 9-11 shows the average minimum in each Census region.

The second qualifying requirement specifies a minimum amount of time employed in the base period. Table 9-12 gives, by Census region, the probability that a covered worker will be subject to this requirement since it is applicable only in some of the states. Then the table shows further the amount of work time required for an individual to be eligible, expressed in hours. Thus, in this module if a worker is covered but he has not had sufficient earnings in the base period, he will not receive compensation for the current unemployment spell. Similarly, if a covered worker is simulated to be subject to a minimum hours requirement and he has not worked at least the minimum number of hours, he will not receive compensation.

Finally, some workers are disqualified from receiving benefits because they voluntarily quit work without good cause, were discharged

TABLE 9-12

MINIMUM HOURS WORKED REQUIREMENT

Region	Probability of Residing Where Minimum Work Rules Apply	Hours Needed for Eligibility
North Central	.490	595
Northeast	.546	665
South	.108	700
West	.220	595

Source: Derived from Table 301, *Comparison of State Unemployment Income Laws,* Washington, Government Printing Office, 1974.

because of misconduct, or refused suitable work. With few exceptions these disqualifications are applicable in all states. The national denial rate in 1973, .028, is used to simulate this type of disqualification on a purely random basis.

Benefit Amount

The unemployment insurance program seeks to provide eligible unemployed workers with a weekly benefit amount representing at least one-half of their weekly wage loss. However, in each state this replacement is limited by a maximum weekly benefit amount. In the simulation a worker's average weekly wage during the base period is approximated simply as his annual earnings divided by the number of weeks worked. (A 35-hour work week is assumed.) Table 9-13 shows the average wage replacement rate in each Census region. As can be seen, the variation in these rates is quite small. The average maximum weekly benefit in force in 1974 is given in Table 9-14 by region. An unemployed worker's weekly benefit is the smaller of (a) his average weekly wage times the applicable replacement rate, or (b) the weekly maximum for the region in which he lives.

The other component of the annual benefit amount is the number of weeks unemployment compensation was received. The maximum number of weeks for which benefits can be received in most states is 26. Thus a worker's annual benefit is the weekly benefit amount times the number of weeks he was unemployed, or times 26, whichever is smaller. In the simulation model, if a worker is unemployed in two consecutive

TABLE 9-13

AVERAGE WEEKLY WAGE
REPLACEMENT RATE, 1974

Region	Average Rate
North Central	.512
Northeast	.558
South	.460
West	.480

Source: Derived from Table 301, *Comparison of State Unemployment Insurance Laws,* Washington, Government Printing Office, 1974.

198

TABLE 9-14

MAXIMUM BENEFIT PER
WEEK, 1974

Region	Maximum
North Central	$68.00
Northeast	84.00
South	64.00
West	85.00

Source: Derived from Table 301, *Comparison of State Unemployment Insurance Laws,* Washington, Government Printing Office, 1974.

years, this "spell" of unemployment is assumed to be continuous. That is, the total number of weeks for which benefits can be received during this entire period is constrained to the maximum.

Aid to Families with Dependent Children[19]

The Aid to Families with Dependent Children (AFDC) program provides financial assistance to needy children who are deprived of support because of the death, incapacity, or absence of a parent. In 1974 the program served about 3 million American families. While this transfer program has federal requirements, it is state administered and some of the eligibility and benefit conditions are optional at the state level. All of the state program variability has been collapsed into regional variability. State AFDC participation data for 1967, 1971, and 1974 were used for this purpose. Each state share of the AFDC caseload was calculated as the number of AFDC participants in the state divided by the total number of AFDC participants in that region. These shares and the mean for the three years of data are shown in Table 9-15. In many cases the region of residence should adequately capture the program variability because the state's rules tend to be similar within region. The AFDC rules in effect in 1970 were used as the model's base, but some major changes in the law since then are also incorporated.

19. Much of this model was drawn from one done by Barbara Boland of The Urban Institute, as described in *Studies in Public Welfare,* Paper No. 12, Washington, D.C., Government Printing Office, November 1973.

Coverage

The unit eligible for AFDC in the simulation is the nuclear family — one or more parents and their minor children. A minor child is defined as one who is under 18 years of age. In most states, the definition is extended to 18–20 years of age for full-time students. Table 9-16 shows regional probabilities of coverage of this latter group. In the simulation, children in this category are eligible for AFDC benefits if a uniform random number is less than or equal to the probability shown for the family's region.

In the model the following five types of families may be eligible for AFDC if a minor child is present:
1. Female headed family.
2. Unemployed father family. The father must be unemployed for at least three months. Only about half of the states provide assistance to

TABLE 9-15

STATE SHARE OF AFDC CASELOAD WITHIN REGION

| Regions and States | RATIO OF AFDC PARTICIPATION IN STATES COMPARED TO REGION AS A WHOLE[a] | | | |
	1967[b]	1971[c]	1974[d]	Average Ratio for the 3 Years
NORTH CENTRAL				
Indiana	.047	.061	.062	.057
Illinois	.225	.243	.254	.241
Iowa	.046	.039	.029	.038
Kansas	.035	.039	.026	.033
Michigan	.173	.197	.223	.198
Minnesota	.062	.059	.050	.057
Missouri	.104	.092	.093	.096
Nebraska	.021	.020	.014	.018
North Dakota	.009	.006	.005	.007
Ohio	.208	.180	.180	.189
South Dakota	.014	.010	.008	.011
Wisconsin	.057	.054	.055	.055
NORTHEAST				
Connecticut	.043	.038	.042	.041
Maine	.016	.021	.026	.021
Massachusetts	.098	.101	.114	.104
New Hampshire	.004	.005	.009	.006
New Jersey	.098	.147	.148	.131
New York	.532	.457	.424	.471
Pennsylvania	.183	.207	.211	.200
Rhode Island	.020	.017	.018	.018
Vermont	.006	.006	.007	.006

(notes at end of table on next page)

TABLE 9-15 (continued)

Regions and States	RATIO OF AFDC PARTICIPATION IN STATES COMPARED TO REGION AS A WHOLE[a]			
	1967[b]	1971[c]	1974[d]	Average Ratio for the 3 Years
SOUTH				
Alabama	.053	.063	.050	.055
Arkansas	.027	.025	.030	.027
Delaware	.011	.010	.010	.010
District of Columbia	.016	.026	.033	.025
Florida	.110	.103	.096	.103
Georgia	.076	.111	.119	.102
Kentucky	.079	.055	.050	.061
Louisiana	.080	.082	.076	.079
Maryland	.078	.065	.075	.073
Mississippi	.070	.049	.058	.059
North Carolina	.077	.059	.054	.063
Oklahoma	.066	.044	.031	.047
South Carolina	.021	.028	.039	.029
Tennessee	.069	.070	.065	.068
Texas	.077	.129	.137	.114
Virginia	.030	.048	.056	.045
West Virginia	.064	.035	.020	.040
WEST				
Alaska	.004	.005	.007	.005
Arizona	.037	.026	.033	.032
California	.706	.726	.683	.705
Colorado	.051	.044	.049	.048
Hawaii	.017	.014	.022	.018
Idaho	.011	.008	.010	.010
Montana	.009	.009	.012	.010
Nevada	.006	.008	.007	.007
New Mexico	.034	.025	.029	.029
Oregon	.037	.045	.047	.043
Utah	.024	.017	.019	.020
Washington	.058	.069	.078	.068
Wyoming	.004	.003	.004	.004

a. Number of state AFDC participants divided by total for region where state is located.
b. Calculated from Table 1, AFDC Families by Type of Residence, 1967, "Findings of the 1967 AFDC Study," NCSS (National Center for Social Statistics), U.S. Dept. of Health, Education and Welfare, 1970.
c. Calculated from Table 7, Recipients of Money Payments and Amount of Payments by State, "AFDC: Selected Statistical Data on Families Aided and Program Operations," NCSS, U.S. Dept. of Health, Education and Welfare, 1971.
d. Calculated from "Recipients of Public Assistance Money Payments and Amount of Such Payments by Program, State and County," NCSS, U.S. Dept. of Health, Education and Welfare, 1974.

TABLE 9-16

PROBABILITY OF AFDC COVERAGE
OF CHILDREN AGE 18–20 IN
SCHOOL BY REGION

Region	Coverage Probability
North Central	.792
Northeast	.957
South	.658
West	.926

Source: Calculated from "Characteristics of State Public Assistance Plans Under the Social Security Act," Washington, D.C., Department of Health, Education and Welfare, 1973.

this type of family. A regional coverage probability, presented in Table 9-17, was computed by summing the caseload shares for those states which do cover unemployed fathers. In the simulation, this type of family will be eligible for AFDC if a uniform random number drawn is less than or equal to the probability for their region of residence as shown below in Table 9-17.

3. Incapacitated father family. The father must be out of the labor force for at least three months and disabled.
4. Parentless children. In the simulation model, it is possible for minor children to be in nuclear families alone because of the death of their parents. It is these families which will be eligible for AFDC. In reality many of these children live with other relatives such as grandparents or aunts and uncles and they are eligible regardless of the income of their relatives. While this situation is not simulated, such living arrangements do exist on the original survey but are not discernible in the microsimulation. This may tend to bias the number of eligibles downward. However, one may suppose that such families with adequate incomes do not often apply for AFDC, and those with inadequate incomes will often be eligible under one of the other family types.
5. Male headed families with no spouse. The federal law merely specifies the "absence from the home of a parent"[20] for categorical AFDC eligibility, not the sex of the remaining parent. This type of eligible family has been relatively rare and accounts for only a fraction of a percent of the participating caseload. But it was included because of the possibility of an increase in its incidence in the future.

20. "Studies in Public Welfare," Paper No. 2, *Handbook of Public Income Transfer Programs,* Joint Economic Committee, U.S. Congress, October 16, 1972.

In reality, families with stepfathers may also be eligible for AFDC depending on the child support laws in some states. This group, which accounts for less than 3 percent of the caseload, has been omitted because of the difficulties in capturing its incidence in the microsimulation.

TABLE 9-17

PROBABILITY OF AFDC COVERAGE
FOR UNEMPLOYED FATHER
FAMILY BY REGION

Region	Coverage Probability
North Central	.775
Northeast	.951
South	.195
West	.902

Source: Calculated from "Characteristics of
State Public Assistance Plans Under
the Social Security Act," Washington,
D.C., HEW, 1973.

Economic Eligibility

Once it is determined that a family is categorically eligible for AFDC assistance, a determination of economic eligibility is made. The first test is a consideration of the family's assets. All states permit ownership of a home and only thirteen states set limits on the value of the home or the family's equity in it, if it is mortgaged. In the model, no eligibility screen is made on the basis of home value because of the test's infrequence and the assumption that it is relatively unimportant for the categorically eligible families. The model, however, does include a screen on other assets besides the home. In general, the states allow assets valued from $150 to $3,000 per family. Table 9-18 gives the weighted means of allowable assets by region.

The last test of family AFDC eligibility involves a comparison of the family's current income with the state's standards of need. This standard represents the state's assessment of what is required by a family of a given size, with no other income, to meet its basic needs. The annualized standards of need by family size for 1970 are shown in Table 9-19, along with the standard deviation for each Census region. A simulation family's current income is computed as the sum of unearned income

TABLE 9-18

AFDC ASSET LIMITATIONS BY REGION

Region	Assets
North Central	$ 688
Northeast	970
South	1431
West	780

Source: Calculated from "Characteristics of State Public Assistance Plans Under the Social Security Act," Washington, D.C., HEW, 1973.

TABLE 9-19

STATE ANNUAL STANDARDS OF NEED FOR AFDC
BY REGION

Region	ANNUAL AMOUNT FOR FAMILY SIZE OF ONE		FURTHER AMOUNT PER ADDITIONAL FAMILY MEMBER	
	Average for Region	Standard Deviation[a]	Average for Region	Standard Deviation[a]
North Central	$1,982	$162	$489	$ 32
Northeast	1,952	276	677	46
South	1,356	51	482	16
West	2,301	471	792	168

a. This signifies the amount by which individual states may differ from their regional average. For example, in the North Central region the state standards may range from $162 more than or $162 less than $1,982 per year; whereas the increment for additional persons in the family may range from $32 more or $32 less than $489.

Source: Derived from "Public Assistance Programs: Standards for Basic Needs," NCSS Report D-2, U.S. Department of Health, Education and Welfare, 1970.

(other transfer payments except food stamps plus any earnings from assets) plus earned income minus any work expenses. Allowable annual work-related and child care expenses are shown in Table 9-20. The child care expenses are allowed only if the family has a single parent. Only expenses for the part of the year worked are used (i.e., expenses times weeks worked divided by 52). Finally, if the family's current income is less than the regional mean standard of need,[21] an AFDC benefit calculation is made.

21. Optionally, the mean standard of need plus a normal random number times the standard deviation is used.

TABLE 9-20

AVERAGE ALLOWANCES FOR ANNUAL WORK-RELATED AND CHILD CARE EXPENSES FOR AFDC BY REGION

Region	Work-Related Expenses	Child Care Expenses
North Central	$ 671	$819
Northeast	926	914
South	389	575
West	1,111	733

Source: Calculated from Table 72 in "Findings of the 1971 AFDC Survey, Part II, Financial Characteristics," NCSS (National Center for Social Statistics), HEW, 1972.

Benefit Calculation

The benefit calculation is similar to the full standard test with two major exceptions: legislation in 1969 established a work incentive feature in which some earnings are disregarded, and some states do not pay according to the full standard. In simulation years beyond 1968, the first $360 and 33 percent of annual earnings above this are excluded from the family's current income.[22] Many states are either fiscally unable or do not desire to pay the difference between the standard of need and a family's resources. Often the full standard is reduced, a final benefit reduction is made, or the benefit is subject to a maximum for a particular family size. The first two reduction methods are treated alike in this model, although, in reality, the full standard reduction is more stringent for families who have some personal income. Families are subject to a regional probability of receiving a benefit reduction, and if the stochastic decision is positive, the mean rate of reduction for the appropriate region is applied. These probabilities and reduction rates are shown in Table 9-21.

Benefits may be subject to a maximum. Again, a stochastic decision is made as to whether the AFDC benefit is subject to a maximum for a particular model family. If so, the maximum is applied according to the formula shown in Table 9-22 for a particular family size. All of the parameters shown represent the law in 1970. However, the regional changes in the standards of need and the maximum up to 1974 are also

---

22. The administrative law requires that $30 each month be excluded (the "30 and 1/3" rule). Since the distribution of hours worked is unknown in the model, the parameter was annualized.

incorporated in the model. In addition, a user of the model may alter these values in years outside of this range.

TABLE 9-21

AVERAGE AFDC BENEFIT REDUCTION RATE

Region	Probability of Use	Average Rate Applied
North Central	.282	.79
Northeast	.006	.90
South	.720	.65
West	.104	.78

Source: Calculated from Tables 2 and 3 of "State Maximums and Other Means of Limiting Money Payments," NCSS Report D-3, HEW, 1970.

TABLE 9-22

AFDC ANNUAL MAXIMUM FORMULA

Region	Probability of Use	WHEN MAXIMUM BENEFITS APPLY, THE LIMITS ARE:	
		For Family Size of One	For Each Additional Child
North Central	.171	$1,080	$312
Northeast	.021	912	396
South	.514	1,596	120
West	.811	1,800	312

Source: Calculated from Table 4 of "State Maximums and Other Means of Limiting Money Payments," NCSS Report D-3, HEW, 1970.

Supplemental Security Income

In 1974, the Supplemental Security Program (SSI) replaced three state based public assistance programs, Aid to the Permanently and Totally Disabled, Aid to the Blind, and Old Age Assistance. The categorical eligibility criteria are basically the same under the new program as the old ones. The program covers individuals who are disabled, blind, or over age 65. However, the new program, unlike the old ones, establishes a uniform floor under which income for those who qualify cannot fall. States that previously provided greater income to eligible persons than they receive under SSI must supplement the federal benefit to maintain the old level. In this program module, the administrative rules under the national SSI program are simulated.

Coverage

To be eligible for benefits a person must be age 65 or older, disabled, or blind. By law, a person is disabled if he is unable to engage in any substantial gainful activity for a period of at least 12 months. In this module a person who is age 65 or disabled and earns less than $1,680 may qualify for benefits. Dependents are not automatically eligible—one must qualify in his or her own right.

There is also a limitation on the assets a person may have to qualify.[23] A person may not have more than $1,500 in resources. If a couple is eligible, they may not have more than $2,250 in resources. By resources is meant the value of all assets over and above that of the following exceptions: a home of reasonable value, household goods, and one automobile. In the simulation, these exceptions are set at $25,000; if other wealth assets exceed the maximum allowable resources, a person is not eligible for SSI benefits.

Benefits

Basically the benefit provided is the national income floor plus any state supplementation payment less a person's or couple's "countable" income. Countable income is the sum of other transfer income and asset income less an income disregard, plus earnings less an earnings disregard. The income disregard is $60 per quarter, used in the model as an annual amount of $240. From earnings is subtracted $195 per quarter plus one-half of any remainder. Again, this disregard is converted to an annual basis for the model. If a person has only earnings, this income disregard is subtracted from them. The national income floor is $1,752 and $2,628 for one and two eligible persons in a family, respectively.[24] Table 9-23 shows the probability that this basic floor is supplemented by the state and the average annual supplemental payment by Census region. If a person's or couple's countable income exceeds the total

---

23. The resources of a spouse are included whether or not he or she qualifies.

24. This floor is "indexed" after 1975 following changes in the Consumer Price Index. This program feature is incorporated into the model.

TABLE 9-23

STATE BENEFIT SUPPLEMENTATION TO SSI

Region	Probability of Receipt	Supplemental Amount by Family Size	
		One-person	Two-person
North Central	.297	$372	$ 516
Northeast	1.000	732	960
South	.070	180	360
West	.913	924	2,304

Source: Derived from Table 5, "State Supplementation Bulletin," November, 1974.

amount of the income floor (plus state supplement where applicable), no benefit is received.

Food Stamps

The food stamp program supplements the food purchasing power of eligible low-income families. In 1971 eligibility requirements and benefits were nationalized. Using these later administrative standards, a simple function was derived to distribute the dollar value of food stamps to model families on the basis of their income and size.

Coverage

All families who receive AFDC or SSI payments are eligible to receive benefits without regard to their income or resources. Households not receiving public assistance must meet the uniform national income and resource eligibility requirements. The major income components considered in the family eligibility test include earnings, all transfer payments, and wealth income. Other income components, such as educational grants and payments from the work incentive program, are also included but are not simulated in this model. The income described is reduced by the amount of taxes paid, by shelter costs that exceed after-tax income by 30 percent, by medical expenses in excess of $10 per month, by child care costs necessary for employment, and by educational fees. The formula in the model to compute net income (NETY) simplifies the national rules and merely reduces earnings by a 10 percent income tax tate and the amount of income net of taxes by 5 percent as a gross estimate of other deductible expenses. The formula to compute net income is

NETY = .95 [.90 EARNINGS + TRANSFERS +

WEALTH INCOME].

If NETY, computed for families not receiving welfare, does not exceed the maximum allowable income shown in Table 9-24, the family is eligible to purchase food stamps.

TABLE 9-24

FOOD STAMP MAXIMUM
ALLOWABLE NET INCOME

Family Size	Maximum Allowable NETY
1	$2,136
2	2,796
3	3,684
4	4,476
5	5,280
6	6,084
7	6,876
8	7,680
9+	7,680 + $636 per each person more than eight

Source: Studies in Public Welfare, Paper No. 2,
*Handbook of Public Income Transfer
Programs,* Washington, D.C., Govern-
ment Printing Office, page 270, 1972.

Benefit

For all families who receive welfare and those families who pass the income test, a dollar value of food stamp benefits is computed. Under this program, families buy stamps worth more than the purchase amount and in turn use these coupons to purchase food. The value of benefits to the family is the difference between the value of the coupon allotment and the amount paid for them. The coupon allotment varies by family size and the purchase requirement varies by net income and family size — subject to a maximum requirement of 30 percent of net income. The purchase requirement as a percentage of net income increases with the family size. In the model, 20 percent of net income is used as a base

TABLE 9-25

FOOD STAMP ALLOTMENT VALUE
BY FAMILY SIZE

Family Size	Allotment
1	$ 432
2	768
2	1,104
4	1,344
5+	1,344 + $240 per person for each person more than five

Source: Studies in Public Welfare, Paper No. 2, *Handbook of Public Income Transfer Programs,* Washington, D.C., Government Printing Office, page 277, 1972.

purchase requirement, and it is increased by 1 percent for each family member.[25] The value of food stamps is computed as the allotment value shown in Table 9-25 minus the purchase requirement.

25. Studies in Public Welfare, Paper No. 2, *Handbook of Public Income Transfer Programs,* Washington, D.C., Government Printing Office, page 276, 1972.

Chapter 10
PROPERTY INCOME, TAXES, SAVINGS, WEALTH, AND INHERITANCE*

This chapter presents the process by which flows of income are converted to stocks of assets of various types and how these assets are transmitted at death. In addition to labor income and transfer income, dealt with earlier, three broad types of property income are represented in DYNASIM: direct money flows, *realized* gains, and *unrealized* gains. Money yields on capital and realized capital gains are added to labor and transfer income to arrive at total family income, which is then subjected to an income tax. Disposable income is obtained by subtracting income taxes, and remaining income is allocated to consumption and saving. Gross saving (plus or minus) takes five forms: changes in the value of corporate stock, other earning assets, residential housing, other nonearning assets, and debt.[1] (Two types of debt are distinguished: mortgage debt on residential housing, and all other debt.) The statistical basis by which savings are allocated to each of the five asset types shapes the portfolios of wealth-holders in the running model.

We proceed by first laying out essentially in words the process of simulating property income, taxes, savings, and wealth. Following that, a short discussion is given of the data base and the method by which behavioral relationships were estimated. Finally the inheritance process is described.

---

* James D. Smith and Stephen D. Franklin had the main responsibility for this chapter and the work it represents.

1. Earnings assets are those which normally generate an explicit yield in the form of interest, rent, dividends, or profit. Nonearning assets are personal belongings, checking accounts, etc., which do not normally provide a direct return.

Wealth Accumulation

General Statement of Procedures for
Simulating Realized Capital Gains

The first step in the imputation of a capital gain to a family is the assignment of an estimated probability of loss or gain from a sale of corporate stock. The probability is assigned as a function of the occurrence of gain or loss on the sale of stock in the prior year, education and age of the family head, the ratio of the value of a family's stock holdings to the average value of stock held by all families, and the percentile rank of the family in the distribution of all families arrayed by size of debt.

Similarly, capital gains from sales of earning assets other than stock are imputed to family units using estimated probabilities of their occurrence. The probabilities are a function of the occurrence of a gain in the prior year, the percentile rank of a family in the distribution of all families arrayed by size of asset holdings, family percentile rank in the distribution of families by size of debt, family percentile rank in the size distribution of gross income, education of head, age of head, size of community, the ratio of a family's wage income to its income from all sources, and the ratio of a family's earning assets to the mean value of earning assets held by all families.

The model provides for transactions in residential housing and the possible gain or loss on such transactions. If, in a given year, a family owns a home, there is a probability that it will be sold. The probability of such an event has been estimated and found to be a function of the age and education of the family head, the size of the family, the ratio of its wage income to total income, the size of community in which it resides, and its percentile rank in the distributions of gross income, assets and debt, and the ratio of the value of the family's home to the mean value of all homes. When a house is sold, a capital gain will occur if the market value of the house exceeds the purchase price. A capital loss occurs when the purchase price exceeds the market value at time of sale.

Buying homes is also simulated. In the event that a home was sold in the same year, the conditional probability of rebuying in the same year was estimated as a function of the age and sex of the family head, the family's rank in the distrubtions of assets, income and debt, the number of children, and the size of the community of residence. If a family did not sell a house in a given year, the probability of buying a home was estimated as a function of the age and education of the family head, the rank of the family in the distributions of income, debt, and the ratio of its wage income to all sources of income, and the size of the family.

Whenever a house is purchased the purchase price is assigned by an equation estimated from data for home purchasers. The purchase price for a family which sold a house in the same year is a function of the family's rank in the distributions of assets and debt, the ratio of the value of the house it owned in the prior year to the value of all homes, and the value of the house it owned in the prior year. If the family did not own a home at the beginning of the year in which it buys a home, the purchase price of the house is assigned as a function of the family's rank in the distributions of gross income and assets.

At the time of purchase a down payment is assigned and the excess of the purchase price over the down payment is amortized over a twenty-five year period. The mortgage rate of interest is taken as given at the time of purchase and is fixed throughout the period of the mortgage.

Asset Yield Income

The value of a family's corporate stock holdings and the value of its earning assets have yields imputed to them which currently are exogenously specified.

Income Tax

DYNASIM includes an income tax model which captures the main features of the 1972 federal statute. For instance, account is taken of married filers (all married filers are assumed to file joint returns), single filers, and head-of-household filers. Exemptions are provided for each family member, and additional exemptions are provided for heads and wives over age 64. Deductions are calculated according to a formula specified in consideration of the law and the ratio of deductions to adjusted gross income over $8,000 in 1972. The published statutory income tax rates are converted to six functions (two for each marital status). A precise specification of the income tax law is given in the final section of Appendix A.

Simulation Strategy

Saving is simulated in a number of forms, all at the family level. The forms now estimated and their sequence in the model's operation are:
1. Saving in the reduction of mortgage debt.
2. Total saving in all forms.
3. Saving in earning assets other than corporate stock.
4. Saving in nonearning assets.
5. Saving in corporate stock.
6. Saving (+,−) in the form of nonmortgage debt.

Earlier in the chapter, transactions in the housing market were described which result in saving in housing equity and debt level changes due directly to purchases and sales. In the model such savings are balanced by saving or dissaving in some other form. For instance, the purchase of a $10,000 equity in a house may be associated with a $10,000 dissaving in earning assets which were sold to buy the house equity. Saving in housing also takes place as mortgage debt is gradually retired. Saving in the reduced mortgage debt is handled very mechanically (as it is the real world by the vast majority of homeowners) by regular payments to principal on mortgages.

The general simulation strategy is to first generate saving in reduced home mortgage and then to impute the total value of saving in all forms including reduced mortgage debt. Savings in all specific forms are constrained to sum to total saving, by a process which uses nonmortgage debt as a residual balancing category.

The simulations of total saving and saving in each specific form except debt follow the same basic logic. The process is shown schematically in Chart 10-1. In the case of total savings, the probability of saving more than $500[2] is assigned to a family as a function of the age and education of the family head, the family's rank in the size distributions of disposable income, debt, and assets, and wages as a percent of gross income. If, on the basis of the draw of a random number, the family is determined to save not more than $500, the probability of dissaving more than $500 is assigned. If, based upon another draw of a random number, it is determined that the family neither dissaves nor saves more than $500, it is assigned a total saving level of zero for the simulation year.

If it is determined that the family saved more than $500, a value of saving is assigned based on an estimated equation which takes total

2. 1963 dollars.

CHART 10-1

SIMULATION OF TOTAL SAVING

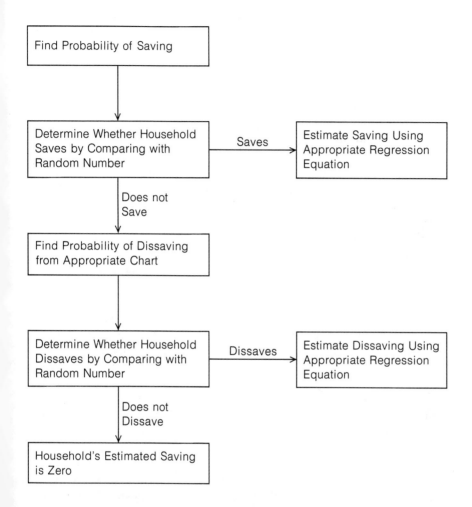

saving to be a function of the ratio of wages to gross income, disposable income rank, an interaction of disposable income rank and asset rank and the level of disposable income, plus a draw from the distribution of an error term calculated in the fitting of the equation.

For families determined to dissave more than $500, a negative value of saving is assigned as a function of the same variable used to assign positive total saving plus the family's rank in the size distribution of debt.

Saving in the form of nonmortgage debt is calculated as the difference between total saving and the sum of saving in each other form. If the difference is larger than current nonmortgage debt, saving in this form is set equal to nonmortgage debt and the remainder of the residual is added to saving in the forms of earning assets, nonearning assets, and corporate stock in shares proportionate to the current values of these assets for the family. Hence, saving in specific forms must sum to a separate estimate of total saving.

Data Base and Details of Estimation
of Saving Operating Characteristic

The data used for the estimation of probabilities and other values used in the operating characteristics of this chapter are from the *Survey of Financial Characteristics of Consumers* (SFCC) which covered the assets and debts of consumers as of December 31, 1962 and from the *Survey of Changes in Family Finances* (SCFF) covering the saving and income of the SFCC respondents during 1963. Saving was computed as the algebraic sum of saving in each net worth component plus saving in the form of retirement plans. Disposable income was estimated as gross income less estimated federal income tax liability. Of 2,164 observations in the SCFF file, 99 were excluded from the analysis of saving because the households had saving which was greater than 90 percent of our estimate of their disposable income. It was assumed that either survey measurement errors or inaccurate estimates of tax liabilities were responsible for these large saving/income ratio estimates, often over 100 percent. In addition, 18 observations were excluded because the respondents reported zero or negative income. (Both the SFCC and the SCFF were conducted by the Board of Governors of the Federal Reserve System.)

Two statistical techniques, automatic interaction detection or AID (see footnote 7) and multiple regression, were used to estimate the operating characteristics used in this part of the model. Although multiple regression methods are widely understood, the use of AID is not widespread and warrants some comment here.

The focus of AID is on reducing variance of a dependent variable by sequentially dividing the data into groups. To use the program one must specify a dependent variable, a set of predictors, and some strategy parameters which are discussed below.

Each predictor variable is coded into a limited number of classes for input to AID. The algorithm calculates the total sum of squares for the entire sample and then systematically examines each predictor to find that split for which the between sum of squares for the two subgroups is maximized. It should be noted that the criterion for determining where to split the sample is one of importance in reducing error, not statistical significance. The process is then repeated on that new group which has the largest within-group sum of squares.

There are several criteria which must be met before a split can occur. First the marginal reduction in error variance which would result from a split must be greater than or equal to some prespecified fraction of the original variance. Secondly, the number of cases in each of the resultant subgroups must be greater than or equal to another pre-specified value (e.g., 25). However, by setting this parameter very small, the user can be alerted to the presence of a few extreme cases that account for a substantial fraction of the variance. Finally a split will not occur if the number of splits has already reached some prespecified maximum (e.g., 30). These criteria are intended to insure that the process stops before unreliable reduction in error variance occurs.

Analysis Strategy for Saving Operating Characteristic

The analysis was designed to develop an estimation procedure that is independent of the level of saving as well as the levels of the major determinants of saving (e.g., income, assets and debt) that characterize the data used to obtain the procedure. With that in mind, saving as a fraction of income was suggested as an appropriate dependent variable. Examination of the effect of using predictor variables in the form indicating the relative positions in the distributions of those variables in place of the actual amounts was also planned. Two indicators of a value's relative position within a distribution were proposed: (1) the value's distance from the mean measured in standard deviations, and (2) the percent of the population having less than the value. The first measure was abandoned due to the fact that the standard deviation of a variable within a sample is very sensitive to extreme cases within the sample distribution.

Traditional regression analysis failed to provide a simple model with much predictive power. However, it was discovered that separate regressions using savers and dissavers were much more satisfactory in every respect than an overall regression. It was felt at this point that a simulation algorithm should be developed to take advantage of this fact by allowing the algorithm to stochastically classify households as saving or dissaving on the basis of probabilities estimated from the SCFF data.

Three savings classes with arbitrary boundaries were decided upon—(1) substantial savers (saving greater than $500), (2) substantial dissavers (dissaving greater than $500), and (3) small savers or dissavers (saving or dissaving up to $500). The computer program, Automatic Interaction Detector (AID), was used to generate probability assumptions for the model in the following way: A dependent variable was created with value 1 for households saving greater than $500 and 0 for others. AID was then used to split the data on a set of predictors so as to maximize reduction in variance of this dummy variable. The result is the AID tree shown in Chart 10-2. A group mean can be considered the probability that a unit with the group's characteristics saves more than $500.

Not surprisingly, of all groups created by splits on income or assets, those with the higher income or asset levels have the larger mean or probability of saving. Also, of the five splits on debt, only once does the group with the lower debt have the larger mean (see groups 8 and 9), indicating that households starting the year with higher debt were more likely to save. The lowest estimated saving probabilities were 0.03 for households with disposable income of at least $3,000, assets and debt both less than $1,000, and whose head has less than 9 years of education (group 26). The highest saving probability of 1.0 was estimated for households with disposable income over $3,000, debt less than $1,000, assets over $10,000, and consisting of one person who is employed by others (group 19).

A second dependent variable was created for units which did not save more than $500. This variable is 1 if the unit dissaved more than $500 and 0 otherwise. Another AID analysis produced the AID tree shown in Chart 10-3. In this case a group mean can be considered the probability that a unit will dissave more than $500 given that it has saved less than $500. Among households that saved less than $500, dissaving was most likely for those having higher assets, higher debt, or more family members. In addition the self-employed had a greater chance of dissaving over $500. The fraction of substantial dissavers among households within final AID groups ranged from 0.06 (group 14) to 0.96 (group 33).

The saving simulation submodel uses these AID results to classify each household in its population as having one of the three types of saving behavior mentioned above. In the simulation model, however, the percentile ranks of assets, debt, and income are used in place of the values shown in the AID charts. For example, an AID group defined as households having assets less than $25,000 and disposable income less than $7500 would be redefined as households with assets within the bottom 77.85 percent and disposable income in the bottom 66.22 percent of the model population's distributions of assets and disposable income respectively. Each household will first be classified as a substantial saver or not a substantial saver by comparing a random variable from a uniform distribution on the interval [0,1] with the appropriate AID group mean (Chart 10-2). Those households that are not substantial savers are

219

CHART 10-2
PROBABILITY OF SAVING > $500

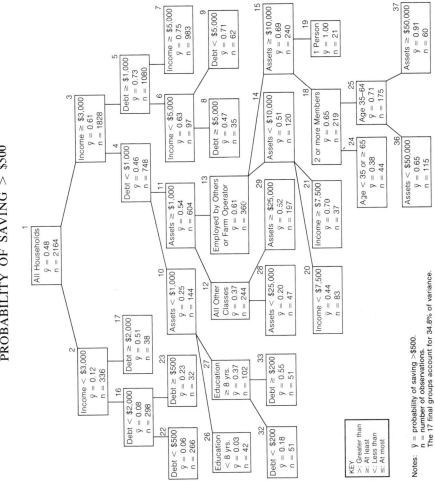

KEY
>: Greater than
≥: At least
<: Less than
≤: At most

Notes: ȳ = probability of saving >$500.
n = number of observations.
The 17 final groups account for 34.8% of variance.

CHART 10-3

PROBABILITY OF DISSAVING > $500
(For Units Saving < $500)

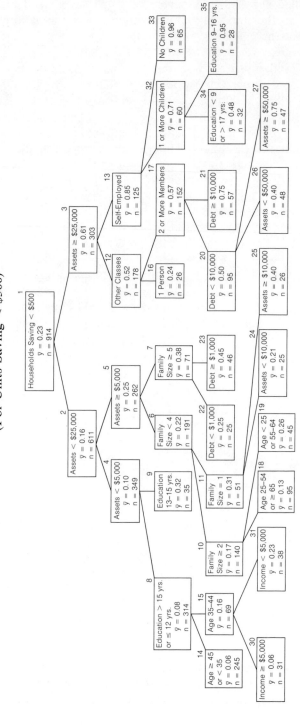

Notes: ȳ = probability of dissaving > $500.
n = number of observations.
The 17 final groups account for 27.8% of variance.

KEY
>: Greater than
≥: At least
<: Less than
≤: At most

then classified substantial dissavers or small savers and dissavers by comparing another random uniform variable with the appropriate AID group mean (Chart 10-3).

The strategy for the remainder of the analysis is to use regression and AID jointly to predict saving or dissaving. Regression equations were estimated to predict the ratio of saving to income for households saving more than $500 and to predict the ratio of income plus assets to dissaving for households dissaving more than $500. Residuals from each regression were then used as dependent variables in AID analyses. The simulation model predicts saving or dissaving using the appropriate regression equation plus a random error term from a distribution which should approximate the distributions of errors in the appropriate final AID group. Most of these error distributions within AID groups were found to be approximately normal by examining normal probability plots. The rest were skewed to the right and could be "normalized" by trimming the upper tail. For units associated with an AID group that does not require "trimming," the error term that is added to the regression prediction is a random normal deviate from a distribution with mean and standard deviation of the residuals in that AID group. Error terms generated for units associated with AID groups having skewed distributions of residuals are either (1) a random normal deviate from a distribution with mean and standard deviation of the "trimmed" distribution or (2) the mean of the extreme residuals. In this case the mean outlier is used as an error term with probability equal to the sum of the sampling weights associated with those outliers divided by the total sum of weights for the group.

Analysis for Household Saving Greater Than $500

There were 1,151 households in the SCFF file whose saving was over $500 and not more than 90 percent of estimated disposable income for 1963. These observations were used in regression analysis with ratio of saving to income as the dependent variable and the following predictors: wages as a percent of gross income coded into five classes and the percentile ranks of assets, debt, and disposable income. In addition, the predictive power of the three variables — assets, debt, and income — was compared with that of the percentile ranks of these variables.

Residuals from the model, regressing the ratio of saving to income on a linear function of predictors, showed increasing dispersion as the predicted value increased. To obtain predicted values that have constant variance about the regression line, the same model was fit using weights of the squared inverse of the original predicted value. Results from regressions, using actual amounts and percentile ranks of assets,

TABLE 10-1

REGRESSIONS WITH DEPENDENT VARIABLE AS THE RATIO OF SAVING TO DISPOSABLE INCOME FOR HOUSEHOLDS SAVING GREATER THAN $500

Equation 1		
Variable	Coefficient	t-Ratio
1. Constant	0.4375	10.65
2. Wages/gross income*	−0.0161	−4.17
3. Percentile rank of assets/1000	0.0659	0.10
4. Percentile rank of debt/1000	−0.2355	−1.36
5. Percentile rank of income/1000	−3.2833	−6.46
6. (Variable 3) × (Variable 5)	27.2192	3.37
$R^2 = 18.6\%$		

Equation 2		
Variable	Coefficient	t-Ratio
1. Constant	0.3412	20.79
2. Wages/gross income*	−0.0253	−6.86
3. Assets/100,000	0.0061	2.70
4. Debt/100,000	0.0560	3.03
5. Income/100,000	0.0769	1.97
6. (Variable 3) × (Variable 5)	−0.0047	−4.47
$R^2 = 7.7\%$		

* Coded as follows: 0 = (0), 1 = (>0, <0.25), 2 = (≥0.25, <0.50), 3 = (>0.50, <0.75), 4 = (≥0.75, <1), 5 = (1).

debt, and income as predictors, including an asset-income interaction, are shown in Table 10-1. Assets and debt become nonsignificant variables in ranked form but income appears to be a more powerful predictor when transformed to ranks. A surprising result is the reversal in signs of the income and asset-income coefficients. Using ranked variables, the results imply that the share of income saved decreases as income rises and increases as the product of income and assets rises. Just the opposite is implied when the actual amounts of income and assets are used as predictors. In both models the coefficient of assets is positive.

Table 10-2 shows results from fitting both models without the debt and asset terms. Eliminating these variables from either equation results in only slight reduction in the amount of variance explained in the saving/income ratios or in actual saving, demonstrating that their impor-

TABLE 10-2

REGRESSIONS EXCLUDING TERMS FOR ASSETS AND
DEBT WITH DEPENDENT VARIABLE AS THE RATIO OF
SAVING TO DISPOSABLE INCOME FOR HOUSEHOLDS
SAVING MORE THAN $500

Equation 3		
Variable	Coefficient	t-Ratio
1. Constant	0.4371	18.89
2. Wages/gross income*	−0.0136	−3.65
3. Percentile rank of income	−3.5996	−7.47
4. (Variable 3) × (Percentile rank of assets)	29.2830	8.07
R² = 18.5%		

Equation 4		
Variable	Coefficient	t-Ratio
1. Constant	0.3508	21.63
2. Wages/gross income*	−0.0265	−7.19
3. Disposable income/100,000	0.0961	3.16
4. (Variable 3) × (Assets/100,000)	−0.0009	−3.89
R² = 6.6%		

* Coded as before (Table 10-1).

tance in either model is minimal. Although the ranked predictors can explain more of the variance in the saving/income ratios, it is not necessarily true that the predicted ratios from this model explain more of the variance in actual saving than predicted ratios from the other model. In fact, Equation 3 for which R^2 was 18.5 percent accounts for 56.1 percent of the variance in saving while Equation 4 with R^2 of 6.6 percent accounts for 63.6 percent of the variance in saving.

Residuals from Equation 3 were analyzed by AID with results shown in Chart 10-4. Assets, debt, number of children, housing status, education of head, age of head, and wages as a percent of income were used to split the residuals into 11 final groups accounting for 7.3 percent of the variance. Other predictors which were available were income, family size, urbanization and employment status. The AID results indicate that within certain subsets of the population, households with the following characteristics have larger saving/income ratios — households

CHART 10-4

RESIDUAL SAVING RATIO

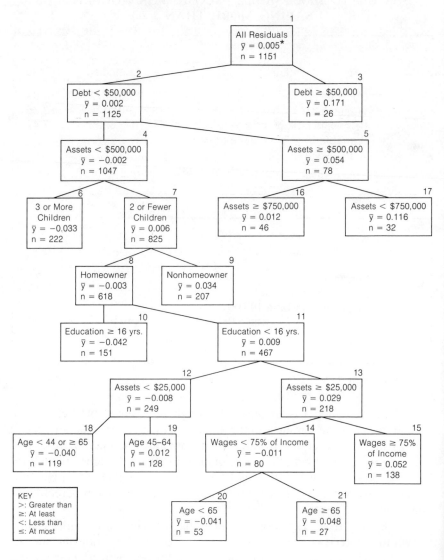

Notes: ȳ = residuals from regression (see text).
n = number of observations.
* Mean residual is not 0 because residuals were calculated for several cases excluded from the regression.
The 11 final groups account for 7.3% of variance.

with two or fewer children, households not owning home, households whose head does not have a college degree (education of 15 years or less) and households with wages at least 50 percent of gross income.

Analysis for Households Dissaving Greater Than $500

   Three hundred twenty-six households in the SCFF file dissaved at least $500. After experimentation with several candidate dependent variables, including functions of the ratio of dissaving to income, to assets, and to the sum of income and assets, the selected form was the ratio of dissaving to the sum of income and assets. Weighted least squares were again used to fit models that produce predicted values with constant variance about the regression lines. The predictors for this estimation were the same used previously and the regression results are compared in Table 10-3. Equation 5 was fit without an asset-income interaction term and Equation 6 was fit without wages/gross income be-

TABLE 10-3

REGRESSIONS WITH DEPENDENT VARIABLE AS THE
RATIO OF ASSETS PLUS INCOME TO DISSAVING FOR
HOUSEHOLDS DISSAVING OVER $500

Equation 5

Variable	Coefficient	t-Ratio
1. Constant	−5.0116	−6.76
2. Wages/gross income*	0.3741	4.63
3. Percentile rank of assets	0.2767	10.44
4. Percentile rank of debt	0.0750	4.37
5. Percentile rank of income	0.1003	6.87
R^2 = 83.7%		

Equation 6

Variable	Coefficient	t-Ratio
1. Constant	17.8574	9.94
2. Assets/10,000	0.4960	6.60
3. Debt/10,000	−0.7118	−3.34
4. Income/10,000	3.4516	3.81
5. (Variable 2) × (Variable 4)	−0.0319	−4.70
R^2 = 16.8%		

* Coded as before (Table 10-1).

226

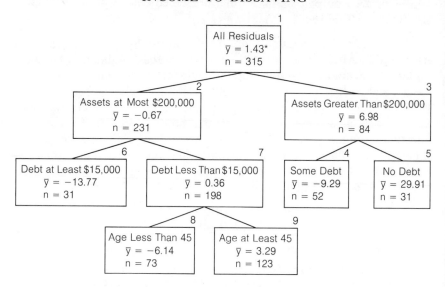

CHART 10-5

RESIDUAL RATIO OF ASSETS PLUS INCOME TO DISSAVING

Nôtes: ȳ = residual of the ratio of assets plus income to dissaving estimated from regression (see text).
n = number of observations.
* Mean residual is not zero because residuals were calculated for several cases excluded from the regression.
The 5 final groups account for 10.7% of variance.

cause those variables were statistically nonsignificant. Ranked predictors explain a much greater portion of the variance in the dependent variable and also explain more of the variance in dissaving. Debt appears to be more important in determining dissaving than it is in determining saving but its effect on dissaving as a ranked predictor is opposite from its effect when the actual value is used.

Again the residuals from Equation 5 were analyzed by AID. Results are shown in Chart 10-5. Assets, debt, and age were able to explain 10.7 percent of the variance in the regression residuals. Negative residuals were more likely for households that had higher debt, indicating that the effect of the percentile rank of debt was overstated by the regression model. Very few splits were generated by AID due to the relatively small number of observations available within the constraint that the minimum group size was 25.

Some Simulation Results

Household saving was simulated for one year using a population consisting of a random sample of 6,008 households from the *1960*

Census Public Use Sample to which assets and debt had been assigned previously. This simulation model used earlier AID results which differ slightly from those presented here but the final version of the model should produce output similar to that presented below. Table 10-4 com-

TABLE 10-4

PERCENTAGE DISTRIBUTIONS OF HOUSEHOLDS SAVING MORE THAN $500 BY SIZE OF SAVING/INCOME RATIO

Ratio	SCFF % of units	SCFF* % of units	Simulation % of units
0 < 0.10	9.22	9.70	6.69
0.10 < 0.15	16.62	17.50	12.73
0.15 < 0.20	16.09	16.95	14.03
0.20 < 0.25	12.44	13.11	14.03
0.25 < 0.30	9.89	10.42	13.54
0.30 < 0.40	14.30	15.06	17.13
0.40 < 0.50	7.82	8.23	8.63
0.50 < 0.70	6.68	7.03	10.59
≥ 0.70	6.93	1.99	2.64
% of all units saving > $500	46.89		47.05

* Excluding 99 cases where ratio was greater than 0.90.

PERCENTAGE DISTRIBUTIONS OF HOUSEHOLDS DISSAVING MORE THAN $500 BY SIZE OF DISSAVING/(ASSETS + INCOME) RATIO

Ratio	SCFF % of units	Simulation % of units
0 < 0.010	1.93	1.86
0.010 < 0.025	17.06	18.35
0.025 < 0.04	15.59	18.76
0.04 < 0.07	16.97	20.83
0.07 < 0.10	10.01	12.91
0.10 < 0.15	9.49	10.54
0.15 < 0.25	16.01	6.93
0.25 < 0.40	7.84	3.77
≥ 0.40	5.10	6.04
% of all units dissaving > $500	12.97	11.55

pares the percentage distributions of households by size of saving/income ratios and dissaving/(assets + income) ratios from the SCFF and the simulation population. A comparison of the percentage distributions of households and saving by level of income is presented in Table 10-5.

TABLE 10-5

PERCENTAGE DISTRIBUTIONS OF HOUSEHOLDS AND
SAVING BY LEVEL OF DISPOSABLE INCOME

Income	SCFF		SCFF*		SIMULATION	
	% of units	% of saving	% of units	% of saving	% of units	% of saving
$ < 1,000	7.73	−3.90	7.65	−7.73	13.72	−7.94
1,000 < 2,000	10.02	−3.32	10.05	−7.17	10.20	−1.79
2,000 < 3,000	8.73	1.08	8.93	1.75	10.78	−0.35
3,000 < 4,000	10.57	4.23	10.61	3.55	9.13	3.77
4,000 < 5,000	8.63	6.98	8.59	7.66	9.70	10.60
5,000 < 6,000	7.82	9.15	7.85	10.25	10.08	13.61
6,000 < 7,500	12.69	13.39	12.86	21.24	14.02	24.19
7,500 < 10,000	19.89	28.06	19.89	34.38	14.45	29.37
10,000 < 15,000	9.88	27.23	9.67	28.78	5.63	13.25
≥ 15,000	4.07	17.10	3.90	7.30	2.30	15.28
Total saving	$49.0 billion		$27.7 billion		$34.9 billion	

* Excluding 99 cases where saving/income ratio was greater than 0.90.

The Intergenerational
Transmission of Wealth

Better government data and greater access to it have spurred a renewed interest in the analysis of income and wealth distributions. For the most part this interest picked up where the work of the late thirties and early forties left off—with cross-sectional distributions. Of growing interest, however, has been the intergenerational transmission of wealth, that is, how the wealth of those who die is passed on to their heirs, in what amounts, and with what implications for the concentration of wealth in society. Questions of how much of the observable cross-sectional distribution can be accounted for by inheritance and how much by saving out of earnings have been matters of speculation and some empirical work by Soltow,[3] Morgan[4] and Projector.[5] However, as Brittain points out, research has not been well structured to capture the importance of inheritance.[6] The issue of inheritance has been, for the most part, a peripheral one in studies concerned with other economic behavior.

In this chapter data from several sources are used to model the transmission and taxing of wealth at death. The general schematics of the process as modeled are shown in Chart 10-6. Deaths, of course, are generated by parts of the overall model described in Chapter 3.

1. *Cost of last illness.* Nearly all deaths impose medical costs on the estates of the decedents. In cases where there is a terminal illness of prolonged length, the medical costs may be substantial. The medical costs deducted for purposes of calculating taxable estate on the federal estate tax return provided a data base to estimate the relation of the cost of last illness to other characteristics of decedents. The cost of last illness was analyzed using AID-III.[7]

In Chart 10-7 the result of the AID analysis is shown. The five final groups (Groups 5–9) explain 5.4 percent of the variance in the cost of terminal illnesses as reported on federal estate tax returns. One would not expect to explain a great deal of the variance with the variables available to us, but there is a systematic, positive relationship between net worth and cost of last illness. The only other variable which contributed significantly to reducing the original variance was age of decedent. Thus only these two characteristics of decedents were used in the attribution of last illness costs. The actual attribution of the cost was the expected value within each characteristic class.

2. *Attorney's fees.* Attorney's fees are a deductable item in the federal estate tax. Consequently, they are available from the estate tax re-

3. Lee Soltow, *Toward Income Equality in Norway,* Madison, Wisconsin, University of Wisconsin Press, 1965.

4. Robin Barlow, Harvey E. Brazer, and James N. Morgan, *Economic Behavior of the Affluent,* Washington, D.C., Brookings Institution, 1966.

5. Dorothy Projector and Gertrude S. Weiss, *Survey of Financial Characteristics of Consumers,* Federal Reserve Technical Papers, August 1966.

6. John A. Brittain. "The Intergenerational Transmission of Wealth: Prospects for a Research Program," mimeo, December 1971.

7. AID-III is a data searching algorithm which sequentially splits a population into pairs such that the sum of the variance around the mean of the pair or the expected value of a regression is the smallest possible proportion of the variance around the expected values of the group from which the pair was derived. The technique has the advantage over regression in not requiring an additive set of independent variables. It also imposes no linearity restrictions on relations between variables. For a detailed discussion of AID-III see, Sonquist, Baker and Morgan, *Searching for Structure,* Institute for Social Research, Ann Arbor, Michigan, 1971.

CHART 10-6

GENERALIZED SCHEMATIC OF INHERITANCE MODEL

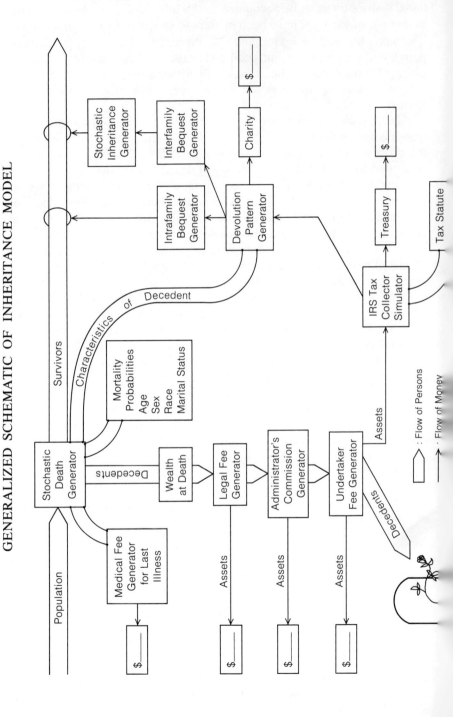

CHART 10-7

MEDICAL EXPENSES OF LAST ILLNESS

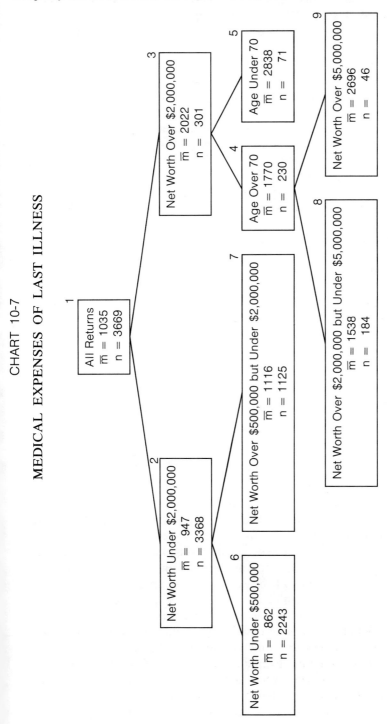

1

All Returns
m̄ = 1035
n = 3669

2

Net Worth Under $2,000,000
m̄ = 947
n = 3368

3

Net Worth Over $2,000,000
m̄ = 2022
n = 301

4

Age Over 70
m̄ = 1770
n = 230

5

Age Under 70
m̄ = 2838
n = 71

6

Net Worth Under $500,000
m̄ = 862
n = 2243

7

Net Worth Over $500,000 but Under $2,000,000
m̄ = 1116
n = 1125

8

Net Worth Over $2,000,000 but Under $5,000,000
m̄ = 1538
n = 184

9

Net Worth Over $5,000,000
m̄ = 2696
n = 46

Notes: m = Mean cost in dollars.
n = Number of observations in group.
Sex was an eligible variable but did not contribute to a significant reduction in variance.
The five final groups account for 5.4% of variance.

turns of 1969. Using AID to split the population into groups such that a regression of attorney's fees on gross estates within groups would produce the greatest reduction of variance relative to a regression on the total set of observations, 51.1 percent of the variance was explained. Age and marital status of decedent were the only other variables which were able to provide a basis for splitting the population with a significant reduction in variance. In Chart 10-8 it can be seen that a simple regression of attorney's fees on gross assets (measured in thousands of dollars) would produce coefficients of $549 and 15.66. The predicted value of $3,645 is the expected attorney's fee when the mean value of the group's gross assets ($198,000) is plugged into the equation.

3. *Executor's fees* (EXCOM). The cost of executor's fees was estimated using two regression equations and data from the 1962 federal estate tax file.

EXCOM = $a + b_1$(NETWORTH) + b_2(MS1) + b_2(MS2) + b_4(MS3), where net worth is measured in $1,000s, MS1 is a dummy for married decedents, MS2 is a dummy for never married decedents, and MS3 is a dummy for all other marital statuses. The equation was fitted separately for decedents with net worth under $200,000 and those with net worth of $200,000 or more. The estimated coefficients for the two equations are:

	Net Worth Under $200,000	Net Worth $200,000 and Over
a	$172.50	$2,517.80
b_1	14.8	17.3
b_2	−843.5	−3,575.0
b_3	575.5	4,223.4
b_4	268.0	− 648.1
	$R^2 = 0.179$	$R^2 = 0.322$

4. *Funeral expenses*. In the simulation, funeral expenses are attributed to decendents' estates on the basis of eight regression equations fitted in the process of an AID run on the 1962 estate tax file. The combined splitting of the population into eight final groups and the simple regression of funeral expenses on net worth within each final group explained 19.2 percent of the variance of funeral expenses. In Chart 10-9 we show the results of the AID run with group regressions.

In some cases the total costs of dying exceeds the assets of the decedent. This is frequently the case when children die. Although they will not generally incur legal or administration fees of any significance, the cost of last illness and funeral will diminish estates of children as well as of adults. Whether a child or an adult, the cost of last illness, administration fees, lawyer's fees, and funeral expenses are all deducted from their estates in accordance with the AID analyses above. When these costs result in a negative estate, it is transferred to the decedent's

CHART 10-8

ATTORNEY'S FEES FOR SETTLING ESTATES

(dollars)

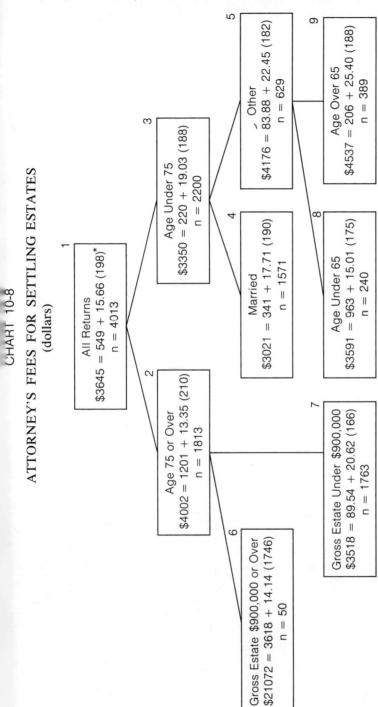

1
All Returns
$3645 = 549 + 15.66 (198)*
n = 4013

3
Age Under 75
$3350 = 220 + 19.03 (188)
n = 2200

2
Age 75 or Over
$4002 = 1201 + 13.35 (210)
n = 1813

5
, Other
$4176 = 83.88 + 22.45 (182)
n = 629

4
Married
$3021 = 341 + 17.71 (190)
n = 1571

9
Age Over 65
$4537 = 206 + 25.40 (188)
n = 389

8
Age Under 65
$3591 = 963 + 15.01 (175)
n = 240

6
Gross Estate $900,000 or Over
$21072 = 3618 + 14.14 (1746)
n = 50

7
Gross Estate Under $900,000
$3518 = 89.54 + 20.62 (166)
n = 1763

Notes: n = number of observations in group.
* The predicted value of the equation in each group is the value of attorney's fees estimated when gross estate measured in 1000s of dollars was at its mean for the group.
Sex was also an eligible variable, but could not produce a significant reduction in variance.
The overall regression R^2 = 46.8%. Total R^2 = 51.1%.
Marginal variance explained by subgroup regression = 4.3%.

CHART 10-9

FUNERAL EXPENSES

(dollars)

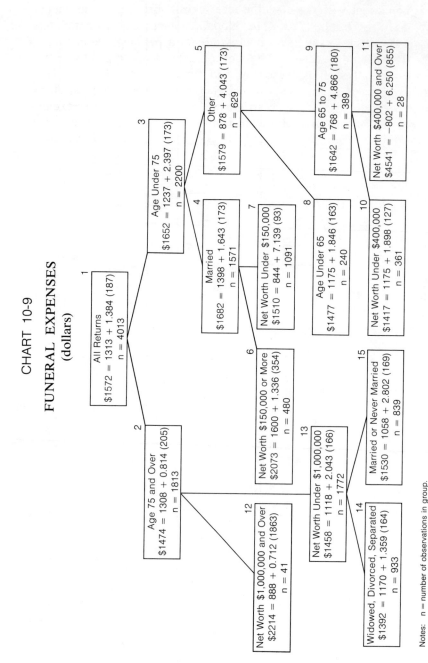

1
All Returns
$1572 = 1313 + 1.384 (187)
n = 4013

2
Age 75 and Over
$1474 = 1308 + 0.814 (205)
n = 1813

3
Age Under 75
$1652 = 1237 + 2.397 (173)
n = 2200

12
Net Worth $1,000,000 and Over
$2214 = 888 + 0.712 (1863)
n = 41

13
Net Worth Under $1,000,000
$1458 = 1118 + 2.043 (166)
n = 1772

6
Net Worth $150,000 or More
$2073 = 1600 + 1.336 (354)
n = 480

5
Other
$1579 = 878 + 4.043 (173)
n = 629

4
Married
$1682 = 1398 + 1.643 (173)
n = 1571

14
Widowed, Divorced, Separated
$1392 = 1170 + 1.359 (164)
n = 933

15
Married or Never Married
$1530 = 1058 + 2.802 (169)
n = 839

7
Net Worth Under $150,000
$1510 = 844 + 7.139 (93)
n = 1091

8
Age Under 65
$1477 = 1175 + 1.846 (163)
n = 240

9
Age 65 to 75
$1642 = 768 + 4.866 (180)
n = 389

10
Net Worth Under $400,000
$1417 = 1175 + 1.898 (127)
n = 361

11
Net Worth $400,000 and Over
$4541 = -802 + 6.250 (855)
n = 28

Notes: n = number of observations in group.
         Dependent variable in parenthesis is the estimated value of funeral expenses when the independent variable in parenthesis, net worth, measured in $1000,
         is at the mean for the group.
         The overall regression R² = 9.3%. Total R² = 19.2%.
         Marginal variance explained by subgroup regression = 9.9%.

heirs in the same manner as a positive valued estate. This conceptualization is consistent with the actual process of cost-bearing for decedents.

5. *Existing Estate Tax.* The model captures the essential features of the federal estate tax. It provides for a personal exemption of $60,000 for each decedent's estate, and a marital deduction of the actual amount bequeathed a spouse or one-half the estate, whichever is less. Charitable bequests, costs of last illness, legal fees, and administrator's commissions are deductable in arriving at taxable estate. After exemptions and deductions are subtracted from the net worth of estates, the remainder is taxed in accordance with current federal estate tax rates. (See Table 10-6.)

Some minor features of the federal estate tax are not included. These are the credits for state and foreign death taxes, the reduction in rates applicable to assets which have been taxed in another estate within the previous ten years, the assets given away in contemplation of death, and certain other life-time transfers which are constructively part of the estate for federal estate tax purposes.

6. *Bequest patterns.* Little information is available about the pattern of transfers set in motion by death. Data available from the IRS identify amounts going to charity and in some years to the spouse, but no information is available on the division of bequests between members of the decedent's family living at home, or, for that matter, on the total amount remaining in the decedent's family vs. what goes to noncharitable recipients outside the immediate family. In order to estimate the pattern of estate distribution, a file constructed by Smith from estate tax returns filed in the District of Columbia in 1969 was used.[8] The statutes of the District of Columbia require an estate tax return to be filed for the estates of all decedents with gross assets of $1,000 or more. Thus the file provided nearly the complete range of estate sizes. Further, the file was constructed to provide information about the distribution of assets among spouse, children, other relatives, nonrelatives, and charities (including gifts to governments). The processes of estimating the pattern of estate distribution in a form suitable for Monte Carlo applications is depicted in Chart 10-10.

The first step was to use AID to estimate the probability that a bequest was made outside the family. A family is defined for this purpose as a head, wife, and children, wherever the latter are living. All never married persons were excluded from the estimation on the grounds that we would follow the arbitrary rule that never married persons had neither spouse nor children and that all their wealth would flow outside the family as defined. The results of the AID analysis is

8. James D. Smith, "White Wealth and Black People: The Distribution of Wealth in Washington, D.C., 1967," in James D. Smith, *Personal Distributions of Income and Wealth,* National Bureau of Economic Research.

TABLE 10-6

FEDERAL ESTATE TAX SCHEDULE

Taxable estate equal to or more than—	Taxable estate less than—	Tax on amount in column (1)	Rate of tax on excess over amount in column (1)
(1)	(2)	(3)	(4)
$ 0	$ 5,000	$ 0	3%
5,000	10,000	150	7
10,000	20,000	500	11
20,000	30,000	1,600	14
30,000	40,000	3,000	18
40,000	50,000	4,800	22
50,000	60,000	7,000	25
60,000	100,00	9,500	28
100,000	250,000	20,700	30
250,000	500,000	65,700	32
500,000	750,000	145,700	35
750,000	1,000,000	233,200	37
1,000,000	1,250,000	325,700	39
1,250,000	1,500,000	423,200	42
1,500,000	2,000,000	528,200	45
2,000,000	2,500,000	753,200	49
2,500,000	3,000,000	998,200	53
3,000,000	3,500,000	1,263,200	56
3,500,000	4,000,000	1,543,200	59
4,000,000	5,000,000	1,838,200	63
5,000,000	6,000,000	2,468,200	67
6,000,000	7,000,000	3,138,200	70
7,000,000	8,000,000	3,838,200	73
8,000,000	10,000,000	4,568,200	76
10,000,000	—	6,088,200	77

Note: Total tax is column (3) plus amount calculated by using column (4).

Source: Federal Estate Tax Return, Form 706 (Revised Sept. 1963).

237

CHART 10-10

ESTIMATION SEQUENCE FOR IDENTIFYING PATTERNS OF WEALTH FLOWS AT DEATH

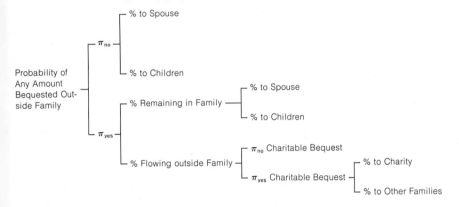

Note: π = probability.

shown in Chart 10-11. The combination of being married and having a net worth of under $100,000 resulted in a probability of .142 of making a bequest outside the family. If a decedent were not married and had $35,000 or more, on the other hand, the probability of making an outside

CHART 10-11

PROBABILITY OF MAKING A BEQUEST OUTSIDE THE FAMILY

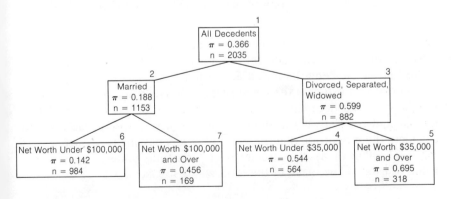

Notes: π = probability.
n = number of observations in group.
Age and sex were also eligible variables but did not contribute to a significant reduction in variance.
The four final groups accounted for 22.4% of variance.

TABLE 10-7

WEALTH BEQUEATHED TO SPOUSE AS A PERCENT OF TOTAL WEALTH BEQUEATHED TO SPOUSE AND CHILDREN, BY SEX AND VALUE OF TOTAL NET ESTATE OF DECEDENTS, WASHINGTON, D.C., 1967

Value of Net Estate $000	MEAN OF RATIO $\left(\dfrac{\text{Spouse}}{\text{Spouse + Children}}\right)$		RATIO OF AGGREGATES OF WEALTH $\left(\dfrac{\Sigma\ \text{Spouse}}{\Sigma\ \text{Spouse + Children}}\right)$	
	Males	Females	Males	Females
From: To:				
0 5	86.7	79.0	85.7	82.7
5 10	90.4	87.3	90.9	86.1
10 15	91.7	82.3	92.1	82.9
15 20	90.6	86.3	90.9	86.9
20 25	95.5	79.9	95.1	80.5
25 30	90.7	90.9	91.0	89.7
30 35	97.7	83.4	97.7	82.9
35 50	96.0	81.3	96.3	81.6
50 75	82.9	75.2	82.3	75.6
75 100	91.0	66.6	90.9	63.0
100 250	79.4	59.0	79.8	55.8
250 and over	72.1	52.7	75.3	41.8

Note: In example for male decedents with estates worth from $10,000 to $15,000, 91.7 percent of the portion of the estate left to the spouse and children went to the spouse. The remaining 8.3 percent went to the children.

bequest was .695. The four end groups numbered 4 through 7 in Chart 10-11 accounted for 22.4 percent of the variance around the mean probability of outside bequests for all decedents.

In order to estimate the mean share of assets going to the spouse, a sample of 1,090 decedents (who were residents of the District of Columbia and married at the time of their death in 1967) was used to calculate the proportion that the value of assets passing to spouse was of the total value of assets passing to children plus spouse, by sex and value of estate. The mean of the ratio was also calculated:

$$\frac{\sum_{i=1}^{n}\dfrac{\text{spouse}_i}{\text{spouse}_i + \text{children}_i}}{n}$$

These values are shown in Table 10-7.

PERCENT OF DECEDENT'S ASSETS BEQUEATHED OUTSIDE FAMILY

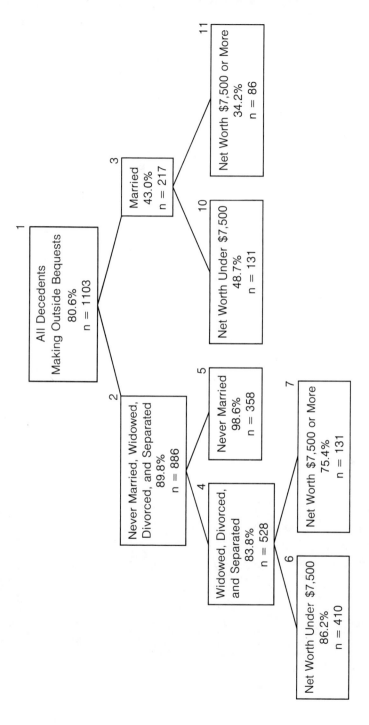

Notes: n = number of observations in group.
Age and sex were eligible variables but did not contribute significantly to the reduction of variance.
For example, 34.2 percent of the wealth of decedents who make outside bequests and who are married and have estates greater than $7,500 went to outside bequests.
The five final groups account for 38.4% of variance.

CHART 10-13

PROBABILITY THAT BEQUEST IS MADE TO CHARITY OR GOVERNMENT
(Given That Some Wealth Was Bequeathed Outside Family)

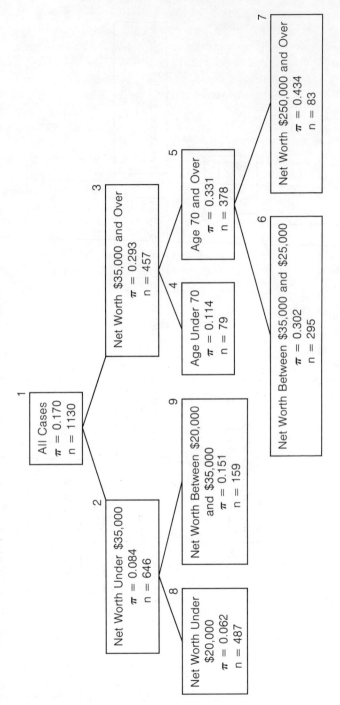

Notes: π = probability.
        n = number of observations in each group.
        For example, given that some wealth was bequeathed outside the family, the probability of a bequest being made to charity or government is .302 for decedents 70 and
        over with net worth between $25,000 and $35,000.
        Sex and marital status were also eligible variables, but could not contribute to a significant reduction in variance.
        The five final groups account for 11.3% of variance.

Females consistently transfer less to their surviving spouse, as a proportion of total transfers to spouse and children, than do males. The distribution of estates between wives and children shifts in favor of children as the total value of estates increase. The observed patterns with respect to the value of the estates are consistent with estate planning strategies to minimize repeated taxation of the same bundle of wealth.

Given that we had a basis for predicting the probability that a bequest would be made outside the family, it was necessary to estimate the share of one's estate which would flow outside (or conversely, remain inside) the family. AID was used again, this time to estimate the proportion of a decedent's assets which were bequested outside the family if any bequests were made. See Chart 10-12.

As might be expected, married decedents give a smaller share outside their family than do decedents who are other than married. The proportion of one's assets given beyond the bonds of the family decreases with increased wealth, but the absolute amount most likely increases.

We next estimated the probability that those decedents transferring wealth outside their family made a bequest to charities or governments. The AID tree shown in Chart 10-13 explained 11.3 percent of the variance in the probability that a charitable transfer took place. The second step in the estimation of charitable bequests was to estimate the share of assets leaving the family which went to charities (including gifts to government) for all decedents making charitable bequests. We were able to explain 13.6 percent in the variance in the share of wealth flowing away from decedents which went to charities. The AID tree of Chart 10-14 shows the result of the AID analysis.

Estimation of Inheritances from Outside Family Unit

The sum of inheritances and gifts received (before death of donor) by 113 families are contained in the SCFF file. The ratio of inheritances generated by estates over $60,000 to the value of gifts greater than $3,000 reported in 1962 statistics of income[9] is about seven to one. On this basis, the value of gifts and inheritances in the SCFF file was treated as inheritances only. Estimation of an inheritance pattern was

9. *Statistics of Income: Fiduciary, Gift, and Estate Tax Returns, 1962,* U.S. Treasury Department and Internal Revenue Service, Government Printing Office, Washington, D.C., 1965.

CHART 10-14

PERCENT OF ESTATE BEQUEATHED TO CHARITY
(Among Decedents Making Charitable Bequests)

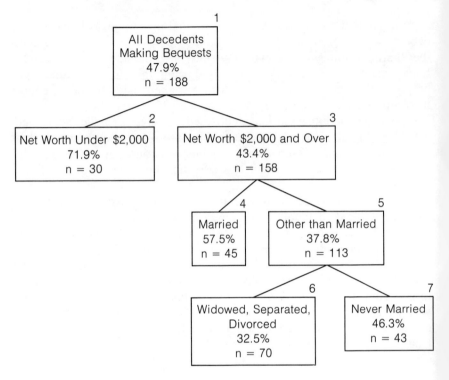

Notes: n = number of observations in group.
"Charity" includes donations to government.
Age and sex were eligible variables but could not significantly reduce the unexplained variance.
The four final groups account for 13.6 % of variance.

done in two stages. First, the probability that a family will receive an inheritance during the simulated year was estimated using AID. The results of the AID analysis shown in Chart 10-15 indicate that inheritance from outside the family unit cannot be predicted very well ($R^2 = 2.3$ percent) with the information that was available. For the simulation, each family was assigned an inheritance probability π equal to one of four values in the final AID groups. The second stage was to estimate an equation to predict the size of inheritance using the 113 SCFF

CHART 10-15

PROBABILITY OF RECEIVING AN INHERITANCE

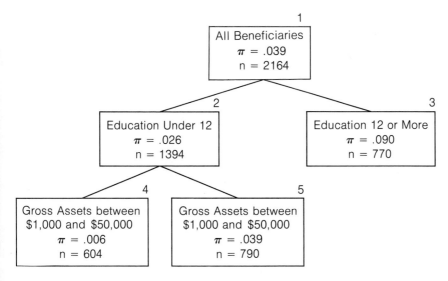

Notes: π = probability.
  n = number of observations in group.
  Income, age, marital status, sex, and race were also eligible variables but did not contribute to a significant reduction in variance.
  The three final groups account for 2.3% of variance.

families which received an inheritance. The resulting equation has the form:

$$\ln (\text{INHERITANCE}) = a + b_1 (\text{GROSS ESTATE})$$
$$+ b_2 (\text{AGE}) + b_3 (\text{ED})$$

where GROSS ESTATE is measured in $1,000's and AGE and ED are the age and number of years of education of the head of the family respectively. The estimated coefficients are:

$$a = 3.58$$
$$b_1 = 0.0007$$
$$b_2 = 0.027$$
$$b_3 = 0.17$$
$$R^2 = 21.9 \text{ percent}$$

PART IV.
EXPLORATIONS
WITH THE MODEL

The simulations described in the remainder of this volume were conducted while DYNASIM was still evolving. Since several different versions of the model were used, not all of the findings could necessarily be produced with the 1975 version of DYNASIM. However, in most cases the results would be similar.

Chapter 11
MONTE CARLO VARIABILITY*

There are two major sources of variability in the predictions of the model which are not a function of the behavioral relations imbedded in the model but rather of the methods that have been used to solve the model. These are (1) the variance related to the specification of the initial population on which the behavioral functions are to operate, and (2) the variance associated with the sampling approach for selecting the particular members of the model population whose status changed each year of the simulation. In running DYNASIM experiments we have generally used the same initial population for multiple runs. This minimizes run-to-run variation of the first type. In addition, we have developed a method of controlling the Monte Carlo variation of the second type. This was described in Chapter 1.

This chapter reports on the efforts to measure the components of sampling error in the model's predictions when special efforts are *not* being made to control the variation. Discussed in turn are the sources of sampling variability; the Monte Carlo component of the error for four samples of 1,000 persons; the Monte Carlo error for a larger sample; and the relation of the variance for samples of different sizes. A discussion of small-sample bias concludes the chapter.

The analysis leads to several important conclusions. First, the variance of predictions from the model are not-large even for samples with as few as 1,000 persons. Second, there is no substantial evidence that the variance in predicted outcomes grows rapidly after about the third or fourth year of simulation. Third, preliminary analysis suggests that the variance of the model's predictions is roughly inversely proportional to sample size. Thus, as the sample size is doubled, the variance is reduced by about one-half. Finally, there is no indication of small-sample bias in the predictions.

---

* Gary Hendricks had the main responsibility for this chapter and the work it represents.

247

248

Sources of Variation

Solving the model, it will be recalled, consists of three steps. First an initial population is specified. In solving the model we have used a representative sample of the U.S. population based on a public use sample from the 1960 census.

This sample differs somewhat from an exact representation of the U.S. population. This difference will affect the predictions of the model.[1]

Second, we compute the probability that an event will occur for each person or family for each potential event included in the model. For each potential event, the sum of the probabilities multiplied by the population weight yields the predicted number of occurrences of that event for the year. Thus, the model yields specific aggregate predictions for each event simulated, such as total deaths, marriages, births, and divorces, number of labor force participants, etc. Other aggregate statistics, such as average wage rate and average hours worked, can also be produced.

The final step in the solution process is to update the sample micropopulation's characteristics. This final step, the actual assignment of changes in status, is necessary in order to provide for each decision making unit the set of attributes required for calculating transition probabilities in the next simulation period.

The assignment of changes in status yields a further set of predictions from the model. After all changes in status are recorded, an updated sample of the population is available from which tabular, regression, and other types of survey statistics can be derived.

The most straightforward way to assign events in accordance with predicted probabilities is to compare each probability with a random number drawn from a 0–1 uniform distribution and assign the appropriate event to a unit whenever the random number is less than the predicted probability. This is called the Monte Carlo method. In essence, the Monte Carlo method of solving the model is a sampling technique whereby individuals and families are selected for changes in status on the basis of probabilities that reflect what research leads us to believe are the real world probabilities of the changes actually occurring. Viewed in this way, a particular prediction or statistic produced by a single run of the model should be regarded as a sample estimate of the true prediction of the model. Rerunning the identical model with a different set of random numbers will yield another set of predictions which will differ somewhat from the first set. The difference between the two solutions is the Monte Carlo sampling variability. The primary focus of

1. In addition to the variance associated with the initial sample used, variation arises in the specification of the initial population because of the need to assign attributes which were not ascertained for the original sample but are needed for the simulation. Initial assignments are based upon known correlations and are made stochastically.

this chapter is to estimate the Monte Carlo sampling variance of the model.

Approach to Measuring Monte Carlo Variance

We measure the Monte Carlo sampling variance by obtaining several solutions of the model using different sets of random numbers. The mean of a large number of individual solutions is the true prediction of the model, and the variance of the individual estimates around the mean is an estimate of the variance of a single solution.

Our first effort to estimate the Monte Carlo variance was made using an early version of the demographic model and a sample of 500 households containing 1,562 persons. The model included the death, birth, marriage, and divorce operating characteristics. Ten runs were made with a different set of random numbers for each run.

The objective of these experiments was to measure the Monte Carlo variance and its annual rate of increase. For each major output of the demographic model, the mean prediction and the standard deviation were computed for each simulation year. The yearly ratios of the standard deviations to the means are shown in Table 11-1.

The predicted number of events in the first year differs hardly at all from one run to another. This is because the predictions of the model are

TABLE 11-1

COEFFICIENTS OF VARIATION FOR PREDICTIONS OF
THE DEMOGRAPHIC MODEL[1]
(Estimates are based on 10 replications of the same initial
sample of 1,564 persons)

	DEMOGRAPHIC EVENT			
Year	Predicted Deaths	Predicted Divorces	Predicted Marriages	Predicted Births
1960	.000	.009	.004	.001
1961	.018	.020	.074	.066
1962	.018	.019	.061	.082
1963	.030	.031	.072	.040
1964	.037	.045	.053	.065
1965	.028	.042	.083	.090
1966	.033	.044	.038	.072
1967	.026	.054	.051	.095
1968	.031	.057	.067	.072
1969	.033	.057	.070	.078

1. The coefficient of variation is the ratio of the standard error to the mean prediction.

250   *Policy Exploration Through Microanalytic Simulation*

the sum of the expected probabilities (across individuals) of events occurring and the sums are virtually identical until the population is altered by deaths, marriages, and births. Thus, it is the years 1961–1969 that are of most interest.

The Monte Carlo variance differs substantially among the different demographic events. For deaths the standard error in 1961 and 1962 is less than 2 percent of the mean; for 1963–69, the standard error ranges from 3.0 to 3.7 percent of the mean prediction of the 10 runs. The standard errors relative to the mean prediction for births are higher than for deaths. They range from 4 percent to over 9 percent. The relative variances of marriages and divorces lie somewhere between deaths and births. After the third or fourth year, the growth of the Monte Carlo variance is slow.

Experiments with a More Developed Model

The next Monte Carlo experiments were performed with a version of the model containing a labor sector and a macro model. They had three objectives: (1) measuring the magnitude of the Monte Carlo variance for the aggregate outputs of the demographic model, the labor force model, and the macro model; (2) examining the relation of Monte Carlo variance to initial sample size; and (3) testing for a small sample bias. Objectives (1) and (2) were fulfilled by making multiple runs with a small sample and then multiple runs with a larger sample. The two sample sizes chosen were 1,000 and 4,000 persons.

For the smaller sample estimates we partitioned the larger sample into four samples of approximately 1,000 persons each. The Monte Carlo variance was then estimated for the larger sample and for each of the smaller samples. Since the larger sample is the sum of the smaller ones, we were able to explore the possibility of a small-sample bias.

Three runs were made for each of the smaller samples and for the larger sample. Each run used a different set of random numbers. For each simulation year and for each sample, the mean prediction and the estimated variance were calculated for a selected set of aggregate outputs. These sets of sample means and their variances are the basic data on which the analysis is based.

Method of Presentation of Experimental Results

While one of the most attractive features of DYNASIM is the richness of its output, this richness causes some difficulty in analyzing errors. There is a large number of statistics for which a variance may be calculated and, since the statistics are time series, the variance can be calculated for each year of simulation.

Omitting the first simulation year, a simple way of reducing the amount of detail is to average the individual-year estimates of the variance of a time series such as total deaths. The square root of this average can then be used as an estimate of the standard error of the individual-year predictions of the time series. Any tendency of the Monte Carlo variability to grow over time can be taken into account by using a regression to estimate the variance rather than a simple mean. The simplest regression to estimate is:

$$(\text{Variance of Time Series X})_t = a + a_1 t$$

where t is time. This is the form in which the estimates of variance in this chapter are presented. We have chosen to show the slope coefficients (a_1) even when their standard errors are large. In addition, since the mean of the individual-year estimates of the variance is the best single estimate of the variance in most instances, t in the regressions has been specified as the actual year minus 1965. Using year minus 1965 as the independent variable means that the constant term (a_0) in the regression is equal to the mean of the 1961–1969 estimates. The square root of the constant term is the estimated standard error of the prediction for 1965.

Estimates of the Monte Carlo Error
for Samples of 1,000 Persons

Table 11-2 shows the results of the regressions of estimated variance on time for the four samples of 1,000 persons. Thirteen series were chosen for analysis. The demographic series include deaths, births, marriages, divorces, and total population. Three of the time series from the macro model are included. Gross national product and gross private domestic investment (both in billions at 1958 prices) were selected because the equations in the macro model determining these are direct points of entry for two of the time series from the micro model—total persons in the labor force and change in total population. Total labor income (also in billions at 1958 prices) was selected since it is an important input into the labor force section of the micro model. Five series from the labor force model are singled out for study—total persons in the labor force and average earnings of four major population groups, white and nonwhite males and females. The constant terms and slope coefficients shown in Table 11-2 are the mean of the four individual estimates. The sampling variability (one standard error) of the means is shown in parentheses.

TABLE 11-2

REGRESSION ESTIMATES OF THE VARIANCE OF PREDICTIONS OF THE MODEL FOR SAMPLES OF 1,000 PERSONS AND STANDARD ERRORS OF THE PREDICTIONS FOR 1965

Time Series	REGRESSION RESULTS[1]		MONTE CARLO VARIABILITY FOR 1965[2]	
	Constant Term	Slope Coefficient	One Standard Error	Coefficient of Variation
Total Deaths (in thousands)	4,534(1,521)	1,060(422)	67	.036
Total Divorces (in thousands)	182(60)	50(29)	13	.025
Total Marriages (in thousands)	11,840(2,859)	−18(1,169)	109	.060
Total Births (in thousands)	126,620(33,197)	4,457(4,307)	356	.081
Total Population (in millions)	3.592(1.077)	.864(.293)	1.895	.010
Gross National Product (in billions of $'s)	$21.0(3.4)	3.6(.5)	4.6	.007
Gross Domestic Private Investment (in billions of $'s)	$8.8(1.8)	.8(.7)	3.0	.030
Total Labor Income (in billions of $'s)	$10.4(1.7)	1.3(.3)	3.2	.008
Total Persons in the Labor Force (in millions)	.299(.051)	.017(.018)	0.547	.006
Average Annual Earnings (in dollars):				
White Males	$16,404(2,613)	95(404)	128	.021
Nonwhite Males	$111,660(2,711)	7,130(8,142)	334	.097
White Females	$18,362(3,945)	−1,151(1,409)	135	.053
Nonwhite Females	$30,896(8,845)	3,781(1,877)	176	.133

1. Constant terms and slope coefficients are the mean of the separate regression estimates obtained for each of four samples of approximately 1,000 persons each. Numbers in parentheses are standard errors of the means.

2. The standard errors in column 3 are the square root of the predicted values (variances) for 1965 of the regressions reported in columns 1 and 2. The coefficient of variation is the ratio of the standard error to the mean prediction for 1965 across all 12 runs of the samples of 1,000 persons.

The slope coefficients, which indicate the extent of the increase in the variance over time, are generally small relative to their sampling errors. In fact, for five of the slope coefficients, zero is included in the range of one standard error. The slope coefficients are also small relative to the magnitude of the average level of Monte Carlo variability (indicated by the constant terms). The estimated sampling errors of the constant terms are relatively small — only one-third to one-seventh as large as the estimated level of Monte Carlo variability.

A clearer notion of the magnitude of the Monte Carlo error for a small sample and of its probable impact on evaluating experimental results is given by examining the estimated standard errors and their relation to the mean predictions. Table 11-2 column 3 shows the standard error of the prediction for 1965 for each of the 13 series whose variance was analyzed. The standard errors are the square root of the constant term of the regressions (shown in column 1). The ratio of the standard error to the mean prediction for 1965 is shown in the last column of the table.

After 5 years of simulation, the sampling errors of the aggregate predictions of the demographic model are probably no larger than those one might expect for a sample survey based on a similarly small number of observations. For the macro model time series, the Monte Carlo variability is less than one percent of the mean prediction for GNP and total labor income in 1965. The variability for gross private domestic investment is relatively larger — about 3 percent of predicted investment.

Although there is a strong trend in the variance of GNP and total labor income (both in constant dollars), these two income aggregates were growing rapidly over the period 1961–1969. Thus, the magnitude of the error relative to the mean was not changing rapidly over the course of the simulation. For example, in 1969 predicted GNP (in constant 1958 dollars) for the first sample was $837 billion. The estimated variance (from Table 11-4) is 50.6 and the standard error $7.1 billion dollars. The coefficient of variation, then, is .008 for 1969 which is not different from the coefficient of variation in 1965.

As expected the standard error for earnings in 1965 is smallest for white males, the largest subgroup in the labor force. For nonwhite participants in the labor force, the standard errors on earnings is $135 for males and $176 for females. In a sample of 1,000 persons, from 100 to 120 persons are likely to be nonwhite.

Monte Carlo Error for a Sample of 4,000

One of the reasons for using different sample sizes was to examine the relation between Monte Carlo variability and initial sample size. Our ex-

TABLE 11-3

REGRESSION ESTIMATES OF THE VARIANCE OF PREDICTIONS OF THE MODEL FOR A SAMPLE OF 4,000 PERSONS AND STANDARD ERRORS OF THE 1965 PREDICTIONS

Time Series[1]	REGRESSION RESULTS[2]		MONTE CARLO VARIABILITY FOR 1965[3]		Standard Error Ratios of 4000 to 1000 Samples
	Constant Term	Coefficient	One Standard Error	Coefficient of Variation	
Total Deaths	1511	371	39	.021	.582
Total Divorces	10	3	3	.006	.231
Total Marriages	4679	−475	68	.037	.624
Total Births	51746	6566	227	.054	.638
Total Population	.336	−.076	.6	.003	.306
Gross National Product	3.420	−.103	1.8	.003	.403
Gross Domestic Private Investment	2.045	−.397	1.4	.014	.481
Total Labor Income	1.645	−.040	1.3	.003	.398
Total Persons in the Labor Force	.062	.0006	.250	.003	.457
Average Annual Earnings:					
White Males	6472	1657	80	.013	.625
Nonwhite Males	25438	2050	159	.046	.476
White Females	6163	1484	78	.030	.578
Nonwhite Females	4751	370	69	.048	.392

1. Total deaths, divorces, marriages and births are in thousands of persons. Total population and persons in the labor force are in millions. Gross national product, gross private domestic investment and total labor income are in billions of dollars at 1958 prices. Average earnings are in dollars.

2. The regressions were Variance of Series X in Year $t = a_0 + a_1$ (Year − 1965).

3. The standard errors in column 3 are the square root of the predicted values (variances) for 1965 of the regressions reported in columns 1 and 2. The coefficient of variation is the ratio of the standard error to the mean prediction for 1965 across all 12 runs of the samples of 1,000 persons.

pectation was that Monte Carlo error, like other sources of sampling variance, would be related to the size of the sample. Moreover, as a first approximation it seems reasonable to assume that the variance due to Monte Carlo error of the distribution of any particular prediction of the model would be inversely proportional to the size of the initial sample.

The results of the regression of the variance of the annual predictions on time for the sample of 4,000 persons are shown in columns 1 and 2 of Table 11-3. Since only one sample of 4,000 persons was used to derive the estimates, sampling errors are not shown. The standard error of the mean prediction of the model for 1965 is shown in column 3 and the coefficient of variation for 1965 in column 4. The last column of Table 3 shows the ratios of the 4,000 person sample estimates of the Monte Carlo variability to the smaller sample variability. The comparison made is between the standard errors of the predictions of the model for 1965, that is, the square roots of the constant terms of the regressions shown in Tables 11-2 and 11-3.

The ratios of standard errors range from .231 to .638. For five of the 13 time series the ratios are above .50, the expected ratio for a fourfold increase in sample size. The remaining 8 ratios are below .50 and four of these are below .40, indicating that the Monte Carlo variance fell faster than in proportion to the increase in sample size. The mean of all 13 ratios is .477.

Tests of Small Sample Bias

The runs made to compare the Monte Carlo component of the sampling variance for samples of different sizes also provide the data necessary to test for any substantial bias in the predictions obtained from running the model using a small initial sample.[2] Since the sample of 4,000 persons is the composite of the four samples of approximately 1,000 persons each, the mean of the predictions from the four smaller samples should equal the prediction derived from the larger sample. In the absence of any small-sample bias in the techniques used for solving the model, the only difference between the two sets of predictions will be that arising from the unsystematic sampling variability owing to the random number draws.

For the time series of each of the 13 variables examined in this chapter, two separate regressions on time were fit, one using the mean of the small-sample predictions (across all 12 small sample runs) as the

2. Bias here refers to systematic differences in predictions which are the result of applying the Monte Carlo solution technique to a large complex model on a small initial sample. Differences which result because of differences in the joint distribution of decision making unit attributes among initial samples are not biases but rather sampling variability.

dependent variable and the other using the mean annual predictions from the three larger sample runs. The results of the two sets of regressions are compared in Table 11-4. The regressions include only years 1961–1969. As with the regressions shown elsewhere in this chapter, time (the independent variable) is year minus 1965. The standard errors of the regression coefficients and the standard error of estimate are shown as indicators of how much variance there is in the time series. The standard errors are very small and the adjusted R^2's (not shown) were generally .90 or greater.

TABLE 11-4

REGRESSIONS OF THE MEAN PREDICTION OF THE MODEL ON TIME FROM MULTIPLE RUNS OF FOUR SAMPLES OF 1,000 PERSONS AND MULTIPLE RUNS OF THE COMBINED SAMPLE OF 4,000 PERSONS

Time Series[1]	CONSTANT TERM		SLOPE COEFFICIENT		STANDARD ERROR OF ESTIMATE	
	1000 Sample	4000 Sample	1000 Sample	4000 Sample	1000 Sample	4000 Sample
Total Deaths	1844 (8.9)	1834 (7.9)	24 (3.1)	24 (2.7)	28	25
Total Divorces	498 (1.6)	503 (2.0)	29 (0.6)	30 (0.7)	5	6
Total Marriages	1844 (13.6)	1855 (8.9)	75 (4.7)	76 (3.1)	43	28
Total Births	4322 (60.4)	4292 (60.2)	167 (21.0)	170 (21.0)	191	190
Total Population	194 (0.2)	194 (0.2)	3 (0.1)	3 (0.1)	1	1
Gross National Product	653 (0.8)	654 (1.1)	33 (0.3)	33 (0.4)	2.6	3.4
Gross Private Domestic Investment	99 (0.6)	98 (0.5)	4 (0.2)	4 (0.2)	2.0	1.5

(note at end of table on next page)

TABLE 11-4 (continued)

Time Series[1]	CONSTANT TERM		SLOPE COEFFICIENT		STANDARD ERROR OF ESTIMATE	
	1000 Sample	4000 Sample	1000 Sample	4000 Sample	1000 Sample	4000 Sample
Total Labor Income.	400 (0.5)	401 (0.6)	24 (0.2)	24 (0.2)	1.6	2.0
Total Persons in the Labor Force	94.1 (0.3)	94.5 (0.3)	2.4 (0.1)	2.4 (0.1)	0.8	0.9
Average Earnings of White Males	5974 (13)	5955 (16)	261 (4)	239 (6)	40	51
Average Earnings of Nonwhite Males	3332 (46)	3308 (34)	72 (16)	120 (12)	146	109
Average Earnings of White Females	2490 (9)		82 (3)		27	
Average Earnings of Nonwhite Females	1481 (29)		40 (10)		93	

1. Total deaths, divorces, marriages and births are in thousands of persons. Total population and persons in the labor force are in millions. Gross national product, gross private domestic investment and total labor income are in billions of dollars at 1958 prices. Average earnings are in dollars.

There is almost no difference between the small and large sample predictions. For none of the time series do the two constant terms differ by as much as 5 percent and in only one instance (total births) do they differ by more than one percent. Except for average earnings, the same statement is true for the slope coefficients.

The fact that no small-sample bias is apparent is an important finding with implications for how one might carry out experiments using the model. If there is no small-sample bias, a larger sample could be partitioned into several smaller samples. For each of the smaller samples a single control run estimate and a single estimate with the application of the treatment could be obtained. The best estimate of the effect of the treatment would be some measure of the difference between the control and treatment runs for the total or larger sample. In the absence of small-sample bias, such an estimate would be obtained by taking the difference between the means of the smaller sample estimates for the control and the treatment runs or by averaging the differences obtained from

258 Policy Exploration Through Microanalytic Simulation

each of the smaller sample runs.[3] Whichever procedure were used, the variance or standard error of the difference could be calculated from the four smaller sample estimates comprising the mean estimate. This multistage procedure for estimating experimental results would be advantageous as long as sampling variability does not fall more than in proportion to increase in sample size.

Conclusions

The single most impressive finding from the Monte Carlo experiments described in this chapter is how small the impact of a specific random number stream is on the results of the model. DYNASIM is very complex and involves a large number of stochastic decisions for each person each year. Yet, with samples of only 1,000 to 2,000 persons the standard errors of most aggregate statistics from the model are less than 5 percent of the prediction. With samples of 4,000 persons the errors are, in many cases, less than 1 percent.

The problem of selecting the appropriate sample size for a particular policy application of DYNASIM will always be present. However, the findings of this chapter and other recent developments greatly diminish the priority researchers need place on sampling variance due to the application of Monte Carlo techniques in DYNASIM.

As discussed in Chapter 1, a new capability has been added to DYNASIM to control for the Monte Carlo variation in simulation experiments. In addition, improvements to the software environment (MASH) in which DYNASIM operates have made the use of initial samples of 20,000 or 30,000 persons practical for many applications. Further improvements will make even larger initial samples practical.

3. Whether one would choose the difference between the mean prediction from the control runs and the mean of the treatment runs or the mean of the differences for each sample would depend upon which had the smaller variance. Both variances could be calculated.

Chapter 12
MARRIAGE, DIVORCE, AND DEATH SENSITIVITY STUDIES*

Five demographic experiments were performed for the purpose of exploring the properties of the model. In each experiment a single demographic process was altered. The alterations were not intended to simulate likely real world occurrences. The primary purpose of the five experiments was to explore the properties of the model, rather than to project the likely real world effects of realistic potential policies or social trends. In effect, the experiments begin not with policies themselves but rather with certain hypothetical initial consequences of a policy or social trend on a single demographic process. Each experiment asks the question: given an hypothesized alteration in a *single* demographic process, what additional demographic, microeconomic and macroeconomic consequences does the model project?

Demographic changes were found to have substantial effects upon the economic sector of the model. This suggests the importance of demographic phenomena in policy issues involving the economy.

Alignment

Before the experiments were conducted, annual aggregate totals of marriages, divorces, deaths, births, and total persons in the labor force in the base run were forced to align as closely as possible with corresponding aggregate totals found in official vital statistics. The adjustment factors used to accomplish this alignment, together with comparisons between the simulated values generated using these adjustment factors and the corresponding historical data, are given in Table 12-1.

As can be seen in Table 12-1, the total number of deaths simulated over the entire decade 1960–1969 without using an adjustment factor

---

* Steven B. Caldwell had the main responsibility for this chapter and the work it represents.

TABLE 12-1

COMPARISON OF HISTORICAL VS. SIMULATED DEATHS, MARRIAGES, DIVORCES, BIRTHS AND TOTAL LABOR FORCE[1]

Year	(1) Simulation Results (in 000's)	(2) Historical Values (in 000's)	(3) Difference: Standard Minus Historical (in 000's)	(4) % Difference $\frac{(1)-(2)}{(2)} \times 100$	(5) Adjustment Factor Used
			DEATHS		
1960	1,777	1,712	65	3.7	1.0
1961	1,706	1,702	4	0.2	1.0
1962	1.719	1,757	−38	−2.2	1.0
1963	1,739	1,814	−75	−4.1	1.0
1964	1,790	1,798	−8	−0.4	1.0
1965	1,784	1,828	−44	−2.4	1.0
1966	1,854	1,863	−9	−0.5	1.0
1967	1,886	1,851	35	1.9	1.0
1968	1,919	1,930	−11	−0.6	1.0
1969	1,947	1,922	25	1.3	1.0
TOTAL	18,121	18,177	−56	−0.3	
			MARRIAGES		
1960	1,464	1,523	−59	−3.9	0.95
1961	1,516	1,548	−32	−2.1	0.95
1962	1,630	1,577	53	3.4	0.95
1963	1,657	1,654	3	0.2	0.95
1964	1,709	1,725	−16	−0.9	0.95
1965	1,808	1,800	8	0.4	0.95
1966	1,881	1,857	24	1.3	0.95
1967	1,963	1,927	36	1.9	0.95
1968	2,056	2,069	−13	−0.6	0.95
1969	2,155	2,145	10	0.5	0.95
TOTAL	17,839	17,825	14	0.07	
			DIVORCES		
1960	394	393	1	0.3	1.05
1961	405	414	−9	−2.2	1.05
1962	416	413	3	0.7	1.02
1963	428	428	0	0	0.99
1964	448	450	−2	−0.4	0.97

TABLE 12-1 (continued)

Year	(1) Simulation Results (in 000's)	(2) Historical Values (in 000's)	(3) Difference: Standard Minus Historical (in 000's)	(4) % Difference $\frac{(1)-(2)}{(2)} \times 100$	(5) Adjustment Factor Used
DIVORCES (continued)					
1965	475	479	−4	−0.8	0.97
1966	501	499	2	0.4	0.97
1967	529	523	6	1.1	0.97
1968	584	584	0	0	1.00
1969	639	639	0	0	1.03
TOTAL	4,819	4,822	−3	−0.06	
BIRTHS					
1960	4,251	4,258	−7	−0.2	0.68
1961	4,149	4,268	−119	−2.8	0.68
1962	3,906	4,167	−261	−6.3	0.68
1963	3,869	4,098	−229	−5.6	0.68
1964	3,697	4,027	−330	−8.2	0.64
1965	3,498	3,760	−262	−7.0	0.60
1966	3,349	3,606	−257	−7.1	0.56
1967	3,305	3,521	−216	−6.1	0.52
1968	3,470	3,502	−32	−0.9	0.49
1969	3,706	3,565	141	4.0	0.47
TOTAL	37,200	38,772	−1,572	−4.1	
TOTAL LABOR FORCE[1]					
1960	84,848	84,718	130	0.2	1.03
1961	84,213	84,535	−322	−0.4	0.97
1962	85,983	86,772	−789	−0.9	0.96
1963	87,718	87,776	−58	−0.1	0.94
1964	89,570	89,576	−6	−0.0	0.94
1965	90,622	90,314	308	0.3	0.92
1966	92,840	93,047	−207	−0.2	0.92
1967	95,202	95,312	−110	−0.1	0.92
1968	96,915	97,504	−589	−0.6	0.92
1969	98,665	99,674	−1,009	−1.0	0.92
TOTAL	906,576	909,228	−2,652	−0.3	

1. Total labor force is defined to include all persons who participated in the labor force at any time during the year.

(i.e., with the adjustment factor equal to 1.0) was barely 0.3 percent less than the historical value. Consequently, no adjustment to *mortality* was necessary. However, a proportional (unchanged) reduction of 0.95 for all ten years was applied to the *marriage* probabilities generated by the model. Using this adjustment led to a slight 0.07 percent excess of simulated over reported marriages for the decade. For *divorce* a time series of adjustments varying over the decade but with a mean of 1.0 was employed. These adjustments resulted in a slight deficit of 0.06 percent in simulated compared to reported divorces for 1960–69.

The adjustment made to *birth* probabilities was more substantial. However, the greater share of this adjustment was made in order to account for the elimination during the runs from the birth function of dependence on interval since last birth. This temporary simplification of the birth function was made to decrease the variance in births. After the adjustment due to the lack of dependence on interval is accounted for, the remaining adjustment corresponds to the pure alignment factor. After alignment the number of simulated births in the decade was 4.1 percent lower than the actual number.

Finally, a small alignment was made to the total number of *persons in the labor force* sometime during the year. This alignment succeeded in bringing the simulated total within at least 1 percent of the actual total for all years, and within 0.3 percent for the decade as a whole.

The purpose of these adjustment factors was to increase the validity of the sensitivity experiment results by preventing aggregate errors in one process from leading to errors in other processes. For example, an excess of simulated marriages would lead by itself to an excess of births. Note that comparisons between simulated and historical *aggregate* totals constitute a relatively less important test of the validity of the model than *distributive* comparisons; the major focus of the model is predicting the distribution of events according to the characteristics of micro units rather than predicting the total number of events across all micro units. Aggregate adjustments are simple to apply. Therefore, assuming that small adjustments do not significantly bias the distributive aspects of the functions, the use of such adjustments can be justified as a way of restricting the spread of one particular type of discrepancy.

Comparing the 1970 Census to the 1970 Simulated Population

One test of the validity of the model is to compare the *real* population as reported in the 1970 Census with the *simulated* population for 1970.

TABLE 12-2

COMPARING SIMULATED AND REAL DISTRIBUTIONS OF THE U.S. POPULATION IN 1970 BY RACE, SEX, AND AGE

(000,000's of persons)

Age	WHITE MALE		WHITE FEMALE		BLACK MALE		BLACK FEMALE		TOTALS	
	10-Year Simulation	1970 Census	10-Year Simulation	1970 Census	10-Year Simulation	1970 Census	10-Year Simulation	1970 Census	10-Year Simulation	1970 Census
0–4	6.72	7.37	7.64	7.05	1.38	1.37	1.24	1.36	16.98	17.15
5–14	16.19	17.67	16.83	16.91	2.58	3.09	2.58	3.07	38.18	40.75
15–24	16.88	15.23	14.40	15.42	2.76	2.32	2.71	2.47	36.75	35.44
25–34	10.49	10.77	9.98	11.00	1.43	1.44	1.56	1.69	23.45	24.91
35–44	9.38	9.98	9.94	10.35	0.92	1.25	1.24	1.51	21.47	23.09
45–54	10.08	10.09	10.35	10.76	1.29	1.11	1.66	1.26	23.37	23.22
55–64	7.64	7.96	9.52	8.85	0.60	0.83	0.78	0.94	18.56	18.59
65–74	5.61	4.91	6.39	6.37	0.41	0.52	0.55	0.63	12.97	12.44
75–84	2.21	2.24	4.78	3.43	0.37	0.19	0.09	7.25	7.45	6.12
85+	0.60	0.49	0.83	0.89	0.09	0.06	0.14	0.08	1.66	1.51
TOTAL	85.78	86.72	90.66	91.03	11.82	12.19	12.56	13.27	200.81	203.21

Sources: 10-Year Simulation: Base run of the model.
1970 Census: U.S. Bureau of the Census, Census of Population: 1970, *General Population Characteristics*, Final Report PC(1)-B1, United States Summary, Table 52.

TABLE 12-3

COMPARING SIMULATED AND REAL DISTRIBUTION OF THE U.S. WHITE POPULATION IN 1970:
MARITAL STATUS BY SEX AND AGE

(000,000's of persons)

WHITE MALE

Age	Single 10-Year Simulation	Single 1970 Census	Married 10-Year Simulation	Married 1970 Census	Widowed 10-Year Simulation	Widowed 1970 Census	Divorced 10-Year Simulation	Divorced 1970 Census	Total 10-Year Simulation	Total 1970 Census
15–24	12.37	11.80	4.51	3.30	—	0.02	—	0.11	16.88	15.23
25–34	1.24	1.58	8.74	8.83	—	0.03	0.51	0.34	10.49	10.78
35–54	1.70	1.34	16.93	17.82	0.33	0.20	0.51	0.71	19.47	20.07
55–74	1.10	0.86	10.68	10.84	0.60	0.79	0.88	0.44	13.26	12.93
75+	0.05	0.22	2.12	1.69	0.60	0.77	0.05	0.07	2.82	2.75
Total	16.15	15.80	42.13	42.48	1.49	1.80	1.89	1.67	62.88	61.75

WHITE FEMALE

Age	Single 10-Year Simulation	Single 1970 Census	Married 10-Year Simulation	Married 1970 Census	Widowed 10-Year Simulation	Widowed 1970 Census	Divorced 10-Year Simulation	Divorced 1970 Census	Total 10-Year Simulation	Total 1970 Census
15–24	8.37	9.72	5.93	5.42	—	0.06	0.09	0.21	14.39	15.42
25–34	0.64	0.99	8.60	9.44	0.14	0.12	0.60	0.48	9.98	11.00
35–54	0.73	1.13	17.52	17.87	1.34	1.03	0.69	1.09	20.28	21.11
55–74	1.06	1.10	9.79	9.15	4.09	4.34	0.97	0.67	15.91	15.26
75+	0.37	0.39	1.52	0.92	3.54	2.90	0.18	0.10	5.61	4.32
Total	11.17	13.33	43.39	42.79	9.10	8.46	2.53	2.56	66.19	67.13

Sources: 10-Year Simulation: Base run of model.
1970 Census: U.S. Bureau of the Census, Census of Population: 1970, *General Population Characteristics*, Final Report PC(1)-B1, United States Summary, Table 53.

The simulated population is created by taking a sample drawn from the 1960 Census and simulating its behavior for ten years using the model's standard set of operating characteristics. Ten years of simulated behavior in the base run generates, in effect, a simulated public use sample for 1970 which can be compared to the actual 1970 Census Public Use Sample. A limited set of such comparisons between the population of the base run in 1970 and the 1970 Census is presented in Tables 12-2 through 12-4 to illustrate how this kind of validation exercise is carried out.

Table 12-2 shows that the age-race-sex distribution of the simulated population compares reasonably well with the distribution in the actual 1970 population. For example, the number of persons 15 and over in the simulation is just 360,000 more than the number reported in the 1970 Census. Note that the relative size of the discrepancies is larger for small population groups (e.g., nonwhite males aged 75–84). Differences between the distributions can arise either from sampling errors in the initial population or from errors introduced by particular components of the model (i.e., deaths, births, or net immigration).

Comparison of the marital status distributions for whites by age and sex is given in Table 12-3. In general the results are reassuring. However, the simulated number of never-married females was less than the number in the 1970 Census for all age groups. For males, the discrepancy varies by age, but the total number of single males in the simulation at all ages was greater than the Census number. Finally, the regional dis-

TABLE 12-4

COMPARING SIMULATED AND REAL DISTRIBUTIONS OF
THE U.S. POPULATION IN 1970: RACE BY
REGION OF RESIDENCE

Region	WHITE		BLACK AND OTHER NONWHITE		TOTAL	
	10-Year Simulation	1970 Census	10-Year Simulation	1970 Census	10-Year Simulation	1970 Census
Northeast	42.31	44.31	2.40	4.73	44.71	49.04
North Central	49.26	51.64	4.27	4.93	53.53	56.57
South	53.45	50.42	14.72	12.38	68.17	62.80
West	31.41	31.38	2.99	3.43	34.40	34.80
Total	176.43	177.75	24.37	25.46	200.81	203.21

Sources: 10-Year Simulation: Base run of model.
    1970 Census: U.S. Bureau of the Census, Final Report PC(1)-B1, Table 60.

tribution (Table 12-4) indicates a deficit in the simulation of nonwhite migrants (and, to a lesser extent, white migrants) from the South and to the Northeast. Comparisons such as these are useful in locating which parts of the model most need attention.

Five Demographic Experiments

Below are descriptions of five demographic experiments performed on the model with brief selected results from each experiment. The purpose is to illustrate possible kinds of analyses, rather than to present exhaustive analyses of each experiment.

1. *Mortality Equalization.* In this experiment we assigned to all persons the same mortality probabilities by age and marital status as those assigned in the control to white females with college education. Racial, sexual, and class (using educational attainment as a proxy of class) differences in mortality probabilities are thereby eliminated in order to explore what further consequences follow from equalization.

The effects on annual totals of deaths, births, marriages, persons in the labor force, and selected other aggregates are given in Table 12-5. The primary effect is a major reduction in the number of deaths. The slight increase in the number of divorces is a consequence of the longer period at risk for many married couples due to increased longevity. Some increases in employment were detected, along with a sizable increase in GNP.

Further insights are gained by comparing the age-race-sex distribution of the population in the experiment after ten years with the comparable population of the control. Table 12-6 shows that the main beneficiaries of equalization are older persons.

2. *Constant Divorce Probability.* This experiment assigns to all marriages a divorce probability (specific to duration of marriage, age at marriage, and number of children) equivalent to that assigned only marriages consummated in 1948 in the control. The sharply upward trend in divorce evidenced during the 1960s for more recent marriage cohorts is thereby eliminated.

The decline in divorces generated by this alteration has significant secondary impacts on the number of children involved in divorce, the number of marriages, the number of female-headed families, the total persons in the labor force and total employment, and GNP (Table 12-7). Note that about 800,000 fewer children were involved in about 400,000

TABLE 12-5

EQUAL MORTALITY BY RACE, SEX, AND EDUCATION EXPERIMENT: TIME TREND IN THE ANNUAL PERCENTAGE IMPACT AND TOTAL ABSOLUTE IMPACT ON SELECTED VARIABLES

% change in $X = a_0 + a_1 (YEAR - 1960)$

X	a_0***	a_1***	S.E.E.[1]	Total absolute impact 1960–70
Deaths	−41.87	0.86	0.33	6,953,000
	(187)	(23.3)		
Births	2.52	0.61	4.21	
	(0.7)	(1.3)		
Total Population	0.34	0.44	0.09	8,500,000**
	(1.6)	(44.1)		
Marriages	−0.76	−0.03	1.32	
	(0.8)	(0.2)		
Divorces	0.67	0.31	0.89	98,000
	(0.6)	(3.1)		
Children in Divorce	−3.11	1.04	2.26	134,000
	(2.7)	(4.2)		
Female-Headed Families	−2.13	−0.68	4.97	*
	(0.4)	(1.2)		
Total Persons in Labor Force Any Time	−0.14	0.31	0.30	10,800,000
	(2.2)	(9.2)		
Total Employment	−0.20	0.29	0.29	9,100,000
	(2.5)	(9.1)		
Average Earnings of Full-Time Black Males	−4.35	1.31	8.10	*
	(1.0)	(1.5)		
GNP	−0.19	0.51	0.33	$166.0 billion
	(3.1)	(14.1)		

* Impact considered not statistically significant if t-statistics for both slope and intercept < 3.0.
** Difference between experiment and base in 1969.
*** t-statistics in parentheses.
1. Standard error of estimate.

fewer divorces, an indication of the fact that the rise in divorce during the 1960s affected couples in the child-rearing ages particularly heavily.

3. *Zero Remarriage.* This experiment sets remarriage probabilities equal to zero for both widowed and divorced persons.

TABLE 12-6

ELIMINATING MORTALITY DIFFERENCES BY RACE, SEX, AND EDUCATION: NUMBER (IN MILLIONS) AND PERCENT (OF TOTAL FOR EACH SEX) OF POPULATION BY AGE, RACE, AND SEX FOR EXPERIMENTAL COMPARED TO CONTROL SIMULATION IN 1969 AFTER TEN YEARS OF SIMULATION

Age		MALE						FEMALE					
		White		Black		Total		White		Black		Total	
		Exp.	Base	Exp.	Base	Exp.	Base	Exp.	Base	Exp.	Base	Exp.	Base
0–14	N	23.09	22.46	4.37	3.87	27.46	26.33	24.80	23.99	3.96	3.74	28.77	27.73
	%	22.6	23.5	4.3	4.1	26.9	27.5	24.0	23.7	3.8	3.7	27.9	27.4
15–34	N	27.01	26.83	4.14	4.10	31.16	30.93	23.90	23.90	4.14	4.19	28.05	28.09
	%	26.5	28.0	4.1	4.3	30.6	32.3	23.1	23.6	4.0	4.1	27.2	27.8
35–54	N	19.61	19.07	2.21	2.16	21.82	21.24	19.97	19.88	2.88	2.84	22.86	22.73
	%	19.2	19.9	2.2	2.3	21.4	22.2	19.3	19.7	2.8	2.8	22.1	22.5
55–75	N	15.15	12.98	1.30	0.99	16.46	13.98	15.74	15.60	1.44	1.30	17.18	16.91
	%	14.9	13.6	1.3	1.0	16.1	14.6	15.2	15.4	1.4	1.3	16.6	16.7
75+	N	4.64	2.75	0.40	0.45	5.05	3.20	5.99	5.50	0.40	0.22	6.40	5.72
	%	4.6	2.9	0.4	0.5	5.0	3.3	5.8	5.4	0.4	0.2	6.2	5.7
TOTAL	N	89.52	84.11	12.44	11.59	101.97	95.70	90.42	88.89	12.85	12.31	103.27	101.20
	%	87.8	87.9	12.2	12.1	100	100	87.6	87.8	12.4	12.2	100	100

Statistically significant consequences detected in this experiment included fewer marriages, divorces and children in divorce, considerably more female-headed families, more persons in the labor force and total employment, and a slightly increased GNP (Table 12-8). Table 12-9 compares the marital status distribution of the experiment and control populations after ten years. The number of widowed persons is relatively unchanged, but a large increase in the divorced population occurred in the experiment. This indicates that remarriage primarily affects divorced persons whose marriages generally terminate at younger ages.

4. *Cohort Decline in First Marriage Probabilities.* Beginning with males born in 1940 and females born in 1942, the experiment reduces first marriage probabilities by 5 percent in each successive birth cohort. The effect is to introduce a decline in age at first marriage and proportion ever married in a gradual way.

Table 12-10 shows that among the significant consequences were fewer marriages, slightly fewer divorces, slightly fewer deaths, and slightly increased male earnings.

5. *Delay in Age at First Marriage.* This experiment increases the average age of first marriage by four years.

Secondary consequences from this experiment were widespread (Table 12-11). Marriages declined nearly 44 percent in the first year and only slightly less each succeeding year. Divorces declined slightly in the first year and the decline increased over the decade. Nearly seven million fewer births occurred over the decade, which in turn contributed to a slight decline in deaths. Employment dropped initially, then increased, until by the end of the decade it was higher in the experiment. GNP was slightly lower. Table 12-12 compares the quite different marital status distributions of the experiment and control after ten years.

The more substantial effects of this age-related first marriage experiment as compared to the previous cohort related experiment are due largely to the timing of the initial impact. The cohort-specific change was introduced quite gradually; only by the decade's end were many of its consequences beginning to emerge. The age shift in first marriage, however, had its sharpest initial impact in the very first year. Thus its secondary consequences emerged more quickly.

Conclusions

Taken together these experiments on the model perhaps begin to illustrate its usefulness in exploring the implications of particular demographic changes.

(*text continues on page 278*)

TABLE 12-7

DIVORCE PROBABILITY CONSTANT ACROSS COHORTS EXPERIMENT: TIME TREND IN THE ANNUAL PERCENTAGE IMPACT AND TOTAL ABSOLUTE IMPACT ON SELECTED VARIABLES

% change in $X = a_0 + a_1$ (YEAR $-$ 1960)

X	a_0***	a_1***	S.E.E.[1]	Total absolute impact 1960–70
Divorces	−2.79 (6.1)	−1.30 (32.0)	0.36	−443,000
Children in Divorce.	−6.26 (2.1)	−1.27 (3.3)	3.55	−828,000
Marriages	0.73 (1.2)	−0.59 (3.2)	1.66	−379,000
Births	3.06 (1.2)	0.27 (0.7)	3.54	*
Deaths	1.36 (1.5)	−0.41 (2.2)	1.73	*
Total Population	−0.06 (2.9)	0.08 (10.9)	0.07	1,300,000**
Female-Headed Families	6.67 (3.9)	−1.26 (3.9)	2.96	−505,000**
Total Persons in Labor Force Any Time	−0.80 (3.1)	0.13 (2.6)	0.44	−1,900,000
Total Employment	−0.73 (3.0)	0.11 (2.5)	0.41	−1,400,000
Average Earnings of Full-Time Black Males	1.77 (0.3)	0.64 (1.02)	5.68	*
GNP	−0.97 (3.7)	0.16 (3.3)	0.44	−9.8 billion

* Impact considered not statistically significant if both t-statistics <3.0.
** Difference between experiment and base in 1969.
*** t-statistics in parentheses.
1. Standard error of estimate.

TABLE 12-8

ZERO REMARRIAGE EXPERIMENT: TIME TREND IN THE ANNUAL PERCENTAGE IMPACT AND TOTAL ABSOLUTE IMPACT ON SELECTED VARIABLES
% change in $X = a_0 + a_1$ (YEAR $-$ 1960)

X	a_0***	a_1***	S.E.E.[1]	Total absolute impact 1960–70
Marriages	−24.72	−0.17	0.87	−4,553,000
	(41.2)	(1.7)		
Divorces	−0.48	−1.49	0.50	−377,000
	(2.9)	(26.9)		
Births	−0.57	−0.50	3.78	*
	(0.03)	(1.2)		
Deaths	0.52	−0.11	1.12	*
	(0.8)	(0.9)		
Total Population	0.02	−0.05	0.05	*
	(2.1)	(9.4)		
Children in Divorce	−2.39	−1.34	2.14	−597,000
	(0.7)	(5.7)		
Female-Headed Families	0.29	5.26	3.64	1,471,000**
	(2.0)	(13.1)		
Total Persons in Labor Force Any Time	−0.20	0.11	0.19	2.800,000
	(2.5)	(5.5)		
Total Employment	−0.19	0.10	0.15	2,100,000
	(2.8)	(5.9)		
Average Earnings of Full-Time Black Males	−4.45	0.58	5.25	*
	(1.4)	(1.0)		
GNP	−0.19	0.09	0.16	$18.3 billion
	(2.6)	(5.2)		

* Value judged not statistically significant if both t-statistics are <3.0.
** Difference between experiment and base in 1969.
*** t-statistics in parentheses.
1. Standard error of estimate.

TABLE 12-9

ZERO REMARRIAGE EXPERIMENT: NUMBER (IN MILLIONS) AND PERCENT (OF TOTAL FOR EACH SEX) OF POPULATION BY SEX, AGE, RACE, AND MARITAL STATUS FOR EXPERIMENTAL COMPARED TO CONTROL SIMULATION IN 1969 AFTER TEN YEARS OF SIMULATION

MARITAL STATUS, FEMALE

Age		Single, Never Married		Married		Widowed		Divorced		TOTAL	
		Exp.	Base	Exp.	Base	Exp.	Base	Exp.	Base	Exp.	Base
15–34.	N	10.46	10.95	14.97	16.05	0.40	0.27	2.21	0.81	28.05	28.09
	%	14.4	14.9	20.7	21.9	0.6	0.4	3.1	1.1	38.7	38.2
35–54.	N	0.99	0.94	17.99	19.48	1.48	1.57	2.16	0.72	22.64	22.73
	%	1.4	1.3	24.9	26.5	2.1	2.1	3.0	1.0	31.3	30.9
55–74.	N	1.12	1.17	10.32	10.50	3.92	4.19	1.21	1.03	16.59	16.91
	%	1.6	1.6	14.2	14.3	5.4	5.7	1.7	1.4	22.9	23.0
75+...	N	0.31	0.36	1.35	1.48	3.24	3.69	0.22	0.18	5.14	5.72
	%	0.4	0.5	1.9	2.0	4.5	5.0	0.3	0.2	7.1	7.8
TOTAL	N	12.89	13.44	44.64	47.53	9.06	9.74	5.81	2.75	72.43	73.46
	%	17.8	18.3	61.7	64.7	12.5	13.3	8.0	3.7	100	100

TABLE 12-9 (continued)

MARITAL STATUS, MALE

15–34.	N	16.10	15.87	12.58	14.52	0	0	1.98	0.54	30.66	30.93
	%	23.0	22.9	18.0	20.9	0	0	2.8	0.8	43.9	44.6
35–54.	N	1.93	2.03	17.27	18.40	0.27	0.31	1.93	0.49	21.42	21.24
	%	2.8	2.9	24.7	26.5	0.4	0.5	2.8	0.7	30.7	30.6
55–74.	N	0.99	1.17	11.50	11.18	1.26	0.67	0.85	0.94	14.61	13.98
	%	1.4	1.7	16.5	16.1	1.8	1.0	1.2	1.4	20.9	20.2
75+...	N	0.18	0.04	2.21	2.34	0.67	0.76	0.09	0.04	3.15	3.20
	%	0.3	0.1	3.2	3.4	1.0	1.1	0.1	0.1	4.5	4.6
TOTAL	N	19.21	19.12	43.56	46.45	2.21	1.75	4.87	2.02	69.86	69.36
	%	27.5	27.6	62.4	67.0	3.2	2.5	7.0	2.9	100	100

TABLE 12-10

COHORT SPECIFIC DECLINE IN FIRST MARRIAGE
EXPERIMENT: TIME TREND IN THE ANNUAL
PERCENTAGE IMPACT AND TOTAL ABSOLUTE
IMPACT ON SELECTED VARIABLES
% change in $X = a_0 + a_1$ (YEAR $-$ 1960)

X	a_0**	a_1**	S.E.E.[1]	Total absolute impact 1960–70
Marriages	−1.89	−2.13	1.08	−2,185,000
	(0.3)	(18.0)		
Divorces	1.32	−0.82	1.11	−132,000
	(2.8)	(6.7)		
Births	1.06	−0.51	4.99	*
	(0.5)	(0.9)		
Deaths	0.74	−0.65	1.09	−412,000
	(1.9)	(5.4)		
Total Population	−0.05	0.00	0.08	*
	(0.8)	(0.5)		
Children in Divorce	−2.34	0.17	2.07	*
	(1.8)	(0.8)		
Female-Headed Families	−1.42	−0.10	5.27	*
	(0.4)	(0.2)		
Total Persons in Labor Force Any Time	−0.29	0.06	0.32	*
	(1.6)	(1.8)		
Total Employment	−0.32	0.07	0.29	*
	(2.0)	(2.1)		
Average Earnings of Full-Time Black Males	−3.47	1.49	4.23	$151
	(1.7)	(3.2)		
GNP	−0.31	0.05	0.30	*
	(1.8)	(1.7)		

* Value judged not statistically significant if both t-statistics are <3.0.
** t-statistics in parentheses.
1. Standard error of estimate.

TABLE 12-11

FOUR-YEAR DELAY IN AGE AT FIRST MARRIAGE EXPERIMENT: TIME TREND IN THE ANNUAL PERCENTAGE IMPACT AND TOTAL ABSOLUTE IMPACT ON SELECTED VARIABLES

% change in $X = a_0 + a_1$ (YEAR $- 1960$)

X	a_0**	a_1**	S.E.E.[1]	Total absolute impact 1960–70
Marriages	−43.73 (34.6)	2.27 (10.6)	1.95	−5,851,000
Divorces	−3.18 (0.3)	−2.65 (10.0)	2.40	−784,000
Births	−5.62 (1.1)	−3.02 (8.2)	3.36	−6,882,000
Deaths	−0.42 (0.4)	−0.62 (7.9)	0.71	−590,000
Total Population	0.20 (8.1)	−0.39 (33.2)	0.11	−6,292,000
Children in Divorce	0.31 (2.8)	−2.62 (15.7)	1.51	−832,000
Female-Headed Families	−8.57 (1.5)	0.90 (0.9)	9.52	*
Total Persons in Labor Force Any Time	−0.64 (7.4)	0.15 (8.8)	0.17	296,000
Total Employment	−0.64 (7.6)	0.14 (8.6)	0.15	250,000
Average Earnings of Full-Time Black Males	−2.80 (1.3)	1.44 (2.8)	4.75	*
GNP	−0.61 (5.6)	0.01 (0.4)	0.16	−$39.9 billion

* Impact considered not statistically significant if t-statistics for both slope and intercept are <3.0.
** t-statistics in parentheses.
1. Standard error of estimate.

TABLE 12-12

FOUR-YEAR DELAY IN AGE ON FIRST MARRIAGE EXPERIMENT: NUMBER (IN MILLIONS) AND PERCENT (OF TOTAL FOR EACH SEX) OF WHITE POPULATION BY AGE, SEX, AND MARITAL STATUS FOR EXPERIMENTAL COMPARED TO CONTROL SIMULATION IN 1969 AFTER TEN YEARS OF SIMULATION

WHITE MALES

Age		Single, Never Married		Married		Widowed		Divorced		Total	
		Exp.	Base	Exp.	Base	Exp.	Base	Exp.	Base	Exp.	Base
15–24	N	18.13	14.25	0.94	4.96	0	0	0.04	0.04	19.12	19.25
	%	26.1	20.5	1.4	7.2	0	0	0.1	0.1	27.6	27.8
25–34	N	3.65	1.62	7.89	9.56	0	0	0.22	0.49	11.77	11.68
	%	5.3	2.3	11.4	13.8	0	0	0.3	0.7	17.0	16.8
35–44	N	0.76	1.03	9.11	8.79	0.04	0.09	0.22	0.18	10.14	10.10
	%	1.1	1.5	13.1	12.7	0.1	0.1	0.3	0.3	14.6	14.6
45+	N	2.03	2.21	23.85	23.13	1.57	1.66	0.90	1.30	28.36	28.32
	%	2.9	3.2	34.4	33.4	2.3	2.4	1.3	1.9	40.9	40.8
TOTAL	N	24.57	19.12	41.80	46.45	1.62	1.75	1.39	2.03	69.40	69.36
	%	35.4	27.6	60.2	67.0	2.3	2.5	2.0	2.9	100.0	100.0

TABLE 12-12 (continued)

WHITE FEMALES

15–24	N	14.52	10.05	2.07	6.58	0	0	0.04	0.13	16.64	16.77
	%	19.8	13.7	2.8	9.0	0	0	0.1	0.2	22.7	22.8
25–34	N	1.30	0.90	9.20	9.47	0.13	0.27	0.63	0.67	11.27	11.32
	%	1.8	1.2	12.6	12.9	0.2	0.4	0.9	0.9	15.4	15.4
35–44	N	0.36	0.45	9.78	9.92	0.40	0.27	0.40	0.31	10.95	10.95
	%	0.5	0.6	13.4	13.5	0.6	0.4	0.6	0.4	15.0	14.9
45+	N	2.07	2.03	21.60	21.55	9.11	9.20	1.62	1.62	34.41	34.41
	%	2.8	2.8	29.5	29.4	12.4	12.5	2.2	2.2	47.0	46.8
TOTAL	N	18.26	13.44	42.66	47.53	9.65	9.74	2.70	2.75	73.28	73.46
	%	24.9	18.3	58.3	64.7	13.2	13.3	3.7	3.7	100.0	100.0

277

The impacts of demographic changes are not limited to the process directly affected but spread to other processes—demographic and economic—as well. Thus, declines in divorce probabilities lead not only to fewer divorces but also to fewer female headed families, fewer marriages, and fewer persons in the labor force.

In some later research reported on in Chapter 15, a version of DYNASIM which included a government transfers module was used. When divorce rates were altered, the result was a significant impact upon both the cost and caseload of the Aid to Families with Dependent Children program and upon the overall distribution of income in the United States.

It is these kinds of reverberations that make it important for policy makers to try to take into account the powerful and volatile demographic processes taking place in society.

Chapter 13
EXPLORATION OF MODEL INTERACTIONS*

This chapter describes a series of simulations that were carried out to investigate how changes in the probability of a particular event occurring affect other outcomes in the model. An early version of DYNASIM was used in these simulations. Thus, the results are not necessarily the same as they would be with the version of DYNASIM described elsewhere in this volume. However, with a few exceptions we would expect the current version of DYNASIM to exhibit the same properties.

One way to examine interactions is to make a fixed change in the probability function for one operating characteristic and to follow the resulting changes in the outputs of other operating characteristics over the course of the simulation. In six different ten-year simulations, a 30 percent reduction was made separately in the probabilities for mortality, fertility, marriage, divorce, labor force participation, and in the unemployment rate.

These simulations have been analyzed by comparing the values of selected aggregate variables in the reduction run with their values in the corresponding year in the base run. In examining the results we have focused attention on the time dependence of relative change as well as on the level of relative change.

The results of these experiments have been analyzed by examining the time dependence of the elasticity of the response of selected variables to the change in the treatment variable. For each year in an experimental run the percentage deviation of the value of a given variable from its value in the base run was calculated. This percentage change was converted to an elasticity by dividing it by -30 since the response was obtained from a 30 percent reduction in the treatment variable. This elasticity was the dependent variable in a linear regression equation with a time trend which was estimated by ordinary least squares. The equation estimated is

$$\text{Elasticity of } X = a_0 + a_1 (\text{TIME} - \overline{\text{TIME}})$$

where $\overline{\text{TIME}}$ is the average value of TIME. TIME was taken to be 1 for 1960, the first year of the simulation, and ranges up to 9 for 1969, the last year of the simulation.

* Gerald Peabody was responsible for this chapter and the work it represents.

TABLE 13-1

ELASTICITIES OF SELECTED VARIABLES WITH RESPECT TO A CHANGE IN THE ALTERED VARIABLE

Dependent Variable	Coefficient[1]	ALTERED VARIABLE					
		Death	Birth	Marriage	Divorce	Labor Force	Unemployment
Total Deaths	Mean	.851	.058	.047	.106		
	Trend	-.029	.012*	.013	-.013		
Total Births	Mean	—	.708	.306	-.129*		
	Trend	—	-.030*	.051	—		
Total Marriages	Mean	—	—	.768	.184		
	Trend	—	—	-.050	.031		
Total Divorces	Mean	-.037	-.044	.269	.979		
	Trend	-.006*	-.008	.047	—		
Population Size	Mean	-.049	.085	.026	-.009		
	Trend	-.009	.012	.006	-.004		
Labor Force	Mean	-.017	—	—	—	.938	-.032
	Trend	-.005	-.003	—	—	-.012	.002
Gross National Product	Mean	-.035	.032	-.009	—	1.106	-.103
	Trend	-.009	.003	—	—	.006	.004
Investment	Mean	-.152	.205	.076	-.042	1.318	-.119
	Trend	-.012	-.012	.010	-.015	-.060*	.013
Capital Stock	Mean	-.043	.070	.020	-.008	.440	-.043
	Trend	-.009	.009	.005	-.003	.056	-.004
Labor Income	Mean	-.041	.039	.011	—	1.351	-.133
	Trend	-.011	.004	—	—	—	—

1. Coefficients with a t-statistic of less than two are indicated by a dash. The corresponding term was eliminated from the equation and the equation was re-estimated. Coefficients with a t-statistic in the range from two to three have a t-statistic greater than three.
Source: 10-year DYNASIM simulation.

The results of these estimations for the six experimental runs are contained in Table 13-1. As the equation is specified, a_0 is the mean value of the response and is so labeled in the table. The time trend is given by the coefficient a_1 which is labeled "trend" in the table.

A discussion of the results for each run will be given below, but first it is useful to overview the major results from these experiments. Within the demographic component of the model there are a number of significant interactions. In particular, changes in marital status — either changes in marriage rates or divorce rates — have important consequences for other demographic processes. In the version of the model used for these runs, changes in the rates for demographic events have a modest effect upon macroeconomic variables apart from investment.[1] Investment is moderately affected by changes in mortality and fertility. The most significant interactions observed in the model result from a change in the size of the labor force. A 1 percent change in the size of the labor force leads to slightly larger changes in GNP, investment, and labor income.

Mortality Reduction

The first column of Table 13-1 contains the changes that resulted from a reduction in the mortality probabilities. Using the mean and the trend in the elasticity formula above, the data imply that in the first year a 1 percent reduction in the mortality probabilities would have led to a 1 percent decline in the total number of deaths. The negative coefficient for the time trend indicates that the magnitude of the change in deaths relative to the base run diminished over the course of the simulation.

Changes in other variables are consequences of changes in the stock of people alive rather than changes in the mortality probability itself. The elasticity for population size has both a negative mean and a negative time trend. Consequently the decline in mortality rates gave rise to a population increase over time. The elasticity for total labor force size also has a negative time coefficient indicating that the mortality reduction led to an increasing size of the labor force due to the increasing stock of people alive who are potential labor force participants.

The initial mortality rates for women in the child-bearing age are sufficiently low and the sampling variability for births is sufficiently high that the reduction in mortality rates does not lead to a statistically significant increase in births. From the data in Table 13-1 it appears that there was a small effect on the number of divorces over time, but there was no detectable effect on the number of marriages. The elasticities for the four macroeconomic variables — GNP, investment, capital stock, and labor

---

1. This result may not hold true for the current version of DYNASIM.

income — have negative time trends as might be expected since both the population and the labor force do also.

Fertility Reduction

In some respects the situation for fertility is analagous to that for mortality in that a reduction in the number of births in one year gives an increase in the size of the stock of women who are at risk for a birth in the next year. Women who want to have a birth in a given year but do not do so because of the reduction in their birth probability will still want to have one the next year. Consequently, there will be more women who want to have a birth in the next year, and relative to the base run there will be slightly more births in the second year than in the first. Women who do not want a birth will simply have their birth rates reduced. The results for the fertility reduction experiment are shown in the second column of Table 13-1.

The reduction in births leads to a reduction in mortality since there are fewer newborns at risk for death. There is no effect upon marriage, as expected, and there is a slight increase in the number of divorces with time. This latter result is also expected since the probability of divorce increases when there are fewer children in the family. The population in the experimental run is smaller than the base run in 1960, and the relative population size falls in each year.

Labor force participation is affected by fertility through the number of children in the family under six years of age. Women with children under six are much less likely to be in the labor force than those without such children. The model incorporates a smaller effect in the opposite direction for men as well as indirect effects through other variables such as divorce. In this experiment the decline in fertility gave a small increase in labor force participation over time, although the mean effect was zero.

Marriage Reduction

The third column contains the results of the marriage reduction experiment. The positive coefficients for total births elasticities indicates that births were reduced as expected. They were reduced substantially in the first year, and the reduction became larger over time.

The change in the total number of deaths is affected by two factors. Married people within the model have lower mortality probabilities than do unmarried people, so the reduction in the number of marriages would lead to an increase in the number of deaths. We expect this effect to be very small, however, because of the low mortality rates typical of people who are marrying. The decline in the number of births, on the other hand, gives fewer infants at risk for death and so would give a decrease in the number of deaths.

The time trend in the total number of marriages follows the pattern observed with the total number of deaths in the mortality reduction experiment. The reduction in the number of marriages in the first year leads to an increased stock of people in the second year who are at risk for marriage. While all of these people have a reduced marriage probability, the magnitude of the marriage reduction is decreased slightly over time from the initial 30 percent because of the increased stock of people.

Divorces are reduced in the second year and continue to fall in subsequent years. Since the number of marriages is reduced in every year, the stock of married people in the experimental run relative to the base run falls in every year. The result is a steady decline over time in the number of divorces.

Decreasing marriages reduces the number of births each year more than it reduces the number of deaths, because the marriage-associated deaths are almost entirely infant deaths. The population size in the experimental run thus declines relative to the base run population.

The labor force showed virtually no difference between the base and experimental run. Most males that marry will become a family head and their probability of labor force participation will increase by roughly 7 percent (for whites). Women who marry have a very small change in their participation rate immediately. However, as soon as they have a child their probability drops by 15 percent (for white women). Since not all women have children immediately after marriage, the number who leave the labor force shortly after marriage is less than 15 percent. The results appear to indicate that men who enter the labor force because they marry tend to be offset by women who leave because they have children, and a change in the marriage rate has little *net* effect upon the size of the labor force.

Divorce Reduction

The results from the divorce reduction experiment are shown in the fourth column of Table 13-1. The reduction in divorces is reasonably stable over the ten-year run. The constancy in the divorce figures can be explained by the relation between divorce and remarriage. The annual probability of remarriage is roughly .5 for men and women in the age range 14–24 and is close to .2 for women and .3 for men between 25 and 44. Consequently, among the ages at which most divorces occur there is a reasonable chance of remarriage. Reducing the number of divorces, therefore, does not increase the stock of married people by the same amount. Many of those who would have divorced would also have remarried soon. While we may expect some increase in the stock of married people, it will be a smaller increase than the decrease in the number of divorces.

Further, the stock of married people after the divorce reduction will have a different distribution by duration of marriage and, consequently, a different distribution by divorce probabilities than the stock before the reduction. With a lower divorce rate, more marriages will survive a longer time. These longer duration marriages have a lower probability of divorce, as long as they survive past three years. Also, with a lower divorce rate there are fewer newlyweds since there are fewer remarriages. Reducing the number of newlyweds lowers the average probability of divorce since divorce probabilities are highest in the first three years of marriage.

Consequently, there are two counteracting effects occurring. The stock of married people increases with a decrease in the divorce rate which would, other things remaining the same, lead to a future increase in the number of divorces. However, this larger stock of married couples contains fewer newlyweds (remarrieds) and more longer duration marriages so the average divorce probability for the stock is lower, The constancy in the divorce rates for the ten-year simulation with reduced divorce probabilities indicates that these two factors cancel one another out.

The divorce reduction led to an increase in the mean relative number of births over the ten-year run. The increase was probably a result of women who remained married completing their families faster than they would have had they divorced. Deaths were decreased by the divorce reduction as expected, since married people have lower mortality probabilities. However, the magnitude of the decrease seems large, and more analysis is required to fully understand it. Marriages were also decreased reflecting the reduced number of people remarrying.

The labor force size was apparently not affected by the divorce reduction and neither were GNP or labor income. The net effect of the changes in fertility and mortality led to slight increases in population size, investment, and capital stock.

Labor Force Reduction

The results for the reduction in the probability of labor force participation are shown in the fifth column. Effects on the aggregate variables for the demographic processes are not shown, since, as the model was initially constructed, no such effects occur. The microlevel probabilities for the demographic processes in this early version of DYNASIM do not depend upon labor force activity, income, or macroeconomic conditions. In the current version of DYNASIM, both marriage and divorce probabilities depend upon economic variables (see Chapters 4 and 5).

The negative time trend for the labor force size elasticity means that the magnitude of the decline in the size of the labor force decreased slowly over the ten-year period of the simulation. This time trend can be accounted for by the slight increase in the participation rates for married women whose husbands had a decline in earnings. That earnings did decline significantly in this experiment is indicated by the figures for labor income in column five.

Reducing the size of the labor force has a very significant effect upon other macroeconomic variables. GNP, investment, and labor income all declined by more than 1 percent per 1 percent decline in labor force size.

Unemployment Reduction

The results for the final run in this series of six reduction experiments are given in Table 13-1, column six. In this run the aggregate unemployment rate was reduced by a factor of 30 percent. Again there is no effect possible on the demographic variables. All macroeconomic variables are significantly increased by reducing the unemployment rate.

Chapter 14

EARNINGS OF WOMEN: IMPLICATIONS OF EQUALITY IN THE LABOR MARKET *

Women's earnings are considerably less than men's (U.S. Department of Commerce, 1972). This is because women are less likely to work than men, are less likely to work full-time if they do work, and on average, are paid lower wage rates than men (Fuchs, 1974, and U.S. Department of Labor, 1974).

The consequences of this disparity are not limited to women. Over the past decade there has been a dramatic increase in families dependent solely upon women for their income (Ross and MacIntosh, 1973).

One way of handling the income insufficiency in families headed by women is to provide transfer payments. However, the dramatic increase in transfer payments to families with dependent children has caused great controversy and is not viewed as an acceptable solution by a large sector of the population.

Another way for society to deal with this insufficiency of income is to move toward equality for women in the labor market. This approach would not necessarily solve the entire problem of income insufficiency by families headed by females any more than it would guarantee a relatively high level of earnings for all women. However, it would reduce the need for transfer payments.

The purpose of this chapter is to explore the potential payoffs of women achieving equality in the labor market. In the experiments, particular attention is paid to the impact upon families headed by women. (The separate question of *how* women should achieve equality, however, is not the issue being addressed here.)

* Richard F. Wertheimer II had the main responsibility for this chapter and the work it represents.

TABLE 14-1

ANNUAL EARNINGS BY RACE AND SEX FOR BASE RUN AND HISTORICAL COMPARISONS
(1958 Dollars)

	WHITE FEMALE AVERAGE EARNINGS		WHITE MALE AVERAGE EARNINGS		NONWHITE FEMALE AVERAGE EARNINGS		NONWHITE MALE AVERAGE EARNINGS	
	Base Run	Historic	Base Run	Historic	Base Run	Historic	Base Run	Historic
1960	$2,280	$2,270	$4,590	$4,590	$1,160	$1,140	$2,750	$2,740
1961	2,200	2,260	4,710	4,710	1,160	1,160	2,630	2,690
1962	2,260	2,340	4,860	4,860	1,210	1,240	2,740	2,690
1963	2,360	2,410	5,070	5,020	1,360	1,280	2,830	2,850
1964	2,290	2,510	5,150	5,170	1,460	1,460	2,840	3,020
1965	2,440	2,620	5,360	5,410	1,690	1,510	2,830	3,120
1966	2,430	2,700	5,690	5,710	1,820	1,740	3,060	3,390
1967	2,400	2,750	5,760	5,780	1,720	1,940	3,240	3,700
1968	2,580	2,840	5,970	5,990	2,170	2,050	3,670	3,970
1969	2,690	2,850	6,140	6,160	2,330	2,260	3,830	4,110
1970	2,660	2,880	6,210	6,130	2,420	2,440	3,760	4,070
1971	2,750	2,900	6,320	6,120	2,750	2,490	4,030	4,120
1972	2,670	2,920	6,540	6,380	2,670	2,740	3,830	4,350

Performing the Experiments

The method used to perform the experiments was as follows. First, the model was run from 1960 to 1972 with all parameters set to our best estimate of their values in the real world. A sample of about 4,000 persons drawn from the 1960 Census 1–10,000 Public Use Sample served as the initial population. A limited number of adjustments in parameters were made to align the model more nearly to certain historical aggregate statistics, such as total births, deaths, marriages, divorces, labor force, etc. Aggregate earnings by race and sex from this base run and historical comparisons are given in Table 14-1.

Three experiments were designed to explore the implications of female equality in the labor market. In Experiment 1 women were assigned the same wage rate function as men. (This means a woman was given the same wage rate as a comparable man, i.e., a man with the same education, age, race, and location.) In Experiment 2 women were assigned the same participation and hours functions as men.[1] In Experiment 3 women were assigned both the same wage rate and the same participation and hours functions as men. In all three experiments the education levels, age distributions, and occupational distributions were the same as in the base run.

Critical Assumptions and Limits of Study

The results of this study depend upon several assumptions embedded in DYNASIM and the way the experiments were carried out. The assumptions impose limits upon the degree to which the results should be taken literally.

First is the assumption that adjustments, which in the real world would occur as a long-run process, take place in the experiments within a single year. The most drastic of these instantaneous adjustments are the absorption by the economy in Experiments 2 and 3 of vast new additions to the labor force without any disruptions: the aggregate unemployment rate is held to actual levels of the 1960s and early 1970s throughout the experiment. By imposing higher rates of unemployment which gradually decline, a researcher could produce a more realistic adjustment process, but we have chosen to ignore this process.

Second, wage rate changes did not induce labor supply responses in the version of the model used.[2] Thus, Experiment 1 is somewhat unrealistic: it disregards the real world expectations that sharp increases in women's wages would bring forth additional labor from women (and that the absolute decreases in men's wage rates might cause a decrease in their labor supply, particularly among the very old and the very young.)

Third, the occupational distribution has been held to its base run values in each of the three experiments. Since the crowding of women into particular occupations is one aspect of wage discrimination against women, the experiments have not fully moved women to equality in the labor market. However, since the occupational categories in this version of the model are broad and since, in Experiments 1 and 3, women are being paid the same as men within each occupation, the impact of this restriction may not be large. In any case, it would be easy to impose a shift in occupational distributions in another experiment.

Fourth, wage rates in DYNASIM are a function of age rather than

---

1. The participation function determines the probability that a person participates in the labor force, while the hours function determines how many hours per year they participate.

2. This deficiency was corrected in a later version.

work experience. One might expect that the increased work experience associated with Experiment 2 might increase wage rates for women.

Finally, there is no feedback from the economic sector of the model to the demographic sector in this version of the model. One might suspect that the changes in labor market activity implied by Experiments 2 and 3 would have affected child bearing and perhaps marriage and divorce. Equal pay for equal work might have changed educational patterns — increasing women's education level and decreasing men's. Yet these would seem to constitute only a second-order problem for the following reasons: these adjustments in demographic behavior would only have a gradual effect on the demographic characteristics of the population; the interest in this particular study is not in the demographic responses per se but rather in their impact upon the economic sector; and the simulation is for only 13 years.

Results

In order to explore the results of the simulation experiments the sample was divided first by sex and then, for the women, into three categories — women who head families with at least one child under age 18, wives, and all other women. The men were divided into two categories — family heads with children and all others.

Since families are generally economic units which pool their earnings, total family earnings were tabulated as well as personal earnings. Tabulation by family gives a better picture of the economic resources available to a child. Female-headed families usually can draw upon only one earner, while husband-wife families can often draw upon two earners. Tabulation by person, on the other hand, is a better gauge of progress towards equality for women. Results are given in Tables 14-2 through 14-13. All earnings statistics are in 1958 dollars.

Experiment 1: Equal Pay for Equal Work

Experiment 1 gave women the same relative wage rates as comparable men but had no effect on the total labor income to be distributed. Thus, the experiment resulted solely in redistribution of earnings from men to women. It could be considered an "equal pay for equal work" experiment.

Table 14-2 shows a comparison of 1964 simulated earnings distributions for six categories of women in the base run and in the experiments.

For all six categories, the percentage of women with earnings less than $3,000 is lower in Experiment 1 than in the base run. There is an increase of over 40 percent in the mean earnings of each group. The level of earnings is still quite low even in Experiment 1 — especially for nonwhites. However, the figures are being kept down, in part, by the women who are not working at all.

Tables 14-3 and 14-4 give the same statistics for the years 1969 and 1972. A similar picture emerges, but the levels of earnings are higher as time progresses. In fact, by 1972 mean earnings of white women heading families are $3,629 in Experiment 1 (compared with $2,526 in the base run).

Tables 14-5 through 14-7 show the family earnings of these women. The picture is quite different. In the base run family earnings are much higher for the wives than for the female heads since the wives have the earnings of their husbands added in. (In 1964, comparing mean *person* earnings in Table 14-2 with mean *family* earnings in Table 14-5, the female heads account for about two-thirds of their families' earnings, while the wives account for only one-fifth of their families' earnings.) Tables 14-5, 14-6, and 14-7 show that Experiment 1 increases the family earnings of the females who head families but decreases slightly the family earnings of the wives. For example, as Table 14-5 shows, mean family earnings of white females who head families increased by about 33 percent under Experiment 1, while mean family earnings of white wives declined by about 2 percent.

The results for the men and their families mirror the results for the women. (See Tables 14-8 through 14-13.) Experiment 1 increases the fraction of men in the lower earnings categories and substantially lowers their mean earnings. For example (see Table 14-8), earnings of nonwhite male family heads with children declined in 1964 from $2,807 in the base run to $2,474 in Experiment 1.

However, since many men with children have working wives who benefit from the experiment, *family* earnings for these men remained roughly unchanged in each year. The families which lost the most in Experiment 1 were the families of men with no children. This includes childless couples and men living alone; presumably the men living alone are the bigger losers. However, even for this group the decline in mean earnings was modest — never more than $200.

In summary, giving women the same wage rate function as men imposes a redistribution of earnings which on net transfers earnings away from single men and towards female-headed families. Husband-wife families experience virtually no change in their pooled earnings, although wives would be contributing a greater share. Thus, equal pay for equal

(*text continues on page 316*)

TABLE 14-2

SIMULATED EARNINGS OF WOMEN, 1964

Percentage Distributions and Means

(1958 Dollars)

NONWHITE WOMEN

Earnings Class	Family Heads with Child[b]				Wives				Others			
	Base Run	Exp 1	Exp 2	Exp 3	Base Run	Exp 1	Exp 2	Exp 3	Base Run	Exp 1	Exp 2	Exp 3
0–$999	75%	71%	67%	63%	79%	67%	48%	29%	78%	74%	65%	62%
$1000–2999	25	21	29	13	15	19	31	40	15	12	23	17
$3000–4999	0	8	4	25	4	13	17	23	5	11	8	12
$5000–7999	0	0	0	0	2	2	4	6	1	2	2	6
$8000–9999	0	0	0	0	0	0	0	2	1	1	1	1
$10,000–$14,999	0	0	0	0	0	0	0	0	0	0	2	2
$15,000 plus	0	0	0	0	0	0	0	0	0	0	0	0
Mean	$567	$890	$899	$1412	$709	$1004	$1577	$2134	$654	$933	$1116	$1491
N[a]	24	24	24	24	48	48	48	48	105	106	106	106

TABLE 14-2 (continued)

WHITE WOMEN

Earnings Class	Family Heads with Child				Wives				Others			
	Base Run	Exp 1	Exp 2	Exp 3	Base Run	Exp 1	Exp 2	Exp 3	Base Run	Exp 1	Exp 2	Exp 3
0–$999	52%	48%	50%	44%	55%	51%	28%	24%	67%	64%	58%	55%
$1000–$2999	22	20	24	19	28	26	28	23	21	18	22	17
$3000–$4999	19	11	19	22	12	11	23	18	8	10	12	14
$5000–$7999	6	17	4	11	5	9	15	21	3	6	6	9
$8000–$9999	2	2	2	2	0	3	3	8	1	1	1	2
$10,000–$14,999	0	2	2	2	0	1	3	5	1	1	1	2
$15,000 plus	0	0	0	0	0	0	0	2	0	0	0	1
Mean	$1708	$2393	$1818	$3298	$1349	$1927	$3062	$4212	$1038	$1452	$1527	$2034
N[a]	54	54	54	54	468	468	468	468	822	822	822	822

a. N is the number of persons in the sample in each particular category in each experiment. Where N is small (say, less than 50), the results must be viewed with caution.
b. In this and succeeding tables, "child" includes one or more children.
Exp 1 = Wage equalization
Exp 2 = Participation and hours equalization
Exp 3 = Wage, participation, and hours equalization

TABLE 14-3

SIMULATED EARNINGS OF WOMEN, 1969

Percentage Distributions and Means

(1958 Dollars)

Earnings Class	Family Heads with Child				NONWHITE WOMEN Wives				Others			
	Base Run	Exp 1	Exp 2	Exp 3	Base Run	Exp 1	Exp 2	Exp 3	Base Run	Exp 1	Exp 2	Exp 3
0–$999	64%	59%	32%	23%	64%	59%	28%	22%	69%	67%	53%	52%
$1000–$2999	32	23	46	32	16	16	29	17	21	15	30	20
$3000–$4999	5	18	23	27	12	9	17	24	8	9	11	19
$5000–$7999	0	0	0	18	9	16	16	24	3	6	3	4
$8000–$9999	0	0	0	0	0	2	7	7	0	2	2	3
$10,000–$14,999	0	0	0	0	0	0	2	3	0	1	0	2
$15,000 plus	0	0	0	0	0	0	2	2	0	0	1	1
Mean	$869	$1142	$1835	$2782	$1306	$1824	$3310	$3614	$936	$1369	$1570	$2075
N[a]	22	22	22	22	58	58	58	58	117	117	117	117

TABLE 14-3 (continued)

WHITE WOMEN

Earnings Class	Family Heads with Child				Wives				Others			
	Base Run	Exp 1	Exp 2	Exp 3	Base Run	Exp 1	Exp 2	Exp 3	Base Run	Exp 1	Exp 2	Exp 3
0–$999	35%	37%	28%	25%	50%	46%	27%	24%	70%	67%	60%	57%
$1000–$2999	39	28	39	25	28	19	23	15	17	13	18	15
$3000–$4999	9	14	18	26	12	17	23	20	7	9	11	11
$5000–$7999	7	11	9	16	6	11	15	21	4	6	7	8
$8000–$9999	4	0	0	2	2	3	5	7	2	1	3	3
$10,000–$14,999	7	4	7	0	2	3	6	8	1	3	2	4
$15,000 plus	0	7	0	7	0	2	1	7	0	1	0	2
Mean	$2621	$3567	$2961	$3871	$1856	$2636	$3702	$5017	$1179	$1642	$1768	$2301
N[a]	57	57	57	57	463	463	463	463	936	936	936	936

a. N is the number of persons in the sample in each particular category in each experiment. Where N is small (say, less than 50), the results must be viewed with caution.
Exp 1 = Wage equalization
Exp 2 = Participation and hours equalization
Exp 3 = Wage, participation, and hours equalization

TABLE 14-4

SIMULATED EARNINGS OF WOMEN, 1972

Percentage Distributions and Means

(1958 Dollars)

					NONWHITE WOMEN							
	Family Heads with Child				Wives				Others			
Earnings Class	Base Run	Exp 1	Exp 2	Exp 3	Base Run	Exp 1	Exp 2	Exp 3	Base Run	Exp 1	Exp 2	Exp 3
0–$999	41%	41%	27%	27%	67%	64%	25%	26%	65%	63%	56%	55%
$1000–$2999	27	9	23	9	21	12	34	13	22	19	20	14
$3000–$4999	32	18	41	18	8	16	20	28	8	10	12	14
$5000–$7999	0	23	9	36	0	7	10	16	3	6	7	11
$8000–$9999	0	9	0	0	3	0	3	8	2	1	3	3
$10,000–$14,999	0	0	0	9	0	2	5	5	0	1	0	2
$15,000 plus	0	0	0	0	0	0	3	3	1	1	1	1
Mean	$1950	$3218	$2778	$4397	$1099	$1489	$3587	$4505	$1192	$1528	$1684	$2109
N[a]	22	22	22	22	61	61	61	61	118	118	118	118

TABLE 14-4 (continued)

Earnings of Women

WHITE WOMEN

Earnings Class	Family Heads with Child				Wives				Others			
	Base Run	Exp 1	Exp 2	Exp 3	Base Run	Exp 1	Exp 2	Exp 3	Base Run	Exp 1	Exp 2	Exp 3
0–$999	36%	32%	26%	23%	53%	48%	26%	25%	70%	67%	61%	59%
$1000–$2999	34	26	30	21	26	21	23	12	17	14	19	14
$3000–$4999	19	13	26	25	11	14	24	22	6	8	10	11
$5000–$7999	4	17	8	19	7	9	15	22	4	7	6	9
$8000–$9999	4	4	6	4	2	3	5	7	1	1	2	3
$10,000–$14,999	2	4	2	6	1	4	5	7	1	2	2	3
$15,000 plus	2	4	2	4	0	1	2	5	0	1	0	2
Mean	$2526	$3629	$3352	$4351	$1778	$2512	$3785	$5131	$1161	$1594	$1645	$2163
N[a]	53	53	53	53	499	499	499	499	963	963	963	963

a. N is the number of persons in the sample in each particular category in each experiment. Where N is small (say, less than 50), the results must be viewed with caution.
Exp 1 = Wage equalization
Exp 2 = Participation and hours equalization
Exp 3 = Wage, participation, and hours equalization

TABLE 14-5

SIMULATED *FAMILY* EARNINGS OF WOMEN, 1964

Percentage Distributions and Means

(1958 Dollars)

| | NONWHITE WOMEN'S FAMILIES | | | | | | | | | | | | | | | |
| | Family Heads with Child | | | | Wives | | | | Others | | | | | | | |
Earnings Class	Base Run	Exp 1	Exp 2	Exp 3	Base Run	Exp 1	Exp 2	Exp 3	Base Run	Exp 1	Exp 2	Exp 3
0–$999	67%	67%	63%	58%	6%	6%	6%	4%	36%	32%	26%	24%
$1000–$2999	25	17	29	13	35	35	19	21	32	35	27	25
$3000–$4999	8	13	4	21	33	35	40	42	20	19	27	28
$5000–$7999	0	4	4	4	19	17	21	19	9	10	11	13
$8000–$9999	0	0	0	4	4	4	8	8	1	0	5	5
$10,000–$14,999	0	0	0	0	2	2	6	6	1	2	3	4
$15,000 plus	0	0	0	0	2	0	0	0	2	2	2	2
Mean	$833	$1218	$1273	$1780	$3811	$3789	$4798	$4838	$2479	$2646	$3483	$3775
N[a]	24	24	24	24	48	48	48	48	106	106	106	106

TABLE 14-5 (continued)

WHITE WOMEN'S FAMILIES

Earnings Class	Family Heads with Child				Wives				Others			
	Base Run	Exp 1	Exp 2	Exp 3	Base Run	Exp 1	Exp 2	Exp 3	Base Run	Exp 1	Exp 2	Exp 3
0–$999	50%	48%	46%	43%	3%	3%	1%	1%	31%	26%	30%	29%
$1000–$2999	22	20	26	20	9	11	6	7	16	15	14	13
$3000–$4999	17	9	17	20	15	17	11	12	13	15	12	13
$5000–$7999	6	15	6	9	31	30	22	22	18	18	14	15
$8000–$9999	6	2	2	2	15	15	17	17	8	8	9	10
$10,000–$14,999	0	7	4	6	20	18	28	25	12	12	15	13
$15,000 plus	0	0	0	0	8	9	15	16	3	4	7	8
Mean	$1980	$2636	$2122	$2652	$8009	$7879	$9884	$9885	$4732	$4944	$5527	$5708
N[a]	54	54	54	54	468	468	468	468	822	822	822	822

a. N is the number of persons in the sample in each particular category in each experiment. Where N is small (say, less than 50), the results must be viewed with caution.
Exp 1 = Wage equalization
Exp 2 = Participation and hours equalization
Exp 3 = Wage, participation, and hours equalization

TABLE 14-6

SIMULATED *FAMILY* EARNINGS OF WOMEN, 1969

Percentage Distributions and Means

(1958 Dollars)

NONWHITE WOMEN'S FAMILIES

Earnings Class	Family Heads with Child				Wives				Others			
	Base Run	Exp 1	Exp 2	Exp 3	Base Run	Exp 1	Exp 2	Exp 3	Base Run	Exp 1	Exp 2	Exp 3
0–$999	55%	55%	23%	18%	9%	7%	3%	2%	30%	29%	23%	22%
$1000–$2999	36	23	46	32	17	19	10	10	26	23	21	17
$3000–$4999	5	18	27	23	21	21	14	17	17	19	18	17
$5000–$7999	5	5	5	27	17	17	24	22	18	16	17	18
$8000–$9999	0	0	0	0	12	10	7	10	3	5	8	11
$10,000–$14,999	0	0	0	0	24	26	33	33	5	6	10	12
$15,000 plus	0	0	0	0	0	0	9	5	2	2	3	3
Mean	$1222	$1539	$2271	$3263	$6271	$6208	$8369	$8415	$3555	$3806	$5022	$5432
N[a]	22	22	22	22	58	58	58	58	117	117	117	117

TABLE 14-6 (continued)

WHITE WOMEN'S FAMILIES

Earnings Class	Family Heads with Child				Wives				Others			
	Base Run	Exp 1	Exp 2	Exp 3	Base Run	Exp 1	Exp 2	Exp 3	Base Run	Exp 1	Exp 2	Exp 3
0–$999	26%	30%	18%	16%	3%	3%	1%	1%	28%	28%	27%	26%
$1000–$2999	39	26	40	28	8	9	5	5	13	12	11	11
$3000–$4999	16	19	25	26	13	14	11	11	11	12	11	11
$5000–$7999	9	14	9	21	19	20	15	16	17	15	13	14
$8000–$9999	2	0	2	0	13	12	14	14	7	7	9	8
$10,000–$14,999	9	4	7	2	24	22	25	23	15	15	17	16
$15,000 plus	0	7	0	7	20	20	28	29	9	10	12	15
Mean	$3027	$3948	$3385	$4251	$9990	$9863	$11,792	$11,766	$5934	$6177	$6855	$7080
N[a]	57	57	57	57	463	463	463	463	936	936.	936	936

a. N is the number of persons in the sample in each particular category in each experiment. Where N is small (say, less than 50), the results must be viewed with caution.
Exp 1 = Wage equalization
Exp 2 = Participation and hours equalization
Exp 3 = Wage, participation, and hours equalization

TABLE 14-7

SIMULATED *FAMILY* EARNINGS OF WOMEN, 1972

Percentage Distributions and Means

(1958 Dollars)

	NONWHITE WOMEN'S FAMILIES												
	Family Heads with Child				Wives				Others			
Earnings Class	Base Run	Exp 1	Exp 2	Exp 3	Base Run	Exp 1	Exp 2	Exp 3	Base Run	Exp 1	Exp 2	Exp 3
0–$999	41%	41%	27%	27%	8%	8%	5%	5%	27%	27%	24%	24%
$1000–$2999	23	9	18	9	15	13	7	5	27	24	18	14
$3000–$4999	32	14	41	18	18	23	15	15	10	15	15	14
$5000–$7999	5	27	14	32	25	30	26	25	17	14	20	20
$8000–$9999	0	9	0	5	15	8	10	13	7	8	9	11
$10,000–$14,999	0	0	0	9	15	12	21	21	9	8	11	10
$15,000 plus	0	0	0	0	5	7	16	16	3	4	4	7
Mean	$2133	$3391	$2958	$4552	$6829	$6628	$9374	$9369	$4361	$4611	$5363	$5644
N[a]	22	22	22	22	61	61	61	61	118	118	118	118

TABLE 14-7 (continued)

WHITE WOMEN'S FAMILIES

Earnings Class	Family Heads with Child				Wives				Others			
	Base Run	Exp 1	Exp 2	Exp 3	Base Run	Exp 1	Exp 2	Exp 3	Base Run	Exp 1	Exp 2	Exp 3
0-$999	31%	28%	21%	19%	4%	5%	3%	3%	28%	28%	27%	26%
$1000-$2999	34	25	30	19	6	5	3	4	13	11	11	10
$3000-$4999	15	15	25	26	11	12	6	7	13	13	11	11
$5000-$7999	9	15	13	19	22	24	18	18	14	15	13	15
$8000-$9999	6	6	4	8	12	11	15	15	7	8	9	8
$10,000-$14,999	4	6	6	4	24	21	26	26	14	13	15	15
$15,000 plus	2	6	2	6	20	21	29	28	11	13	15	16
Mean	$3113	$4197	$3292	$4866	$10,129	$10,033	$12,094	$12,131	$6326	$6563	$7182	$7391
N[a]	53	53	53	53	499	499	499	499	963	963	963	963

a. N is the number of persons in the sample in each particular category in each experiment. Where N is small (say, less than 50), the results must be viewed with caution.
Exp 1 = Wage equalization
Exp 2 = Participation and hours equalization
Exp 3 = Wage, participation, and hours equalization

TABLE 14-8

SIMULATED EARNINGS OF MEN, 1964

Percentage Distributions and Means

(1958 Dollars)

NONWHITE MEN

Earnings Class	Family Heads with Child				Others			
	Base Run	Exp 1	Exp 2	Exp 3	Base Run	Exp 1	Exp 2	Exp 3
0–$999	19%	21%	19%	21%	52%	56%	52%	57%
$1000–$2999	40	40	36	49	24	22	23	24
$3000–$4999	26	32	28	26	16	17	16	14
$5000–$7999	15	6	17	4	7	4	8	5
$8000–$9999	0	0	0	0	1	1	1	0
$10,000–$14,999	0	0	0	0	0	0	0	0
$15,000 plus	0	0	0	0	0	0	0	0
Mean	$2807	$2474	$2893	$2363	$1686	$1468	$1737	$1395
N[a]	47	47	47	47	112	112	112	112

TABLE 14-8 (continued)

WHITE MEN

Earnings Class	Family Heads with Child				Others			
	Base Run	Exp 1	Exp 2	Exp 3	Base Run	Exp 1	Exp 2	Exp 3
0–$999	6%	7%	6%	7%	42%	45%	42%	45%
$1000–$2999	16	20	16	21	19	19	19	20
$3000–$4999	19	24	18	26	16	16	15	17
$5000–$7999	29	27	30	26	12	11	12	11
$8000–$9999	12	11	12	10	5	4	6	3
$10,000–$14,999	14	8	15	7	5	4	5	4
$15,000 plus	4	3	4	3	1	1	2	1
Mean	$6356	$5660	$6512	$5399	$3089	$2742	$3165	$2612
N[a]	469	469	469	469	862	862	862	862

a. N is the number of persons in the sample in each particular category in each experiment. Where N is small (say, less than 50), the results must be viewed with caution.
Exp 1 = Wage equalization
Exp 2 = Participation and hours equalization
Exp 3 = Wage, participation, and hours equalization

TABLE 14-9

SIMULATED EARNINGS OF MEN, 1969

Percentage Distributions and Means

(1958 Dollars)

	NONWHITE MEN							
	Family Heads with Child				Others			
Earnings Class	Base Run	Exp 1	Exp 2	Exp 3	Base Run	Exp 1	Exp 2	Exp 3
0–$999	16%	16%	16%	18%	54%	55%	54%	55%
$1000–$2999	16	23	16	26	18	21	18	22
$3000–$4999	35	37	35	37	14	13	15	15
$5000–$7999	21	12	21	9	9	7	7	6
$8000–$9999	4	5	4	5	3	2	3	2
$10,000–$14,999	9	7	9	5	2	2	2	1
$15,000 plus	0	0	0	0	1	0	1	0
Mean	$4413	$3862	$4392	$3601	$2141	$1853	$2127	$1721
N[a]	57	57	57	57	123	123	123	123

TABLE 14-9 (continued)

WHITE MEN

Earnings Class	Family Heads with Child				Others			
	Base Run	Exp 1	Exp 2	Exp 3	Base Run	Exp 1	Exp 2	Exp 3
0–$999	9%	10%	9%	10%	38%	40%	38%	41%
$1000–$2999	11	14	10	16	18	19	18	21
$3000–$4999	18	19	18	21	15	16	15	16
$5000–$7999	22	24	23	25	14	13	15	12
$8000–$9999	12	10	12	9	5	5	5	5
$10,000–$14,999	18	15	18	14	3	2	3	1
$15,000 plus	11	8	10	7	3	2	3	1
Mean	$7727	$6839	$7666	$6372	$3741	$3309	$3715	$3087
N^a	464	464	464	464	936	936	936	936

a. N is the number of persons in the sample in each particular category in each experiment. Where N is small (say, less than 50), the results must be viewed with caution.
Exp 1 = Wage equalization
Exp 2 = Participation and hours equalization
Exp 3 = Wage, participation, and hours equalization

TABLE 14-10

SIMULATED EARNINGS OF MEN, 1972

Percentage Distributions and Means

(1958 Dollars)

| | NONWHITE MEN | | | | | | | |
| | Family Heads with Child | | | | Others | | | |
Earnings Class	Base Run	Exp 1	Exp 2	Exp 3	Base Run	Exp 1	Exp 2	Exp 3
0–$999	15%	15%	15%	18%	48%	49%	47%	49%
$1000–$2999	20	22	20	18	19	28	20	30
$3000–$4999	18	23	17	28	17	13	17	12
$5000–$7999	28	33	32	28	13	8	13	7
$8000–$9999	12	2	10	3	2	2	2	1
$10,000–$14,999	7	5	7	3	1	1	1	1
$15,000 plus	0	0	0	0	0	0	0	0
Mean	$4773	$4232	$4760	$3937	$2172	$1861	$2181	$1720
N[a]	60	60	60	60	136	136	136	136

TABLE 14-10 (continued)

	WHITE MEN							
	Family Heads with Child				Others			
Earnings Class	Base Run	Exp 1	Exp 2	Exp 3	Base Run	Exp 1	Exp 2	Exp 3
0–$999	10%	11%	10%	11%	38%	40%	38%	41%
$1000–$2999	10	13	10	15	17	18	17	19
$3000–$4999	16	17	15	17	14	14	14	16
$5000–$7999	23	26	23	27	14	14	14	12
$8000–$9999	12	9	13	8	6	5	6	5
$10,000–$14,999	17	13	17	14	7	6	7	5
$15,000 plus	12	10	11	8	2	3	4	3
Mean	$7932	$7110	$7879	$6610	$4012	$3598	$3988	$3347
N[a]	500	500	500	500	943	943	943	943

a. N is the number of persons in the sample in each particular category in each experiment. Where N is small (say, less than 50), the results must be viewed with caution.
Exp 1 = Wage equalization
Exp 2 = Participation and hours equalization
Exp 3 = Wage, participation, and hours equalization

TABLE 14-11

SIMULATED *FAMILY* EARNINGS OF MEN, 1964

Percentage Distributions and Means

(1958 Dollars)

NONWHITE MEN'S FAMILIES

Earnings Class	Family Heads with Child				Others			
	Base Run	Exp 1	Exp 2	Exp 3	Base Run	Exp 1	Exp 2	Exp 3
0–$999	6%	6%	6%	4%	23%	24%	18%	19%
$1000–$2999	36	36	19	21	31	33	27	27
$3000–$4999	32	34	40	43	27	27	28	30
$5000–$7999	19	17	21	19	16	13	20	17
$8000–$9999	4	4	6	6	1	0	6	5
$10,000–$14,999	2	2	6	6	1	2	1	2
$15,000 plus	0	0	0	0	1	1	1	1
Mean	$3806	$3799	$4722	$4748	$3008	$2936	$3755	$3650
N^a	47	47	47	47	112	112	112	112

TABLE 14-11 (continued)

WHITE MEN'S FAMILIES

Earnings Class	Family Heads with Child				Others			
	Base Run	Exp 1	Exp 2	Exp 3	Base Run	Exp 1	Exp 2	Exp 3
0–$999	3%	3%	1%	1%	17%	17%	15%	16%
$1000–$2999	9	10	6	7	15	15	13	14
$3000–$4999	15	17	11	12	17	18	16	16
$5000–$7999	31	29	22	22	21	20	18	19
$8000–$9999	15	15	17	17	12	10	11	10
$10,000–$14,999	20	18	28	25	13	12	16	14
$15,000 plus	8	9	15	16	5	7	10	11
Mean	$8000	$7869	$9881	$9883	$6006	$5927	$6996	$6887
N[a]	469	469	469	469	862	862	862	862

a. N is the number of persons in the sample in each particular category in each experiment. Where N is small (say, less than 50), the results must be viewed with caution.
Exp 1 = Wage equalization
Exp 2 = Participation and hours equalization
Exp 3 = Wage, participation, and hours equalization

TABLE 14-12

SIMULATED *FAMILY* EARNINGS OF MEN, 1969

Percentage Distributions and Means

(1958 Dollars)

	NONWHITE MEN'S FAMILIES							
	Family Heads with Child				Others			
Earnings Class	Base Run	Exp 1	Exp 2	Exp 3	Base Run	Exp 1	Exp 2	Exp 3
0–$999	9%	7%	4%	2%	21%	22%	18%	18%
$1000–$2999	18	19	11	11	24	23	14	17
$3000–$4999	21	21	14	18	15	21	24	16
$5000–$7999	18	18	25	23	20	17	17	23
$8000–$9999	12	11	7	11	8	2	7	8
$10,000–$14,999	23	25	32	32	11	15	15	14
$15,000 plus	0	0	9	5	2	1	5	4
Mean	$6123	$6082	$8259	$8342	$4699	$4556	$5919	$5955
N[a]	57	57	57	57	123	123	123	123

TABLE 14-12 (continued)

WHITE MEN'S FAMILIES

Earnings Class	Family Heads with Child				Others			
	Base Run	Exp 1	Exp 2	Exp 3	Base Run	Exp 1	Exp 2	Exp 3
0–$999	3%	3%	1%	1%	15%	17%	14%	15%
$1000–$2999	8	9	5	5	12	12	10	11
$3000–$4999	13	14	11	11	13	15	13	13
$5000–$7999	19	20	15	16	21	18	18	16
$8000–$9999	13	12	14	14	8	9	10	9
$10,000–$14,999	24	22	25	23	19	19	21	19
$15,000 plus	20	20	28	29	11	11	14	17
Mean	$10,000	$9871	$11,768	$11,768	$7442	$7339	$8436	$8298
N[a]	464	464	464	464	936	936	936	936

a. N is the number of persons in the sample in each particular category in each experiment. Where N is small (say, less than 50), the results must be viewed with caution.
Exp 1 = Wage equalization
Exp 2 = Participation and hours equalization
Exp 3 = Wage, participation, and hours equalization

TABLE 14-13

SIMULATED *FAMILY* EARNINGS OF MEN, 1972

Percentage Distributions and Means

(1958 Dollars)

NONWHITE MEN'S FAMILIES

Earnings Class	Family Heads with Child				Others			
	Base Run	Exp 1	Exp 2	Exp 3	Base Run	Exp 1	Exp 2	Exp 3
0–$999	8%	8%	5%	5%	17%	17%	15%	15%
$1000–$2999	15	13	7	5	19	23	15	21
$3000–$4999	18	23	15	15	22	21	21	13
$5000–$7999	25	30	27	25	17	18	20	18
$8000–$9999	15	8	10	13	10	10	6	7
$10,000–$14,999	15	12	22	22	11	7	14	15
$15,000 plus	3	5	15	15	4	5	9	10
Mean	$6471	$6300	$9068	$9121	$5665	$5507	$6982	$6759
N[a]	60	60	60	60	136	136	136	136

TABLE 14-13 (continued)

WHITE MEN'S FAMILIES

Earnings Class	Family Heads with Child				Others			
	Base Run	Exp 1	Exp 2	Exp 3	Base Run	Exp 1	Exp 2	Exp 3
0-$999	4%	5%	3%	3%	17%	17%	15%	15%
$1000-$2999	6	5	3	4	11	11	9	11
$3000-$4999	11	12	6	7	14	15	12	12
$5000-$7999	22	24	18	18	18	17	18	18
$8000-$9999	12	11	15	15	10	9	10	9
$10,000-$14,999	24	21	26	26	17	16	19	18
$15,000 plus	20	22	29	28	14	14	17	16
Mean	$10,165	$10,066	$12,125	$12,155	$7684	$7594	$8670	$8529
Nª	500	500	500	500	943	943	943	943

a. N is the number of persons in the sample in each particular category in each experiment. Where N is small (say, less than 50), the results must be viewed with caution.
Exp 1 = Wage equalization
Exp 2 = Participation and hours equalization
Exp 3 = Wage, participation, and hours equalization

work would benefit children in female-headed families as well as the women themselves.

Experiment 2: Equal Hours in the Labor Force

Experiment 2 gives women the same labor force participation probability function and the same hours in the labor force function as men. This leads to a substantial increase in aggregate labor income since the macro model makes the implicit assumption that the average productivity for new entrants to the labor force is the same as the overall average productivity of labor. Thus, in the base run real labor income in 1972 was $480 million, but this increased in Experiment 2 to $559 million. Some of this increase in aggregate labor income is more apparent than real since some fraction of this increase represents payments by working wives and mothers to other women for providing housekeeping and child-care services. Presumably, these services were being provided in the base run in the form of housework, which does not get included in the national income accounts.

For female family heads with children, Experiment 2 resulted in increases in earnings roughly equivalent to those in Experiment 1 for nonwhites but somewhat smaller for whites. For both races Experiment 1 appears to put more women in the higher earnings categories than Experiment 2. Moreover, part of the gains from Experiment 2 are only apparent, as indicated earlier, since many women who increase their degree of labor force participation thereby incur a substantial cost to pay for housekeeping and child-care services they used to perform themselves.

Wives gain considerably more from Experiment 2 than from Experiment 1. Average earnings more than double. This difference between the heads and the wives presumably occurs because the wives' level of labor force participation is lower than the heads' in the base run.

Family earnings of female family heads go up by slightly more than person earnings—just as in Experiment 1. For wives, family earnings increase by much more than in Experiment 1. This differs from Experiment 1 because, in Experiment 2, the gains of the wives are not counterbalanced by losses of their husbands.

The personal earnings of men are left virtually unchanged by Experiment 2. However, family earnings of men increase due to the increase in earnings of women in many of their families.

In summary, increasing women's participation in the labor market to the point where they work for as many hours as comparable men yields its greatest benefit to husband-wife families and much less of a benefit to female-headed families.

Experiment 3: Equal Hours and Equal Pay

Equal hours and equal pay are much more than additive in their impact upon nonwhite female heads' earnings. Experiment 1 increases the fraction of nonwhite female family heads earning over $3,000 per year in 1964 from zero in the base run to 8 percent; Experiment 2 increases the fraction to 4 percent; but Experiment 3 increases the fraction to 25 percent—with the mean real earnings increased to two and one-half times their base run level. By 1972 nearly one-half of all nonwhite female family heads earn more than $5,000 per year in Experiment 3. (These figures need to be viewed with caution because of the rather small sample size.)

The results for white female family heads are not quite so dramatic but are still quite impressive. Mean real earnings for white female family heads in 1972 are $4,351 in Experiment 3 compared with $2,526 in the base run.

Wives, both nonwhite and white, also receive larger increases from Experiment 3 than from Experiments 1 and 2 combined. Since wives tend to work less than female heads, the combination of working as many hours and earning at the same wage rates as comparable men is quite potent. By 1972, 63 percent of the white wives had real earnings of over $3,000 (compared with 21 percent in the base run, 31 percent in Experiment 1, and 51 percent in Experiment 2).

Family earnings for nonwhite female family heads were up quite sharply in Experiment 3 compared with Experiments 1 and 2. These results reflect the sharply increased earnings of the heads themselves—other earners making only a minor contribution to total family earnings. Similarly, family earnings for white female family heads increased by roughly the same amount as the earnings of the heads themselves.

The impact of Experiment 3 upon men's earnings is about the same as Experiment 1—the equal pay experiment. Women get the net increase in real labor income, while men lose their privileged place in the relative wage distribution. Consequently, their earnings decline.

Unlike Experiment 1, however, Experiment 3 results in an increase in family earnings for male family heads with children. This is because their own earnings loss is more than counterbalanced by the large increase in their wives' earnings. In fact, every family category has higher mean real earnings in Experiment 3 than in the base run for all three years. (There is still the qualification that some of this increase is only apparent.)

In summary, the results of Experiment 3 are an amalgam of Experiment 1 and Experiment 2. Both female family heads and wives experience substantial earnings gains—partially at the expense of men, partially due to the increase in aggregate labor income. For some groups a strong positive interaction effect is present. This is due to the fact that women's earnings in Experiment 3 consist of the total of four components—(1) the base run wage rates times the base run hours, (2) the base run wage rates times the added comparable-to-male hours, (3) the base run hours times the higher comparable-to-male wage rates, and (4) the added hours times the higher wage rates. It is the fourth item which accounts for the positive interaction.

A Comparison of Male and Female Earnings

Up to this point we have focused on the gain or loss in earnings for various person and family groups. In this section we shall examine briefly the degree of movement towards equality in earnings between men and women implied by the three experiments. Table 14-14 gives the ratio of mean female earnings to mean earnings by race for all persons who participated in the labor force each year and the grand mean for each ratio over the whole period.

On the base run white females' mean earnings were only 44 percent of white males over the period 1960–1972, while nonwhite females' earnings were 56 percent of nonwhite males' earnings. These differences reflect differences in personal characteristics but also reflect differences in the number of hours worked and differences in wage rates paid for comparable individuals of each sex.

For nonwhites the equal pay for equal work experiment has a dramatic impact—raising the female-male earnings ratio from 1960–1972 average of .56 up to an average of .91. In fact, during the last three years of the Experiment I run, nonwhite women surpass nonwhite men in average earnings—the result, in part, of a strong upward trend in the ratio that appears in both the base run and the experiments.

For white women the results of Experiment 1 are quite significant but not as dramatic. The average ratio rises from .44 in the base run to .70. Part of the reason the results are less spectacular is that the experiments are superimposed upon a declining trend in the ratio. (Fuchs has shown that this decline is misleading. He found that the female-male

TABLE 14-14

SIMULATED FEMALE-MALE MEAN EARNINGS RATIO

	BASE RUN		EXPERIMENT 1		EXPERIMENT 2		EXPERIMENT 3	
	Non-white	White	Non-white	White	Non-white	White	Non-white	White
1960	.42	.50	.71	.81	.55	.68	.93	1.08
1961	.44	.47	.77	.76	.57	.63	1.01	1.03
1962	.44	.46	.78	.75	.62	.61	1.09	1.01
1963	.48	.46	.80	.74	.63	.60	1.08	1.00
1964	.52	.44	.85	.70	.64	.60	1.09	.98
1965	.60	.45	.99	.71	.78	.60	1.32	.97
1966	.59	.43	.97	.66	.73	.58	1.22	.92
1967	.53	.42	.88	.64	.74	.56	1.22	.90
1968	.59	.43	.89	.67	.82	.59	1.30	.95
1969	.61	.44	.99	.68	.81	.59	1.29	.94
1970	.65	.43	1.03	.67	.92	.58	1.46	.92
1971	.68	.44	1.05	.67	.96	.59	1.50	.95
1972	.70	.41	1.09	.63	.95	.57	1.52	.91
1960–1972 Mean	.56	.44	.91	.70	.75	.60	1.23	.97

earnings ratio for *comparable* men and women actually increased by 4.8 percent between 1959 and 1969.)

The impact of Experiment 2 — giving women the same participation rate and hours functions as comparable men — was smaller. The average value of the ratio for nonwhites went up from .56 to .75, while the ratio increased from .44 to .60 for the whites. The comparison between Experiments 1 and 2 becomes even less favorable to Experiment 2 when one considers that for many women the increase in earnings is counterbalanced by an increase in housekeeping and child-care expenses.

Experiment 3 raises the earnings ratio to an average of 1.23 for nonwhite women. They surpass the men presumably because of their higher average level of educational attainment. The increase is more than the sum of the increases from Experiments 1 and 2.

Experiment 3 brings white women to near equality with white men. The average value of the ratio is .97 over the period of simulation. Part of the reason why white women do not achieve full parity is their lower occupational status than men.

In summary, giving women equal pay for equal work moves women in the direction of parity in earnings more than having them work as much as men. A comparison of Experiment 1 with Experiment 3 demonstrates that working as much as comparable men has a much stronger effect after women have already achieved wage rate parity with comparable men.

Conclusion

Several criteria have been implied in evaluating the results of these experiments. Among the most important were (1) the desirability of changes which improve the economic welfare of families with children dependent upon a woman for earnings, and (2) the value of moving women towards earnings parity with men. Using these two criteria, given a choice between policies which tend to equalize wage rates and those which tend to make women work more hours in the labor force, comparison of the results of Experiment 1 and 2 indicates that moving toward equality in wage rates is more effective. However, because of the interaction effect, moving on both fronts at once is even better, as the results of Experiment 3 demonstrate.

Chapter 15
IMPACT OF DIVORCE ON THE DISTRIBUTION OF INCOME *

As is well known, there is a strong trend toward increased family instability in the United States. In 1974 there were 63 divorced persons for every 1,000 currently married persons.[1] This was nearly double the level of 35 per 1,000 in 1960. Furthermore, the ratio of divorced persons to married persons increased more rapidly during the first years of the 1970s than during the 1960s. While this rapid acceleration in divorces has many implications, one of the more serious is the corresponding growth in the number of families headed by women with children under 18. The female-headed family usually has only one potential earner — the mother — who has relatively low expected earnings. She is therefore often dependent on the public transfer program, Aid to Families with Dependent Children (AFDC), for support.

DYNASIM is well suited for quantitative analysis of the effects of marital disruption. As discussed in previous chapters, families[2] are actually created and dissolved in the simulation via the processes of divorce, marriage, and remarriage. Thus, the full dynamics of the process can be observed. In particular, changes in the economic "well-offness" of persons involved in divorce can be assessed.

This chapter reports on the results of two simulation runs in which the demographic and economic effects of two different divorce probabilities were observed. In the first run, called Simulation I, the *probability of divorce* for persons with a given set of demographic characteristics was held constant after 1974. In the second run, referred to as Simulation II, the probability of divorce was increased each year by the average percentage increase which occurred in the early 1970s — 5 percent.

The initial population of the model was drawn by taking a 50 per-

---

* Sheila Zedlewski and Sheila Larkin were responsible for this chapter and the work it represents.
 1. "Marital Status and Living Arrangements: March 1974," *Current Population Reports*, Series P-20, No. 271, 1974.
 2. Throughout this chapter "family" corresponds to a nuclear family concept — that is, families consisting of a married couple and their children. Single persons, whether previously married or not, and their children, if any, are included as nuclear families.

cent sample of the 1970 1-in-10,000 Census Public Use Sample. This smaller sample (approximately 10,000 persons) was then moved forward by the model through 1974, the end of the period for which actual historical events could be tracked. Afterwards, the two simulations mentioned above proceeded through 1984. The parameters of the model for these two simulations differed in only the one respect mentioned—the probability of divorce.[3] Thus, the differences which are observed between Simulation I and Simulation II may be entirely attributed to the difference in the probability of divorce since any Monte Carlo variability was also held constant.[4]

Results

Demographic Events

The aggregate number of divorces in the United States which occur in each simulation is shown in Table 15-1. One can see the divergence in the number of divorces between Simulation I and II beginning in 1975. In 1984 alone about 60 percent more divorces occur in the second simulation than in the first. In the total population[5] over 4 million more divorces would occur during the entire 1975–1984 period in the increasing divorce rate simulation.

A divorce may trigger various further outcomes. For example, one or both of the parties may remarry. This phenomenon is reflected in the substantial increase in the number of marriages which occur in Simulation II as shown in Table 15-1. In the ten-year period after 1974, 2.4 million more marriages take place than in I. Some persons no doubt were divorced and remarried more than once. However, not all of the parties of divorce remarry. The male party forms a new nuclear family of his own when the divorce occurs, and he may remain single for varying periods of time. Similarly, the female party, who continues to remain in the original nuclear family with her children (if any), may remain single indefinitely. In fact, 2.6 million more family units exist in Simulation II than in Simulation I by 1984. The decline in the number of

3. The divorce module incorporated in these simulations is not the one described earlier in this book because that module was not available at the time this experiment was carried out. An older module was used, and the basic difference is that no economic variables affect a family's divorce probability. This earlier module is described by Steven Caldwell in Guy Orcutt, et al., "Microanalytic Simulation Through Policy Exploration," Urban Institute Working Paper 509-5, 1974.

4. This procedure is fully described in Chapter 1.

5. The numbers reported have been blown up to equal U.S. population totals.

TABLE 15-1

AGGREGATE COUNTS OF MAJOR DEMOGRAPHIC EVENTS
UNDER DIFFERENT ASSUMPTIONS, TOTAL
U.S. POPULATION
[in thousands]

Year	DIVORCES I	DIVORCES II	BIRTHS I	BIRTHS II	DEATHS I	DEATHS II	MARRIAGES I	MARRIAGES II
1970	696		3,657		1,965		2,162	
1971	725		3,475		2,005		2,160	
1972	798		3,265		1,972		2,262	
1973	880		2,884		1,960		2,248	
1974	949		2,900		1,968		2,310	
1975	998	1,070	2,962	2,955	1,974	1,974	2,417	2,431
1976	1,042	1,164	3,047	3,042	2,018	2,019	2,501	2,538
1977	1,086	1,273	3,152	3,156	2,020	2,028	2,615	2,671
1978	1,129	1,382	3,187	3,236	2,008	2,020	2,649	2,745
1979	1,187	1,529	3,272	3,207	2,044	2,054	2,686	2,857
1980	1,239	1,665	3,373	3,285	2,092	2,108	2,763	3,021
1981	1,294	1,803	3,474	3,409	2,120	2,136	2,766	3,096
1982	1,346	1,951	3,548	3,445	2,151	2,179	2,806	3,207
1983	1,402	2,109	3,579	3,511	2,217	2,233	2,878	3,311
1984	1,439	2,279	3,540	3,400	2,224	2,246	2,908	3,494

I = Flat divorce rate after 1974.
II = Increasing divorce rate after 1974 of 5 percent per year.

births which occur in Simulation II is caused by this increase: simply fewer two-parent families exist to bear children. While births may occur in the simulation to single women, the probability of such births is relatively low. The small increase in the aggregate number of deaths in Simulation II is due to the fact that single persons have higher death probabilities than married ones. The effect is slight, however, because younger persons who have the greatest risk of divorce also have low death probabilities.

Distribution of Income

Of particular interest are any changes in the distribution of income which occur because of an increase in marital instability. For analytical purposes the types of families in the simulation population have been grouped by the sex of the head of the family and whether or not there are dependent children under 18 years of age in the unit. In the simulation model the children involved in a divorce always remain with the mother. We have divided families into four categories.

Category 1: Families which contain children and are headed by men. (A wife may or may not be present.)

Category 2: Families which contain children and are headed by women. (Husband *not* present.)

Category 3: Families which contain no children and are headed by men. (This category therefore includes all single, widowed, and divorced men, as well as childless couples.)

Category 4: Families which contain no children and are headed by women. (This category therefore includes all single, widowed, and divorced women with no children.)

When a divorce splits up a Category 1 family, the wife and children will constitute a Category 2 family, while the husband will constitute a new Category 3 family. When a divorce splits up a Category 3 family (childless couple), the wife will constitute a Category 4 family, while the husband will constitute a new Category 3 family.

Table 15-2 shows the distribution of total family income in 1984 for Simulations I and II by type of family. Total family income includes the earnings, transfer income, and asset income of all members of the family. It is shown in 1958 dollars.[6] At first glance the distribution of income appears very similar in the two runs. This reflects the fact that although shuffling among family types has occurred, the new families tend to resemble others of their same type. We do see, however, that the mean income for all families has dropped by about $300. This occurs because in Simulation II there are 2.6 million more families overall, but the number of families in the highest mean income group—male heads with children—has dropped by 2 million.

The absolute change in the number of families falling in each income interval is shown in Table 15-3. This table shows more clearly the changes discussed above. The number of female-headed families with children has increased by 1.8 million in the high divorce rate simulation. More than half of these new families fall in the lowest two income intervals—$4,000 and under. The increase in the total number of families who fall in the lowest income interval is 1.3 million or about one-half of the new family units. All of these families are poor with total family income $2,000 or below.

Perhaps a more interesting picture of family economic well-being is

6. The GNP price deflators used for years 1975 through 1984 were 1.84, 1.96, 2.09, 2.22, 2.32, 2.42, 2.51, 2.61, 2.72, and 2.83, respectively.

TABLE 15-2

DISTRIBUTION OF TOTAL FAMILY INCOME[a] IN 1984, BY TYPE OF FAMILY, UNDER TWO DIVORCE RATE ASSUMPTIONS

Income (1958 $)	ALL FAMILIES		CATEGORY 1[b]		CATEGORY 2[c]		CATEGORY 3[d]		CATEGORY 4[e]	
	I	II	I	II	I	II	I	II	I	II
0– 2,000	13.1%	14.2%	3.5%	3.5%	26.5%	26.2%	8.9%	10.0%	31.5%	31.7%
2,001– 4,000	15.6	15.6	9.4	9.5	34.4	32.5	12.8	12.4	24.6	24.0
4,001– 6,000	11.3	11.5	10.1	10.6	11.2	12.7	11.5	11.1	12.7	13.3
6,001– 8,000	10.5	10.5	10.5	9.8	10.9	10.5	11.4	11.6	8.5	8.8
8,001–10,000	8.6	8.5	10.3	10.4	6.9	8.6	8.8	9.0	6.4	5.2
10,001–12,000	7.1	7.2	8.8	8.8	2.1	2.0	8.1	8.4	4.2	4.5
12,001–14,000	6.8	6.7	9.6	9.6	1.4	1.4	7.3	7.6	3.4	3.1
14,001–16,000	5.7	5.4	9.3	8.3	0.8	1.2	5.6	5.7	2.4	2.5
16,001–18,000	4.5	4.6	6.7	7.1	2.1	2.3	5.7	5.3	0.9	0.8
18,001–20,000	3.1	2.9	4.6	4.8	1.8	1.2	3.4	3.2	0.5	0.7
More than 20,000	13.5	12.8	17.2	17.6	1.8	1.4	16.7	15.6	4.9	5.3
Mean	$10,931	$10,660	$13,116	$13,249	$5,086	$5,112	$12,590	$12,244	$6,200	$6,216
N (000)	93,026	95,607	27,449	25,404	5,701	7,497	40,151	42,217	19,725	20,489

I = Flat divorce rate of 1974 extended to 1984.
II = Increasing divorce rate at 5 percent annually from 1974 to 1984.
a. Includes earnings, transfer income, and asset income.
b. Families which contain children and are headed by men.
c. Families which contain children and are headed by women.
d. Families which contain no children and are headed by men.
e. Families which contain no children and are headed by women.

TABLE 15-3

ABSOLUTE DIFFERENCES IN NUMBER OF FAMILIES BY INCOME INTERVAL FROM BETWEEN
SIMULATION I TO II IN 1984

[Numbers in thousands]

Income (1958 $)	All Families	Category 1[a]	Category 2[b]	Category 3[c]	Category 4[d]
0– 2,000	+1,345	–62	+455	+681	+268
2,001– 4,000	+433	–186	+475	+83	+62
4,001– 6,000	+537	–62	+309	+63	+228
6,001– 8,000	+225	–412	+166	+330	+144
8,001–10,000	+103	–206	+249	+248	–186
10,001–12,000	+246	–187	*	+310	+104
12,001–14,000	+60	–186	*	+248	*
14,001–16,000	–187	–433	*	+166	*
16,001–18,000	+164	*	*	+145	*
18,001–20,000	–83	*	*	–83	*
More than 20,000	–268	–268	*	–124	+103
TOTAL	+2,581	–2,045	+1,796	+2,066	+764

* Change represented 2 or fewer simulation cases.
a. Families which contain children and are headed by men.
b. Families which contain children and are headed by women.
c. Families which contain no children and are headed by men.
d. Families which contain no children and are headed by women.

shown in Table 15-4 which gives the total income available per person. Ignoring the fact that there are economies of scale in group living arrangements, families with young children (Categories 1 and 2) have lower resources per person than those without young children (Categories 3 and 4). The third column under "All Families" gives the percentage difference in the fraction of families which fall into each income interval, comparing Simulations I and II. Newly created families fall disproportionately into the lowest and the highest income per person intervals. The newly created female-headed families with children have a high chance of falling into the lowest income interval—$1,000 or less— but the newly created male-headed families without children have a high chance of falling into the highest income interval—greater than $10,000. In Simulation II, 3.5 million children have "moved" from male-headed families where their share of family income was $3,426 to female-headed families where their share is $1,987. But other male heads have moved from a situation where their income share was also $3,426 to one where it is $7,042. These results must be viewed with caution, however, because the model does not simulate private transfers of alimony and child support. Correcting for this lack should change the analysis only slightly because of the irregularity and paucity of these types of transfer. (This issue is addressed more fully in the next section in connection with changes that have occurred in the major components of total family income—earnings and transfers.)

Major Income Components

We have seen that, as a result of an increased rate of divorce, far more female-headed families with children under 18 (Category 2 families) exist in the population. In addition, it has been shown that this type of family has the lowest income available to them relative to other families, whether measured on a per family or per person basis. A closer look at the components of total family income helps clarify the basis for the plight of these families.

It has already been mentioned that one of the reasons why the income of families with no children and headed by a woman (Category 2) is relatively low is that only one potential earner exists. In contrast, the income of male-headed families, particularly those with children, is often a combination of the earnings of the husband and wife. A second contributing factor is that, as is well known, the earnings of females are lower than those of their male counterparts.[7] Their expected wage rates

---

7. This issue is discussed in greater detail in Chapter 12.

TABLE 15-4

DISTRIBUTION OF TOTAL INCOME PER CAPITA IN 1984 BY TYPE OF FAMILY

Income (1958 $)	ALL FAMILIES			CATEGORY 1[a]		CATEGORY 2[b]		CATEGORY 3[c]		CATEGORY 4[d]	
	I	II	Percent Difference[e]	I	II	I	II	I	II	I	II
0– 1,000	9.4%	10.5%	+15	12.2%	12.6%	40.6%	41.6%	4.2%	4.8%	7.2%	8.3%
1,001– 2,000	18.4	18.0	*	20.8	20.6	28.3	26.7	11.4	11.2	26.6	25.6
2,001– 3,000	15.1	14.5	–2	19.7	19.3	10.9	10.7	12.0	11.3	16.2	16.4
3,001– 4,000	12.4	11.7	–3	16.0	15.2	9.1	8.0	11.5	11.1	10.2	10.0
4,001– 5,000	9.7	9.7	+3	12.0	11.9	6.2	6.9	9.6	9.5	7.7	8.5
5,001– 6,000	7.6	7.6	+2	7.8	8.5	1.4	1.9	8.7	8.6	6.8	6.6
6,001– 7,000	5.8	5.7	+1	4.6	4.1	0.7	1.1	7.8	7.6	4.6	5.3
7,001– 8,000	4.3	4.2	+2	2.6	3.3	0.7	0.6	6.4	6.2	3.5	2.7
8,001– 9,000	3.2	3.3	+5	1.1	1.3	1.4	1.4	5.2	5.4	2.6	2.2
9,001–10,000	2.8	2.5	–5	1.1	1.1	0.4	0.6	4.4	3.9	2.5	2.3
More than 10,000	11.4	12.3	+12	2.4	2.5	0.4	0.6	18.6	20.4	12.0	12.0
MEAN	$5,303	$5,357		$3,426	$3,479	$1,923	$1,987	$6,966	$7,042	$5,507	$5,448
N (000)	93,026	95,607		27,443	25,404	5,701	7,497	40,151	42,217	19,725	20,489

I = Flat divorce rate of 1974 extended to 1984.
II = Increasing divorce rate at 5 percent annually from 1974 to 1984.
a. Families which contain children and are headed by men.
b. Families which contain children and are headed by women.
c. Families which contain no children and are headed by men.
d. Families which contain no children and are headed by women.
e. This column compares the numbers of families in each income interval in Simulation II with those in Simulation I, expressed as a percentage. Note that there may be differences in these numbers of families even when the percentage distributions for each simulation are the same, since there are more families in Simulation II.
* Change represents 2 or fewer simulation cases.

and their level of participation in the work force both tend to be lower than for males.

Table 15-5 shows the relative labor force experience of five groups of persons over 18 years of age in the population for Simulations I and II in 1984. The groups are males who head families with children, all other males, females who head families with children, married females, and all other females. It should be mentioned again that one can see little change from Simulation I and II because the composition of the groups has remained about the same, although their relative numbers have changed. Because the unemployment rate is exogenous, the labor market model assumes that any additions to the labor force, in this case more female heads of families with children, are absorbed.

Table 15-5 shows that over 80 percent of the female heads with children do participate in the labor force. This is about the same rate as that for the other male category and 15 percent lower than that for male heads with children. One of the things that holds this rate down to 80 percent is that some of these women have just made the transition from nonworking wives to self-supporting family heads. The lack of participation in the previous year depresses a woman's probability of working in the current year, although the transition to family head does significantly increase her probability of working. To use a point suggested by Saw-hill,[8] a woman's "employment" by her husband does little to aid her in finding employment in the labor market. Thus, the woman may not work—at least temporarily. Table 15-5 also shows that married women have a 50 percent chance of working. Therefore, for about half of the male-headed families with children, total family income, as examined earlier, is comprised of some earnings of the husband and of the wife. The relatively low rates of participation of all other females shown here are due in a large part to their age. This group includes many older women whose primary source of income is social security.

Among people who work, males tend to work more hours per year than females. But a higher proportion of female family heads with children work more than 2,000 hours per year as compared with other females or married females. The presence of a child under six years of age in the family has a depressing effect on the number of hours a woman works, whether married or not. It appears that some change in the composition of this group may have occurred from Simulation I to Simulation II. In the latter, the high divorce rate run, more women are working over 2,000 hours. Younger women (age less than 44) and those with older children are more likely to work full time. With higher divorce probabilities one expects a somewhat broader group of families at risk

8. Isabel Sawhill, "Discrimination and Poverty Among Women Who Head Families," paper presented at the Conference on Occupational Segregation, Wellesley College, May 1975.

TABLE 15-5

EMPLOYMENT AND EARNINGS IN 1984 OF PERSONS 18 YEARS OF AGE AND OLDER
[in thousands]

	MALE HEADS WITH CHILDREN		OTHER MALES		FEMALE HEADS WITH CHILDREN		MARRIED FEMALES		OTHER FEMALES	
	I	II	I	II	I	II	I	II	I	II
Participating in the Labor Force										
Number	26,458	24,475	41,948	44,117	4,523	6,072	26,809	25,735	13,219	13,198
Percent	97%	97%	83%	84%	81%	82%	50%	50%	49%	48%
Hours of Participation										
Number not working	929	867	8,778	8,592	1,074	1,322	26,871	25,384	13,941	14,602
Percent not working	3%	4%	17%	16%	19%	18%	50%	50%	51%	53%
Number working 1 to 2,000 hours	8,117	7,704	20,923	22,100	3,387	4,348	23,070	22,203	9,697	9,666
Percent working 1 to 2,000 hours	30%	30%	41%	42%	61%	59%	43%	43%	36%	34%
Number working more than 2,000 hours	18,341	16,771	21,026	22,017	1,136	1,714	3,738	3,532	3,523	3,532
Percent working more than 2,000 hours	67%	66%	42%	42%	20%	23%	7%	7%	13%	13%
MEAN EARNINGS (1968 $)	$9,000	$9,055	$6,046	$6,129	$3,207	$3,304	$1,739	$1,785	$1,997	$1,947

I = Flat divorce rate simulation.
II = Increasing divorce rate simulation.

for divorce, since there is only a finite group each year with the peak divorce probability. Thus, this type of difference may show itself here. Women's lower participation in the labor force tends to depress their mean earnings. But aside from this, women's earnings on the average are much lower than men's. A tabulation of mean earnings in 1984 by sex for only persons who participate reveals that earnings for men would be about $8,000 while those for females would be about $3,700.

The most interesting aspect of family transfer income in these simulations is the role which AFDC plays in reducing the income insufficiency of the female-headed families with children under 18. Although this program also serves families in which the father is disabled or, in some states, unemployed, the major group aided is families with a female head and dependent children. In the early 1970s this group accounted for about 80 percent of the program's caseload. Thus, the growth of this group of families significantly affects the cost of this program to the government. Figure 15-1 shows the dramatic difference in the growth of female-headed families with children under 18 under the two different

FIGURE 15-1

GROWTH OF FEMALE-HEADED FAMILIES
WITH CHILDREN
1970–1984
(1970 = 100)

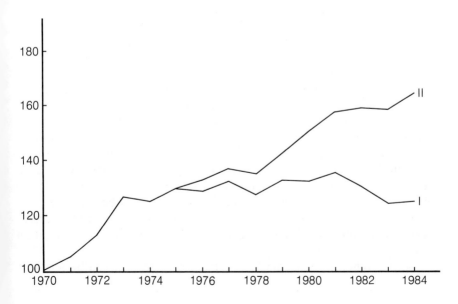

I = Flat Divorce Rate (after 1974).
II = Increasing Divorce Rate.

divorce rate assumptions. The number of families of this type grows by 64 percent from 1970 to 1984 under the increasing divorce rate assumption, while their number levels off under the flat divorce rate assumption.

Although the type of family under discussion is categorically eligible for AFDC payments, it must also meet economic eligibility standards. The income and resources of such a family may not exceed the "standard of need" for that particular family size. Before turning to the change in the AFDC caseload between Simulation I and II, the significance of the omission from the simulations of private transfers in the form of child support and alimony must be examined. This type of family income is taken into account in the determination of eligibility for AFDC. Unfortunately, data for this type of transfer are conspicuously lacking on a nationwide basis.[9] Tabulations from one year (1970) of the Panel Study of Income Dynamics survey reveal that 29 percent of all female-headed families with children under 18 receive some support in the form of private transfers from ex-husbands.[10] On the average this type of income amounted to $300 per year (in 1958 dollars) for *all* families of this type. Considering only the families receiving this type of payment, the average was $1,032 per family. One can see that, on the average, this amount is not in itself enough to keep a female-headed family out of poverty. This type of family would still remain the least well-off in terms of per person or per family income. This income must be supplemented by earnings, a public transfer, or both.

The lack of child support and alimony income in the model does affect the measurement of the number of families who can qualify for AFDC. But the size of the error can be judged only subjectively because of its interrelationship with the assumed program standard of need. It is the author's view that the standard chosen for the 1980s is probably so conservative that it completely offsets this lack of income. Only a 27 percent increase in the need standard spread out gradually over the entire 1974–1984 period was assumed to occur. In the simulation, in order to qualify for benefits the income of a family of three could not exceed an annual income of $1,653 in 1984. Even with this conservative standard of need, nearly a half a million more families in 1984 are simulated to receive benefits in the run with an accelerating divorce rate (Simulation II) compared with the run with a constant divorce rate (Simulation I). The annual difference in AFDC caseloads between the two simulation runs is shown in Figure 15-2. Obviously a higher standard of need would pull more families on to the AFDC rolls in both simulation runs.

Other differences in transfer payment receipts between Simulations

9. This is one of the primary reasons why this type of transfer is not yet incorporated into the simulation model.
10. Weighted tabulations done by the author.

FIGURE 15-2

ANNUAL DIFFERENCE IN AFDC CASELOADS
BETWEEN SIMULATION I AND
SIMULATION II, 1974-1984[1]

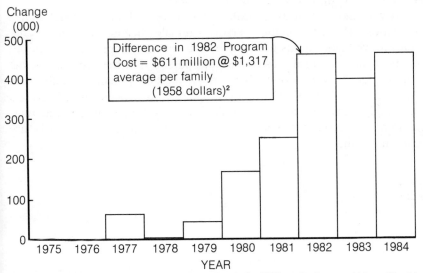

1. Because of the small sample size some fluctuations in the AFDC caseload occur which would not be expected in the real world. This phenomenon arises because different marriage matches may take place in Simulation I than in Simulation II, and, therefore, female-headed families may have different characteristics.
2. One example of how caseload differences translate into cost differences.

I and II also occur but are not shown. Under the law as it operated in 1975, any family eligible for AFDC is eligible to purchase food stamps. The participation rate among these eligible families has been around 40 to 50 percent. Thus, the food stamp caseload increase is about one-half that of the AFDC increase. In the longer run—a period longer than the duration of these simulations—one would also expect some change to occur in the receipt of social security retirement benefits. With a higher divorce rate, fewer women may be entitled to receive benefits based on their husbands' earnings.

Conclusions

Under a divorce rate which accelerates after 1974 at a rate of 5 percent per year, 2.6 million more family units would exist in the population after a 10-year period than if the divorce rate remained static. Of these new family units 1.8 million are families headed by a female and contain children. By either a per family or per person measure of income, this type of family is economically the least well-off in the population. Even under a conservative estimate of what the AFDC economic eligibility cut-off will be in 1984, the program's caseload would be almost a half million families larger under the accelerating divorce rate assumption than under the static divorce rate assumption.

It was shown that as a result of the increased marital instability in Simulation II, 4.5 million persons—female heads and their children—moved from a position where their income share was $3,426 per person to one where it was $1,987 per person. On the other hand, the average per person income share of 1.5 million persons—single male heads—moved from $3,426 to $7,042. Thus, as a result of projecting a continually growing rate of divorce, the new female heads and their children are economic losers while the new single male heads are economic gainers.

Appendix A
TWO GLOSSARIES AND FUNCTIONAL SPECIFICATIONS

Glossary for Micro Variables*

Variable	Description
$AFDC_{kt}$	This variable represents the part of family income received from the aid to families with dependent children program.
AGE_{it}	This variable represents the age in years of the ith individual during year t.
$BIRTH_{it}$	This variable indicates whether the ith female gave birth during year t.
$BIRTH\ YEAR_{it}$	This variable indicates the year in which the ith female gave birth to her last child.
$CHILDSIX_{kt}$	This variable indicates whether the family contains a child whose age is less than six.
$DEATH_{it}$	This variable indicates if the ith person dies during year t.

* The subscript k is used to indicate that the variable applies to the kth family. The subscript i indicates that the variable applies to the ith individual. The subscript t indicates that the variable was obtained in year t.

335

Variable	Description
DESIRE CHILD$_{it}$	This variable indicates if the ith woman desires a child in year t.
DISABLED$_{it}$	This variable indicates whether the individual is disabled during year t. It is the output of an operating characteristic module and is used in both current and lagged form.
DIVORCE$_{it}$	This variable indicates if the ith person is divorced in year t.
EARNS$_{it}$	This variable represents the earnings of the individual obtained through labor force participation. It is calculated by multiplying the number of hours worked by the hourly wage. This variable is used in current, one-lag, and two-lag form.
ENTER SCHOOL$_{it}$	This variable indicates if a child who is 5, 6, or 7 years old enters school in year t.
FAMILY EARNINGS$_{kt}$	This variable represents the part of family income which is earned through labor force participation. It is used in both current and lagged forms.
FAMILY SIZE$_{kt}$	This variable indicates the total number of family members.
FAMILY INCOME$_{kt}$	This variable represents total family income. It is the sum of family income obtained from earnings and transfer payments. This variable is used in current, one-lag, and two-lag form.
FRACTION UNEMPLOYED$_{it}$	This variable indicates the frac-

Variable	*Description*
	tion of total hours spent in the labor force during which the individual is unemployed. It is used in both current and lagged forms.
GRADE COMPLETED$_{it}$	This variable indicates the highest grade completed by the ith individual. This variable is used in both current and lagged form.
HOURS$_{it}$	This variable indicates the hours which the ith individual spends in the labor force. It represents the sum of hours at work and the hours unemployed. This variable is used in both current and lagged form.
HOURS WORKED$_{it}$	This variable indicates the hours worked. It is calculated from HOURS$_{it}$ and from FRACTION UNEMPLOYED$_{it}$.
KIDSBORN$_{it}$	This variable indicates the number of children to whom the ith woman has given birth. The variable ranges from 0 to 5. The 5 code indicates that the woman has had 5 or more children.
LEAVES HOME$_{it}$	This variable indicates if the ith person leaves home during year t.
LABOR FORCE$_{it}$	This variable indicates whether the ith person participates in the labor force during year t. It is used both in lagged and current form.
MARRY$_{it}$	This variable indicates if the ith individual is flagged to enter the marriage pool during year t. It applies only to never married individuals.
MIGRATE$_{kt}$	This variable indicates if the family changes its REGION by moving out of its current area.

Variable	*Description*
$MOVE_{kt}$	This variable indicates if the kth family moves during year t. Movement may be either within or between REGIONs.
$NUMBER\ BORN_{it}$	This variable indicates the number of children born to the woman in year t.
$FOODSTAMP_{kt}$	This variable represents the part of family income received from the food stamps program.
P_{1kt}	This variable is one of two variables which are added to determine the probability of divorce. It is determined by a function of other variables.
P_{2kt}	This variable is one of two variables which are added to determine the probability of divorce. It is determined by a function of other variables.
$PENSION_{kt}$	This variable represents the part of family income received from pensions other than social security.
$RACE_i$	This variable indicates the race of the ith person.
$REGION_{kt}$	This variable indicates the region in which the kth family lives. Four regions are recognized: Northeast, North Central, South, and West.
$REMARRY_{it}$	This variable indicates if the ith individual is flagged to enter the marriage pool during year t. It only applies to previously married individuals.
SEE_i	This variable represents the stan-

Variable	*Description*
	dard deviation of a standard normal random variable. It is a function of race, sex, and age.
SEX$_i$	This variable indicates the sex of the ith individual.
SCHOOL STATUS$_{it}$	This variable indicates if the ith person is in school in year t.
SMSA SIZE$_{kt}$	This variable indicates the size of the SMSA in which the family lives. Five categories are recognized. These are under 250,000, between 250,000 and 500,000, between 500,000 and 750,000, over 750,000, and outside SMSA. It is used in both current and lagged form.
SOCSEC$_{kt}$	This variable represents the part of family income received from the social security program.
SSI$_{kt}$	This variable represents the part of family income received from the supplemental security income program.
TRANSFER INCOME$_{kt}$	This variable represents the part of family income received from transfer programs. The value of this variable is obtained by summing the outputs of the social security, pension, unemployment compensation, AFDC, SSI, and food stamp income modules. It is used in current, single-lag, and double-lag form.
UNCOMP$_{kt}$	This variable represents the part of family income received from

Variable	*Description*
	unemployment compensation payments.
UNEMPLOYMENT$_{it}$	This variable indicates whether the ith individual experienced any unemployment in year t. It is present in both current and lagged form.
WAGE RATE$_{it}$	This variable indicates the hourly wage rate for individual i during year t. This variable is used in both lagged and current form.
WED STATE$_{it}$	This variable indicates if the ith person is never married, widowed, divorced, or married. This variable is used in both current and lagged form.
WED YEAR$_{it}$	Year of most recent change in marital status.
YEAR$_t$	This variable indicates the current year.
YEARS AT CURRENT SCHOOL LEVEL$_{it}$	This variable indicates the number of years an individual who is in school has spent at his current school level.
ϵ_{it}	This variable is a normal random variable with mean zero and standard deviation SEE$_i$.
ρ_i	This variable captures the serial correlation of the ith individual's experience over time. It is a function of race, sex, and age.

Glossary for Macro Variables

Variable	Description	Reference[1]
CCl	Capital consumption in billions of constant dollars (1958 prices)	_____
CCA	Capital Consumption Allowance in billions of current dollars	C14.2
GNP	Gross National Product in billions of current dollars	C14.1
GNPl	Gross National Product in billions of constant dollars (1958 prices)	C14.1/C3.1
Il	Non-inventory gross private domestic investment in billions of constant dollars (1958)	C1.3/C3.1
IBT	Indirect Business Taxes in billions of current dollars	C14.5
Kl	Capital Stock in billions of constant dollars (1958 prices)	_____
L	Total employment (civilian and armed forces) in millions	C24.3 + C24.4
LY	Labor Income in billions of current dollars	C15.2
LY1	Labor Income in billions of 1958 dollars	C15.2/C3.1
NI	National Income in billions of current dollars	C14.8
NNP	Net National Product in billions of current dollars	C14.3
P	Implicit price deflator for GNP where 1958 equals 100	C3.1

1. KEY TO REFERENCES: All entries beginning with "C" are from Appendix C of the 1973 *Economic Report of the President*. The number before the period gives the table number. The number after the period gives the column or row number. Blanks in the column indicate variables for which no historic series is readily available.

Variable	*Description*	*Reference*
POP	Total population	C23.1
U	Unemployment as a fraction of total labor force	C24.8/C24.2
WYl	Wealth income in billions of 1958 dollars	(C14.3 − C15.2) ÷ C3.1

Detailed Functional Specifications

I. MICROPASS SECTOR

A. Demographic Program Block

1. INCREMENTATION

This module updates appropriate attributes by recording the passage of a year. If X is a relevant attribute, incrementation can be represented by

$$X_t = X_{t-1} + 1.$$

2. LEAVING HOME

P(LEAVES HOME) = F_1(SEX$_i$, AGE$_{it}$, RACE$_i$)
where F_1 is given in Table A-1.

TABLE A-1

PROBABILITY OF YOUNG ADULT LEAVING PARENTAL
FAMILY AND FORMING NEW FAMILY BY AGE, RACE,
AND SEX OF YOUNG ADULT

Age	White Male	Nonwhite Male	White Female	Nonwhite Female
14–17	.02	.02	.01	.01
18–19	.02	.02	.01	.01
20–24	.05	.05	.04	.04
25–29	.05	.05	.05	.05
30–34	.02	.02	.00	.00
35+	0	0	0	0

These probabilities are arbitrary approximations, designed to leave in their parental families roughly the number of young adults found there in national surveys, after taking into account the very large effect of marriage in taking young adults from parental families.

3. DIVORCE

P(DIVORCE) = $P_{1kt} + P_{2kt}$
$P_{1kt} = F_1$(WED YEAR$_{it}$, YEAR$_t$)
$P_{2kt} = P_{1kt} + F_2[$RACE$_i$(of head), AGE$_{it}$(of head), DIS-ABLED$_{it-1}$(of head), UNEMPLOYMENT$_{i,t-1}$ (of head), EARNS$_{i,t-1}$(of wife), REGION$_{k,t-1}$, SMSA SIZE$_{k,t-1}$, WED YEAR$_{it}]$
  F_1 is given in Table 5-5.
  F_2 is given in Table 5-6.

4. BIRTH

Step 1

P(DESIRE CHILD) = 0 if unmarried
= $F_1(\text{KIDSBORN}_{i,t-1})$ if married

Step 2

P(BIRTH) = $[.36\ e^{[-.105\{\max(0,\text{AGE}_{it}-24)\}]}]$
if desires a child

= $[.36\ e^{[-0.20\{\max(0,\text{AGE}_{it}-24)\}]}] \times$
$[1\text{-}F_2(\text{RACE}_i,\text{GRADE COMPLETED}_{i,t-1})]$
if does not desire a child

Step 3

P(NUMBER BORN$_{it}$) = $F_3(\text{RACE}_i)$

Step 4

CHILD'S RACE$_i$ = MOTHER'S RACE$_i$
CHILD's SEX$_i$ = F_4 (RACE$_i$)
F_1 is given in Table A-2.

TABLE A-2

PROBABILITY OF DESIRING
ANOTHER CHILD (F_1)

KIDSBORN$_{it-1}$	$F_1(\text{KIDSBORN}_{it-1})$
0	.96
1	.96
2	.70
3	.30
4	.20
5 or more	.20

F_2 is given in Table A-3.

TABLE A-3

CONTRACEPTION EFFICIENCY (F_2)

GRADE COMPLETED	RACE	
	White	Nonwhite
>12	.975	.75
12	.985	.80
<12	.99	.85

F_3 is given in Table A-4.

TABLE A-4

PROBABILITY OF MULTIPLE
BIRTHS (F_3)

	NUMBER BORN$_{it}$		
Race$_i$	1	2	3
Nonwhite	.9760	.0237	.0003
White	.9812	.0185	.0003

F_4 is given in Table A-5.

TABLE A-5

PROBABILITY OF
MALE BIRTH (F_4)

Race$_i$	Male
Nonwhite	.5059
White	.5134

5. DEATH

$$P(DEATH_{it}) = [F_{11} + F_{12} \cdot e^{F_{13} \cdot (year-1950)}] \cdot F_2 \cdot F_3 \cdot F_4$$

where:
F_{11}, F_{12}, and F_{13} are given in Table 3-1 and are each functions of RACE$_i$, SEX$_i$, AGE$_{it}$.
F_2 is given in Table 3-3 and is a function of RACE$_i$, SEX$_i$, WED STATE$_{it}$, and AGE$_{it}$.
F_3 is given in Table 3-4 and is a function of RACE$_i$, SEX$_i$, AGE$_{it}$, and GRADE COMPLETED$_{i,t-1}$.
F_4 is given in Table 3-5 and is a function of SEX$_i$, AGE$_{it}$, WED STATE$_{i,t-1}$ and KIDSBORN$_{i,t-1}$.

6. FIRST MARRIAGE SELECTION

$P(MARRY) = 0$ if AGE$_{it} \leq 14$ or if AGE$_{it} \geq 34$.
F_1 is a function of YEAR$_t$, RACE$_i$, AGE$_{it}$ and SEX$_i$.
F_2 is a function of RACE$_i$, AGE$_{it}$, SEX$_i$, GRADE COMPLETED$_{i,t-1}$, HOURS WORKED$_{i,t-1}$, WAGE RATE$_{i,t-1}$, and AFDC$_{k,t-1}$, FOODSTAMP$_{k,t-1}$, and UNCOMP$_{k,t-1}$.

F_1 for males with $AGE_{it} \leq 17$ is given in Table A-6.
F_1 for all females and males with $AGE_{it} > 17$ is given in Tables 4-2 and 4-3.
F_2 for persons with $AGE_{it} \leq 17$ or $AGE_{it} > 27$ is zero.
F_2 for persons for whom $AGE_{it} > 17$ and $AGE_{it} \leq 27$ is given in Table 4-6.

TABLE A-6

PROBABILITY OF FIRST MARRIAGE FOR
MALES WITH $AGE_{it} \leq 17$ (F_1)

Age	15	16	17
Nonwhite	.002	.005	.015
White	.001	.004	.015

7. REMARRIAGE SELECTION

$$P(REMARRY_{it}) = F_1(SEX_i, AGE_{it}, WED\ STATE_{it}, WED\ YEAR_{kt}, YEAR_t)$$

F_1 is presented in Table 4-7.

8. EDUCATION

Step 1

$$P(ENTER\ SCHOOL) = F_1(AGE_{it})$$

F_1 is given in Table A-7.

TABLE A-7

PROBABILITY OF
ENTERING SCHOOL
(F_1)

AGE_{it}	$F_1(AGE_{it})$
Less than 5	0
5	.09
6	.945
7	1
8 or greater	0

Step 2

Four school levels are recognized: grade school (first through eighth grade), high school (ninth through 12th grade), college (13th through 16th grade), and graduate school (17th and 18th grade). When applied to a person in grade school, high school, or college, this program module determines whether or not the person (a) continues on at the same school level, (b) drops out of school, (c) graduates from the school level but does not go on to the next school level, or (d) goes on to the next school level.

The probability functions are given in Tables 6-1 through 6-9. Each probability is a function of some combination of $RACE_i$, SEX_i, AGE_{it}, YEARS AT CURRENT SCHOOL LEVEL$_{i,t-1}$, and GRADE COMPLETED$_{it}$ (of head). When applied to a person in graduate school, it is assumed that the person spends exactly two years in graduate school before he successfully graduates.

9. LOCATION

Step 1

$$P(MOVE_{it}) = F_{11}(SEX_{it}(\text{of head}_t), AGE_i(\text{of head}_t), WED \\ STATE_{it}(\text{of head}), WED\ YEAR_{kt})$$

Step 2

If MOVE:
$$P(MIGRATE_{kt}) = F_{12}(SEX_{it}(\text{of head}), AGE_i(\text{of head}) \\ GRADE\ COMPLETED_{it}(\text{by head}))$$

Step 3

If MIGRATE:
$$REGION = F_{13}(REGION_{k,t-1}, RAGE_i)$$
$$SMSA\ SIZE_k = F_{14}(SMSA\ SIZE_{k,t-1})$$
Functions F_{11}, F_{12}, F_{13}, and F_{14}, are given in Tables 7-1 through 7-5.

10. DISABLED

If not DISABLED$_{t-1}$:
$$P(DISABLED_{it}) = F_{D1}(RACE_i, SEX_i, AGE_{it}, WED\ STATE_{it})$$
If DISABLED$_{t-1}$:
$$P(DISABLED_{it}) = F_{D2}(RACE_i, SEX_i, AGE_{it}, GRADE\ COM- \\ PI\ ETED_{it})$$
F_{D1} and F_{D2} are given in Table 9-1.

B. Labor Program Modules

11. WAGE RATE[1]

if not in LABOR FORCE$_{t-1}$:
  WAGE RATE$_{it}$ = $[F_{Wt} + \epsilon_{it}/(1 - \rho_i)]$
if in LABOR FORCE$_{t-1}$
  WAGE RATE$_{it}$ = $[\rho_i \cdot$ WAGE RATE$_{i,t-1}$ + $F_{Wt} - \rho_i \times$
    $F_{W,t-1} + \epsilon_{it}]$
  F_{Wt} is a function of RACE$_i$, SEX$_i$, AGE$_{it}$, WED STATE$_{it}$,
  DISABLED$_{it}$, GRADE COMPLETED$_{it}$, and REGION$_{kt}$.
  ϵ_{it} is a normal random variable with mean zero and standard deviation SEE$_i$.
  Both ρ_i and SEE$_i$ are functions of RACE$_i$, SEX$_i$, and AGE$_{it}$.
  The values of all functions are given in Table 8-6.

12. LABOR FORCE PARTICIPATION

P(LABOR FORCE$_{it}$) = F_{LF1}(LABOR FORCE$_{i,t-1}$, RACE$_i$, SEX$_i$,
    AGE$_{it}$, WED STATE$_{it}$, DISABLED$_{it}$,
    TRANSFER INCOME$_{k,t-1}$, NON-WIFE
    INCOME$_{k,t-1}$, CHILDSIX$_{kt}$) +
    F_{LF2}(RACE$_i$, SEX$_i$, AGE$_{it}$, U$_{t-1}$).

F_{LF1} is presented in Table 8-2.
F_{LF2} is presented in Table A-8.

TABLE A-8

IMPACT OF THE UNEMPLOYMENT RATE
ON LABOR FORCE PARTICIPATION (F_{LF2})

Attributes	
Men 14–20	$-1.19 U_{t-1} + .04$
Men Aged 21–64	$-0.24 U_{t-1} + .01$
Persons over 65	$-1.72 U_{t-1} + .06$
Nonwhite Women Aged 21–64	0
White Women Aged 21–64	$-0.50 U_{t-1} + .02$
Women 14–20	$-0.73 U_{t-1} + .03$

13. HOURS IN LABOR FORCE[2]

If not in LABOR FORCE$_{t-1}$:
  HOURS$_{it}$ = $F_{Ht} + \epsilon_{it}/(1 - \rho_i)$
If in LABOR FORCE$_{t-1}$:
  HOURS$_{it}$ = $\rho_i \cdot$ HOURS$_{i,t-1}$ + $F_{Ht} - \rho_i \cdot F_{H,t-1} + \epsilon_{it}$

1. In the 1975 version of DYNASIM, $F_{W,t-1}$ is approximated by using F_{Wt}.
2. In the 1975 version of DYNASIM, $F_{H,t-1}$ is approximated by using F_{Ht}.

F_{Ht} is a function of $RACE_i$, SEX_i, AGE_{it}, WED STATE$_{it}$, GRADE COMPLETED$_{it}$, DISABLED$_{it}$, WAGE RATE$_{it}$, FAMILY INCOME$_{i,t-1}$ − EARNS$_{k,t-1}$, TRANSFER INCOME$_{k,t-1}$, and CHILDSIX$_{kt}$.

ϵ_{it} is a normal random variable with mean zero and standard deviation SEE$_i$. Both ρ_i and SEE$_i$ are functions of $RACE_i$, SEX_i, and AGE_{it}.

All functions are contained in Table 8-4.

14. FRACTION OF HOURS UNEMPLOYED[3]

Step 1

$$P(UNEMPLOYMENT_{it}) = F_{U1}(RACE_i, \ AGE_{it}, \ WED \ STATE_{it}, \ GRADE \ COMPLETED_{it})$$

Step 2

If UNEMPLOYED$_t$ and not UNEMPLOYED$_{t-1}$:
FRACTION UNEMPLOYED$_{it}$ = $F_{U2t} + \epsilon_{it}/(1 - \rho_i)$
If UNEMPLOYED$_t$ and UNEMPLOYED$_{t-1}$:
FRACTION UNEMPLOYED$_{it}$ = (FRACTION
UNEMPLOYED$_{i,t-1}$) +
$F_{U2t} - \rho_i F_{U2,t-1} + \epsilon_{it}$

F_{U2t} is a fraction of $RACE_i$, AGE_{it}, WED STATE$_{it}$, GRADE COMPLETED$_{it}$, DISABLED$_{it}$, CHILDSIX$_{it}$ and REGION$_{kt}$.

ϵ_{it} is a normal random variable with mean 0 and standard deviation equal to SEE$_i$. ρ_i and SEE$_i$ are both functions of $RACE_i$, SEX_i and AGE_{it}. F_{U1} is in Table 8-8. F_{U2}, SEE$_i$, and ρ_i are in Table 8-9.

15. EARNINGS

$$EARNS_{it} = WAGE_{it}[HOURS_{it}(1 - UNEMPLOYMENT_{it} \times FRACTION \ UNEMPLOYED_{it})]$$
FAMILY EARNINGS$_{kt}$ = Σ_iEARN$_{it}$
where summation is over persons in family k.

C. Transfer Block

16-22. See Chapter 9.

D. Taxes and Wealth Block[4]

23. WEALTH INCOME

See Chapter 10.

---

3. In the 1975 version of DYNASIM $F_{U2,t-1}$ is approximated by using F_{U2t}.
4. Not included in the 1975 version of DYNASIM.

24. FEDERAL INCOME TAXATION AND DISPOSABLE INCOME

The income tax is computed in simulation for each family filer or unattached individual by the following steps:

a. Determination of adjusted gross income (AGI).

AGI = WAGES + PROPINC − ADJUST

AGI is roughly equivalent to the concept used by the Internal Revenue Service. PROPINC is income from property. ADJUST is a variable which can be used to model various tax provisions such as sick pay and moving expenses.

b. Determination of taxable income (TAXINC).

TAXINC = AGI − EXEMPT (FAMSIZE
        + H + W) − DDUCT

EXEMPT is a variable which can be set to represent the value of personal exemptions under the law. It was set in 1975 at $750. FAMSIZE is the total family size of each filer unit. H is a dummy variable set to 1 if the family head is 65 or older and otherwise to 0. W is set to 1 if the wife of the family head is 65 or older and otherwise to 0.

DDUCT is the value of claimed deductions. It is determined by the equation DDUCT = 1300 + Z(AGI − 8667), where Z is the ratio of deductions to AGI. Z = 0.2434, based on calculations from the 1972 returns of persons with AGI in excess of $8,000.

c. Levying tax (FEDTAX).

FEDTAX = TAXINC[(FDTXRT1)(MS1)(LEVEL1)
        + (FDTXRT2)(MS1)(LEVEL2)
        + (FDTXRT3)(MS1)(LEVEL1)
        + (FDTXRT4)(MS2)(LEVEL2)
        + (FDTXRT5)(MS3)(LEVEL1)
        + (FDTXRT6)(MS3)(LEVEL2)]

MS1 = 1 if filer is married, otherwise 0.
MS2 = 1 if filer is unmarried and living with others, otherwise 0.
MS3 = 1 if filer is single, otherwise 0.
LEVEL1 = 1 if filer's income is over $8,000, otherwise 0.
LEVEL2 = 1 if filer's income is $8,000 or less, otherwise 0.
FDTXRT1 = −16.7088 + 13.1770 (Log TAXINC/1000)
FDTXRT2 = 14.1906 + 1.1187 (Log TAXINC/1000)

$$\text{FDTXRT3} = -13.3524 + 13.0228 \text{ (Log TAXINC/1000)}$$
$$\text{FDTXRT4} = 14.4187 + 1.6405 \text{ (Log TAXINC/1000)}$$
$$\text{FDTXRT5} = -9.8655 + 12.8403 \text{ (Log TAXINC/1000)}$$
$$\text{FDTXRT6} = 14.7284 + 2.0641 \text{ (Log TAXINC/1000)}$$

d. Disposable income determination (DI).

$$\text{DI} = \text{AGI} - \text{FEDTAX}$$

25. SAVING AND WEALTH

See Chapter 10.

II. MARRIAGE UNION SECTOR

People who have entered the marriage pool through the marriage module or the remarriage module are ranked and matched according to the ranking shown in Table A-9, which has age, education, region, and race as inputs.

III. MACROMODEL SECTOR

The Macromodel Equations

1. Gross National Product, in billions at 1958 prices:

$$\text{GNP1}_t = 345.0 + 0.297 \text{ K1}_{t-1} + 8.293 \text{ L}_t + u_t$$

where $u_t = 0.8 \, u_{t-1}$ and $u_0 = 0$.

2. Non-inventory gross private domestic investment, in billions at 1958 prices:

$$\text{I1}_t = -8.0 + 0.397 \text{ I1}_{t-1} + 0.083 \text{ GNP1}_t$$
$$+ 0.195(\text{GNP1}_t - \text{GNP1}_{t-1})$$
$$+ 3.224(\text{POP}_t - \text{POP}_{t-1}) + u_t$$

where $u_t = 0.5 \, u_{t-1}$ and $u_0 = 0$.

3. Capital consumption, in billions at 1958 prices:

$$\text{CC1}_t = 0.040 \text{ K1}_{t-1}$$

where $\text{K1}_{29} = 611$.

4. Non-inventory capital stock, in billions at 1958 prices:

$$\text{K1}_t = \text{K1}_{t-1} - \text{CC1}_t + \text{I1}_t$$

5. Implicit price deflator for GNP, where 1958 value equals one:

$$P_t = P_{t-1} + 0.214 + 0.313(P_{t-1} - P_{t-2}) - 0.113 \, U_t$$
$$- 0.402(U_t - U_{t-1}) + u_t$$

where $u_t = 0.3 \, u_{t-1}$ and $u_0 = 0$.

TABLE A-9

MATE MATCHING: THE RANK ORDERING ALGORITHM

Rank Order Code	Race	Region	Education	Age	Rank Order Code	Race	Region	Education	Age
1	NW	all	17+	35+	68	W	S	13–16	35+
2	NW	all	17+	25–34	69	W	S	12–	35+
3	NW	all	17+	22–24	70	W	S	12–	25–34
11	NW	S	13–16	22–24	75	W	NE	12–	25–34
12	NW	S	13–16	19–21	76	W	NE	12–	35+
13	NW	S	13–16	18–	77	W	NE	13–16	35+
14	NW	S	12–	18–	78	W	NE	13–16	25–34
15	NW	S	12–	19–21	79	W	NE	12–	22–24
16	NW	S	12–	22–24	80	W	NE	12–	19–21
17	NW	S	13–16	25–34	81	W	NE	12–	18–
18	NW	S	13–16	35+	82	W	NE	13–16	18–
19	NW	S	12–	35+	83	W	NE	13–16	19–21
20	NW	S	12–	25–34	84	W	NE	13–16	22–24
21	NW	non-S	12–	25–34	90	W	NC	13–16	22–24
22	NW	non-S	12–	35+	91	W	NC	13–16	19–21
23	NW	non-S	13–16	35+	92	W	NC	13–16	18–
24	NW	non-S	13–16	25–34	93	W	NC	12–	18–
25	NW	non-S	12–	22–24	94	W	NC	12–	19–21
26	NW	non-S	12–	19–21	95	W	NC	12–	22–24
27	NW	non-S	12–	18–	96	W	NC	13–16	25–34
28	NW	non-S	13–16	18–	97	W	NC	13–16	35+
29	NW	non-S	13–16	19–21	98	W	NC	12–	35+
30	NW	non-S	13–16	22–24	99	W	NC	12–	25–34
51	W	all	17+	35+	105	W	W	12–	25–34
52	W	all	17+	25–34	106	W	W	12–	35+
53	W	all	17+	22–24	107	W	W	13–16	35+
61	W	S	13–16	22–24	108	W	W	13–16	25–34
62	W	S	13–16	19–21	109	W	W	12–	22–24
63	W	S	13–16	18–	110	W	W	12–	19–21
64	W	S	12–	18–	111	W	W	12–	18–
65	W	S	12–	19–21	112	W	W	13–16	18–
66	W	S	12–	22–24	113	W	W	13–16	19–21
67	W	S	13–16	25–34	114	W	W	13–16	22–24

6. Gross National Product, in billions at current prices:

$$GNP_t = P_t \cdot GNP1_t$$

7. Capital consumption allowance, in billions at current prices:

$$CCA_t = 0.891\ CCA_{t-1} + 0.014\ GNP_t$$

8. Net National Product, in billions at current prices:

$$NNP_t = GNP_t - CCA_t$$

9. Indirect business tax and nontax liability, in billions at current prices:

$$IBT_t = 3.6 + 0.592\ IBT_{t-1} + 0.051\ NNP_t + u_t$$

where $u_t = 0.5\ u_{t-1}$ and $u_0 = 0.$

10. National Income, in billions at current prices:

$$NI_t = -2.5 - 0.001\ NI_{t-1} + 1.006(NNP_t - IBT_t) + u_t$$

where $u_t = 0.6\ u_{t-1}$ and $u_0 = 0.$

11. Labor income, in billions at current prices:

$$LY_t = LY_{t-1} - 1.8 + 0.322(LY_{t-1} - LY_{t-2}) + 0.621(NI_t - NI_{t-1})$$

12. Labor income, in billions at 1958 prices:

$$LY1_t = LY_t/P_t$$

13. Wealth income, in billions at 1958 prices:

$$WY1_t = GNP1_t - CC1_t - (IBT_t/P_t) - LY1_t$$

Appendix B
RELATION TO OTHER DEMOGRAPHIC MODELING EFFORTS*

DYNASIM can be compared with other modeling efforts at two levels. First, individual operating characteristics can be compared with other attempts to represent the same demographic or economic processes. Second, the entire model can be compared with other modeling efforts of similar scope. Included in this latter category are a proposed microsimulation model of the health care system which includes a demographic model by Yett et al. (1970), a microanalytic demographic model developed by Michielutte and Sprehe (1971) to serve as the first step in the development of a set of social indicators, and a general demographic model constructed by Hyrenius, Holmberg, and Carlsson (1967). Probably the best known recent effort of this kind is the model known as POPSIM. Since POPSIM is still operative and since it is quite comparable to our work, we will focus on a comparison between it and DYNASIM. The particular version of POPSIM used as a basis for comparison is described in a user's manual published early in 1973 (National Center for Health Statistics, 1973).

DYNASIM and POPSIM can be compared along the following dimensions:

a. *Sampling Units*. Individuals are the only units in POPSIM, while DYNASIM has two units: individuals and nuclear families. These two units allow a more realistic description of the life flow of persons among important family groupings.

b. *Closed vs. Open Population*. POPSIM uses an "open" population, while DYNASIM uses a "closed" population. In an open population model, when marriage takes place, a spouse is created with the appropriate characteristics. It is assumed that this individual is available in the population being represented, though he may not be present in the computer population. In a closed pop-

---

* Steven Caldwell and Gerald Peabody share the main responsibility for this appendix and the work it represents.

356 *Policy Exploration Through Microanalytic Simulation*

ulation, the spouse must come from the computer population. Persons who marry are then linked together to form a new nuclear family in the computer population. Finally, a closed model maintains family ties between successive generations.

c. *Generation of Initial Population.* POPSIM has been designed so that it is sufficiently general to be applied to a wide variety of national populations. As one consequence, since many nations do not have appropriate records available, POPSIM generates an initial population by using data on the interrelationships between the characteristics of the population and on the statistical distributions of these characteristics rather than using a representative sample population drawn from a census or survey. In DYNASIM the operating characteristics have been specifically designed to apply only to the U.S. population. To represent the U.S. population, a self-weighting sample is drawn from a national census or survey. This procedure captures, within the limits of sampling error, all the covariances of all the attributes presented in the survey describing the population.

d. *Specification of Operating Characteristics.* DYNASIM incorporates a much broader range of independent variables in each operating characteristic than does POPSIM, as the following examples illustrate. The marriage probability in POPSIM is dependent upon age, marital status, and sex. In DYNASIM this probability is dependent upon these three variables but also upon race, education, cohort, period, and a variety of socioeconomic characteristics. Divorce in POPSIM depends only upon duration of marriage, while in DYNASIM it is also dependent upon marriage cohort, age at first marriage, number of children, and a variety of socioeconomic characteristics. Mortality in POPSIM depends upon age, sex, and marital status. In DYNASIM the death probability includes these three independent variables along with race, education, parity (for females), and a time trend. The fertility model in POPSIM uses birth probabilities dependent upon age, marital status, and parity and has a family planning module with which specific contraceptive devices may be included. DYNASIM includes variations in fecundity within the population as well as contraception use (without specifying the device) and effectiveness dependent upon race, education, and marital status.

e. *Scope of Model.* Both POPSIM and DYNASIM simulate marriage, divorce, fertility, and mortality. In addition, DYNASIM simulates geographic mobility, schooling attainment, labor force participation, hours worked, wage rate, earned income, transfer income, disability, and a macromodel of the economy.

Thus, in the demographic area where the two models are most comparable, DYNASIM incorporates a richer set of independent variables in each operating characteristic. In large part this difference reflects the different purposes behind the construction of each model. POPSIM was designed to be sufficiently general that it could be applied to a variety of nations, while DYNASIM has been designed to apply only to the United States. The second major difference between the two models is the combination of operating characteristics for simulating both demographic and economic processes in DYNASIM.

In the area of fertility, Hyrenius and Adolfsson (1964), Ridley and Sheps (1966), Jacquard (1967) and Barrett (1969) have each developed simulation models similar to our fertility operating characteristic. A major difference between their work and that reported here is the detail with which they simulate the biological process of fertility. These models generally follow a woman in monthly intervals and specifically simulate conception, miscarriage, still and live births, and the period of post-partum infecundity. While these factors have been accounted for in our operating characteristic, only live birth is explicitly simulated. The latest version of REPSIM, described by Clague and Ridley (1972), allows a woman to use contraception, either to affect her spacing of births or to limit her total number of births, and explicitly represents the various marital statuses of the woman. Thus, REPSIM is close in specification to the fertility operating characteristic incorporated in DYNASIM.

In developing the fertility operating characteristic the goal has been to adequately account for the biological basis of reproduction while also incorporating psychological and social variations in the reproduction process (Davis and Blake, 1956). The operating characteristic has been specified to represent the contemporary period in the United States and incorporates variations in fertility by race, educational attainment, and other variables. In the fertility models discussed above, the parameter specification is more general and does not include these variations with social status. The fertility operating characteristic provides a capability for detailed analyses of the fertility experience in the United States which has been achieved at the expense of some generality and the exclusion of some details of the biological process.

There has been some interest by economists in population issues for a considerable time. At the micro level Leibenstein (1957) and Becker (1960) have applied the economic theory of consumption behavior to fertility, and most of the recent work on individual fertility behavior follows this approach. (See Schultz, 1973, for a review of recent literature of this kind.) This work has contributed valuable understanding concerning the role of income, the costs of children, and women's labor force activity in the fertility process. However, the approach taken to fertility in our work implies that this microeconomic conceptualization of fertility is inadequate. The major limitations of this approach include an almost complete absence of accounting for the biological basis of fertility and an inadequate behavioral model inherent in the utility maximization approach.

One important macro approach to the economics of fertility has been developed by Easterlin (1968); more recent research includes that by Phillips, Votey and Maxwell (1969) and by Gregory, Campbell, and Cheng (1972). These studies have attempted to account for year-to-year variations in the birth rate for the nation or for smaller geographic areas using selected economic variables. Such highly aggregate approaches at best only suggest the individual behavioral relationships which are important for analyzing the impact of public policies on individuals and families. Further, concentration on the birth rate alone does not give a complete picture of the likely completed rates of fertility for different cohorts. Birth rates in a particular year can change in response to changes in the timing pattern of births as well as to changes in desired fertility levels. These two factors affect the cohort fertility levels quite differently and must be separately analyzed in order to understand the course of fertility.

One approach that is closer in spirit to ours is the demographic-economic model for Puerto Rico described by Nerlove and Shultz (1970). Since their simultaneous equations model uses small geographic units as the unit of analysis, it suffers to some extent from the limitations of all macro approaches. However, their model does represent a wide range of demographic activity, including migration and marital status changes, though it is not as comprehensive as DYNASIM.

Appendix C
RECALCULATING
THE KITAGAWA-HAUSER
DIFFERENTIAL
MORTALITY RATIOS
FOR USE IN THE MODEL

The differential mortality ratios calculated by Kitagawa and Hauser are not quite appropriate for our mortality submodel. This appendix explains how their ratios have been converted to better fit the particular needs of DYNASIM.

The desired parameters for the model to generate mortality differentials by educational attainment categories would have the following property: within a given age, race, and sex class, each category of educational attainment would have associated with it a ratio which, when multiplied by the death probability specific to the age-race-sex group, would yield the actual death probability for that specific education group. (The same kind of parameters are needed for the model to produce mortality differentials by marital status, income, and parity.)

If P_{ijk} is the generated mortality probability for the ith age group, jth race group, and kth sex group, in which there are N_{ijk} living persons, then there are $P_{ijk} \cdot N_{ijk}$ *expected deaths* in the ith age, jth race, and kth sex population.

If the probability of death did not vary across educational classes within the age, race, and sex subpopulation, then for the mth educational class containing $N_{ijk:m}$ persons (where $m = 1,2,3 \ldots n$, given a total of n educational attainment classifications) there would be $P_{ijk} \cdot N_{ijk:m}$ expected deaths. But to reflect the mortality differentials by education which do exist, it is necessary to estimate a correction factor based on the actual number and the expected number of deaths as follows:

If the actual number of deaths in the education, age, race, and sex class is $A_{ijk:m}$ as compared with the expected, $E_{ijk:m} = P_{ijk} \cdot N_{ijk:m}$, then the proper adjustment factor is estimated by dividing the actual number of deaths by the expected number:

$$\frac{A_{ijk:m}}{E_{ijk:m}}$$

If this ratio is multiplied by P_{ijk} (the death probability for the entire age, race, and sex class), the result is a probability which yields the true number of expected deaths for the educational group m, $A_{ijk:m}$, when multiplied by the number in the group, $N_{ijk:m}$.

Kitagawa and Hauser, however, compute the expected number of deaths for a given education, age, race, and sex group using death probabilities adjusted only for the age composition of the group, and not the race and sex composition. Their purpose in doing so was "to enable direct comparison of the size and pattern of education and income differentials in different subgroups of the population" (Kitagawa, 1971). However, the operation of the model requires comparisons *within* race and sex groups, rather than between them.

The indices Kitagawa and Hauser compute can be represented as

$$\frac{A_{ijk:m}}{P_i \cdot N_{ijk:m}}$$

that is, the actual number of deaths in a given age, race, sex, and education group is divided by the expected number, given by 1960 age-specific (not sex- or race-specific) mortality rates applied to the number of persons in the age, race, sex, and education class. (Actually, since the two age groupings are so large, i.e., 25–64 and 65 and older, the expected number of deaths is gotten in an age-standardized fashion by using the age-specific rates in smaller age classes–namely, 25–34, 35–44, 45–54, and 55–64 for the first, and 65–74 and 75 and over for the second — to the population in each group respectively; then the expected number is the sum of the expected in each age group.)

Once the indices, which may be defined as the age-adjusted ratios of actual deaths to expected deaths in which expected deaths for each education class are computed by multiplying 1960 age-specific death rates for the total United States population by the age composition of the sex, race, education subpopulation, mortality ratios are then taken to be the index for each education class of a subpopulation divided by the mortality index for the total subpopulation. The mortality ratio for the mth educational class in the ith, jth, and kth age, race, sex subpopulation is thus:

$$R_{ijk:m} = \frac{I_{ijk:m}}{I_{ijk}}$$

and, substituting, we get

$$R_{ijk:m} = \frac{A_{ijk:m} \cdot N_{ijk}}{N_{ijk:m} \cdot A_{ijk}}$$

BIBLIOGRAPHY

Chapter 1

Adelman, I. "Economic Processes," in *International Encyclopedia of the Social Sciences,* David L. Sills, ed., Macmillan and the Free Press, vol. 14, pp. 268–274, 1968.

Barrett, J. C. "A Monte Carlo Study of Reproduction," presented at the Society for Human Biology Symposium, London, 1967.

Bergmann, B. R. "Labor Turnover, Segmentation and Rates of Unemployment: A Simulation-Theoretic Approach," Project on the Economics of Discrimination, University of Maryland, August 1973.

――――. "A Microsimulation of the Macroeconomy with Explicitly Represented Money Flows," *Annals of Social and Economic Measurement,* July 1974 (3,3), pp. 475–490.

Bryan, W. R., and W. T. Carleton. "Short-Run Adjustments of an Individual Bank," *Econometrica,* April 1967, vol. 35, pp. 321–347.

Carleton, W. T., and W. R. Bryan. "Deposit Expansion and Federal Reserve Banking System Interaction: A Micro Unit Simulation," mimeographed, 1971.

Clark, C. "A System of Equations Explaining the U.S. Trade Cycle 1921–41," *Econometrica,* 1949, vol. 17, pp. 93–124.

Clarkson, G., and H. Simon. "Simulation of Individual and Group Behavior," *American Economic Review,* vol. L, December 1960.

Duesenberry, J. S., G. Fromm, L. R. Klein, and E. Kuh, eds., *The Brookings Quarterly Econometric Model of the United States,* Chicago, Rand McNally, 1965.

Duesenberry, J., O. Eckstein, and G. Fromm. "A Simulation of the United States Economy in Recession," *Econometrica,* October 1960.

Edwards, J. B., and G. H. Orcutt. "Should Aggregation Prior to Estimation Be the Rule?" *Review of Economics and Statistics,* November 1969.

Foster, P. F., and L. Yost. *Population Growth and Rural Development in Buganda: A Simulation of a Micro-Economic System,* Misc. Publication 621, Agricultural Experiment Station, University of Maryland, 1968.

Giesbrecht, F. G., and G. Ranney. Demographic Microsimulation Model POPSIM I: Manual for Program to Generate the Initial Population, Closed Core Model, Research Triangle Institute, 1968.

――――, G. Ranney, and J. R. Chromy. Demographic Microsimulation Model POPSIM II: Manual for Programs to Generate the Initial Population, Open Core Model, Research Triangle Institute, 1968.

――――, and L. Field. Demographic Microsimulation Model POPSIM II: Manual for Programs to Generate Vital Events, Open Core Model, Research Triangle Institute, 1969.

Guetzkow, H., ed. *Simulation in Social Science: Readings,* Prentice Hall, 1962.

Holmberg, I. *Demographic Models: DM4,* Demographic Institute, University of Göteborg, Sweden, 1968.

Horvitz, D. G., F. G. Giesbrecht, B. V. Shah, and P. A. Lachenbruch. "Popsim, A Demographic Microsimulation Model," *International Union for the Scientific Study of Population,* General Conference, London, 1969.

Hyrenius, H., and I. Adolffson. *A Fertility Simulation Model,* Demographic Institute, University of Göteborg, Sweden, 1964.

――――, I. Holmberg, and H. Carlsson. *Demographic Models: DM3,* Demographic Institute, University of Göteborg, Sweden, 1967.

361

Klein, L. "The use of Econometric Models as a Guide to Economic Policy," *Econometrica,* April 1947, vol. 15, pp. 111–51.

——. *Economic Fluctuations in the United States 1921–41,* Cowles Commission Monograph 11, London, 1950.

——, and A. Goldberger. *An Econometric Model of the United States, 1929–1952,* North-Holland, Amsterdam, 1955.

Lansing, J., and J. Morgan. *Economic Survey Methods,* Institute for Social Research, University of Michigan, Ann Arbor, 1971.

Leontief, W., et al. *The Structure of the American Economy,* New York, Oxford University Press, 1951.

——. "Static and Dynamic Theory," in *Studies in the Structure of the American Economy,* New York, Oxford University Press, 1953.

Mirer, T. "The Effects of Macroeconomic Fluctuations on the Distribution of Income," *Review of Income and Wealth,* series 19, no. 4, December 1973.

Nelson, R. and S. Winter. "Toward an Evolutionary Theory of Economic Capabilities," *American Economic Review,* May 1973.

Orcutt, G. "A New Type of Socio-Economic System," *Review of Economics and Statistics,* May 1957, vol. 58, pp. 773–97.

——. "Simulation of Economic Systems," *American Economic Review,* vol. L, December 1960.

——, M. Greenberger, J. Korbel, and A. Rivlin. *Microanalysis of Socioeconomic Systems: A Simulation Study,* Harper & Row; New York, 1961.

——. "Research Strategy in Modeling Economic Systems," in *The Future of Statistics,* Donald G. Watts, ed., Academic Press, 1968.

——, H. W. Watts, and J. B. Edwards. "Data Aggregation and Information Loss," *American Economic Review,* September 1968, vol. 58, pp. 773–787.

Pechman, J. A. "A New Tax Model for Revenue Estimating," reprinted in *Studies in Government Finance,* Brookings Institution, Washington, D.C., 1965.

Pryor, F. L. "Simulation of the Impact of the Social and Economic Institutions on the Size Distribution of Income and Wealth," *American Economic Review,* March 1973, vol. 63, pp. 50–72.

Ridley, J. C., and M. C. Sheps. "An Analytic Simulation Model for Human Reproduction with Demographic and Biological Components," *Population Studies,* March 1966, pp. 297–310, vol. 19.

Ruggles, Nancy and Richard Ruggles. "A Proposal for a System of Economic and Social Accounts," in *The Measurement of Economic and Social Performance, Studies in Income and Wealth,* no. 38, National Bureau of Economic Research, 1973.

Sadowsky, G. *MASH: A Computer System for Microanalytic Simulation for Policy Exploration,* The Urban Institute, Washington, D.C., 1976.

Schulz, J. H. *The Economic Status of the Retired Aged in 1980: Simulation Projections,* U.S. Department of Health, Education and Welfare, Social Security Administration, Office of Research and Statistics, Research Report no. 24, 1968.

Shubik, M. "Simulation of the Industry and the Firm," *American Economic Review,* vol. L, December 1960.

——. "Bibliography on Simulation, Gaming and Allied Topics," *Journal of American Statistical Association,* vol. 50, December 1960.

Smithies, A. "Economic Fluctuations and Growth," *Econometrica,* vol. 25, pp. 1–52, January 1957.

Sprehe, J. T. and R. L. Michielutte. "Simulation of Social Mobility: Toward the Development of a System of Social Accounts," prepared for Eastern Sociological Society, April 1969.

——. "Simulation of Large-Scale Social Mobility: Toward the Development of a System of Social Accounts." Final Report on NSF Grant no. GS-2311, 1971.

Suits, D. "Forecasting and Analysis with an Econometric Model," *American Economic Review*, vol. 52, March 1962, pp. 104–132.

Stone, Richard. *Mathematics in the Social Sciences and Other Essays*, Chapman and Hall, London, 1966.

Tinbergen, J. *Statistical Testing of Business-Cycle Theories*, Society of Nations, Geneva, 1939.

Wilensky, G. R. "An Income Transfer Computational Model," *The President's Commission on Income Maintenance Programs — Technical Studies*, U.S. Government Printing Office: 1970, 0-379-518, pp. 121–134.

Watts, Harold. "Graduated Work Incentives: An Experiment in Negative Taxation," *American Economic Review*, vol. 59, no. 2, May 1969.

Chapter 3

Bourgeois-Pichat, Jean. "Eassai sur la Mortalite 'Biologique' de l'Homme," *Population* (Paris), vol. 7, no. 3, pp. 381–394, July-September 1952.

Carter, H., and P. C. Glick, *Marriage and Divorce: A Social and Economic Study*, Harvard University Press, 1970.

Demeny, Paul, and Paul Gingrich. "A Reconsideration of Negro-White Mortality Differentials in the United States," *Demography*, vol. 4, pp. 820–837, 1967.

Farley, Reynolds. The Quality of Demographic Data for Nonwhites. *Demography*, vol. 5, 1968, pp. 1–10.

Kitagawa, Evelyn, and Philip M. Hauser. "Methods Used in a Current Study of Social and Economic Differentials in Mortality. In *Emerging Techniques of Population Research*, Annual Conference of the Milbank Memorial Fund, New York, 1962.

———. "Education Differentials in Mortality by Cause of Death: United States, 1960," *Demography*, vol. 5, no. 1, 1968, pp. 318–353.

———. *Differential Mortality in the United States: A Study in Socioeconomic Epidemiology*, American Public Health Association, Cambridge, Mass., Harvard University Press, 1973.

Madigan, F. C. "Are Sex Mortality Differentials Biologically Caused," *Milbank Memorial Fund Quarterly*, vol. 35, 1957, pp. 1–22.

McCann, J. C. "Differential Mortality and the Formation of Political Elites: The Case of the U.S. House of Representatives," *American Sociological Review*, 1972, vol. 37.

Moriyama, Iwao M. "Problems in the Measurement of Health Status," *Indicators of Social Change*, Eleanor Bernert Sheldon and Wilbert E. Moore, eds., Russel Sage Foundation, New York City, 1968.

National Center for Health Statistics. *United States Life Tables, 1969*. Public Health Services, vol. II, section 5, Government Printing Office, Washington, D.C., 1972.

———. "Vital and Health Statistics," series 20, no. 2, *Mortality Trends in the United States, 1954–63*.

———. *The Change in Mortality Trend in the United States*, Washington, Department of Health, Education and Welfare, Public Health Service, 1964.

———. *Infant Mortality Trends: United States and Each State, 1930–1964*, Washington, Department of Health, Education and Welfare, Public Health Service, 1965.

———. *Vital Statistics Rates in the United States, 1940–1960*, Washington, Department of Health, Education and Welfare, Public Health Service, 1968.

Orcutt, G. H., M. Greenberger, J. Korbel and A. M. Rivlin. *Microanalysis of Socioeconomic Systems: A Simulation Study*, Harper & Row, New York, 1961.

Peabody, Gerald E. "A Simulation Model of Fertility in the United States," The Urban Institute, Washington, working paper 709-5, 1971.

Preston, S. H., Nathan Keyfitz and Robert Schoen. *Causes of Death: Life Tables for National Populations,* New York, Seminar Press, 1972.

Shyrock, Henry, Jacob Siegel, et al. *The Methods and Materials of Demography,* vol. 2, Government Printing Office, Washington, D.C., 1971.

Sutton, Gordon F. "Assessing Mortality and Morbidity Disadvantages of the Black Population of the United States," *Social Biology,* vol. 18, December 1971, pp. 369–383.

Thornton, Russell G., and Charles B. Nam. "The Lower Mortality Rates of Nonwhites at the Older Ages: An Enigma in Demographic Analysis," *Research Reports on Social Science,* Florida State University, pp. 1–8, 1968.

U.S. Bureau of the Census. *A Method of Projecting Mortality Rates Based on Postwar International Experience,* by Arthur A. Campbell, International Population Reports, Series P-91, no. 5, Government Printing Office, Washington, D.C., 1958.

————. *Current Population Reports,* Series P-25, No. 493, "Projections of the Population of the United States, by Age and Sex: 1972 to 2020," Government Printing Office, Washington, D.C., 1972.

United States Public Health Service. *Mortality by Occupation and Industry Among Men 20 to 64 Years of Age: United States, 1950,* Lillian Guralnick. Vital Statistics Special Reports, vol. 53, no. 2, Government Printing Office, Washington, D.C., 1962.

Chapter 4

Akers, Donald S. "On Measuring the Marriage Squeeze." *Demography,* vol. 4, pp. 907–924, 1967.

Baltes, P. B. "Longitudinal and Cross-sectional Sequences in the Study of Age and Generation Effects." *Human Development,* vol. 11, pp. 145–171, 1968.

Buss, A. R. "Generation Analysis: Description, Explanation and Theory," *The Journal of Social Issues,* vol. 30, no. 2, pp. 55–72, 1974.

Carlsson, G. and K. Karlson. "Age, Cohorts and the Generation of Generations," *American Sociological Review,* vol. 35, pp. 710–717, 1970.

Carter, Hugh, and Paul C. Glick. *Marriage and Divorce: A Social and Economic Study,* American Public Health Association, Vital Statistics Monographs, Cambridge, Mass., Harvard University Press, 1970.

Feeney, Griffith. "A Model for the Age Distribution of First Marriage," mimeographed, Population Institute, University of Hawaii, March 1972.

Frieden, Alan. "The United States Marriage Market," *Journal of Political Economy,* vol. 82, pp. 544–552, 1974.

Hastings, Donald W., and J. G. Robinson. "A Re-examination of Hernes' Model on the Process of Entry into First Marriage for United States Women, Cohorts 1891–1945," *American Sociological Review,* vol. 38, no. 1, pp. 138–142, 1973.

Hernes, Gudmund. "The Process of Entry into First Marriage," *American Sociological Review,* vol. 37, no. 1, pp. 173–182, 1972.

Hirschman, Charles, and Judah Matras. "A New Look at the Marriage Market and Nuptiality Rates," *Demography,* vol. 8, no. 4, pp. 549–596, 1971.

Jamison, Ellen L., and Donald S. Akers. "An Analysis of the Difference Between Marriage Statistics from Registration and Those from Census and Surveys," *Demography,* vol. 5, pp. 460–474, 1968.

Johnson, A. L., M. S. Brekke, M. P. Strommen, and R. C. Underwager. "Age Differences and Dimensions of Religious Behavior," *The Journal of Social Issues,* vol. 30, no. 3, pp. 43–68, 1974.

Land, K. C. "Social Indicator Models: An Overview," *Social Indicator Models,* K. C. Land and S. Spilerman, eds., New York, Russell Sage Foundation, 1975.

Laufer, R. S., and V. L. Bengtson. "Aging and Social Stratification: On the Development of Generational Units," *The Journal of Social Issues,* vol. 30, no. 3, pp. 181–206, 1974.

Mason, K., H. Winsborough, W. Mason, and W. Poole. "Some Methodological Issues in Cohort Analysis of Archival Data," *American Sociological Review,* vol. 38, pp. 242–257, 1973.

McFarland, D. D. "Comparison of Alternative Marriage Models," *Population Dynamics,* T. N. E. Greville, ed., New York, Academic Press, pp. 89–106, 1972.

Morgan, James. *Five Thousand American Families—Patterns of Economic Progress,* vol. I, Institute of Social Research, University of Michigan, Ann Arbor, Michigan, 1974.

Porter, Richard D. "On the Use of Survey Sample Weights in the Linear Model," *Annals of Economic and Social Measurement,* vol. 2, no. 2, pp. 141–158, 1973.

Riley, N. W., M. Johnson, and A. Foner. *Aging and Society: A Sociology of Age Stratification,* vol. 3, New York, Russell Sage Foundation, 1972.

Ryder, N. B. "The Cohort as a Concept in the Study of Social Change," *American Sociological Review,* vol. 30, pp. 843–861, 1965.

_____. "The Emergence of a Modern Fertility Pattern: United States, 1917–66," *Fertility and Family Planning,* S. J. Behrman, L. Corsa and R. Freedman, eds., pp. 99–123, University of Michigan, Ann Arbor, Michigan, 1970.

Saveland, Walt, and Paul C. Glick. "First Marriage Decrement Tables by Color and Sex for the United States in 1958–60," *Demography,* vol. 6, pp. 243–260, 1969.

Schaie, K. W., and C. R. Strother. "The Effect of Time and Cohort Differences on the Interpretation of Age Changes in Cognitive Behavior," *Multivariate Behavioral Research,* vol. 3, pp. 259–294, 1968.

U.S. Bureau of the Census. *U.S. Census of the Population: 1960. Subject Reports: Age at First Marriage,* Final Report PC(2)-4D, Washington, D.C., Government Printing Office, 1966a.

_____. *U.S. Census of the Population. Subject Reports: Marital Status,* Final Report PC(2)-4E, Washington, D.C., Government Printing Office, 1966b.

_____. *Current Population Reports,* Series P-20, no. 223, "Social and Economic Variations in Marriage, Divorce and Remarriage: 1967," Washington, D.C., Government Printing Office, 1971.

Chapter 5

Bumpass, Larry, and James Sweet. "Differentials in Marital Instability," *American Sociological Review,* vol. 37, no. 6, pp. 754–766, December 1972.

Caldwell, Steven. First Marriage and Divorce in the United States: Combining Over Time and Cross-section Evidence, unpublished doctoral dissertation, Cornell University, 1975.

Carlsson, G., and K. Karlson. "Age, Cohorts and the Generation of Generations," *American Sociological Review,* vol. 35, pp. 710–717, 1970.

Carter, Hugh, and Paul C. Glick. *Marriage and Divorce: A Social and Economic Study,* American Public Health Association Vital Statistics Monographs, Cambridge, Massachusetts, Harvard University Press, 1970.

Farley, Reynolds, and A. T. Hermalin. "Family Stability: A Comparison of Trends Between Blacks and Whites," *American Sociological Review,* vol. 36, no. 1, pp. 275–296, February 1971.

Land, K. C. "Some Exhaustible Poisson Process Models of Divorce by Marriage Cohort," *Journal of Mathematical Sociology,* vol. 1, pp. 213–232, July 1971.

––––––. "Social Indicator Models: An Overview," *Social Indicator Models,* K. C. Land and S. Spilerman, eds., New York, Russell Sage Foundation, 1975.

Mason, K., H. Winsborough, W. Mason, and W. Poole. "Some Methodological Issues in Cohort Analysis of Archival Data," *American Sociological Review,* vol. 38, pp. 242–257, 1973.

Morgan, James. *Five Thousand American Families – Patterns of Economic Progress,* vol. I, Ann Arbor, Michigan, Institute of Social Research, University of Michigan, 1974.

Porter, Richard D. "On the Use of Survey Sample Weights in the Linear Model," *Annals of Economic and Social Measurement,* vol. 2, no. 2, pp. 141–158, 1973.

Ryder, N. B. "The Cohort as a Concept in the Study of Social Change," *American Sociological Review,* vol. 30, pp. 843–861, 1965.

Sawhill, Isabel, and Heather Ross. *Time of Transition: The Growth of Families Headed by Women,* Washington, D.C., The Urban Institute, 1976.

U.S. Bureau of the Census. *U.S. Census of the Population. Subject Reports: Marital Status,* Final Report PC(2)-4E, Government Printing Office, Washington, D.C., 1966.

––––––. *Current Population Reports,* Series P-20, No. 223, "Social and Economic Variations in Marriage, Divorce and Remarriage: 1967," Government Printing Office, Washington, D.C., 1971.

Chapter 6

Adams, Walter. "Academic Self-Image as a Strong Determinant of College Entrance and Adult Prospects," *American Journal of Economics and Sociology,* vol. 29, 1970, p. 199.

Becker, Gary. *Human Capital,* New York City, Columbia, 1964.

Berls, Robert H. "Higher Education Opportunity and Achievement in the United States," in *The Economics and Financing of Higher Education in the United States,* Joint Economic Committee, U.S. Congress, 1969, p. 145.

Bowles, Samuel. "Schooling and Inequality from Generation to Generation," *Journal of Political Economy,* p. S119–S251, vol. 80, no. 3, part II, May/June 1972.

Eckland, Bruce K. "College Dropouts Who Come Back," *Harvard Educational Review,* vol. 34, p. 402–420, Summer 1964a.

––––––. "Social Class and College Graduation: Some Misconceptions Corrected," *American Journal of Sociology,* vol. 70, 1964b, p. 36.

Folger, J. K., H. S. Astin, and A. E. Bayer. *Human Resources and Higher Education,* New York, Russell Sage, 1970.

Jaffe, A. J., and W. Adams. "Trends in College Enrollment, *The College Board Review,* Winter, 1964–65.

––––––. *American Higher Education in Transition,* New York City, Bureau of Applied Social Research, Columbia University, 1969.

Marshall, K. T., and R. M. Oliver. "A Constant-Work Model for Student Attendance and Enrollment," *Operations Research,* vol. 18, 1970, p. 193.

Peabody, Gerald E. "Schooling Attainment and Social Class," Washington, D.C., The Urban Institute, Working Paper 504-4, 1972.

Sewell, W. H., and V. P. Shah. "Socioeconomic Status, Intelligence, and the Attainment of Higher Education," *Sociology of Education*, vol. 40, 1967, p. 1.

―――. "Social Class, Parental Encouragement, and Educational Aspirations," *American Journal of Sociology*, vol. 73, 1968, p. 559.

Spady, W. G. "Educational Mobility and Access: Growth and Paradoxes," *American Journal of Sociology*, vol. 73, 1967, p. 273.

Trent, J. W., and L. L. Medsker. *Beyond High School*, San Francisco, Jossey-Bass, 1968.

U.S. Bureau of the Census. *Current Population Reports*, Series P-20, No. 132, "Educational Change in a Generation: March 1962," Washington, D.C., U.S. Government Printing Office, 1964.

―――. *Current Population Reports*, Series P-20, No. 167, "School Enrollment: October 1966," Washington, D.C., GPO, 1967.

―――. *Current Population Reports*, Series P-20, No. 169, "Educational Attainment: March 1967," Washington, D.C., GPO, 1968.

―――. *Current Population Reports*, Series P-20, No. 185, "Factors Related to High School Graduation and College Attendance: 1967," Washington, D.C., GPO, 1969.

―――. *Current Population Reports*, Series P-20, No. 207, "Educational Attainment: March 1970," Washington, D.C., GPO, 1970.

Chapter 7

Apgar, W. C. "Migration as Investment: Some Further Considerations," Discussion Paper #64, Harvard Program on Regional and Urban Economics, 1970.

Blanco, C. "The Determinants of Interstate Population Movements," *Journal of Regional Science*, 5, 77–84, 1963.

Bowles, S. "Migration as Investment: Empirical Tests of the Human Investment Approach to Geographical Mobility," *Review of Economics and Statistics*, 52, 356–362, 1970.

Fabricant, R. A. "An Expectational Model of Migration," *Journal of Regional Science*, 10, 13–24, 1970.

Ginsberg, R. B. "Critique of Probabilistic Models: Application of the Semi-Markov Model to Migration," *Journal of Mathematical Sociology*, 2, 63–82, 1972a.

―――. "Incorporating Causal Structure and Exogenous Information With Probabilistic Models: With Special Reference to Choice, Gravity, Migration and Markov Chains," *Journal of Mathematical Sociology*, 2, 83–103, 1972b.

Greenwood, M. J. "Lagged Response in the Decision to Migrate," *Journal of Regional Science*, 10, 375–384, 1970.

Hagerstrand, T. "Migration and Area: Survey of a Sample of Swedish Migration Fields and Hypothetical Considerations on Their Genesis," *Land Studies in Geography*, no. 13, 1957.

Kelley, A. C., and L. W. Weiss. "Markov Processes and Economic Analysis: The Case of Migration," *Econometrica*, vol. 37, no. 2, April 1969, 280–297.

Land, K. "Duration of Residence and Prospective Migration: Further Evidence," *Demography*, 6, 133–140, 1969.

Lansing, J. B., and Eva Mueller. *The Geographic Mobility of Labor*, Survey Research Center, Institute for Social Research, Ann Arbor, 1967.

Lee, E. S. "A Theory of Migration," *Demography,* 3, 47–57, 1966.
———. "Needed Research in Migration," draft, June 16, 1971.
Long, L. H. "Migration Differentials by Education and Occupation: Trends and Variations," *Demography,* May 1973, 243–258.
Lowry, I. S. *Migration and Metropolitan Growth: Two Analytical Models,* Chandler, San Francisco, 1966.
Morrison, P. A. "Duration of Residence and Prospective Migration: The Evaluation of a Stochastic Model," *Demography,* 4, 553–561, 1967.
———. "Chronic Movers and the Future Redistribution of Population," *Demography,* 8, 171–184, 1971.
———. *Population Movements and the Shape of Urban Growth: Implications for Public Policy,* The Rand Corporation, Santa Monica, California, 1972.
———. "Theoretical Issues in the Design of Population Mobility Models," *Environment and Planning,* vol. 5, no. 1, 1973, 125–134.
Olvey, L. D. *Regional Growth and Inter-Regional Migration—Their Pattern of Inter-Action,* Ph.D. dissertation, Harvard University, Cambridge, Massachusetts, 1970.
Shryock, H. S., and C. B. Nam. "Educational Selectivity of Interregional Migration," *Social Forces,* 43, 1965, 299–310.
Stouffer, S. A. "Intervening Opportunities and Competing Migrants," *Journals of Regional Science,* 2, 1960, 1–25.
Taeuber, K., L. Chiazze, and W. Haenszel. *Migration in the United States: An Analysis of Residence Histories,* Public Health Monograph No. 77, Public Health Service, U.S. Department of Health, Education, and Welfare, 1968.
Tarver, J. D., and W. R. Gurley. "A Stochastic Analysis of Geographic Mobility and Population Projections of the Census Divisions in the United States," *Demography,* 2, 134–139, 1965.
ter Heide, H. "Migration Models and Their Significance for Population Forecasts," *Milbank Memorial Fund Quarterly,* 41, 1963, 56–57.
Wertheimer, R. F. *The Monetary Rewards of Migration Within the U.S.,* The Urban Institute, Washington, D.C., 1970.
Wolpert, Julian. "The Basis for Stability of Interregional Transactions," paper presented at the London meeting, British section, Regional Service Association, 1967.

Chapter 8

Becker, Gary. *Human Capital,* New York, National Bureau of Economic Research, 1964.
Boskin, Michael J. "The Economics of Labor Supply," Memorandum no. 110, Stanford University Research Center on Economic Growth, 1970.
Cain, Glen G. "Unemployment and the Labor-Force Participation of Secondary Workers," *Industrial and Labor Relations Review,* January 1967, pp. 275–297.
Cain, Glen G., and Harold W. Watts, eds. *Labor Supply and Income Maintenance: Econometric Studies,* Chicago, Markham Press, 1973.
Fleisher, Belton M., and Richard D. Porter. "Assets, Nonemployment Income, and Alternative Models of Labor Supply," Ohio State University Center for Human Resource Research, 1971.
Freeman, Richard B. "Changes in the Labor Market for Black Americans, 1948–72," *Brookings Papers on Economic Activity,* 1973, pp. 67–120.

Gramlich, Edward M. "The Distributional Effects of Higher Unemployment," *Brookings Papers on Economic Activity,* 1974, pp. 293–341.

Greenberg, David H., and Marvin Kosters. "Income Guarantees and the Working Poor: The Effect of Income Maintenance Programs on the Hours of Work of Male Family Heads," The Rand Corporation, R-579-OEO, 1970.

Hall, Robert E. *Wages, Income and Hours of Work in the U.S. Labor Force.* Department of Economics, University of California, Berkeley, 1970.

_____. "Turnover in the Labor Force," *Brookings Papers on Economic Activity,* 1972.

Hill, C. R. "The Determinants of Labor Supply for the Working Urban Poor," University of Michigan Institute of Public Policy Studies, Discussion Paper no. 14, 1970.

Jencks, Christopher. *Inequality,* New York, Basic Books, 1972.

Kalachek, E., and F. Raines. "Labor Supply of Lower Income Workers and the Negative Income Tax," in *Technical Reports of the President's Commission on Income Maintenance Programs,* Washington, D.C., U.S. Government Printing Office, 1970.

Kosters, Marvin. "Income and Substitution Effects in a Family Labor Supply Model," unpublished dissertation, University of Chicago, 1966.

Perry, George. "Unemployment Flows in the U.S. Labor Market," *Brookings Papers on Economic Activity,* 1972, pp. 245–278.

Ruggles, Nancy and Richard. "The Anatomy of Earnings Behavior," National Bureau of Economic Research, May 1974.

Sawhill, Isabel. "The Economics of Discrimination Against Women: Some New Findings," *Journal of Human Resources,* vol. VIII, no. 3, Summer 1973, pp. 383–396.

Smith, Ralph, and Charles Holt. "A Job Search-Turnover Analysis of the Black-White Unemployment Ratio," *Proceedings of the Twenty-third Annual Meeting of the Industrial Relations Research Association,* 1971, pp. 76–86.

Survey Research Center. *A Panel Study of Income Dynamics, 1968–1973 Interviewing Years,* Ann Arbor, Institute for Social Research, 1974.

Thurow, Lester. *Poverty and Discrimination,* Washington, D.C., The Brookings Institution, 1969.

Weiss, Randall. "The Effect of Education on the Earnings of Blacks and Whites," *Review of Economics and Statistics Within the U.S.,* May 1970, pp. 150–159.

Welch, Finis. "Black-White Differences in Returns to Schooling," *American Economic Review,* December 1973, vol. 63, pp. 893–907.

Wertheimer, II, Richard F. *The Monetary Rewards of Migration Within the U.S.,* Washington, D.C., the Urban Institute, 1970.

_____. "Employment and Earnings Operating Characteristics," Washington, D.C., Urban Institute Working Paper 0980-6, March 1975.

Chapter 14

Fuchs, Victor R. "Recent Trends and Long-run Prospects for Female Earnings," *American Economic Review,* vol. 64, May 1974.

Ross, Heather L., and Anita MacIntosh. "The Emergence of Households Headed by Women," Washington, D.C., The Urban Institute, Working Paper 776–01, June 1973.

U.S. Department of Commerce. "Money Income in 1971 of Families and Persons in the United States," *Consumer Incomes, Current Population Reports* (Series P-60, no. 85, December 1972).

U.S. Department of Labor. *1974 Manpower Report of the President,* Washington, D.C., Government Printing Office, 1974.

Appendix B

Barrett, J. C.   "A Monte Carlo Study of Reproduction," *Genus,* 1969.

Becker, G. S.   "An Economic Analysis of Fertility," in *Demographic and Economic Change in Developed Countries,* National Bureau of Economic Research, Princeton, 1960.

Clague, A. S., and J. C. Ridley.   "The Assessment of Three Methods of Estimating Births Averted," paper prepared for a conference on the uses of computer simulation in human population, Pennsylvania State University, June 1972.

Davis, K., and J. Blake.   "Social Structure and Fertility: An Analytic Framework," *Economic Development and Cultural Change,* vol. 4, p. 211, 1956.

Easterlin, R. A.   *Population, Labor Force, and Long Swings in Economic Growth: The American Experience,* New York, Columbia University Press, 1968.

Gregory, P. R., J. M. Campbell, and B. S. Cheng.   "A Simultaneous Equation Model of Birth Rates in the United States," *Review of Economics and Statistics,* vol. 54, no. 4, pp. 374–380, November 1972.

Jacquard, M. A.   "La reproduction humane en regime Malthusien," *Population,* vol. 22, pp. 897–920, 1967.

Hyrenius, H., and I. Adolfsson.   *A Fertility Simulation Model,* Report no. 2, Demographic Institute, University of Göteborg, Sweden, 1964.

Hyrenius, H., I. Holmberg, and M. Carlsson.   *Demographic Models: DM3,* Report no. 5, Demographic Institute, University of Göteborg, Sweden, 1967.

Leibenstein, H.   *Economic Backwardness and Economic Growth,* John Wiley, 1956.

Michielutte, R., and J. T. Sprehe.   *Simulations of Large-Scale Social Mobility: Toward the Development of a System of Social Accounts,* Final Report: National Science Foundation, 1971.

National Center for Health Statistics.   *User's Manual for POPSIM,* U.S. Department of Health, Education, and Welfare, 1973.

Nerlove, M., and T. P. Schultz.   *Love and Life Between the Censuses: A Model of Family Decision Making in Puerto Rico, 1950–1960,* Rand, 1970.

Phillips, L., H. L. Votey, and D. E. Maxwell.   "A Synthesis of the Economic and Demographic Models of Fertility: An Economic Test," *Review of Economics and Statistics,* vol. 51, no. 3, pp. 298–308, August 1969.

Ridley, J. C., and M. C. Sheps.   "An Analytical Simulation Model for Human Reproduction with Demographic and Biological Components." *Population Studies,* March 1966.

Schultz, T. P.   "A Preliminary Survey of Economic Analyses of Fertility," *American Economic Review,* vol. 53, p. 71, 1973.

Yett, D. E., M. Intrilligator, L. Kimbell, and L. Drabek.   "The Development of a Microsimulation Model of Health Manpower Supply and Demand," in *Proceedings of a Conference on Health Manpower Simulation Models,* vol. I, U.S. Department of Health, Education and Welfare, 1970.